VICTORIOUS INSURGENCIES

VICTORIOUS INSURGENCIES

Four Rebellions That Shaped Our World

Anthony James Joes

THE UNIVERSITY PRESS OF KENTUCKY

Scholarly publisher for the Commonwealth,
serving Bellarmine University, Berea College, Centre
College of Kentucky, Eastern Kentucky University,
The Filson Historical Society, Georgetown College,
Kentucky Historical Society, Kentucky State University,
Morehead State University, Murray State University,
Northern Kentucky University, Transylvania University,
University of Kentucky, University of Louisville,
and Western Kentucky University.
All rights reserved.

Editorial and Sales Offices: The University Press of Kentucky
663 South Limestone Street, Lexington, Kentucky 40508-4008
www.kentuckypress.com

14 13 12 11 10   1 2 3 4 5

Library of Congress Cataloging-in-Publication Data

Joes, Anthony James.
  Victorious insurgencies : four rebellions that shaped our world / Anthony
James Joes.
    p.   cm.
  Includes bibliographical references and index.
  ISBN 978-0-8131-2614-2 (hardcover : alk. paper)
  1. Insurgency—History—20th century. 2. Guerrilla warfare—
History—20th century. 3. Insurgency—China—History—20th
century. 4. Guerrilla warfare—China—History—20th century.
5. Insurgency—Vietnam—History—20th century. 6. Guerrilla
warfare—Vietnam—History—20th century. 7. Insurgency—
Cuba—History—20th century. 8. Guerrilla warfare—Cuba—
History—20th century. 9. Insurgency—Afghanistan—History—
20th century. 10. Guerrilla warfare—Afghanistan—History—
20th century. I. Title.
  D431.J65 2010
  355.02'1809—dc22
                                                    2010023315

This book is printed on acid-free recycled paper meeting
the requirements of the American National Standard
for Permanence in Paper for Printed Library Materials.

♾ ♻

Manufactured in the United States of America.

   Member of the Association of
       American University Presses

To all who serve

Contents

INTRODUCTION

Who Cares about Yesterday's Wars?

This book is about four insurgencies whose success changed the structure of world politics.

For the past six decades, the most common type of conflict has been insurgency, in the form of guerrilla war. Today, such conflicts rage all across the globe, from South Asia to South America, from Sinkiang to Sudan. An influential student of insurgency warned long ago that "guerrilla warfare is what regular armies always have most to dread, and when this is directed by a leader with a genius for war, an effective campaign becomes well-nigh impossible."[1] All major military powers have had difficult, sometimes disastrous, experiences fighting guerrillas. Consider just the French in the Vendée, Spain (where Napoleon lost more soldiers than in Russia),[2] and Vietnam; the British in the Carolinas,[3] South Africa, Cyprus, and Northern Ireland; the Germans in Yugoslavia; the Japanese in China; the Soviets in Afghanistan; the Russians in Chechnya; and, irony of ironies, the Communist Vietnamese in Cambodia.

The question of how to deal effectively with such conflicts has absorbed much attention from the U.S. military in recent years. It is not entirely clear, however, that after a great deal of earnest effort, the United States is really much better prepared to wage successful counterinsurgency today than it was a decade ago. Even the new *Army/Marine Counterinsurgency Field Manual* has received some searing criticism.[4]

The clichés, errors, and shibboleths that dominated American discourse about America's South Vietnam experience distorted U.S.

foreign policy for three decades. Now it seems that many Americans are prepared to erect their Iraq experience—however incomplete, contradictory, and politically motivated their interpretations of it—into a sort of unique template for future conflicts, an "Iraq Syndrome," with consequences potentially as harmful as the apparently fading Vietnam Syndrome.

What is to be done? Across continents and even across millennia, guerrilla insurgencies display patterns, notably patterns of error on the part of the counterinsurgents. The construction of an electorate-convincing, victory-producing, and life-saving U.S. counterinsurgency doctrine therefore clearly requires as broad a base of information about and analysis of these errors as possible.

Consider the following scenario: a superpower, the self-conscious carrier of a universalistic ideology, invades a backward neighbor directly across its border. Gravely underestimating the difficulty of this operation, the superpower commits forces inadequate to the task. To this key error, the invaders add widespread rape, looting, sacrilege, and casual murder. This behavior provokes a determined popular resistance, fueled by xenophobia and religious fervor and sustained by outside aid. The unexpectedly fierce and protracted struggle severely undermines the reputation of the superpower and plays a major role in its ultimate collapse.

Is this a serviceable summary of what happened to the Soviets in Afghanistan in the 1980s? Yes—but it also encapsulates the essence of Napoleonic France's experience of Spain (from which conflict the term *guerrilla* derives). Spain was Napoleon's Afghanistan. (The anti-French *guerrilleros* of Spain employed tactics strikingly similar to those used in the same peninsula against the Romans two thousand years before.)[5]

Many students of war, and especially of insurgency, have warned against the tendencies of Americans to ignore their own and others' experience. The distinguished strategist Bernard Brodie wrote that "the only empirical data we have about how people conduct war and behave under its stresses is our experience with it in the past, however much we have to make adjustments for subsequent changes in conditions." Ian F.W. Beckett states that "the past of guerrilla warfare represents the shadow both of things that have been and of those that will be."[6] Contemporary RAND researchers uphold this view: "Iraq and Afghanistan are consonant with some general characteristics of insurgency and counterinsurgency, and are more similar to than different from many previous insurgencies"; and "in an age when insurgencies have worldwide reach, counterinsurgents can ill-afford not to examine the complexities of past cases and the continuities among them, *especially since the complexities of the insurgency that the counterinsurgents are facing may not be elucidated until much later. . . .* counterinsurgents should continue to learn from the successes and mistakes of other counterinsurgencies to avoid the repetition of mistakes."[7] The recent Army–Marine Corps counterinsurgency manual states that "knowledge of the history and principles of insurgency and COIN provides a solid foundation that informed readers can use to assess insurgencies. . . . All insurgencies are different; however, broad historical trends underlie the factors motivating insurgencies."[8] And William Rosenau observed that "the U.S. Military, despite relatively unambiguous counterinsurgency successes in Viet Nam during the 1960s and in El Salvador during the 1980s, failed to transfer hard-won skills and lessons to Iraq and Afghanistan in an appropriate manner."[9] This volume aligns itself squarely with this position. One is tempted to remark that those who ignore the lessons of counterinsurgency are doomed to repeat them—almost certainly at great expense, and not only in treasure. The insurgencies of both the recent and the distant past are a rich storehouse of wisdom that it would be almost criminal to ignore.

Insurgency is common, but insurgent victory is *not* common. However, when one closely observes those relatively few cases in which insurgents were victorious, one finds that several of them produced consequences that may justly be called world-historical. This book offers an examination of four of those conflicts:

—in China, between Chiang Kai-shek's Nationalists and Mao Tse-tung's Communists in the 1930s and 1940s;

—in Vietnam, between the French and the Viet Minh from 1945 to 1954;

—in Cuba, between the Batista regime and the followers of Fidel Castro, from 1956 to 1959; and

—in Afghanistan, between the Soviet Union and a notably diverse assortment of enemies native and foreign, from 1980 to 1988.

In the tradition of Aristotle, Lenin, Crane Brinton, and Katherine Chorley, this book seeks to make clear both the surprisingly serious internal political weaknesses and the striking military errors of the regimes that lost, or gave up, their counterinsurgency efforts.[10] And following the school of analysis that includes Niccolò Machiavelli, Theda Skocpol, Jeffrey Record, Bard O'Neill, and many others, this study also focuses on the influence of the insurgency's external environment, and especially of outside assistance to the insurgents, both direct and indirect.[11] To anticipate: all four conflicts display a strikingly similar pattern of counterinsurgent weakness and error, despite the fact that they developed in very different geographic and cultural milieus over more than a half century.

In dealing with "the lessons of history," we need of course to be very cautious. It is notoriously hard to foresee all the consequences of a policy. The past is littered with disastrous decisions based on what were at one time considered to be compelling analogies to previous situations. The path ahead is piled high with difficulties and dangers. The great need is for insight derived from careful analysis of concrete cases, each in its particular context. And there is need for humility, derived from the realization that we do not know and cannot know all we need to know and that even well-conceived and well-intentioned policies have produced the gravest consequences.

1

China
The Long War, 1929–1949

Origins of the Chinese Conflict

China, wrote Lucian Pye, is "a civilization pretending to be a state."[1] The sheer massiveness of the country is impressive. In area, China is three times the size of India, six times that of Iran, twenty-five times that of Japan, and twenty-seven times that of Germany. The distance from Beijing to Hong Kong—by no means the longest axis in the country—is roughly equal to the distance between Stockholm and Istanbul. And China's population of 1.25 billion is equal to that of North America and Europe combined. More than one out of every five human beings on this planet is Chinese. Consider also that "a billion or so Europeans in Europe and the Americas live divided into some fifty separate and sovereign states, while more than a billion Chinese live in only one state."[2] It was in this vast and ancient arena that the Nationalist regime of Chiang Kai-shek became the first government in the world to be confronted by a Communist guerrilla insurgency.

Rebellions and civil wars in the middle of the nineteenth century —Taiping, Nien, Muslim, and others—reduced China's population from approximately 410 million in 1850 to 350 million in 1873.[3] "Thus the coercion of China by western gunboats and even the Anglo-French occupation of Peking [the old name of Beijing] in 1860 were brief, small, and marginal disasters compared with the midcentury rebellions that swept over the major provinces. The Europeans and Americans who secured their special privileges in China's new treaty ports were on the fringe of this great social turmoil, not its creators."[4]

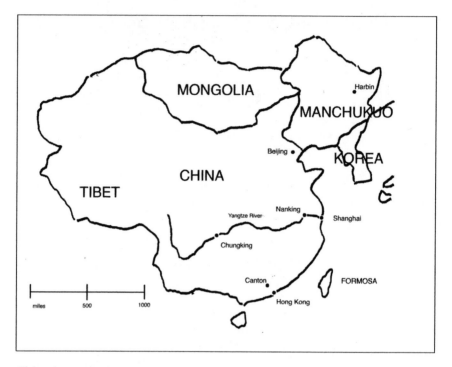

China

Indeed, for most of its existence, China lived in near isolation from Europe, separated from it by boundless deserts, daunting mountains, treacherous seas, primitive communications, and also—not least—by Sinocentrism, a profound indifference to the nature and events of the outside world.[5]

Nevertheless, it would not be much of a distortion to interpret twentieth-century Chinese politics as a reaction on the part of key elements in the population to foreign intrusion. China suffered all the penalties of colonialism without any of the benefits. By 1900 debts and indemnities to foreign states consumed between one-quarter and one-third of Chinese government revenues.[6] As Ernest P. Young writes, "Although never a colony, China was a semi-colony, or in constant danger of being divided into colonies. The steady diminution of formal sovereignty over seventy years had made the Chinese state immensely vulnerable." Consequently, "to prevent an occasion for the partition of the country and to establish more advantageous lines of defense had become the first task of politics."[7]

Military defeat by foreigners was constant and humiliating, from the Opium Wars to the Boxer Rebellion, and especially in the first Sino-Japanese War of 1894–95. The latter conflict revealed China's utter helplessness against a country the Chinese had considered to be their cultural offspring, and the war heralded the overthrow of the Ch'ing dynasty. A decade later the Chinese witnessed at close hand another stunning Japanese victory, this one over the Russians in the war of 1904–5. In that conflict, the first time in modern history that a European power had suffered defeat at the hands of an East Asian state, much of the fighting between the Japanese and the Russians actually took place on Chinese soil. The contrast between a burgeoning Japan, with the might and prestige of its booming industries and modern armed forces, and a decrepit China, economically backward and militarily feeble, astounded and humiliated a whole generation of young Chinese. Fearing that foreign powers would soon carve up China, they concluded that national salvation required new institutions that could impose strong measures.

All this mounting discontent and confusion prepared the way for the Revolution of 1911, the beginning both of contemporary Chinese politics and of forty years of civil and foreign war. The overthrow of the decadent Manchu dynasty in 1911 proved to be unexpectedly easy: "The Revolution of 1911 was essentially a collapse, not a creation," a major reason why it turned out to be so unsatisfactory to everyone.[8] Conservative elements played the major role in this initially cautious revolution, and the former Imperial general, statesman, and military reformer Yuan Shih-k'ai assumed office as president of the revolutionary republic. Yuan believed that if China was ever to be able to defend itself successfully against Japan and other foreign predators, it needed not a contentious and centrifugal republican regime but a strongly centralized government under a constitutional monarchy. Hence in 1916 he proclaimed himself no longer president but henceforth emperor (in the manner of the two Napoleons).[9]

Yuan's assumptions about authority in the Chinese context proved to be correct: republicanism failed in China, opening the way to Communist dictatorship. But at the time, Yuan's imperial pretensions offended many and provoked new rebellions, the principal one of which was led by the remarkable Sun Yat-sen. Born in

1866, educated at an Anglican college in Honolulu, and awarded a medical degree by a Hong Kong hospital, Sun nevertheless devoted all his energies to revolutionary politics. He was prominent in the Revolution of 1911, and though at first a supporter of Yuan, he opposed Yuan's emergent monarchism. In his search for a formula for republican stability, Sun developed a political theory based on nationalism, socialism, and democracy (as he understood those terms) and in 1912 organized the Kuomintang (the National People's Party, the KMT) as a vehicle for the realization of these principles. Sun labored incessantly to establish a new republican regime, but its authority did not extend much beyond the city of Canton. Then the death of Yuan in 1916 inaugurated the chaotic warlord era, in which provincial military governors exercised semisovereign powers in accord with or in defiance of the central Peking regime, making alliances with one another, often under the tutelage of foreign governments.[10] By 1924 more than 1.5 million men were under arms, mainly in the service of the warlords. "The fundamental law of the warlord system was that if any one warlord appeared to be achieving national authority, the others would gang up on him."[11] A decade and more after the overthrow of the Imperial dynasty, China had achieved neither unity nor order, and—not for the first or last time—the country seemed to be on the edge of disintegration. It was in this context that the great competition between the Kuomintang and the Chinese Communist Party began, a contest to determine which of them would emerge as the savior—or at least the ruler—of China.

In the early 1920s, the Chinese Communist Party (CCP) followed an impeccably orthodox Leninist line, according to which the next stage of China's evolution would be bourgeois national development. Hence the CCP had to support the leadership of the bourgeois KMT. After 1925, however, KMT rebuffs to the Communists, including assaults and arrests in several places, caused the CCP to reconsider this strategy. The irresistible attraction of the Leninist coup in St. Petersburg, the doubling of the Chinese proletariat between 1916 and 1922 (to 2 million), the impressive growth of the CCP itself (from 400 members in 1923 to 93,000 in 1927), the belief in the "hegemony of the proletariat" and a corresponding tendency to view the peasantry as cannon fodder—all these combined to turn the CCP to a Leninist strategy of urban insurrection. The disastrous failure of that strategy in 1927, followed by a similar catastrophe in 1930, discredited the Leninist line. Meanwhile, population increases in the countryside, along with a decrease in the total area under cultivation, enormously stimulated peasant indebtedness and discontent. These factors united to bring new leaders to the fore in the CCP, principally Mao Tse-tung, with an orientation toward a strategy of rural revolution. Ultimately, this new leadership appealed successfully to growing numbers of peasants by promising them what they wanted: improvement in their material and social condition. In essence, the CCP learned to offer to the peasant the KMT program, which the KMT had failed to put effectively into practice. Not only did Mao shift the locus of struggle in Chinese revolutionary politics from the city to the countryside; he also redefined the importance of that struggle. In the strict Leninist view, the battle against imperialism in the colonialized periphery of the world (including China) was merely a stimulus to the "real" revolution in Europe. Mao, however, elevated the fight of the Chinese Communists against the KMT and later the Japanese to central historical importance, in effect proclaiming it the dress rehearsal for the global uprising of the world's backward societies.[12] Herein lay one of the principal roots, or at least justifications, of the Sino-Soviet rift that altered the shape of world politics in the 1960s and after.

The Kuomintang

Sun Yat-sen, the father of modern Chinese nationalism, founded the Kuomintang to advance his vision of a rejuvenated and republican China. The KMT soon became one of the two great contenders—the other being the CCP—for the right to lead China into unity and modernity.[13]

There were then, and still are, two Chinas: interior or heartland China and coastal or maritime China.[14] Although militarily superior foreign states had been invading or imposing themselves upon China for generations, in the year 1910 the great majority of Chinese had never actually even seen a foreigner. The preponderance of China's territory, its interior heartland—remote, impoverished, and immobile—had remained relatively untouched by foreign incursion and influence. The impact of the Europeans and the Japanese had indeed been tremendous, but it had been almost completely confined to the great coastal cities of maritime China and their surrounding hinter-lands. Here, the ever-increasing presence of foreign personnel, ideas, methods, and organizations had developed a significant number of Chinese with "modern," certainly nontraditional, outlooks and aspirations. These persons formed the basis of an emerging middle class and came to constitute the core of the KMT's support.

The KMT program of the early 1920s was both simple and revo-lutionary: first to subdue the warlords and second to expel the im-perialists. That meant establishing an effective central government, one that could maintain order and collect taxes. It meant restoring the integrity of China, specifically by abolishing the unequal trea-ties and territorial concessions that foreign governments had long been able to extract by military force from a backward and divided China. And it meant modernizing the country under the direction of the educated classes.[15]

The KMT wanted, in short, a political revolution, not a social one. The party's base was in Canton, but it received crucial financial support from the great business houses in Shanghai and also from China's numerous and prosperous diaspora—the overseas Chinese, who had long suffered discrimination and worse in their countries of residence because there was no powerful Chinese state to intercede for them.

"The Kuomintang was the party of the bourgeoisie," the party of maritime China.[16] As such, it never understood the desires of the peasantry. It talked about "land to the tiller" but usually forgot about land reform in the midst of other, more pressing demands. The KMT was not the party of the rural elite, the landowners and magistrates of the countryside. But it mistook this rural elite for a stabilizing in-fluence, rather than the profoundly destabilizing force that, because of its exploitation and increasing illegitimacy, it actually was.[17]

The bloody suppression of the prodemocracy demonstrations in Tiananmen Square in Beijing in 1989 was but a reminder of the huge role soldiers and armies have played in contemporary Chinese politics. In the 1920s, the leaders of the KMT realized from the outset that to begin to achieve their goals in a fragmented and violent China, the party needed to create its own army. They therefore established a military academy at Whampoa, near Canton, in June 1924. Sun Yat-sen himself officially inaugurated the school. Soviet general Vasily

Blucher served as chief of staff, and a young man named Chou En-lai filled the office of political commissar.[18] The director of the academy was a young Japanese-trained officer named Chiang Kai-shek.

Like Chiang, the principal Chinese members of the Whampoa faculty were graduates of the Japanese military academy, Shikan Gakko. The initial corps of students comprised 499 chosen from among 3,000 applicants. The original course of instruction consisted of six months' training, based on Leninist principles and stressing political indoctrination above all.[19] After his break with the Chinese Communists, Chiang turned to the German Army (of the Weimar Republic) for assistance and training, and the name of the Whampoa Academy was changed to Central Military Academy. Nevertheless, the early graduates of the school were ever after known as the "Whampoa Clique." The existence and cohesiveness of this group of officers greatly complicated, and even impeded, Chiang's post-1945 campaign against the forces of Mao Tse-tung.

Impressed with the courage and loyalty displayed by Chiang, Sun appointed him his military adviser. This was a major reason for Chiang's rise to prominence in the leadership of the Kuomintang. Another was his willingness and ability to act as the principal liaison between Sun's government and the Soviet regime, the only foreign government friendly to the KMT. In August 1923, Chiang went to Moscow on a political-military mission; among the results of this visit was that the Russians sent one Michael Borodin to be a personal adviser to Sun and political consultant to the Kuomintang.[20]

Russian policy toward China in those days was based on orthodox Marxist-Leninist analysis: in that view, what China needed was unification and independence under the leadership of its bourgeoisie, not a proletarian revolution. To promote these ends (which the Soviets saw as serving their interests against Japanese expansion), the Russians sent military advisers and equipment along with Borodin. For its part, the KMT had from earliest days imitated certain Bolshevik methods, including party cell organization, the political commissar system in the armed forces, and heavy political indoctrination of its troops. After 1924, the KMT adopted the Leninist practice known as "democratic centralism," which meant the complete subordination of lower party organs to higher and the doctrine of party "guidance" (i.e., dictatorship) of the Chinese people. In January 1924, when the KMT held its first party congress at Canton, it endorsed cooperation with the Soviets, a tactical alliance with the Chinese Communist party, and the development of a KMT base of support among industrial workers and peasants.[21]

The Northern Expedition

Chiang Kai-shek, who eventually succeeded Sun as leader of the Kuomintang, later wrote an internationally famous book called *China's Destiny.* The English edition of the work, which considerably toned down the bitterly antiforeign thrust of the original Chinese version, appeared in 1947.[22] In his introduction to that work, Philip Jaffe wrote that one could "describe *China's Destiny* as the political bible of the Kuomintang." In it, Chiang proclaimed that "the target of the Nationalist Revolution [was] the imperialists [foreign powers] and the warlords." These two groups constituted a two-headed monster in his eyes. The abolition of the so-called unequal treaties between China and foreign governments was "the most important objective of the Chinese Nationalist Revolution." Among their many evil effects, these treaties had robbed China of the ability to control tariffs and thus had contributed to the ruin of traditional handicrafts and prevented the industrialization of the country.[23] But more than that, "the secret activities of the imperialists were actually the chief cause of the civil wars among the warlords following the establishment of the Republic."[24] The warlord system interfered with trade, undermined agriculture, and worst of all, invited meddling by both the Japanese and the Russians and pointed toward the permanent disintegration of the Chinese state. Breaking the vicious symbiosis of warlords and imperialists was the essence of the Nationalist vision. Destruction of warlord control over northern China became the chief and most immediate priority of the KMT. Hence the long-planned Northern Expedition by the main KMT army from its base in Canton began in July 1926 under the leadership of Chiang himself (Sun Yat-sen having died in 1925).

The forces of the warlords were no match for the Nationalist army. The warlords recruited their troops largely from impoverished peasants; these forces gave the Chinese military "an extremely bad reputation."[25] Within Chiang's Nationalist forces, promotion for merit and combat ability was more common than in warlord armies or in the former Chinese Imperial armies. KMT party cadres looked after the pay and food of the troops. They taught their men that they were the saviors of China, not social outcasts like traditional soldiers. All of this kept up morale and held down depredations against the civilian population. Thus KMT troops benefited from a good reputation among the peasantry; as Donald A. Jordan observes, "the [KMT army] proved to be far superior to its military opponents in its fighting spirit and political awareness, which were closely related."[26]

The KMT's announced program of national unification alerted all its actual and potential enemies, as well as the armed forces they controlled. Thus, just to get the Northern Expedition started, Chiang had had to enter into alliances with local warlords in the KMT base of Kwangtung Province, the area around Canton. As he progressed north, Chiang offered the warlords in the path of his army a stark choice: resist and be destroyed, or join the KMT. Several warlords prudently chose the latter alternative, bringing their armed followers en masse onto the side of the KMT and in return being confirmed in control of their territories, not as warlords but as legitimate governors recognized by the emerging Nationalist regime.

With their policy of allowing cooperative warlords to ally with it, the KMT could present the Northern Expedition as an instrument not of conquest but of unification. More fundamentally, if Chiang had not been willing to accept the conversion, however reluctant, of at least some of the warlords, the Northern Expedition might well have suffered military defeat. Besides, if the expedition had fought its way across central and northern China victoriously but too slowly, foreign powers would have had excuse to intervene openly to "establish order."

The co-opting of warlords was thus not a bad idea in itself. It was rather the manner in which it occurred that contained the seeds of future trouble. Chiang incorporated several warlord armies into the KMT ranks as whole units, rather than admitting their members on an individual basis. This type of co-option, along with defection from warlord forces and civilian volunteering, increased the KMT army from 100,000 in July 1926 to 1 million in February 1928.[27] The flood of new soldiers into the KMT overwhelmed and disheartened the competent and sincere party cadres. Consequently these new "allies" received very little political indoctrination. Most of them remained the instruments of former warlords who for the time being chose to wear the KMT colors. Additionally, the success of the Northern Expedition attracted great numbers of bureaucrats and political careerists into the KMT. Convinced that he must establish KMT authority over a unified China as quickly as possible, Chiang accepted all these elements in wholesale batches. Herein lay an essential, long-term, and extremely consequential difference between the KMT and the CCP: "Mao purged, Chiang tried to convert."[28]

The KMT forces soon captured Shanghai, the financial and commercial capital of China and also the center of Chinese Communist Party strength. Elements of the CCP leadership had apparently been planning a move against Chiang, and, although his antiwarlord expedition was not yet completed, he chose to end his collaboration with the Communists, turning upon them violently.[29] Thus, "the twenty-two year-long Chinese civil war began in Shanghai in the early morning hours of April 12, 1927."[30] Chiang's preemptive move took them by surprise, and, hobbled by tactical instructions from the Comintern in Moscow—instructions that had more to do with the rivalry between Stalin and Trotsky than with conditions in China—the Communists' reaction was confused and ineffective. In Shanghai and eventually other cities, hundreds of party members were shot by Chiang's supporters and soldiers, and the CCP's small but flourishing urban organization lay in smoking ruins.[31] Soon after the Shanghai affair, the KMT took Nanking, and the Northern Expedition came to an end in June 1928 when Peking fell to Chiang's forces.

The completion of the Northern Expedition and the suppression of the CCP resulted in what appeared to be the unification of China. But such appearances were profoundly deceptive. The expansion of the KMT through the wholesale absorption of warlords and old-style bureaucrats, who usually had views, interests, and aims very different from that party, seriously diluted its cohesiveness and energy. *Chiang never transcended the costs of his too-early and too-easy success.* Perhaps there really had been no alternative to choosing quick victory rather than slow but genuine consolidation; nevertheless, that choice had resulted in the KMT and its armies becoming too large and too heterogeneous. Later events made it impossible for Chiang to undertake a thorough housecleaning of the KMT, the serious weaknesses of which became painfully clear years later when Chiang's forces came to grips with the smaller but more compact and cohesive armies of a resurgent Communist Party under Mao Tse-tung. But all that was many years in the future. For the time being, as his most recent biographer writes, "against all odds and expectations, Chiang Kai-shek had defeated the warlords or brought them under the umbrella of a republican government and a single party—the Kuomintang. It was a historic and impressive achievement."[32]

At the conclusion of the Northern Expedition, Chiang established his capital at Nanking, inaugurating the period of Nationalist rule known as the "Nanking Decade." Now the new regime had to confront the staggering responsibility of dealing with the multiple, deeply rooted, and interconnected pathologies afflicting China. C. Martin Wilbur points out that, "though the politically aware looked forward with hope in 1928, progress toward creating a modern nation-state was sure to be slow even under the most favorable conditions. And such were not to be."[33] Lloyd Eastman notes, "Ten years [was going to be] too brief a time to establish a completely new national administration and to turn back the tide of political disintegration and national humiliation that for a century and a half had assailed the nation. Even if conditions had been ideal, the new government could have done little more than initiate political, social and economic reforms."[34] Conditions were of course far from ideal and became catastrophically worse. Nonetheless, during the Nanking Decade the accomplishments of Chiang's regime were by no means negligible. Its reforms included a centralized system of tax collection; an improved road network; and efforts to increase grain production, control insects, and make education standardized, more extensive, and based on a single form of the language. The regime also made serious strides in the field of women's rights as it worked to abolish forced marriages, concubinage, foot-binding, and other social ills. At the same time, the industrial sector of China's economy experienced an impressive annual growth rate of 6 percent.[35] There is no denying that much progress was made, so that "although today Nationalist China has become a synonym for corruption and ineptitude, to foreign observers at the time it was a truism that the provinces ruled by Nanking [the KMT] were the heart of an emerging modern state which was attracting the loyalty of more and more Chinese."[36] Even as late as 1941, at least one scholar believed that a victory over Japan by Chiang's badly battered regime "would create a nucleus for liberal democracy in Asia."[37] As Robert Bedeski reminds us, during the all-too-brief Nanking Decade, "the KMT regime established the foundations of the modern Chinese State and created an incomplete set of political structures which served as a 'rough draft' for the [Communist regime to come]. The reforms [in Communist China] since 1976 reestablish this lineage but do not acknowledge it."[38]

Mao Tse-tung and Guerrilla Warfare

Mao Tse-tung used to be heralded as one of the world's master political thinkers because he conceived the idea of a revolution based on the peasantry.[39] But consider that the superiority of the weapons of any even semimodern army, and the long period of training necessary to master the effective use of such weapons, have very often led rebels to adopt rural guerrilla warfare. Quite beyond that, special circumstances led Mao to the countryside. The classic Leninist model of the urban coup was totally inappropriate for China, with its vast size, overwhelmingly peasant population, and primitive transportation facilities.[40] Moreover, the CCP had already proved much too weak to confront the armed power of Chiang and the KMT directly, and the Nationalists were firmly in control of all of China's great coastal cities. Mao developed his countryside strategy because he had to: if China was going to have a Communist revolution, it would have to base itself, however incongruously, on the peasantry (of course, always under "the leadership of the proletariat," i.e., of the central committee of the CCP).

The Role of Guerrillas in Maoist Thought

Given conditions in China since the overthrow of the Imperial government, Mao of necessity came to realize that a Communist revolution would require protracted military struggle on a vast scale. Although Mao is known in the West preeminently as the creator of modern guerrilla tactics, it was fundamental in his view that guerrilla war was auxiliary to conventional war; the revolution would not succeed until guerrilla bands had developed into, or had been superseded by, regular large-scale armies with heavy equipment. Guerrillas alone could not achieve victory.[41] "An independent [i.e., Communist] regime must be an armed one"; in addition to setting up guerrilla bands in KMT-controlled (and later Japanese-occupied) territory, the Communists in their base areas (or "soviets," as they were called) must develop substantial conventional forces. "The existence of a regular Red Army of adequate strength," wrote Mao, "is a necessary condition for the existence of Red political power."[42] By 1945, this regular Red Army (exclusive of guerrilla units) totaled nine hundred thousand men, and during the ensuing civil war it grew much larger.

In Mao's thinking, conventional warfare would be primary and decisive. He wrote in "On Protracted War": "Among the forms of warfare in the anti-Japanese war mobile warfare comes first and guerrilla warfare second. When we say that in the entire war mobile warfare is primary and guerrilla warfare supplementary, we mean that the outcome of the war depends mainly on regular warfare, especially in its mobile form, and that guerrilla warfare cannot shoulder the main responsibility in deciding the outcome." In summary, "guerrilla warfare will not remain the same throughout this long and cruel war, but will rise to a higher level and develop into mobile warfare. Thus the strategic role of guerrilla warfare is twofold: to support regular warfare and *to transform itself into regular warfare*."[43]

How then, according to Mao, would guerrillas specifically contribute to final victory? In his *Basic Tactics*, Mao insists that

the principal object of the action of a guerrilla unit lies in dealing the enemy the strongest possible blows to his morale, and in creating disorder and agitation in his rear, in drawing off his principal forces to the flanks or to the rear, in stopping or slowing down his operations, and ultimately in dissipating his fighting strength so that the enemy's units are crushed one by one [by conventional forces] and he is precipitated into a situation where, even by rapid and deceptive actions, he can neither advance nor retreat.[44]

In the late 1930s the CCP was in no conceivable way strong enough to confront the regular armies of the KMT. In these circumstances, Mao developed his theories and techniques of guerrilla warfare, because he had no choice.

Politics First

Foremost among Mao's ideas was the primacy of politics: guerrilla war was above all a political process. The most basic of all political questions is "Who commands?" With regard to this question, the creation and maintenance of armed forces, whether guerrilla or conventional, involved many difficulties and dangers. Not least of these was the specter of excessive influence by military chiefs over the political leadership of the revolutionary movement, or even the complete dominance of the party by its military commanders, as was the case in the KMT. Therefore, as Mao famously declared, "every communist must grasp the truth that 'political power grows out of the barrel of a gun,'" but "our principle is that the party commands the gun, and the gun must never be allowed to command the party."[45] But how can one prevent the command of the party by the gun, the command of the political leadership by the military chieftains— especially if the latter are successful in war? That Mao was always concerned about dangers of this type is shown by his attack, as late as 1937, on what he considered a tendency within the Red Army to move toward warlordism. Mao expended every effort to ensure that in the Chinese Communist armed forces, at least at the higher levels, the regular officers were reliable party members. He also appointed to various strategic posts within the Red Army political officers with direct access to the highest levels of the party. These regimental political officers, however, were not quite like Trotsky's commissars.[46] In the Soviet Army, political commissars were watchdogs set over military commanders of unproven political loyalty, whereas the principal duty of the CCP regimental political officer was not the surveillance of the commander but the indoctrination of the troops (a practice earlier employed by the KMT, owing to Soviet influences at the Whampoa Military Academy).

Once the leadership question has been settled, the next item on the guerrilla agenda must be morale. "Weapons are an important factor in war," Mao wrote, "but not the decisive factor; it is people, not things, that are decisive. The contest of strength is not only a contest of military and economic power, but also a contest of human power and morale."[47]

Morale through Indoctrination

Most students of guerrilla warfare stress the necessity for the guerrillas to have good morale. Without it, how will they endure the physical and psychological hardships involved in months or even years of operating in difficult or unhealthful terrain, deprived of the consolations of normal life, perhaps lacking the most elementary medical care, eating irregularly and often poorly, and pursued by the security forces of the state, who are seeking to kill them?[48]

After experiencing the hardships of such an existence, guerrillas will sooner or later ask themselves and each other: For what cause are we risking our own lives and taking the lives of others and destroying property? How do we know that our acts in furtherance of this cause are noble and not merely criminal? How sure can we be that our sacrifices will not be in vain? And how will the triumph of our cause represent an improvement over the present state of things? How shall these difficulties be overcome, how shall these questions be answered? Mao's response was clear: "The fighting capacity of a guerrilla unit," he insisted, "is not determined exclusively by military arts, but depends above all on political consciousness."[49]

Profoundly convinced of the indissoluble link between "political consciousness" (or conviction) and military morale, Mao sought to build and lead an army of convinced believers through constant political indoctrination, the true essence of the Communist military organization: our cause is just, our enemy is inadequate, and hence our triumph is certain. As Cromwell's army had been a church in arms, so Mao's army was to be a party in arms.

In Mao's famous formulation, the guerrilla, whatever his level of political sophistication, "moves among the people as the fish through the water." A good deal of instruction time for both guerrillas and regulars was therefore devoted to teaching them how to behave properly toward civilians ("Return borrowed articles, be sanitary, be polite," etc).[50] The leaders of Chinese Communism were determined to create forces that would enjoy the genuine sympathy and support of the civil population among whom they operated, and certainly

Mao believed that such support was absolutely vital to the triumph of his revolution. He also perceived that correct beliefs ("political consciousness") would reinforce correct behavior, and vice versa. (Nevertheless, as we shall see, during the civil war after 1945, Mao repeatedly ordered that captured Nationalist and puppet soldiers be incorporated en masse into the ranks of the People's Liberation Army.)

Communist forces, moreover, must engage in ceaseless propaganda, aimed not only at their own soldiers or at civilians, but at the opponent as well. For example, Mao declared that "the most effective method of propaganda directed at the enemy forces is to release captured soldiers and give the wounded [enemy] medical treatment."[51] This was a true and powerful insight: KMT soldiers who knew that capture by the Communists meant decent treatment and eventual release could be expected to give up rather than fight to the death or even to the point of serious danger.

Morale through Victory

Many factors can contribute to good morale: defense of one's hearth, religious exaltation, personal and group loyalties, and perhaps especially the belief that one is risking one's life on behalf of a cause whose triumph is desirable and probable. But there is absolutely no greater morale builder than victory in combat. Mao firmly grasped the truth that nothing attaches a combatant to his cause more securely than the conviction that it is going to be victorious. Clausewitz taught that the morale of a guerrilla movement must be built up by winning early victories against very small numbers of government troops. The first duty of the guerrilla unit is to survive. There must be no needless heroics and absolutely no staking of the existence of the guerrillas on one throw of the dice. But the second duty of the guerrilla unit is to win, no matter how small the encounter. "Many minor victories," wrote Mao, "[make] a major victory. Herein lies the great strategic role of guerrilla warfare in the war of resistance [against Japan]."[52]

Hence, Mao insists in *Basic Tactics*, "if we do not have a 100 per cent guarantee of victory, we should not fight a battle."[53] The guarantee of victory lay in concentrating greatly superior numbers at the critical point and in surprise, two factors that of course almost invariably go together. Guerrillas must therefore never be led into combat unless victory is arithmetically certain, owing either to their locally overwhelming numbers or to other factors, such as notoriously and demonstrably poor enemy morale. Mao insisted on this principle whether in regard to a small guerrilla band attacking an isolated Japanese outpost or (later) the regular Communist army attacking Nationalist main-force units. "We should resolutely fight a decisive engagement in every campaign or battle in which we are sure of victory; we should avoid a decisive engagement in every campaign or battle in which we are not sure of victory; and we should absolutely avoid a strategically decisive engagement on which the fate of the whole nation is staked." Whatever the overall strategic situation, however badly Mao's forces might be outnumbered in the big picture, he always strove to achieve local superiority, to have more men (many times more) at the particular point of action: "Our strategy is to pit one against ten and our tactics are to pit ten against one—this is one of our fundamental principles for gaining mastery over the enemy."[54]

Mao often said, "The enemy advances, we retreat. The enemy camps, we harass. The enemy tires, we attack. The enemy retreats, we pursue."[55] The guerrillas' most important weapon was the unexpected attack: "The peculiar quality of the operations of a guerrilla unit lies in taking the enemy by surprise." Of course, surprise depends upon the guerrillas moving quickly. Here the guerrillas' light armament becomes an advantage: "The great superiority of a small guerilla unit lies in its mobility."[56] (The revealing term the Romans used for the equipment a regular army hauls around with it was *impedimenta*.) Accordingly, "the basic principle of guerrilla warfare must be the [tactical] offensive," and "the sole habitual tactic of a guerrilla unit is the ambush."[57]

These prescriptions proved not very difficult to achieve against the ponderous and less-than-brilliantly-led KMT forces after the end of World War II. But in addition, the Nationalist forces suffered from the classic dilemma of almost all counterinsurgent forces in history: how to properly allocate their troops between hunting guerrillas and providing security to populations and places. The KMT, although its total forces were larger in the beginning, had to garrison or protect all points and areas of potential strategic or tactical value: population centers, arsenals, bridges, main roads, railroads, airfields, training camps, banks, symbolic buildings—everything. Hence, observes F.F. Liu, "the nationalists, defending a large area and holding many critical lines of communication, were particularly susceptible to [Communist] hit-and-run tactics."[58]

Secure Regional Bases

The huge geographic extent of China and its poor communications always seriously hobbled the counterinsurgency efforts of the KMT. These conditions also allowed—almost required—Mao to develop the concept of the secure regional base: a remote area in which to build up and supply guerrilla or conventional units and also to serve as a laboratory for political and social experimentation. Mao established base areas in mountainous districts or marshlands, traditional bandit territory, far from population centers and the reach of the KMT state. In a word, geography trumped economics or sociology. Mao was creating what Samuel P. Huntington many years later called the Eastern Model of Revolution; in this scenario, revolutionary forces do not attempt to seize power at the center (in contrast to the French or the Leninist model). Instead, they establish themselves in a place relatively safe from government interference and then seek to spread out gradually from this base, taking over one new area after another, until at last they isolate the government in its capital city (this is the mirror image of the classic "clear-and-hold" method of counterinsurgency).[59]

This creation of a freestanding, self-sufficient, peasant-based "Soviet Republic" within and against the larger Chinese state represented a tremendous deviation from earlier CCP strategy, not to speak of traditional Marxist teaching. Mao was insistent on this fundamental point: "Guerrilla warfare could not last long or grow without base areas."[60] He was also keenly aware that the viability of these base areas was utterly dependent on the government's incapacity to deploy and sustain great numbers of its troops against them or to attack them with massive airpower. In "Problems of Strategy in Guerrilla War against Japan," Mao observed that "the vastness of China's territory and the enemy's shortage of troops provide guerrilla warfare in China with this [ability to flourish]"; and it followed ineluctably that "this is an important, even a primary condition, as far as the possibility of waging guerrilla warfare is concerned, and small countries like Belgium which lack this condition have few or no such possibilities."[61]

Two Points to Ponder

An appreciation of Mao's wisdom in emphasizing the role of political conviction in warfare does not require one automatically to assume that all guerrilla forces, especially Communist ones, are or were composed exclusively, or even mainly, of highly motivated ideologues. In analyzing the ability of some guerrilla forces to survive under the most adverse conditions, one must take into account several factors: pride in one's unit, the prospects of severe punishment if captured, fear of reprisal for desertion or substandard performance, a feeling of having been cut off from society at large, and above all the sense of invincibility that results from the fact that well-led guerrillas are permitted to go into combat only when victory is nearly certain. One would expect none of these morale-building factors to survive even the shortest period of confinement behind barbed wire, an expectation borne out in the behavior of Vietcong and Malayan Communist prisoners, for example, who would betray their comrades with impressive facility, especially for material inducements.[62]

In the decades since the end of the fighting in China, disagreement has developed over the question of whether active (as opposed to passive or coerced) civilian support is a necessity, or merely a great advantage, to guerrillas. One distinguished authority has written that "only when the people provide intelligence, guides, recruits, and labor can the rebels set ambushes, avoid mopping-up campaigns, and exercise their extreme mobility. While a rebel army may be able to obtain supplies at gunpoint, it cannot get this positive support from people if it behaves like a bunch of bandits."[63]

This is a reasonable proposition, and it seems to receive direct confirmation from the triumph of Mao and indirect confirmation from the complete eradication of Ernesto Guevara's Bolivian expedition after his ignominious failure to obtain civilian support. But from the self-evident validity of the statement that guerrillas derive incalculable benefits from a friendly civil population and hence should not behave "like bandits," it does not follow that all protracted guerrilla operations by definition enjoy uncoerced civilian support, with the implication that the government against which a guerrilla struggle is being waged must necessarily be repressive and unpopular. Even well-disciplined guerrillas may and do use threats of violence against the civil population. If one were to discount, or even to deny a priori, the use and the effectiveness of terror against civilians, to obtain recruits or intelligence or anything else, or if one were to dismiss the possibility of resigned belief on the part of these civilians that the rebels are probably going to win and therefore must be placated, it would constitute a serious impediment to a broader understanding of guerrilla war, especially in light of the Algerian and Vietnamese experiences.[64] The exact relationship between a given guerrilla movement and its noncombatant environment is a subject to be investigated, not assumed.

But let us return to Mao in the China of the 1930s. The development and effective application of certain basic concepts—the central role of regular armed forces, party supremacy over those armed forces, constant indoctrination of troops, no battle without overwhelming tactical superiority, careful treatment of the civil population, leniency toward prisoners, and the secure territorial base—eventually bore much fruit for the Communist forces confronting a war-battered and demoralized KMT. In the early 1930s, however, the picture was radically different. The large and self-confident KMT army was on the offensive. By the fall of 1934, the fifth of Chiang's "encirclement campaigns" (discussed below) placed in question the very survival of Communism as a viable military force. At that time, the CCP decided to save what could be saved by embarking on the famous Long March: 100,000 Communists set out on the journey from Kiangsi Province. One year later, after meandering six thousand miles through swamps and across mountains, ravaged by hunger and harassed by the KMT, perhaps 5,000 survivors reached what was to become the new base area in Shensi Province.[65] Chiang was preparing a final annihilation campaign for these remnants late in 1936 when a conspiracy among some of his generals resulted in his arrest. His captors insisted that Chiang give up what they viewed as his obsession with destroying the CCP; they demanded instead that he form an alliance with the CCP and turn his attention more fully to the growing menace of Japanese aggression, terms to which Chiang very reluctantly agreed. This episode—the so-called Sian Incident—ensured the survival of a Chinese Communist nucleus and thus changed the history of the whole world.[66] But here we need to backtrack a little.

The Encirclement Campaigns

From the days of the Ming dynasty (1368–1644), the province of Kiangsi in southeastern China had been a stronghold of rebellion against central authority. In this historic crucible of insurgency the Chinese Communist Party had established its main base. And here, from December 1930 to October 1934, Chiang Kai-shek concentrated his efforts, known as the five Encirclement Campaigns, on the final destruction of the CCP. The Communists defeated the first four campaigns. They allowed the Nationalist forces to penetrate deep into their Kiangsi stronghold (Mao wrote: "Boldly lure the enemy troops in deep so as to herd them together and annihilate them" and "The enemy advances, we retreat").[67] Then, by taking advantage of interior lines, effective communications, and good intelligence, the Communists mobilized their whole strength in surprise night attacks against first one relatively small group of KMT troops, then another ("After smashing one column, we should shift our forces to smash another, and by smashing them one by one, shatter the converging attack").[68] Another favorite CCP tactic was to besiege some vital point and then ambush the force sent to the rescue.

It was not, however, just good Communist tactics that accounted for the failures of the first four encirclement campaigns. Personal, factional, and regional antagonisms among the Nationalist commanders undermined Chiang's efforts in Kiangsi, as they would in the coming war against the Japanese.[69] Poor communications and inadequate logistics also played their baleful role. But it was above all a lack of airpower that always severely hampered counterinsurgency operations by the KMT forces.

The First Encirclement Campaign developed in December 1930 and January 1931. Although employing three armies, it wound down in the face of superior Communist tactics. The Second Encirclement

Campaign, in April and May 1931, deployed 200,000 Nationalist troops. Rivalries among Nationalist commanders were the principal cause of their failure.[70] During the Third Encirclement Campaign, unfolding between July and September 1931, Chiang himself, in order to overcome the obvious factionalism that had hampered the first two campaigns, took personal charge, directing 300,000 soldiers. But his efforts met with little success, being distracted by a rebellion of anti-Chiang factionalists in Canton and by the Japanese invasion of distant Manchuria. The Fourth Encirclement Campaign, from January to May 1933, pitted 153,000 Nationalist troops against 65,000 Communists.[71] Fears of renewed Japanese aggression in North China halted this effort.

These first four campaigns had been "modern," in that they employed concepts borrowed from European armies. Their objective had been the annihilation of the enemy forces. In contrast, the strategy of the Fifth Encirclement Campaign, which lasted from October 1933 to October 1934, derived more from traditional Chinese strategic concepts, especially ones developed during the suppression of the bloody and protracted Taiping rebellion in the mid-nineteenth century.[72] This fifth campaign, accordingly, sought not to kill insurgents but to take and hold territory, forcing the guerrillas out and away. This time Chiang deployed about 800,000 troops against 150,000 Communists.[73] The campaign united the strategic offensive with the tactical defensive: that is, KMT forces would move massively into Communist territory while employing self-protective tactics to deter enemy attack. Nationalist troops would often end the day's march in midafternoon, allowing them time to build a fortified camp to discourage night attacks. (Having troops spend the night in a purpose-built fortified camp had been standard procedure in the Roman army in its great days.)

Since the end of the third campaign (September 1931), the Nationalists had constructed many new roads to help overcome the serious supply problems that had hindered their earlier efforts. With this same objective, they had set up telephone units and constructed new airports. They also received another accession of supporters for the Nationalist cause: the radicalization of the CCP land program since 1933 drove key elements of the rural elite, hitherto deeply suspicious of the urban and reformist KMT, to support Chiang.

In this fifth campaign, the Nationalists introduced a major new weapon system against the Communists: blockhouses, an elaboration of the concept of strategic offensive plus tactical defensive. Rural laborers, under supervision of the local elite, constructed lines of these blockhouses, ultimately thousands of small fortifications surrounded by trenches and barbed wire, with interconnecting fields of machine-gun and artillery fire.[74] Some of the largest blockhouses were made of brick and stone and were three stories high; simpler ones went up in from one to three days. After a line of blockhouses had been erected, the troops would advance a few kilometers and, under the protection of the existing blockhouses, erect a new line of them, then advance again. To support all this construction, the KMT built hundreds of miles of roads. These blockhouse lines choked Communist economic activities. They also meant that timely medical care was available for wounded Nationalist soldiers, a provision that was very good for morale. But above all, the blockhouse system deprived the Communists of their greatest advantage, the ability to maneuver. At the same time, the Communist forces could not simply assault the blockhouse lines because of the Nationalists' superior weaponry.[75]

So undeniable were the successes of the fifth campaign that the CCP leadership decided to abandon Kiangsi and embark upon the famous Long March—actually a Long Retreat.[76] The march began in the fall of 1934 and ended with the arrival one year later of the battered remnants of the party in their new home in Shensi Province, in north-central China. (The success of the march depended in no small part on lavish use of the substantial funds the CCP had been receiving from Moscow.) The Nationalist campaign against the Communists in Kiangsi was so thorough that the Communists never tried to reestablish a presence in that province.

By 1936 the Chinese Communist Party was facing extermination at the hands of Chiang's forces. As Lyman Van Slyke wrote:

The Red Army had given a brilliant account of itself [on the Long March]. It is doubtful, however, that it could have continued to maintain itself if Generalissimo Chiang Kai-shek had pursued his policy of military anni-hilation of the Red forces. . . . At the end of 1936 [Chiang] was preparing a new "blockhouse-fortress" campaign around the [CCP] base in Shensi along the lines of the Fifth Campaign in Kiangsi. Had he decided to open this campaign, the Communist forces would almost certainly have been either "exterminated" or forced to begin a new "Long March," probably across Mongolia to Soviet Russia.[77]

But war with Japan changed everything.

Chiang always believed that the Japanese could not succeed in conquering China and that the true menace was to be found in the Chinese Communist Party. His slogan "unification before resistance" encapsulated his desire to stamp out the Communists before dealing with the invading Japanese. But the Sian Incident forced him to turn away from a sixth campaign, away from the final elimination of the CCP.[78] The Nationalists continued to fight the Communists, not without effect, by other tactics, including amnesties and the penetration of Communist apparatuses by KMT intelligence agents.[79] Nevertheless, the Japanese invasion saved the nucleus of Chinese Communism and thus set in motion a series of events that affected the entire globe, and not least Japan itself.

The Second Sino-Japanese War

The Sino-Japanese War that broke out in 1937 was the true beginning of World War II. It soon expanded into a global conflict and profoundly reshaped world politics for the rest of the twentieth century. For David Lu, one can hardly exaggerate the importance of this contest:

> The Sino-Japanese War was the longest war Japan ever fought against any nation. On the question of the withdrawal of Japanese troops from China, the United States and Japan were poles apart in their negotiations, and the fighting there thus constituted one of the major causes of the Pacific war. In destroying the power structure of the Nationalist government and creating a vacuum, the Sino-Japanese War also prepared the way for the eventual triumph of the Communists in China.[80]

Japan's Vision

World War II in the Pacific had been preparing for a very long time. Although that war turned into the greatest naval struggle in the history of the planet, its origins were not rooted in questions of naval dominance or security. On the contrary, observes D. Clayton James, "Japanese leaders from the Meiji Restoration of 1868 onward had envisioned their nation not as a leading maritime state *but rather as the dominant continental power of East Asia.*" Indeed, Japan's "identification of national security and economic prosperity with a hegemonial position in East Asia became an article of faith for the Imperial government that was not compromised until the end of the Pacific War [in 1945]."[81] To attain that hegemony, Japan had already fought two major and victorious wars, against China in 1894–95 (the first Sino-Japanese War) and against Russia in 1904–5.

Thus, explains James B. Crowley, "China policy, not policy toward the United States, the Soviet Union, or Britain, represented the basic axiom and the basic dynamic in Japanese foreign affairs."[82] During the 1930s, Japanese leaders saw the conquest of China as providing their nation with raw materials and markets, an outlet for its surplus population, a bulwark against any Soviet move into China (especially Manchuria), a means of solidifying their own political power, and an opportunity for industrialists to make great profits from war production.[83] But over and above these specifics was "a persistent obsession with status and prestige—or to put it in terms Japanese would more readily recognize, rank and honor [in world affairs]."[84]

In 1931 the Japanese had taken over Manchuria and set up a puppet state called Manchukuo, under the nominal rule of the former and last emperor of China. This state was a substantial enterprise, extending over five hundred thousand square miles and including nearly 40 million inhabitants, most of whom were not ethnically Chinese but Manchurians, Mongols, and Koreans. Protests in the League of Nations over the conquest of Manchuria caused Japan to walk out of that body permanently. The Japanese Empire now included Manchukuo, along with Taiwan, Korea, and island possessions in the Pacific. The move into Manchuria was in part a preparation for what Japanese ruling circles saw as an inevitable struggle with the Soviet Union. But beyond this, the Japanese leadership also intended to bring China proper into its political and economic orbit, into the much-heralded "Greater East Asia Co-Prosperity Sphere," a Japanese Monroe Doctrine for the Far East.

Japanese efforts to manipulate China diplomatically ran into increasingly strong resistance by the middle 1930s, and the prospect of a China unified under the nationalist (and xenophobic) Chiang filled wider and wider circles in Japan with alarm. At the same time, key elements in Japan were gravely worried about the consequences for their country's influence, or even its security, if the Communists should triumph on the Chinese mainland. These factors helped persuade the Japanese, especially the semi-independent armed forces, to invade north and central China in the summer of 1937.

Japan's swift conquest of Manchuria a few years previously had set up expectations for a quick collapse of Chinese resistance. But "contempt [for the Chinese] and overconfidence," in the view of one study, "led the Japanese army to engage in a long, drawn-out war essentially unprepared, and no coherent strategic planning was developed."[85] The armies were waging war on a mammoth front: Chiang set up his wartime capital in Chungking, which was farther away from Tokyo than Ankara is from London. In real terms it was much farther than that, because of China's primitive railroad and highway system. (In 1937 China had seventy-five hundred miles of railroads, less than the state of Illinois, one-sixty-fourth its size.) Without foreign allies, without armaments to match those of the Japanese, Chiang adopted a general strategy of withdrawing into remote southwestern China and waging a war of attrition.

As the war on the mainland turned out to be much more difficult than Japan's leaders had expected, the country's logistic system became strained to a dangerous degree. Hence, the Tokyo government turned its eyes toward Southeast Asia, seeing it as an inexhaustible source of vital oil, rubber, metals, and foodstuffs and weakly defended by the British, the Dutch, and the French, nations at that time fighting for their very existence on the European continent.

Expansion of the War

From the beginning, the administration of Franklin Roosevelt publicly supported Chiang Kai-shek's government against the Japanese and their Chinese collaborationist regimes. As early as the fall of 1938, General Tojo (a future premier) stated that Chinese resistance was being sustained by Soviet, British, and U.S. assistance.[86] Indeed, the Imperial Rescript declaring war on the United States and Britain (December 1941) blamed those countries for keeping Chiang's "fratricidal" regime in Chungking alive.[87]

But before that, an event occurred that was as unforeseen as it was cataclysmic: the fall of France to the Nazis in June 1940. The shockwaves from the French collapse were going to entirely transform the political landscape all across the planet. In Berlin, Hitler and his entourage, and many others, became convinced of his military genius and general infallibility. In Rome, Mussolini reluctantly concluded that Germany would dominate Europe for the foreseeable future, and he therefore brought Italy into the war. In Washington, Congress passed the Two-Ocean Navy Act (July 1940). In Moscow, Stalin decided to annex the Baltic republics and Bessarabia, moves that convinced Hitler that the day of reckoning with Bolshevism must come soon. In London, obtaining the close support of the United States became the most important aim of the British war cabinet, and the Entente Cordial with France, a fundament of British foreign policy since 1904, was eventually replaced by the "special relationship" with the Americans, a relationship lasting into the twenty-first century. And in Tokyo, the now-patent inability of France to mount even a token defense of Indochina prompted the Japanese to occupy northern Vietnam (September 1940), primarily to interdict supplies going to the Nationalist government at Chungking.[88]

At about the same time, to protect itself from American interference with its China campaign and British and American retaliation during and after its planned conquest of Southeast Asia, Japan sought the alliance of Germany and Italy and signed the Axis Pact with those countries. Chiang Kai-shek, much more clear-sighted than the Tokyo government, viewed Japan's joining the Axis as an incalculable boon to himself and his cause: "This is the best thing that could have happened to us," he wrote triumphantly; "the trend toward victory in the war of resistance has been decided."[89]

In late July 1941, the Japanese occupied southern Indochina. The ominous threat to British Malaya, the Dutch East Indies, and the U.S. Philippines represented by this latest aggressive move led President Franklin D. Roosevelt on August 1 to proclaim an oil embargo against Japan. This was an extremely serious blow to the Japanese, because they had to import 88 percent of their petroleum products, of which imports 80 percent came from the United States. Great Britain, Australia, and the Dutch East Indies joined this embargo. (The Japanese had been negotiating for months to buy petroleum from the Dutch.) In Geoffrey Blainey's stark formulation, "the sudden ban on petroleum and other vital supplies undermined Japan's war campaign in central China even more than if Britain, the United States and Australia had combined to send an army of 200,000 and squadrons of military aircraft to assist the Chinese." Not surprisingly, war in the Pacific now became inevitable.[90]

Sino-Japanese Collaboration

As their campaign in China dragged interminably on, the Japanese began setting up puppet regimes there, each under the tutelage of a different Japanese army. In March 1940, these separate entities were combined into the National Government of China, with its capital at Nanking. The leader of this new regime was Wang Ching-wei (1883–1944), a close friend and disciple of Sun Yat-sen, a former leader of the left wing of the KMT and a longtime rival of Chiang. Like many other leaders of the KMT, Wang had studied in Japan.[91]

Initially, Wang's government was not without prospects of attracting popular support, especially in largely apolitical northern China. Wang preached collaboration with Japan, a country whose achievements and status were admired by many Chinese, because in 1940 China was fighting alone with no prospect of foreign assistance or intervention and because resistance to Japan would result not only in tremendous destruction but also in the ultimate victory of the Chinese Communists.[92] At the same time, Wang's ideological stance of uniting exploited East Asia under the leadership of a culturally similar Japan against Western domination and the Bolshevik threat ("Asia for the Asians!") also had great potential appeal.[93] In summary, he offered the Chinese people peace and economic cooperation with Japan instead of what he and others viewed as interminable and suicidal war. The Wang regime used the same party name, the same slogans, and even the same flag as the KMT, causing great confusion among many of the people who lived in Japanese-occupied areas and indirectly aiding the expansion of Communist influence.

The Imperial Japanese Army relied heavily on Chinese cooperation. Collaborationist troops may have numbered as many as 800,000. Of these almost 500,000 were former Nationalists who had been ordered by Chiang to defect to the Wang regime rather than be defeated by the Japanese.[94] Sometimes troops of the puppet state would give aid to the Communist guerrillas. But quite beyond that, the Japanese never allowed Wang's regime enough autonomy for it to gain legitimacy or to protect the millions it claimed to rule from Japanese rapacity. In time it came to be widely viewed by Chinese as merely a cloak for predatory Japanese policies. The disillusioned Wang died in 1944 at Nagoya University hospital of complications from an old gunshot wound.[95]

Fundamentally, the Japanese never had a unified, thought-out military or political program regarding China. On this central subject, as on many others, the Japanese government often spoke with several voices. Right up until the end of the war, some Japanese diplomats and military commanders wished to reach accommodation with Chiang's government, turning it into an ally or at least a friendly neutral in what many Japanese leaders believed to be an inevitable war with the USSR. Chiang himself, because of his fear and detestation of the Communists, was not opposed to some type of compromise with the Japanese. In 1944 the Japanese offered peace and recognition to the Chiang government, but by then it was much too late.[96]

The Japanese Invasion and the KMT

As the conflict developed, the leadership in Tokyo uneasily settled on "a war of political annihilation against the Nationalist government of China."[97] It would be difficult to exaggerate the catastrophic effects—military, political, economic, and moral—of this decision on Chiang Kai-shek's government. The backbone of the KMT was the progressive elements in the great coastal cities: merchants, professionals, students. These people were by no means democrats, nor did they look with enthusiasm on the prospect of social revolution in the countryside, whence many of them derived much of their real income. They were also very distrustful, in the Chinese manner, of grassroots movements. What they did want, and were willing to work for, was a strong and modern Chinese state, able to maintain internal order, deter or repel external aggression, and build the infrastructure of a modern and developing economic life. China had been making real progress toward these goals when the Japanese invaded the coastal areas and severed the KMT government from its natural supporters. Retreating across China, the Nationalists established their new capital at Chungking, in the southwest, an area that was like another world to the KMT, a backward, remote world dominated by local elites and secret societies, hardly touched by the twentieth century. Most of China's industrial base and financial resources had to be left behind.

At Chungking, Chiang was forced to rely for support on the local landowning class. Not only did the KMT regime now have uncongenial supporters; it was also extremely short of revenue. It therefore made the fateful (if understandable) decision to finance the anti-Japanese war through inflation. By 1945, the retail price index was twenty-six hundred times higher than in 1937.[98] Inflation broke the back of much of the middle class, the KMT's natural constituency. Hardest hit were schoolteachers and other government employees. One careful study concludes that "this inequitable distribution of the burden [of inflation] produced widespread graft and corruption among the civil servants, and it undoubtedly was an important factor in the downfall of the Nationalist government." And Suzanne Pepper believes that "monetary inflation probably contributed more than any other single issue during the [subsequent] civil war years to the loss of urban public confidence in the KMT's ability to govern."[99]

The Japanese war also irreversibly damaged the KMT army (to be discussed shortly).

Japanese Forces in China

Mao Tse-tung established his reputation as a master strategist of guerrilla warfare mainly in fighting against the Imperial Japanese Army (IJA) during World War II. But what is the actual validity of that reputation based on that criterion? Clearly, the IJA was strong enough to push the Nationalists out of Nanking and Shanghai and force them to set up their government in remote Chungking. But nobody had ever claimed that the KMT army was a world-class organization, to say the least. And despite all the shortcomings and mistakes of the KMT forces, the Japanese were never able to force Chiang into surrender or accommodation.

Why not? Why did the Japanese not complete the conquest of China, which they had begun so successfully in Manchuria in 1931 and then recommenced in China proper in 1937? This is of course a complicated question, but the heart of the answer lies in Mao's observation that "their [the Japanese] forces [were] inadequate in relation to China's vast territory."[100]

What, first of all, was the actual strength of the Imperial Japanese Army in China proper (excluding Manchukuo, the puppet state established in Manchuria in 1931)? Surprisingly, perhaps, it has not been easy for experts to agree on an exact figure. One distinguished study states that in 1937 the IJA totaled less than 1 million men, of whom about two-thirds were in China; another source estimates that in the fall of 1938 the IJA had 600,000 soldiers in China proper.[101] By 1941 the IJA seems to have had 27 divisions in China, out of a total of 51, for a total of about 1.1 million men.[102] A study by Colin Gray concludes that there were only 23 divisions in China by late 1941. *The Statesman's Yearbook 1944* estimates a mere 14 IJA divisions in China in late 1942. Other authoritative sources suggest that Japanese troops in China proper and Manchukuo numbered between 1 and 1.2 million, of which many were watching the Soviet border rather than operating against guerrillas.[103] The IJA may in fact have had no more than 850,000 men in China in 1943 and but 560,000 in 1944.[104] At the time of the surrender, there were at most 950,000 IJA soldiers in all of China, most of poor quality. Chu Teh, the soldier who under Mao built the Red Army, estimated that Japanese troops in China proper numbered only 580,000 in 1945.[105]

It appears reasonable, then, to estimate that the IJA in China proper rarely if ever reached a total of 1 million troops. One million soldiers to subdue and occupy a country of 480 million, 85 percent of whom were rural, would have been statistically the equivalent of President Lincoln's trying to suppress the Confederate rebellion in 1861 with an army of nineteen thousand men. Most of the Japanese forces were engaged in operations against the Nationalist armies, not against the Communists. The grotesquely inadequate numbers of Japanese troops and the language barrier between them and the surrounding civilians allowed space for Communist guerrillas to operate, anarchy to develop, and disillusionment to spread among those Chinese who initially entertained some pro-Japanese sentiments.[106] In North China, where most Communist guerrilla activity was concentrated, Japanese troop density was usually no greater than four soldiers per ten square kilometers. Mao was quite aware of these facts and their implications: "Japan, though strong, does not have enough soldiers." Therefore, "the enemy, employing his small forces against a vast country, can only occupy some big cities and main lines of communication and part of the plain." Confronting these Japanese forces, the KMT began the war in 1937 with 1.5 million men, a number that increased to 5.7 million by 1941. One must add to that figure the 440,000 mobilized by the Communists by the mid-1940s. Thus Mao could confidently declare that "Japanese imperialism has two basic weaknesses, namely, its shortage of troops and the fact that it is fighting on foreign soil."[107]

As the quantity of Japanese troops against whom Mao made war was insufficient, so the quality of those troops was uneven. A substantial proportion of IJA forces in China were garrison units, not first-line combat troops. Their levels of training and discipline were, on the average, not impressive; Mao himself admitted the less-than-first-rate condition of his Japanese foes many times. In 1939, the Soviet Army was still reeling from the incredibly destructive Stalinist purges of its officer corps; soon that army made a scandalously poor showing against the Finns. Yet—revealingly—when the IJA clashed with this same Soviet Army in Manchuria, during the so-called Nomonhan Incident in the summer of 1939, the IJA came off very badly, losing eighteen thousand soldiers.[108]

The equipment of the Japanese Army also left much to be desired. The standard-issue IJA rifle was a copy of European models and thus was rather too long and heavy for the average Japanese soldier. This rifle, moreover, along with the field artillery and most machine guns, was of World War I design. With regard to mobility and armor, the Japanese forces on the mainland were not an Asian version of a Nazi blitzkrieg force. On the contrary, "the army remained an infantry army, reliant on horses."[109] Most of the army's trucks were imported American models, for which spare parts of course became unavailable. Japanese tanks were few (only four hundred produced in 1944), light, old-fashioned, and intended for infantry support. The Soviet T-34 medium tank carried a 76mm gun and 45mm of armor; the American Sherman tank had a 75mm gun and 75mm of armor; the American Pershing tank, a late entrant into the war, carried a 100mm gun and 105mm of armor; and the German Panther tank came with a 75mm gun and 120mm of armor. In contrast, the most common IJA tank carried a 37mm gun and its armor was so thin that small-arms fire could penetrate it.[110]

The quality of military intelligence regarding China available to the Japanese Army was also inadequate. One study of Japanese intelligence notes that "to be posted to China was a black mark on one's career, a sign that an officer was not suited to learn from German methods or prepare for the real war to come against the Soviet Union." In fact, Japanese intelligence on a great many subjects was inferior to that of other major powers. More ominously, "while Japan's information collection efforts may sometimes have been of high quality, her leaders relied more upon their own, often uninformed, ideas of how potential enemies might respond to Japanese policies. Too frequently, they assumed that those responses would be in accord with Japan's wishes. In short, they engaged in 'best case' analysis."[111]

True enough, the Japanese Army in North China was able to inflict much damage on the Communist forces. Nevertheless, in terms of numbers, equipment, quality, relevant intelligence, and especially its general ability to undertake effective counterinsurgency, the IJA against which Mao made his reputation was notably inadequate.[112]

The Japanese and Communist Expansion

Maoist tactics, no matter how intriguing or self-evident on paper, would have had no effect whatever without men and women to put them into practice. The golden age of Maoist guerrilla warfare was the struggle against the Japanese during World War II. In that contest, it was not the attractions of Communist ideology that produced recruits for Mao's guerrilla forces. Rather it was the barbarous behavior of the Japanese Imperial Army, barbarism partly provoked by the operations of Maoist guerrillas.

By 1937, the Communists had been fighting the KMT for nearly a decade. Their army numbered no more than fifty thousand men, and they had few real links with the peasantry. Their forces were "concentrated in central Shensi province, a backwater of China in the loop of the Yellow River." Before the Japanese invasion, the peasantry was a passive element in political affairs; even the Communists' appeal to its most basic economic interests had little effect.[113] The year before, Mao had embarked on the Long March to Shensi to save the remnants of his shattered following from total destruction at the hands of the conquering KMT. The coming of the Japanese changed all this.

It now appears hard to question that the factor that more than any other saved the fortunes of the Chinese Communist Party and allowed it to become a major contender for supreme power was Japanese brutality against the peasantry. In late 1940, the CCP in northern China launched its Hundred Regiments Offensive. This operation, the largest and most prolonged by the Communists during the entire war, did extensive damage to the Japanese occupation forces. For years, the Japanese armies in Manchuria and North China had fought the guerrillas largely through massive population resettlement and tight control of food.[114] But in response to the Hundred Regiments Offensive, the Japanese, under the command of General Yasuji Okamura, embarked upon the "three alls" campaign: "Kill all, burn all, destroy all." The objective, in Maoist terms, was to dry up the water in which the guerrilla swam, to utterly devastate an area and thus deprive the guerrillas of food, recruits, and intelligence. In carrying out this "policy," the Japanese would surround a district, kill or scatter all persons and animals within it, then burn everything to render the area uninhabitable. Thus, the Japanese themselves created the conditions for the alliance between the CCP and increasing numbers of peasants.

Since Communist guerrillas followed Mao's constant instruction to run away from superior forces, the Japanese rarely encountered them. The people they did encounter were the defenseless and hitherto inactive peasants. Indiscriminate Japanese terror taught the peasants that there was no safety, no living, with the Japanese, even if the peasants did not help the guerrillas, *even if the peasants were opposed to the guerrillas.* For example, if a guarded railroad line was damaged, all the male inhabitants of the nearest village, from age twelve to age forty, were likely to be executed. The terror compelled even the most parochial and pacifist peasants to reassess their situation, to conclude that the only viable course lay in armed resistance, and to recognize that the most effective organizers of armed resistance in northern China were the Communists. (The CCP attracted far fewer recruits in central China, because in those parts it lacked the strength to launch Hundred Regiment–type drives and thereby bring down

Japanese retaliation on the peasants.) Instead of breaking the connections between the peasantry and the Eighth Route Army—the name
Mao gave to the Red Army after 1937—Japanese counterinsurgent
practices drove the two into a close alliance.[115]

For a while, however, it looked as if Japan's deliberately brutal
policy would actually work: Geoffrey Fairbairn concludes that "even
given their lack of understanding of what was politico-military good
sense in northern China, the Japanese and their puppet forces came
close in 1941–1942 to breaking the links between the Red Army and
the peasantry."[116] But over time the major effect of the "three alls"
campaign and similar policies was to turn the Communists into a
powerful force: membership in the CCP was 40,000 in 1937; by 1945 it
was 1.2 million. Thanks to the Japanese, "the masses were mobilized
for war" under the leadership of the CCP.[117] Mao himself was quite
aware how much of his success he owed to "the peculiar barbarity
of Japan's war."[118]

Communism and Nationalism

The superiority of the Japanese enemy to Mao's forces clearly influenced Mao's theory of protracted guerrilla war; it also forced him
to invent new political expedients. After 1937, wishing to stress the
need for unity among all classes in the countryside against the hated
invader, the CCP downplayed agrarian radicalism and abandoned
class war and compulsory redistribution of property in favor of
united national resistance. Class compromise became the new mantra
in Communist-controlled areas: "the Communists . . . eschewed their
old slogans of class warfare and violent redistribution of property
in their post-1937 propaganda and concentrated solely on national
salvation."[119] Mao proclaimed, "We [Communists] must unite the
nation without regard to parties or classes and follow our policy of
resistance to the end."[120] Communists must "oppose the policy of
isolation and affirm the policy of winning over all possible allies."[121]
To be sure, landlords had to lower rents and interest charges, but
peasants still had to pay them. Thus, Mao's basic program began
to resemble that of the KMT. Landless peasants were supposed
to sublimate their economic desires through the prestige of being
identified as the real force of the Red Revolution and through politi-

cal eminence in the Communist Party, from which landlords were excluded. Of course, all this social harmony was merely tactical; once the Japanese were visibly losing the war, Mao became much more radical in his land policy.

Now let us look more closely at this relationship between Japanese invasion and Communist expansion. As a profound student of non-Western politics pointed out years ago, "one of the central features of the great revolution of our times which has brought the modern world into being is that peoples of mankind in successive stages have been swept into a vivid and sometimes all-consuming sense of their existence as nations—or at least the desire to create nations where none existed before."[122]

But why was it not until in the twentieth century that countries like China, India, and Vietnam, such very old societies, were swept by these nationalistic aspirations and convulsions? In part, the answer is that it is almost impossible to make a true revolution—a violent, profound, and lasting change in the power structure of a society, as opposed to mere rebellion—in the absence of the "revolutionary alliance" of intellectuals, with their schemas and their thirst for power, and peasants, with their numbers and their potential to rise from apathy. True revolutions have been notably rare, largely because of the great obstacles in the path of this union of ideas (intellectuals) and mass (peasants). The urban intellectual disdains the peasant as superstitious, ignorant, and dirty; the peasant views the intellectual as contemptuous, unrealistic, and dictatorial. Each group has some good reasons for holding its unflattering view of the other. Therefore, some powerful catalyst is necessary to overcome the mutual distaste of peasants and intellectuals so that a revolution, Communist or otherwise, can occur. In our time, this catalyst has appeared almost exclusively in the form of outraged national feeling.[123] The Communists were well aware of this truth: indeed, as Chalmers Johnson reminds us, "the primary political tactic of communist revolutionaries since the time of Lenin has been the attempt to forge a 'united front' with genuine nationalist movements, thereby hoping to gain mass support for a communist organization not on the basis of the organization's communist values and goals but on the basis of its *tactically adopted* nationalist values and goals."[124]

Since at least the days of the Napoleonic invasion of Spain, the best way for guerrillas to gain the support of the local population has been on the basis of "the defense of the fatherland against alleged domestic traitors or foreign invaders," or both. More directly, in order for politically alienated intellectuals in general, and for the leaders of a given Communist party in particular, to make effective contact with the peasants in the name of vindicating the dignity of the outraged motherland, foreigners must cooperate by carrying out an invasion. This signal, essential service the Japanese performed for the Chinese Communists. Chalmers Johnson writes:

From 1921 to 1937 communism failed in China because the Chinese people, in general, were indifferent to what the Communist party had to offer. After 1937, it succeeded because the population became receptive to one particular kind of political appeal, and the Communist party—in one of its many disguises—made precisely that appeal: it offered to meet the needs of the people for leadership in organizing resistance to the invader and in alleviating war-induced anarchy in rural areas.[125]

Lenin had grasped the dynamic of invasion and revolution:

The fundamental law of revolution is as follows: for a revolution to take place it is not enough for the exploited and oppressed masses to realize the impossibility of living in the old way, and demand changes; for a revolution to take place it is essential that the exploiters should not be able to live and rule in the old way. It is only when the "lower classes" do not want to live in the old way and the "upper classes" cannot carry on in the old way that a revolution can triumph. This truth can be expressed in other words: revolution is impossible *without a nationwide crisis. . . .* that the ruling class should be going through a governmental crisis, which draws even the most backward masses into politics . . . weakens the government and makes it possible for the revolution to rapidly overthrow it.[126]

The Japanese militarists obligingly forced great segments of the peasantry to see that they could not any longer go on "in the old way," and simultaneously they made it impossible for the ruling KMT to continue to rule, in the old way or any other.

The requirements for the conquest and pacification of China far exceeded the human and material capacities of the Japanese military. The KMT forces retreated, and the local gentry fled before the advancing Japanese. Thus the Japanese troops made rapid advances into China, but they lacked the numbers and the technology to sustain these advances and to maintain order behind their lines. The result was anarchy and chaos among the peasantry, partly caused by Communist guerrillas, for which the Japanese could find no better solution than "kill all, burn all, destroy all." Confusion and terror created a vacuum for the Communists to fill; in many areas to the rear of the Japanese forces, the CCP became the real government. When the long and horrific war finally came to an end, northern China had become the stronghold of the Communists. That is, it was not economic or sociological factors, but rather the prolonged presence of CCP forces in a given area that best explained the expansion of Communist control there.[127]

The Anti-Japanese War

In strategic terms, Mao envisioned that the anti-Japanese war would consist of three phases. In his well-known formulation, "the first stage covers the period of the enemy's strategic offensive and our strategic defensive. The second stage will be the period of the enemy's strategic consolidation and our preparation for the counter-offensive. The third stage will be the period of our strategic counter-offensive and the enemy's strategic retreat."[128]

China's primitive communications system was the key weakness for any government or would-be government. The IJA countered guerrilla attacks on its lines of communication with massive construction projects. To guard an important road or railway, the Japanese built broad ditches and walls on both sides, protected by fortified structures. They also thrust these new fortified roads directly into guerrilla-infested areas, cutting the latter up into sectors. By the end of 1942, the IJA had constructed more than nine thousand miles of roads, along with thirty thousand blockhouses and nine thousand forts.[129]

Partly as a response to IJA fortified-road tactics, the guerrillas dug tunnels and tunnel complexes under and sometimes between villages, so that they could attack Japanese units from what at first appeared to be deserted areas. The tunnels also helped the guerrillas escape encirclement efforts.

All this digging aside, after the Hundred Regiments Offensive, Communist forces did not engage in much fighting against the IJA.[130] As a recent study confirms, "Communist guerrillas did create difficulties for the Imperial Army in some areas, but the CCP did not come close to challenging Japanese power in the key regions of China."[131] One reason for this was that they were often poorly equipped. But the main reason was that the Communists were anticipating the end of World War II and the consequent great showdown with the KMT, whose forces they constantly attacked, in contrast to the CCP's usual passivity toward the Japanese. An IJA report from Kwantung in February 1944 stated that the guerrillas did not present much of a threat because they were intent on conserving their strength. Moreover, as the end of the war began to come clearly into view, the CCP began making overtures to the troops of the Chinese collaborationist regime. Because the Communists refrained from attacks on areas occupied by such troops, the IJA turned more and more territory over to them, which of course freed Japanese soldiers for other duties, but it also gave the Communists scope for infiltration and proselytism.[132]

The Nationalist Armies

Lucian Pye noted that "in no country in the world have soldiers dominated politics so extensively and for so long as in China."[133] And in the first half of the twentieth century, no Chinese soldier-politician was more powerful and visible than Chiang Kai-shek, the principal figure in China between 1927 and 1949. Forced in 1937 into a war he believed China was not ready for, Chiang became the national and international symbol of heroic resistance to Axis aggression, a resistance whose tenacity dismayed the Japanese. In November 1943 he met with President Roosevelt and Prime Minister Winston Churchill in Cairo to determine Allied strategy against Japan. His government became one of the founders of the United Nations and one of the five permanent members of the UN Security Council.

In the last analysis, the instrument by which Chiang and the KMT held China together was the army. How the Japanese war affected this army was therefore going to have the most momentous consequences for the future of China.

After his break with the Communists toward the end of the 1920s, Chiang turned for military assistance to republican Germany. German officers served as Chiang's close advisers and also as instructors at Whampoa Academy. (Hitler, with his decision for a Japanese alliance, eventually broke this Chinese connection.) Chiang and his German advisers agreed that in the event of a major Japanese invasion, China's only hope would be a war of attrition, trading space for time, like the Russians' policy against Napoleon.[134] By 1936, Nationalist plans envisioned a strategic retreat to Chungking while inflicting casualties on the Japanese, causing them to overextend their supply lines and burdening them with the administration of vast areas of China.

Nevertheless, at the outbreak of the war in 1937, Chiang and his generals decided that they could not abandon Nanking, their capital, and Shanghai, China's most vital city, without a serious struggle. The August 1937 fight for Shanghai turned into "the bloodiest battle the world had seen since Verdun."[135] More than 270,000 Nationalist troops, the nucleus of Chiang's slowly modernizing army, were killed or wounded. Nanking fell in December, and the city was plunged into the period of indescribable horrors known as "the Rape of Nanking."[136] The Shanghai-Nanking struggle cost the Japanese 70,000 casualties and cost the Chinese 360,000.[137] Many of Chiang's best troops were lost, troops that could have been used much more effectively to counterattack the Japanese in central China.

After the fall of Nanking, Chiang did not want to lose any more precious troops in fruitless positional warfare against the better-armed Japanese; he therefore began a slow retreat into mountainous southwestern China, according to prewar plans. He also caused the relocation into the same area of many factories and their skilled workers, and even entire universities, across distances of two and three thousand miles.

The Nationalist Officer Corps

The Kuomintang had founded the Whampoa Military Academy to produce the officers who would establish a unified China. Between 1929 and 1944, the academy graduated the impressive total of 146,000 officers. The best prepared of them were those who received their commissions between 1929 and 1937. After that period, the quality of the graduates as a group declined gravely because of the Japanese invasion: in the face of the emergency, the three-year academy course was cut to one year. Moreover, during the war many candidates gained admission who in normal times would not have met the educational qualifications. The furious fighting around Shanghai and Nanking at the war's outset had killed 10,000 junior officers, fully one-tenth of the entire officer corps. The Nationalist forces never recovered from that devastation: in 1937, 80 percent of the officers in the typical Nationalist infantry battalion were academy trained; by 1945 the figure had declined to 20 percent. Japanese intelligence estimated that the Nationalist officer corps alone was suffering 54,000 killed, wounded, and missing every year.[138]

It later proved bitterly unfortunate for the Nationalists that "although the quality of junior commanders was generally satisfactory, command at the higher levels was deplorable." Sun Tzu advised that "speed is the essence of war."[139] But as one study of the Nationalist forces puts it, "the Chinese expectation of fighting a 'prolonged war' often fostered a passive mindset among leading commanders who believed that their primary responsibility was to survive the war, thereby vitiating their will to attack"; in general, "the Chinese had given up the initiative on the battlefield and were content to maintain a reactive posture vis-à-vis the invaders." As early as 1943, the Chinese High Command issued its conclusion that "the main reason for their defeat by Japan in many engagements was the Chinese commanders' inability to understand the basic principles of modern warfare."[140]

The Common Soldiers

While the Japanese war undermined the quality of the Nationalist officer corps, the rank and file also suffered seriously. To meet the Japanese threat, the Chinese armies had to rely on conscription. Between 1937 and 1945, KMT China drafted 14 million men, of whom 3.2 million became casualties. During its participation in World War II, the United States also drafted about 14 million; relative to population, the U.S. wartime mobilization rate was much higher than China's.[141]

Chinese conscripts were rarely supplied adequately and were often under the direction of officers who were less than capable.

Sanitary and medical facilities were usually quite primitive. Medical attention for draftees or wounded personnel was rare and superficial: one authority states that the Nationalist forces needed 30,000 army doctors but had in fact only 2,000. Most of the time—wartime—there was only one physician for every 1,700 soldiers.[142]

Inadequate medical attention became all the more serious in light of the malnutrition that existed among many Nationalist units. Many centuries before, Sun Tzu had insisted: "Pay heed to nourishing the troops!"[143] But the average Chinese soldier apparently ate meat only once or twice a month, a situation that of course seriously affected his performance.[144] The Chinese soldier "actually received only a fraction of the food and money allotted him, because his officers regularly 'squeezed' a substantial portion for themselves." Much of this corruption was of course the result of inflation, which had reduced the pay of officers to a fraction of its prewar value. (It should also be noted that such practices were common both in the Imperial Roman Army and also for quite an extensive period in the British Navy.) As a consequence, most nationalist soldiers suffered nutritional deficiencies. An American expert, who in 1944 examined 1,200 soldiers from widely different kinds of units, found that 57 percent of the men displayed "nutritional deficiencies that significantly affected their ability to function as soldiers."[145]

Under these conditions, obtaining and retaining a sufficient number of troops became a major problem in itself. The induction of draftees into the army was "a horrible experience"; perhaps as many as 1 million recruits died from malnutrition or disease before arriving in a battle zone.[146] O. Edmund Clubb grimly notes that "a large proportion of the Nationalist KMT conscripts, often to be seen in Chinese wartime towns roped together to prevent their escape, died even before reaching their assigned units."[147] On one memorable occasion, when confronted with undeniable evidence of the savage maltreatment of conscripts, Chiang Kai-shek publicly beat the head of the local draft board with his cane.[148]

Often hungry or worse, Chinese troops despoiled local civilians. The consequences of such behavior could be grave: in Honan Province in 1944, "when the Chinese troops retreated in defeat, more soldiers were killed by the indignant local population than by the Japanese." In Chiang's words, "the troops were ignorant of the need to protect and unite with the people, even unrestrainedly harassing them, so that military discipline was completely nonexistent."[149] Such relations between the Nationalist troops and the civilian population, stemming from the disastrous supply situation for many army units, accounts at least in part for the difficulty Nationalist forces encountered when trying to operate as guerrillas.[150] Masses of refugees moving from Japanese-occupied areas into Nationalist territory of course aggravated the permanent supply emergency.

The Equipment of the Nationalist Armies

Not surprisingly, the equipment with which the Nationalist armies had to fight the Japanese was often in deplorable condition. Fearful of Japanese aggression into Siberia, Stalin wanted a united anti-Japanese resistance centered upon Chiang Kai-shek. Accordingly, he sent the KMT one thousand aircraft, two thousand pilots, five hundred military advisers, and substantial amounts of gasoline and artillery, and supplied very little to the CCP.[151] But of course, the surprise Nazi invasion of Russia in June 1941 caused such assistance to be closed off.

Help from America arrived in the form of Claire Chennault's famous Flying Tigers, who were active by late 1941 (and paid for by the KMT regime). China participated in President Roosevelt's Lend-Lease project, but during 1941 and 1942 the United States assigned a mere 1.5 percent of such aid to China, and even less in 1943 and 1944.[152] One consequence of this tightfistedness was that "in 1944, China had only about six thousand trucks in the entire country, half of which were out of service due to shortage of parts."[153] Most of the Nationalist divisions had little or no artillery. But Roosevelt did send Chiang an "advisor" in the person of General Joseph Stilwell, possibly the most mean-spirited and self-promoting officer in the American Army.[154]

The most basic tools of modern warfare were unavailable. In Europe, commanders used theater maps whose scale was 1:20,000. Chinese military maps were scaled 1:1,000,000 and were "cluttered with cartographic errors."[155] Even worse, as Ch'i Hsi-sheng observed, "many intelligence branches of [Nationalist] armies and army groups did not even possess wireless transmitters to send intelligence to the headquarters"; therefore, "typically, the Chinese battlefield was marked by chaos. Commanders often did not know where their soldiers were. Troops in transit would recklessly intrude into the positions defended by other units without proper prior identification." In summary, "many battles were lost or their victories failed to be exploited because of the inability of commanders to be kept informed of battlefield conditions or to transmit timely decisions."[156]

China was decades behind Japan in terms of economic modernization and productivity and was at the bottom of the priorities list for help from the Allied Forces. Consequently, Ch'i Hsi-sheng notes:

Their primitive weapons made Chinese troops helpless against enemies entrenched behind hardened fortifications, and their weapons' unreliability further eroded the soldiers' confidence. . . . The lack of modern weapons placed the Chinese entirely at the mercy of their enemies. In the air, Japan's absolute superiority enabled it to bomb and strafe military and civilian targets with impunity. On the ground, Japan's extensive and indiscriminate use of poison gas terrorized Chinese soldiers while its tanks and armored vehicles condemned Chinese infantry soldiers to a position of absolute defenselessness.[157]

Casualty ratios of Chinese to Japanese soldiers, depending on the year and the location of fighting, ran between three to one and ten to one. For China, then, the war was a national crucifixion.

Political Unreliability of the Nationalist Forces

In addition to having widespread professional deficiencies, high-ranking Nationalist officers did not always display the virtue of political reliability. The KMT under Chiang had always been much more an alliance of fairly disparate groups than a centralized, authoritative organization, and the same was true of the Nationalist army. By 1944 that army enrolled close to 3.5 million men, but rather than a united, homogeneous force, it was more like "a coalition of armies which differed in degree of loyalty to the central government as well as in training, equipment and military capabilities."[158] Cliques and factional jealousies were rampant within the KMT, while many important elements in the Nationalist army were the heirs of the old warlord forces dating from before the Northern Expedition. These conditions, of course, severely undermined trust and coordination among Nationalist military leaders.[159] The Japanese invasion offered to outlying provincial commanders an alternative to following Chiang's orders; they could make deals, explicit or implicit, with the Japanese. Indeed, in 1944 a group of former warlords plotted to overthrow Chiang, and between 1941 and 1943 fully sixty-nine Nationalist generals, changing sides with the changing tides, defected to the Japanese, taking five hundred thousand soldiers along with them.[160] Thus, as Tang Tsou summarizes, "the question of what troops would obey whom under what circumstances could not be answered with any certainty."[161] The natural effect of this set of circumstances on Chiang was that when choosing commanders, he placed considerably more emphasis on political reliability than on professional competence. To appreciate properly the pressures that caused Chiang to value politics over merit, one needs to recall that President Abraham Lincoln, especially in the first year of the Civil War, appointed several men to high command in the Union Army precisely and solely because they were prominent figures in the Democratic Party, support from which was essential to the prosecution of the war. Nevertheless, in the last analysis Chiang could count completely only on those troops he commanded directly.

From 1938 up to 1944, battle lines between Nationalist and Japanese forces remained fairly stable overall. But, Ch'i Hsi-sheng points out,

barely eight months before acknowledging defeat to the Allied powers [i.e., in December 1944], Japan delivered a mortal blow to the Nationalist Chinese Army from which she never had time to recover. . . . The consequence was that, unlike other Allies who became stronger as they approached victory, Nationalist China was in a weaker military position on the eve of victory than at any previous point during the war.[162]

This catastrophic blow was called by the Japanese the Ichi-go Offensive, and it involved possibly as many as six hundred thousand soldiers. The offensive inflicted a half million casualties upon the Nationalist forces.[163] Such tremendous losses after so many years of fighting devastated Chiang's regime in terms of morale as well as military strength. A perceptive student of revolutions has written that "even after great loss of legitimacy has occurred, a state can remain quite stable—and certainly invulnerable to internal mass-based revolts—especially if its coercive organizations remain coherent and effective."[164] But the war, even in its last months, had fatally weakened the "coercive organizations" of the KMT. "The general deterioration of the Nationalist army during the war against Japan had momentous consequences," as Lloyd Eastman notes, because "the army was the foundation of Nationalist political power. When it began to crumble, it presaged the overthrow of Chiang Kai-shek and the National [*sic*] government."[165]

Civil War

Thanks to the Japanese invasion and occupation, by 1945, when Chiang was preparing for open civil war with the Communists, he was in command of forces in which a large proportion of the officers were simply not proficient at their tasks. During the new conflict, a tactic that became common to Nationalist units was to retreat behind city walls, where they waited for relief but most commonly found themselves trapped and sometimes wiped out. The People's Liberation Army (PLA), as Mao's regular forces came to be called, normally refused to defend territory, choosing instead to maintain mobility, so that it could constantly take advantage of these Nationalist blunders. Leaving the initiative in the hands of the Communists was very costly in terms of troop losses.[166] "Government commanders," according to Pepper, "had never learned the lessons of speed and decisiveness that had been mastered by their [CCP/PLA] adversaries." Consequently, "they found themselves repeatedly surprised, hemmed in, and immobilized." The U.S. consul general at Changchun informed Washington that the Nationalists were trying to "compensate by defensive measures what the Nationalist commanders and armies lack in offensive spirit."[167] And of course no one was more aware of these grave faults than Chiang himself. As the renewed civil war developed, he declared (in June 1947), "It cannot be denied that the spirit of most commanders is broken and their morality is base." Half a year later he lamented, "[Most officers] don't use their brains and are unwilling to study. Regardless of what the problem may be, they are invariably careless and do not seek a thorough understanding." And as the curtain was falling on the mainland struggle and Chiang had already transferred most of his followers and troops to Taiwan (Formosa), he wrote: "From the latter part of the war against Japan to the present, the corruption and degeneracy within our revolutionary army have been fantastic, simply unimaginable."[168]

The Postwar Nationalist Regime

At the end of World War II, China appeared to be entering a new era of national dignity and international respect. Chiang Kai-shek had obtained the abolition of the detested and humiliating "unequal treaties," the restoration to Chinese control of Manchuria (taken by Japan in 1931) and Taiwan (taken by Japan in 1895), and recognition by Stalin as the legitimate government of China, along with Stalin's promise not to give military assistance to the CCP. In addition, China was now one of the Big Four (with the United States, Britain, and the USSR) and had received a permanent seat on the UN Security Council.

The Nationalist army, moreover, with some of its divisions having been American-trained, was twice as big as the Communist forces and exerted at least some degree of control over more than 300 million of China's 450 million inhabitants. The CCP, in contrast, had little experience beyond guerrilla war, no air force, no navy, and no international recognition.

Presidents Roosevelt and Truman wanted peace between Chiang and the CCP in order to avoid civil war and possible Soviet intervention. But in fact, Stalin did not believe that Mao's Communists had a serious chance of winning a civil war with Chiang's Nationalists. Hence, the Soviets, as well as the Truman administration, exerted pressure on both sides to work out some sort of compromise settlement. Between August and October 1945, Mao himself spent six weeks in Chiang's capital, negotiating and banqueting with him. That Chiang allowed the Communist leader to enter the Nationalists' den and then leave was a sign of his confidence in an ultimate KMT triumph. And in December 1945, General George Marshall arrived in China to assist in finding a peace formula. His mission ended in complete failure.[169]

As a result of Japan's surrender, China had regained its independence and territorial unity. But Mao and his cohorts wanted an independent and unified China *ruled by them*—not at all the same thing. Two de facto governments and two claimants to ultimate power could not coexist peacefully within the same country for long. In July 1946, from Yenan, in northern Shensi Province, their capital ever since the bitter days of the Long March, the leadership of the CCP announced that the Eighth Route Army, the New Fourth Army, and various CCP forces in Manchuria were being combined to form the People's Liberation Army (PLA). It was a proclamation of civil war.

In contrast to the experience of the Communists, the war had been extremely hard on the KMT, exhausted by eight years of fighting the Japanese as well as by infighting and corruption among military leaders. And as the KMT returned to take over control of the coastal areas and Taiwan, it did enormous damage to its cause. KMT plans for administration and economic recovery were inadequate. Those Chinese who, for whatever pressing reasons, had remained behind under Japanese occupation were treated with condescension at best.[170] Widespread and shameless looting took place; in part, this can be explained by the wartime inflation, which made the pay of the KMT soldier worthless and led him often to extort food from civilians. As a general statement, the return or entry of the war-battered KMT into areas previously controlled by the Japanese or their collaborators was a political disaster, characterized by arrogance, incomprehension, corruption, and inflation. The situation was especially bad in Manchuria and on Formosa/Taiwan (where the educated elite spoke Japanese).[171] During the subsequent civil war, Chiang's troops occupied all the great cities, many of which came under land blockade by Communist forces. This caused the price of food and other commodities in urban areas to rise even further and thus aggravated the tendencies of KMT troops to engage in extortion.

The stealing was no doubt stimulated by the suspicion on the part of many who served the KMT that the regime was not going to last very long. At any rate, the abuses that accompanied the KMT return to power in the former Japanese-occupied areas dissipated much of the prestige of the recent victory. Mao, in contrast, had long labored to inculcate into the Communist forces "a respect for the civil population and abstinence from plunder which distinguished the Red Army from all other armies which the Chinese peasantry had seen in the past and contributed greatly toward winning the support of the population."[172]

Throughout the struggle that followed, morale within the PLA seems to have been relatively high, even when the civil war was not going as well as it might have. In part, this was a result of the PLA's emphasis on good relations between officers and men; Mao insisted that officers must lead by example, not by fear and punishment as in the Japanese and czarist armies. And it must have been very important in sustaining Communist morale (as perhaps it has been in all Communist insurgencies since that time) to know that ultimately the PLA had behind it the power of the Soviet Union. Watchful of the morale of their own troops, the leaders of the PLA were untiring in seeking to undermine that of their opponents. Ceaseless propaganda was directed at KMT soldiers, already aware that if they were taken prisoners they would not be shot and might actually be released after a short time.[173] The Communists also enjoyed success in their efforts to convert KMT prisoners and enlist them in the PLA. In fact, captured enemy soldiers soon became a principal source of Communist weapons and recruits.

Above all, the level of morale on both sides depended on the fact that most of the time it was becoming ever clearer to everyone that the KMT was not winning the civil war and might indeed be defeated. This depressing situation stemmed directly from a fundamental strategic decision by Chiang. Because the KMT claimed to be not just *a* government of China but *the* government, Chiang believed it essential to take immediate control of as much territory as possible after the Japanese surrender. This decision proved to be one of the major factors in the undoing of the Nationalist cause. The Reds cared little for holding territory per se, as illustrated by their abandonment of their capital, Yenan, to Nationalist troops in March 1947. They operated against the thinly spread Nationalist forces according to Mao's fundamental principle of always having superior numbers at the point of combat: In Maoist strategy, "the major objective is the annihilation of the enemy's fighting strength, not the holding or taking of cities and places"; hence, "in every battle, concentrate absolutely superior forces—double, triple, quadruple, and sometimes even five or six times those of the enemy—to encircle the enemy, and strive for his annihilation, with none escaping from the net."[174] KMT positional warfare, against which the Reds used concentration of forces at one particular spot after another, had especially catastrophic consequences for the Nationalists in Manchuria.

The KMT Debacle in Manchuria

The surrender of Japan permitted the restoration of KMT authority in its old bases, the great coastal cities and the Yangtze Valley. It also meant the reassertion of Chinese sovereignty over the former puppet state of Manchukuo and also the island of Taiwan, lost in the First Sino-Japanese War of 1894–95. Chiang was especially eager to reestablish KMT control over Manchuria, long a locus of Japanese occupation and aggression and, thanks to Japanese developmental policies there, potentially one of the richest and most productive areas of the country. Besides, wrote Steven I. Levine, "Japan's defeat had removed the one foreign power that was unalterably opposed to [Communist] revolution in Manchuria." Soviet forces had begun entering Manchuria in early August 1945; their occupation was "characterized by destruction, pillage and rape."[175] For somewhat similar reasons, including the considerable industrial base of the region, the presence of Soviet forces there, the proximity of the USSR, and the extreme tenuousness of Nationalist supply lines, Mao was anxious to establish CCP power in Manchuria.

Clearly, the situation called for quick action. Lieutenant General Albert Wedemeyer, commander of American forces in the China Theater, wanted to rush seven U.S. divisions into Manchuria to receive the surrender of Japanese troops there and forestall a potential Communist takeover, but Washington rejected his proposal.[176] Indeed, the lack of comprehension on the part of Washington policymakers about what the facts and the stakes were in China—not to mention repeated slights, insults, and humiliations offered to America's wartime ally Chiang—is truly depressing.[177] In any event, Manchuria, the first major battleground in the renewed Nationalist-Communist civil war, was destined to become the graveyard of KMT military power.

Mao and the other CCP leaders viewed Manchuria as rich, relatively urban, and conveniently right next door to the USSR. Russian troops had been overrunning Manchuria during the waning days of the war, and on August 19, 1945, Russian and Chinese Communist troops linked up for the first time in history. The PLA Army was now pouring some of its best units and political cadres from northern China into Manchuria and with Russian help was seizing enormous amounts of equipment. With Soviet encouragement, Japanese prisoners assisted in the training of Communist forces, and in subsequent battles much of the artillery employed on the Communist side was manned by Japanese gunners.[178]

The KMT wanted to return in strength to Manchuria before the Communists had established their complete domination there, but the center of KMT power was far away in southwest China, and the regime lacked sufficient transport to move enough military units in the required time. In light of this emergency, U.S. aircraft carried many Nationalist troops into Manchuria. Chiang also employed the desperate expedient of using surrendered Japanese and puppet troops on the scene to maintain order and keep the Communists at bay until he could arrive there in strength, a decision that did little to burnish his credentials as the living symbol of Chinese nationalism. The American ambassador characterized the Nationalist regime in the region as incompetent and unpopular, and the KMT entrusted very few Manchurians with office. In part this reflected the fact that Chiang feared the separatist tendencies of northeastern China almost as much as he feared the CCP. To make matters much worse, as large numbers of KMT soldiers began arriving in Manchuria, they treated the soldiers of the former puppet regime there badly. Consequently, about seventy-five thousand of these eventually went over to the PLA.[179]

At roughly the same time, for purposes of economy, the KMT government had decreed a sweeping postwar demobilization, just as civil war loomed darkly on the horizon. More than 1.5 million troops, including 200,000 officers, suddenly found themselves dismissed from the army. Many of these men, jobless, with few prospects, and deeply embittered, joined the PLA.[180]

The contest in Manchuria was no guerrilla conflict. Massive conventional forces confronted each other. The Communists alone conscripted 1 million Manchurians into their forces. The Nationalists made a huge military investment in Manchuria, but they fought their typically defensive and stationary war there, playing into the hands of Mao and his tactics of concentration of forces against one target at a time ("After smashing one column, we should shift our forces to smash another"). Chiang, moreover, sought to conserve the strength of his best units rather than to use them aggressively. As it turned out, the retreat, surrender, and general deterioration of the Nationalist forces provided the Communists with the heavy artillery they had hitherto lacked. The Russians also turned over to them great quantities of weapons left behind by the Japanese.[181] Possessed of these invaluable arms, the Communists were able to make the Manchurian struggle the first in which they employed tanks and artillery in significant numbers; they then used them to carry on conventional warfare against the KMT in China proper.

Within the Nationalist high command, confusion and disorder on a grand scale made all bad situations worse. The cliquishness of the older Whampoa graduates undermined unity of command. Chiang's friends insisted on reporting directly to him instead of to their nominal superiors. Chiang also issued orders over the heads of regional commanders, compounding the chaos. American ambassador J.L. Stuart soon blamed the open rivalry among KMT commanders as the primary cause of Nationalist defeat.[182] In addition, the widespread corruption that had bedeviled the KMT for years continued to do its destructive work: certain generals were pocketing funds that were intended for the purchase of supplies for their ill-tended troops, and some even sold equipment to the PLA, a considerable portion of which equipment had been furnished by the U.S. taxpayer. (But as the conflict went on, supplies provided to the Nationalists from the United States greatly diminished, much to the consternation of General Wedemeyer.)[183]

In March 1948 U.S. Major General David Barr, a senior U.S. adviser to Chiang, realizing that the Nationalists were on the edge of disaster, advised Chiang to cut his losses and evacuate Manchuria. Believing it was politically impossible for him to concede that strategic area to the Communists—it was over Manchuria that the struggle with Japan had begun in 1931—Chiang declined this advice, and the struggle continued. KMT losses, through combat and defection, mounted into many scores of thousands. Finally, in October 1948, Chiang himself undertook to direct the struggle for Manchuria from his headquarters in Peking. It was too late. A major

KMT army, with all of its American equipment, surrendered to the PLA on October 15. Mukden, Manchuria's capital, fell to the Communists on November 1.[184]

The defeat by Communist forces in Manchuria was the beginning of the end for the Nationalists. Not only had the KMT lost nearly 400,000 troops, including some of its best, along with all their equipment, but the Communists now had 360,000 battle-tested soldiers available to be sent into the contest for China proper.[185]

The consequences of the Manchurian battles were momentous. A contemporary Chinese observer explained:

The Chinese Communists had no soldiers in the Northeast [Manchuria]; now they have the soldiers not wanted by the central government. The Chinese Communists had no guns; now they have the guns the central government managed so poorly and [lost] to them, and sometimes even secretly sold to them. The Chinese Communists had no men of ability; now they have the talents the central government has abandoned.[186]

In addition, the economic resources of Manchuria could have contributed to helping the KMT restore control over eastern China without the horrendous inflation that did so much to wreck the regime. Instead, these resources were now in the hands of the KMT's deadly enemies. And of course, the defeats in Manchuria gravely damaged Nationalist morale, which in turn contributed to further defeats. General Barr wrote: "The morale and spirit of the [Communist] troops is very high because they are winning."[187]

The Civil War after Manchuria

The disinclination of Nationalist generals to take the offensive or to coordinate movements, thus allowing their units in Manchuria to be defeated piecemeal by the Communists, together with major defections of KMT forces at decisive moments, had made 1948 a year of Nationalist disasters. General Barr ascribed most of the responsibility for the rapid decay of the KMT military position to "the world's worst [military] leadership."[188]

Immediately after the conquest of Manchuria by Communist forces, the struggle for east-central China (called the battle of Hwai-Hai) began. More than 1 million men on both sides took part in this confrontation. Once again, KMT commanders played into Mao's hands, allowing him to use his favorite tactic of crushing the dispersed Nationalist forces one at a time. When this phase of the war came to an end, the KMT had lost roughly 550,000 troops, including the last of its American-equipped divisions.[189] Many Nationalist units were lacking ammunition for their U.S.-supplied weapons. At this point the KMT had no really first-rate soldiers left with which to prevent the Communists from crossing the Yangtze River (even if it had had the heart for the job). Once the capital of a confident KMT, Nanking now lay open to the Communists.[190] After the capture of Mukden, General Lin Piao moved his Red Army with unexpected rapidity from Manchuria to the gates of Peking.[191] The plans for the defense of this great city had been betrayed to him, and Peking fell to the Communists on January 22, 1949. That same disastrous month, Chiang surrendered his office of president to Vice President Li Zongren, a redoubtable figure who wanted to make a stand on the banks of the Yangtze; if the enemy should nevertheless succeed in crossing the river, Li intended to create a bastion in southwest China. By the spring of 1949, Communist forces had increased during the previous six months from 1.2 million to almost 2.8 million, while KMT forces in the same period had fallen from 2.7 million to 1.5 million; nevertheless, the Nationalists still had sufficient troops with which to continue the struggle. Chiang, however, who commanded most of the KMT armed forces, undercut such plans; he had already secretly decided to abandon the mainland for the island of Taiwan, to which he began moving men and supplies without informing all the relevant commanders. Hence, Li was deprived of the strength he needed to prevent a Communist crossing of the Yangtze, while the normal disarray and confusion within the Nationalist armies increased.[192]

Even at this point, all was not necessarily lost. The well-respected Nationalist general Pai Chung-hsi struck boldly at Lin Piao's army and inflicted a costly defeat on it. But Chiang, for reasons that can only be guessed, caused essential forces on Pai's flanks to be withdrawn, making further aggressive action on Pai's part impossible.[193] On the night of April 20, 1949, therefore, Communist units crossed the Yangtze, assisted in this endeavor by a suitable bribe to the commander of the key Nationalist fortress at Kiangyin.[194] Nanking, capital of the Nationalists, fell to the Red Army on April 22, and Shanghai followed one month later. The collapse of KMT rule continued during the summer, capped by the surrender of a large Nationalist army in Shensi Province on September 19. This event made the cautious Mao confident enough to proclaim at Peking, on October 1, 1949, the existence of a Communist government of all China. Meanwhile, after the fall of Nanking, the KMT government had retreated to Canton, a city with matchless historical associations for them. Even this last continental bastion was lost on October 16. Earlier in the year, Chiang had moved the Nationalist air force, navy, and treasury to Taiwan. By the end of 1949, 2 million KMT supporters, including more than a half million members of the armed forces, had arrived on that island, the last important piece of Chinese territory on which Nationalist rule existed.

Reflection

The causes of the defeat of Chiang and his Nationalists by Mao and the CCP are complex. Some authors have identified these causes as deeply rooted in Chinese history and thus outside both Chiang's control and the scope of this chapter. According to Suzanne Pepper, "the eventual Communist victory was founded upon the weaknesses of the old society and the political establishment which governed it." Mary C. Wright believed the KMT failed because it tried to restore the Confucian social order, a program thoroughly inadequate in the face of China's situation in the twentieth century. But the most recent biography of Chiang states, "Truly, it is [Chiang Kai-shek's] vision, not Mao's, that guides the People's Republic in the twenty-first century."[195]

Other analysts have emphasized more immediate and more concrete explanations for the KMT defeat. The French Air Force general Lionel Max Chassin, in his 1952 study *The Communist Conquest of China*, found the discipline of the Red armies to be admirable, especially regarding conduct toward the civilian population.[196] This discipline he attributed to the high level of morale produced by constant indoctrination in a basic message: justice at home and expulsion of foreign intruders (what Chassin calls the Communists' "xenophobic nationalism"). In contrast, he identifies the lack of political education as the major cause of the Nationalist defeat: simple peasant soldiers understood the necessity to fight the Japanese but could not grasp why they needed to fight peasants like themselves in far-away provinces. "In this," he concludes, "lies the essential reason for the victory of Mao Tse-tung."[197]

There is an undeniable measure of truth in Chassin's view. Surely no one would wish to denigrate the fighting qualities of the People's Liberation Army. But Chassin's analysis slights other powerful contributors to CCP success. For one major example, as Lincoln Li points out, "Japanese brutality motivated the peasantry in the affected areas far beyond what the propaganda and organizing ability of the Chinese Communists could have done."[198]

And then General Chassin himself admits that "the successes of this [Chinese Communist] army were almost always obtained with ease: never in the civil war were the Communists confronted by truly resolute, well-armed, and well-led adversaries."[199] During the civil war, that is to say, the People's Liberation Army hardly ever had to face good-quality troops of the type that had conducted the Encirclement Campaigns. Morale in the Nationalist forces was generally low, due to inadequate training, pay, food, and medical care, and most of all because of a series of bloody defeats at the hands of the Imperial Japanese Army. Besides, the PLA avoided attacking except in circumstances in which it enjoyed numerical superiority. Writes Lincoln Li:

Theirs was a fine fighting force, but historians must nevertheless conclude that in the Communist conquest of the vast mainland of China much of their success must be attributed to the default of the Chinese nationalist military power—a great military force taxed by eight years of supreme effort against Imperial Japan and betrayed from within by corruption, maladministration and dissension in high places.[200]

One can, moreover, easily make too much of political indoctrination of troops. The Communist regime in post–World War II Hungary carefully selected officer candidates from among what it called the proletariat and then heavily indoctrinated them, along with the enlisted personnel. But in a few days in November 1956, this carefully recruited and indoctrinated army instantaneously and almost totally deserted the regime, which thereupon collapsed.[201]

Obviously, military blunders on the part of Chiang and the KMT leadership—retention of incompetent generals, confusion in command structure, overextension of forces, mistreatment of the civilian population, tactics of static defense against a mobile enemy, failure to address peasant aspirations effectively—must take a prominent place in a full explanation of the outcome. Many, indeed all, of these military defects and errors were correctable in principle; if at least some of them had been corrected, even in part, it is far from certain that the civil war would have ended at the time and in the way it actually did. But the KMT would not have had the opportunity to make all these grave military and political blunders—or at least the cost of them would not have been nearly so high—if no major civil war had occurred. If we therefore ask what was the most fundamental and decisive condition that made the great conflict after the conclusion of World War II possible—what was the principal reason why the CCP, on the verge of annihilation in 1936, was in a position to wage a massive conventional struggle in 1945—the answer is and can only be the Japanese invasion. This was the most fundamental reason for the Maoist triumph.

Before World War II, the KMT had passed important land-reform legislation, including restrictions on exorbitant rents and improvement in land tenure.[202] But during the war, pushed out of its natural constituency on the coast, cut off from allies, resting uneasily on a conservative rural base, fighting one war against the Communists and another against the Japanese, the KMT regime in Chungking failed not only to address itself to fundamental land reform but even to hold down the usurious interest rates with which peasants were confronted so often. Thus, it never had a chance to attach to itself the great rural masses. And after the Japanese invasion began, the KMT's tendency to mount anti-Communist operations gradually alienated those elements of the educated classes who had not already lost faith in the ability of the KMT to save China.

The KMT's lack of a popular land program made it all the more imperative that the party deliver, or seem to deliver, on its most basic pledges: national independence and national unity. In a China so long invaded, defeated, and humiliated by its neighbors and other imperial powers, so often torn by peasant rebellion and warlord extortion, any leadership group that managed to achieve independence and unity would have assured itself of historical significance and political popularity. In the 1930s, unity meant bringing all China under KMT rule, which in turn meant the complete extirpation of the Communists. Chiang was clearly on the verge of achieving this very aim when the conquering Japanese burst in. Thus, after 1937, the KMT could deliver neither independence nor unity. On the one hand, it had lost the "Mandate of Heaven," the all-important aura of the eventual winner. On the other hand, between 1937 and 1945, the fight against the Japanese presented the CCP with the time and space to develop from a small and ragtag force on the edge of the country and on the verge of extinction into a major contestant for supreme power and a plausible claimant to the title of paladin of Chinese nationalism.[203] The Japanese invasion, in sum, both made a post-1945 civil war inevitable and ensured that the KMT would fight it under profoundly disadvantageous conditions.

No Japanese War, No Communist Revolution

On this most central question—why did Mao and his Communists wrest control of China from Chiang's Nationalists—an impressive panoply of distinguished authorities have identified the second Sino-Japanese conflict as the key. The following are representative examples from that panoply. Lloyd Eastman writes: "[The Sino-Japanese conflict] lasted eight years. Some fifteen to twenty million Chinese died as a direct or indirect result. The devastation of property was incalculable. And after it was over the Nationalist government and army were exhausted and demoralized. Thus it inflicted a terrible toll on the Chinese people and contributed directly to the Communist victory in 1949. The war with Japan was surely the most momentous event in the history of the Republican era in China." For Jonathan Spence, "the eruption of full-scale war with Japan in the summer of 1937 ended any chance that Chiang Kai-shek might have had of creating a strong and centralized nation-state." That is, declares Walter Laqueur, "the Japanese destroyed the hold of the KMT." In the view of Chalmers Johnson, "the actual source of the Communist party's authority in China today dates from the wartime period when it led the mobilized masses of previously non-Communist areas in their struggle with the Japanese army," and thus "Communism in China has very little meaning apart from the trials China experienced during the war of resistance." Paul K.T. Sih wrote: "Had it not been for the outbreak of the Resistance War against the Japanese invasion in July 1937, China would have been able to attain the status of a new, modern society." In John K. Fairbank's view, "Japan supplied the major circumstance that led to KMT decline and to CCP survival, growth, and victory." For Lincoln Li, the egregious brutality of the Japanese and their elimination of Nationalist forces from large areas played directly into the hands of the Communists. In light of all this, Bard O'Neill writes, "there is reason to question"—to say the very least—"whether Mao's strategy would have been successful against the Kuomintang if the Japanese had not invaded China." In summary, concludes Geoffrey Fairbairn, "there is no very good reason to believe that the CCP and the Red Army would have triumphed had it not been for the Japanese invasion of China and the methods of pacification adopted in support of the consolidation of Japanese politico-military power."[204]

But the Japanese did invade. When their invasion began, the Chinese Communist Party possessed an army of at most 50,000 men. It controlled a territory of 35,000 square miles, 1 percent of the total area of China, with about 1.5 million inhabitants. When the Japanese surrendered eight years later, Mao Tse-tung commanded an army of more than 900,000, and Communist territory extended to 225,000 square miles with 65 million subjects.[205] Thereafter, Mao's military competence and Chiang's military blunders hurled China and the world into a new era.

Let us be clear: it is impossible to deny that from the start of the civil war, Chiang and the KMT made many errors. But they had already been mortally wounded by the Japanese. The Nationalists had had the ill luck to be responsible for China's safety just when Japanese expansionist aspirations were reaching their zenith; the Japanese war would have severely tested, and possibly destroyed, any Chinese regime of any political hue. At war's end, because of the many compromises made during the Northern Expedition and the anti-Japanese resistance, Chiang, although essentially honest himself, felt unable to root out deep-seated corruption and widespread incompetence among major elements of the KMT. Thus the banner of reform went by default to the Communist Party. The CCP could contrast a dismaying Nationalist present with a utopian Communist future. Nevertheless, when growing numbers of Chinese turned toward the Communists for salvation, it was much less a vote for the CCP than an expression of a systemic loss of confidence in the KMT.[206]

Someone Better than Chiang?

It would be difficult to deny that in the last half of the twentieth century, Chiang Kai-shek's reputation in the United States was devastated by criticism that was too often partisan, superficial, and even ignorant. Nevertheless, it is a legitimate question to ask: Would another supreme leader for Nationalist China have done better? In the judgment of Ch'i Hsi-sheng,

the answer to this question is by no means obvious. Chiang was one of the few Chinese generals of his generation to have acquired some grasp of modern military science, a healthy appreciation of Western technology, and a strong commitment to the training and discipline of soldiers. Many of his contemporaries were semiliterate in military affairs and totally ignorant of international relations.[207]

However serious the deficiencies of the Japanese armed forces that became apparent after 1941, it was elements of those armed forces that carried out the tactically brilliant attack at Pearl Harbor. Nor should one forget the Japanese capture of "impregnable" Singapore, where in February 1942, after relatively little fighting, 130,000 British and Empire troops surrendered to a considerably smaller Japanese force, "the worst disaster and largest capitulation in British history."[208] Thus Chiang's Nationalists were not the only ones to suffer under the furious competence of Imperial Japan. And the Chinese did incomparably better in World War II than they had in the Opium War of 1834 or the First Sino-Japanese War of 1894–95 (or than the French did in World War II). Despite the staggering burden of Nationalist defects, the Japanese never succeeded in forcing Chiang to negotiate. According to Lloyd Eastman, "Whatever may be the final judgment on the issue [of Chiang's leadership], it remains a fact that the Nationalist forces persevered for eight long years against an enemy who possessed a vast technological superiority. The political, economic and human costs of this war were enormous.

Yet they [the Nationalists] did not abandon the Allied war effort, and their forcing the Japanese to maintain an army of about one million men in China contributed significantly to the eventual victory."[209] Moreover, after Pearl Harbor Chiang flew to India and persuaded Gandhi not to let his Congress party paralyze the British war effort. Chiang's successful conference with Gandhi, little appreciated at the time or afterward, made a contribution to the Allied war effort that can hardly be calculated.[210]

The Maoist Mystique

The worldwide vogue of Mao's thought that followed upon his victory was based on his (deserved) reputation as the theorist and practitioner par excellence of guerrilla warfare. In the last quarter of the twentieth century, many students, advocates, participants, and opponents of revolution thought that they saw in this Maoist mode of fighting the ultimate, invincible weapon that could be used successfully anywhere against anybody.[211] But the collapse of Maoist insurgencies from the 1960s to the 1980s, in Thailand, the Philippines, Peru, and especially Vietnam, recalls the enduring value of what Lenin identified as "the very gist, the living soul of Marxism—the concrete analysis of a concrete situation."[212] Each revolution, like each insurgency, has aspects that are unique and often decisive. Mao himself insisted on that very point, writing: "China's revolutionary war, whether civil or national war, is waged in the specific environment of China and so has its own specific circumstances and nature distinguishing it both from war in general and from revolutionary war in general. Therefore, besides the laws of war in general and of revolutionary war in general, it has specific laws of its own. Unless you understand them, you will not be able to win China's revolutionary war."[213]

To summarize: The Chinese Communists derived incalculable benefit from the indirect and certainly unintentional aid they received from the Japanese, who severely damaged the Nationalist regime and armies both in their capabilities and in their morale.[214] Then after Japan's surrender, Mao's forces received massive direct assistance from the Soviet Army in Manchuria, which turned over to them great quantities of invaluable modern weapons. It seems to be easily forgotten—or ignored—that the Maoist victory over Chiang's weakened Nationalists was won not by guerrilla bands but by regular armies, massive in size and equipped with modern Russian, Japanese, and American weapons.

The Aftermath

Mao's victory over Chiang signaled the sudden transformation of China from an ally of the United States to an ally of the Soviet Union. No one can know what all the consequences would have been if the KMT had defeated or stalemated the CCP after 1945. But at the very least, without Mao's victory it is extremely difficult to imagine how or why China's intervention in the Korean War—not to speak of the war itself—with its nine hundred thousand Chinese casualties, would have occurred; or why the Americans would have gone to Vietnam. Certainly the people of China would have been spared the Great Leap Forward. In the damning verdict of a distinguished historian, "the national catastrophe of the Great Leap Forward in 1958–1960 was directly due to Chairman Mao. In the end some *twenty to thirty million people* lost their lives through malnutrition and famine because of the policies imposed upon them by the CCP."[215] This figure represents "more Chinese than died in all the famines of the preceding one hundred years."[216] In addition, Mao later incited the "Great Proletarian Cultural Revolution," whose "undeniable madness" led to more millions of deaths, the burning down of the British and Indonesian embassies by mobs of young Red Guards, the closing of all Chinese universities for four years, the irredeemable destruction of much of the priceless patrimony of Chinese culture, and, not least, "a legacy of crime and juvenile delinquency."[217]

Quite aside from the domestic calamities he imposed upon the Chinese people, in foreign affairs Mao managed to alienate at one and the same time the Americans, the Japanese, the Indians, and the Indonesians; and as if the disasters of the Korean War had not been enough, he sent his soldiers into bloody clashes with the armies of the Soviet Union and Communist Vietnam, a truly remarkable record.

On one level, Mao's military victory over the KMT represented the forcible imposition of Leninist-Stalinist concepts and policies, barely thirty years old, on the culture of China, four thousand years old. On another level, it signaled the subordination of urban, maritime China to rural, heartland China. These are the keys to understanding why thirty years of Maoist Communism failed to make China a modern country, while Taiwan, South Korea, Singapore, Hong Kong—even Malaysia—surged forward, and Japan became a global economic power. Mao believed that "only people infected with the evils of bourgeois materialism could want an improved standard of living."[218] In 1989, forty years after Mao proclaimed the People's Republic, Chinese government figures revealed that 100 million persons in the western provinces suffered from malnutrition, while 220 million persons (70 percent of them women) over the age of fourteen did not know how to read or write.[219]

But if there is one single fact above all others to keep in mind about the victory of Mao Tse-tung, it is surely this one: that in the decades *after the civil war came to its end*, Mao was directly responsible for the deaths of more Chinese—many, many millions more—than the Japanese had been.

French Indochina, 1946

2

French Vietnam
A War of Illusions

The Setting: French Vietnam

Many Americans think of Vietnam primarily or solely as a place where American troops once fought. Some journalists and academics write about Vietnam as if that word refers to something that happened to Americans, or even as a series of events that unfolded inside the Beltway.[1] But long before Americans arrived in Vietnam, the French were there, and their experience set the stage for everything that followed.

Lying between China and Australia, Vietnam and the other countries of Southeast Asia constitute the crossroads of the Pacific Basin and the Indian subcontinent. Many people, probably most, in this area have been and still are poor, but the region itself is potentially quite rich, with great quantities of rubber, petroleum, rice, metals, and much else. The compelling desire to possess these strategic resources eventually induced the Empire of Japan to attack Pearl Harbor.

On the eve of World War II, in all Southeast Asia, only Thailand was independent. The American flag flew over the Philippines; the British had Burma, Malaya, and Singapore; the Dutch administered sprawling Indonesia (called then the Netherlands East Indies); and the French ruled, in varying degrees, over French Indochina, which included Laos, Cambodia, and Vietnam, the latter subdivided into Tonkin, Annam, and Cochin China. Within a year after World War II, the Philippines were independent, followed within a short time by all the European possessions in the region—except for French

Indochina. Of the prewar colonial powers, only the French remained committed to retaining their vast empire and sustaining that commitment by armed force; it was a commitment they were to pursue from the steaming forests of Vietnam to the burning sands of Algeria. And because of this commitment, France became the first Western power to confront a Maoist-style revolutionary war.

With an area of 127,000 square miles, Vietnam is the size of Finland, or of Missouri and Arkansas combined. The country is long and narrow. Its northernmost point lies on the latitude of Miami and its southernmost point on the latitude of the Panama Canal. The north-south axis of the country stretches more than one thousand miles, roughly the distance between Rome and Copenhagen, or Boston and Jacksonville. But Vietnam is very slender, 300 miles at its widest, 50 miles at its narrowest. The country is in effect two great deltas, that of the Red River around Hanoi and of the Mekong River around Saigon. Eighty percent of the population lives in these two areas. Hence the Vietnamese compare the geography of their country to two rice baskets on a shoulder pole.

The great distance between north and south, made greater still by primitive communications, produced regional subcultures. And regionalism was reinforced by frequent internal warfare between two Vietnamese states, each based on one of the deltas, with their mutual boundary usually somewhere around the eighteenth parallel. For several centuries before the partition in 1954 (at the seventeenth parallel), one single Vietnamese state had controlled all the country's territory for only about thirty years. "The political, psychological, moral and economic differences between the North and the South" constituted "a profound reality," and therefore the division into North and South Vietnam (1954–75) was "normal, not exceptional."[2]

Origins of the Vietnamese Revolution

Hannah Arendt once observed that the dominant form of revolution in the twentieth century consisted of armed uprisings organized by relatively small groups of full-time revolutionaries.[3] An instructive example of a minoritarian and elitist revolutionary movement, and the ability of such a movement to disguise its true nature, is provided by the Communist Party of Vietnam.

A distinguished Indian historian of Western imperialism wrote that, in the first three decades of the twentieth century at least, French rule in Vietnam was as good as that in any colonial area in the world.[4] It was the French themselves who fostered the indigenous revolutionary elite that formed a Communist party, fashioned an ideology of independence, attracted peasant support, and eventually expelled France from Vietnam. By the end of World War I the French had created, by means of state schools and religious academies, a sizable stratum of European-educated Vietnamese. And during that conflict, many Vietnamese served with the armies of France in Europe and learned much about the great outside world; they returned home to find conditions in their country very disillusioning.

The new potential Vietnamese elite was barred from the positions and power to which it felt entitled by its French education and French military service. Comparative figures on the European presence in Asia are revealing. In 1925, the British were governing 325 million Indians with a force of 5,000 European civil servants; the French employed the same number to govern only 30 million Vietnamese. A decade later, three times as many French held government posts in Vietnam as English in India. There were even French traffic police officers in Hanoi as late as the 1950s. Many positions in the civil service and in private enterprise, and all of the top ones, were closed to Vietnamese. When they did get jobs in those fields, they usually found themselves subordinate to Frenchmen with less education than themselves, and they received one-half to one-fifth the salary paid to the French in similar positions. The French spoke about liberty, equality, and fraternity to their Vietnamese pupils, but the educated Vietnamese was at best a second-class citizen in his own country. If he wished, he could contemplate the situation in the Philippines, an American possession, where almost all the government services—police, health, education—were staffed and run by Filipinos.[5] The future leaders of the Vietnamese revolution were, like those who made the Bolshevik and Nazi revolutions, men who had been frustrated in their desire for upward mobility. Predictably, "for most of those who became revolutionaries, it was clear that their own opportunities for advancement were inseparably bound up with eliminating French rule in Vietnam."[6] The revolutionary icon Ho Chi Minh, although a graduate of a select preparatory school in Hue, had been rejected for government employment. Pham Van Dong, a future premier of Communist North Vietnam, was the son of an Annamese mandarin. Bui Tin, the North Vietnamese Army officer who led the final assault on the Presidential Palace in Saigon in April 1975, was a great-grandson of a provincial governor and cabinet minister. Bui Tin's father, who employed a chauffer and several house servants, possessed a degree in French literature and had also been a provincial governor and cabinet minister.[7]

In a word, the Vietnamese revolution was not organized and led by illiterate paupers and desperate peasants. Our modern obsession with economics and the class struggle has helped to obscure the extent to which the political conflicts of the past hundred years have been fueled by the desire of unhappy intellectuals to get into power. The underemployment and lack of status among educated Vietnamese, along with the roadblocks to positions of authority for them, are at the root of the Vietnamese revolution.[8]

Outside influences—French, Soviet, and especially Chinese, both Nationalist and Maoist—powerfully contributed to and even shaped Vietnamese nationalism. For instance, many of the activists of the new Communist Party that Ho Chi Minh sent into Vietnam, including Pham Van Dong, were graduates of Chiang Kai-shek's military academy at Whampoa. Another example of foreign influence on Vietnamese nationalism is the VNQDD, the Nationalist Party of Vietnam, founded in Hanoi in 1927 under the direct inspiration of Chiang's Kuomintang. Nationalist parties in Vietnam were urban and elitist, with little idea of either the necessity or the means to appeal to the peasantry. The VNQDD's peasant program, for example, seems to have consisted mainly of extorting money from the well-to-do and then lending it to peasants, in order to obligate them to the party. The inability to come up with a long-range and realistic revolutionary strategy resulted in adventurist and premature uprisings; in 1930 one such poorly coordinated effort by the VNQDD, eventually joined by the Communists, resulted in a crushing defeat at the hands of the French. Those VNQDD leaders who escaped arrest fled to Chiang Kai-shek's China, where they remained until the middle of World War II. But many Communists remained in Vietnam and kept their organization alive.[9]

In addition to their mainly urban composition and lack of relevant revolutionary theory, other factors kept non-Communist nationalist groups like the VNQDD weak, thereby opening the way for the capture of the growing nationalist sentiment by Ho and his Communists. Most importantly, the French permitted no channel whereby Vietnamese could peacefully express the desire for political change and opposition to perpetual French domination. In sharpest contrast to the situation in India or the Philippines, public advocacy of independence for Vietnam was treated as treason.[10] This French policy therefore gave a tremendous advantage to those with the will and ability to engage in clandestine organization. VNQDD leadership, having little organizational experience and in a weak condition because of internal factionalism, like the rest of the non-Communist nationalist movement, could not escape the efficient French repression. Non-Communist nationalist organizations were periodically decimated by the French police. The Vietnamese Communists, in contrast, with a party based on tight discipline and a leadership trained abroad in the tactics of Leninist subversion, were able to survive and even expand. Besides, the Vietnamese Communists had ideological allies and defenders in the French Parliament, and the non-Communist nationalists did not. This international Communist linkage assumed major importance when the Communist-backed Popular Front cabinets held power in France in the late 1930s. Finally, when at the end of World War II exiled VNQDD leaders returned to their native country in the van of Chinese Nationalist occupation forces, they soon found themselves thoroughly discredited among their own people by Chinese arrogance and looting. The eventual withdrawal of the Chinese from northern Vietnam left the VNQDD exposed to attack by both the French police and the Vietnamese Communists. By the summer of 1946, they were almost completely destroyed. It is only one of the rich ironies of the whole Vietnamese revolution that the French searched desperately in the 1950s for an effective nationalist alternative to the Communists, an alternative that, by their vigorous persecution from the 1920s to the 1940s, they had all but destroyed.

Ho Chi Minh

The person who above all others benefited from the failure of non-Communist nationalism in Vietnam was Ho Chi Minh. When he was born in 1890, in Nghe An Province, an old-time hotbed of revolution on the central coast, Ho's name (the first of many) was Nguyen Tat Thanh. In his revolutionary career he adopted several aliases until finally settling on Ho Chi Minh, meaning "he who illuminates." Ho was a descendant of scholars and government bureaucrats; his father, an ardent nationalist, sent Ho to the best high school in Vietnam, at Hue. Turned down for a position with the French administration, Ho embarked upon a strange odyssey that carried him all around the world and eventually to total power in Hanoi. In 1911 he took a job on a French steamship and did not return to his country for thirty-three years. During his steamer voyage to Europe, Ho associated with seamen from Brittany and Cornwall. Finding them as illiterate and superstitious as any Vietnamese peasant, Ho lost his awe of white men. He claimed to have worked as a pastry cook for the great Escoffier in London, and he may have spent some time in New York City's Harlem. At Tours, he actually helped found the French Communist Party. Later, in Moscow, he took courses in the certainties of Marxism and the techniques of Leninism at the University of the Toilers of the East. Becoming active in the Comintern, the Moscow-centered Communist International that orchestrated party activities across the globe, he maintained the sensible—almost self-evident—proposition that the Asian revolution would have to be based on the peasantry, not on Marx's urban proletariat, thus anticipating Mao Tse-tung by several years.[11] He visited Vietnamese settlements in Thailand disguised as a Buddhist monk, and he fled from Chiang's China to Stalin's Soviet Union by crossing the forbidding Gobi Desert. Arrested in Hong Kong in 1932 and held for extradition to French Vietnam, he was defended all the way to the Privy Council in London by none other than Sir Stafford Cripps.[12] Cripps got Ho out of prison by presenting him as a political refugee and thus not subject to extradition. This was very fortunate indeed for Ho, because the French had him under sentence of death. In Moscow once more, he learned much about the arts of deception at the famous Lenin School. Reentering China, he spent time with Mao's Eighth Route Army. During these adventures, he learned to speak passable Russian, English, and Mandarin Chinese, in addition to his own Vietnamese tongue and French, which he had learned as a boy. Ho's experience of the outside world was not only incomparably greater than that of any other Vietnamese leader; it far surpassed that of any of the major Communist demigods, including Stalin and—most especially—Mao Tse-tung.

Ho first entered upon the world political scene when, still a young man, he attempted to petition President Woodrow Wilson at Versailles to consider the subject of Vietnamese independence. Brushed aside by the statesmen of the victorious Allied Powers, he nevertheless won for himself much notoriety and prestige among the sizable group of Vietnamese resident in France. And here, perhaps for the first time, Ho was attracted to Communism, because that ideology—and its Soviet proponents who had come recently to power—seemed to provide the only international support for Vietnamese national aspirations.[13] Lenin was indeed interested in independence for the Asians, but for rather complicated reasons. Like all Marxists born in the nineteenth century, Lenin was totally Eurocentric. When he, like Marx, used phrases like "the history of all peoples," he meant "the history of the Europeans." Lenin and other Marxists had long been puzzled by the continuing failure of the European proletariat, even after the Russians had given them the example in 1917, to rise up and carry out the revolution, the inevitability of which had been so convincingly laid out by Marx himself. Lenin's explanation for this proletarian failure was that the ruling capitalists of Europe had bribed the upper strata of their respective proletariats with some of the loot stolen from the subject peoples of their colonial empires. Clearly, then, reasoned Lenin, if the overseas empires could be broken up, the European proletariat would be deprived of its imperialist bribes and sink back into "immiseration." Then the long-desired European revolution would arrive. That is what Trotsky meant when he said, "The road to Paris and Berlin lies through the towns of Punjab and Afghanistan," sometimes more succinctly rendered as "The road to Paris lies through Peking."[14] In the summer of 1920, Ho read Lenin's "Theses on the National and Colonial Question," and this probably more than anything else first turned him to Communism.[15] Of course, Lenin never applied his ideas about the liberation of oppressed nationalities to the oppressed nationalities of Soviet Russia; by definition, oppression was another capitalist monopoly. Nevertheless, Communism "seemed to offer racial equality to subject peoples," and that was its fundamental appeal in Vietnam, not only after World

War I but after World War II as well.[16] In December 1920 Ho became a delegate to the Eighteenth Congress of the French Socialist Party at Tours, where he participated in the walkout that resulted in the foundation of the French Communist Party. Ho was thus the first Vietnamese Communist.

Ho remained unmarried and ascetic throughout his life; his one personal indulgence seems to have been chain-smoking American cigarettes. His image as one who sacrificed all personal comforts and private desires in an unquenchable patriotic fire, willing to struggle for his principles at no matter what cost in death and destruction, paradoxically endeared him in the 1960s to American and European students whose lifestyles were anything but ascetic, who viewed the patriotism of their own countrymen as a contemptible anachronism, and who found the shedding of blood for any political cause obscene. The image of Ho as a self-sacrificing ascetic, however, is not accepted in its entirety by all commentators. One American scholar has recorded his opinion that "mendacity was a cornerstone of Ho's career."[17] During his wanderings Ho had had several incredibly narrow escapes from Western prisons, stimulating accusations that from time to time he had purchased his freedom by acting as a police informer. More specifically, some maintain that Ho betrayed non-Communist Vietnamese revolutionaries, including Trotskyists, to the French authorities for money.[18] One of those believed to have been thus betrayed was the nationalist hero Phan Boi Chau, called by Bernard Fall "Vietnam's Sun Yat-sen." Fall also questioned the truth of Ho's saintly self-denial: the Hanoi regime told the world that Ho lived and slept in a small peasant hut right beside the former French governor's palace, but Fall said that in July 1962 he walked all around the grounds of that palace but failed to find that little hut.[19]

The Communist Party of Vietnam

To act always under the guidance of correct revolutionary theory was of the utmost concern to Marxist revolutionaries. Lenin said, "No revolutionary theory, no revolution." He meant it, and his followers all across the globe believed it, with good reason. Thus all the tremendous changes in the strategy and tactics of the Vietnamese revolution had to be fitted in, somehow, with correct Marxist theory as interpreted by Lenin and understood by the directors of the Comintern. Ho Chi Minh was no theorist; responsibilities for theoretical orthodoxy fell principally to his collaborator Truong Chinh. But no matter how winding the roads over which he led his followers, Ho never lost control. His dominance was based on his vast experience of the world, his good contacts in Moscow, and his international reputation as a revolutionary leader. But above all, his contribution to Vietnamese Communism lay in his genius as an organizational tactician. When it came to building fronts, cementing alliances, attaching non-Communist organizations to his own party, simply swallowing up rival groups whole, or having the leaders of such groups murdered, Ho had no equals, certainly not in Vietnam.

Ho Chi Minh floated to power on a wave of nationalist sentiment, but the craft that carried him was the Communist Party of Vietnam. This craft did not look at all seaworthy as the decade of the 1920s came to an end; it was broken into three sections, each claiming to represent authentic Marxism-Leninism. On orders from Moscow, the three squabbling factions came together in January 1930 to form the Indochinese Communist Party, with a membership of 211.[20] Then the tiny, newly united party was nearly wiped out by its involvement with the ill-prepared nationalist uprisings of 1930. French police repression, vigorous and effective, was aided to a considerable extent by betrayal within the party: "Virtually the entire Party Central Committee," writes Douglas Pike, "had been sold out by fellow Communists."[21]

Vietnamese Communism differed from all other anti-French organizations in the country because "it was a subversive movement launched from outside Vietnam by the Soviet Government as an instrument for embarrassing France."[22] In the 1930s and after, the close association of the Vietnamese Communists with foreign Communist states was of enormous, even decisive, advantage to it. The Comintern gave them money, training in Moscow in the arts of subversion, an external source of discipline and doctrine, and the morale-building belief that they were part of a worldwide movement led by a major European power and assured of ultimate triumph by Marxian analysis.

But subservience to Moscow was not without its costs. The strategy of Vietnamese Communism was made in Moscow, and Moscow refused to allow East Asian realities to intrude on its total absorption with the European scene.[23] In terms of promoting world revolution, Moscow's leadership, institutionalized in the Communist International, was a total failure, especially in western and central Europe. In those areas, Moscow's ferocious attacks on the socialist parties and labor unions both divided the working classes and isolated the local Communists. After twenty years of Comintern direction, European Communism was weaker in 1939 than it had been in 1919. Moscow expected Asian Communist parties as a matter of course to jump and dance to every change in its international line, regardless of what disasters that line might provoke in their respective countries.

Living outside Vietnam during the 1930s, Ho was spared the humiliation and political damage that would have resulted from having to explain and enforce the ever-changing Moscow directives. Reflecting deeply on the trauma of the 1930 uprisings and their suppression, he derived two fundamental lessons from that experience. First, no force generated inside Vietnam alone could defeat the French; some international upheaval would be necessary, such as World War I, which had made possible the Bolshevik seizure of power in Russia. Second, the party must be ready for such an eventuality by perfecting a tightly disciplined, tested organization of armed revolutionaries.

In 1936, the party received unexpected and spectacular assistance with its preparations: the Popular Front cabinet came to power in France with Communist backing and soon proclaimed a general amnesty for political prisoners in Vietnam. All the subversives, including Communists, so painstakingly rounded up after 1930, were now released and permitted to organize openly and insert themselves into the mainstream of Vietnamese politics—all this with the blessings of the rhetoricians in the National Assembly at Paris.

Even while deriving usable lessons from the past, even while receiving valuable favors from friends in France, the Vietnamese Communists, like the nationalists, remained a very small operation indeed. Pre–World War II nationalism in Vietnam was almost exclusively an urban affair, which is to say that it affected hardly at all the great majority of the population. The power of Marxism-Leninism in colonial and underdeveloped areas, in the 1930s as in the 1980s, lay not in popularity among the peasantry, nor even among the proletariat (which of course was very small), but rather in its attraction for the urban intellectuals. Many of these intellectuals found themselves excluded from participation in the capitalist economy, where important positions were reserved for Europeans. Because capitalism in Vietnam wore an alien face, Marxist condemnation of capitalism and consignment of it to oblivion struck a responsive chord.[24] Excluded from full participation in the world of the French, Vietnam's intellectuals were at the same time cut off by their education, aspirations, and style of living from traditional Vietnamese culture. Marxism provided a psychological as well as political haven for many such persons: "To be a Marxist represented a grand gesture of contempt for the corrupt past as well as the humiliating present."[25] Most of all, Marxism-Leninism represented for Vietnamese intellectuals a vision—indeed, a promise—of power, the power from which they were excluded. In those days Communist revolutionary theory, even in peasant societies such as Vietnam, insisted on "the leadership role of the proletariat," which meant the leadership role of the party—that is, of the intellectuals who were and remained its core and soul.

In the Vietnam of the late 1930s, Communism derived little benefit from its attraction for the small urban educated class. The party remained hardly more than a sect centered in Hanoi and a few other cities. Then in August 1939, the world was amazed, stupefied, by the Hitler-Stalin pact. Dutiful Communists in France and in Vietnam supported Moscow's alliance with the former hated Nazi menace and hence became openly the enemies of the French state. In November 1940 elements of the small Communist Party actually staged an armed insurrection, which was quickly suppressed.[26] French authorities in Hanoi reacted with predictable speed and severity, casting party leaders and members alike into prison. Those who escaped had to leave the comfort of their cafés and teahouses to shelter in the despised and unfamiliar countryside, an exodus that in the not-distant future produced the most momentous consequences.[27]

The Japanese and the Viet Minh

One can hardly exaggerate the influence on political developments in Vietnam exerted by foreign powers (excluding France, in this context, from that category). A primary example is the crucial role performed by the Japanese in the Vietnamese revolution. As Peter M. Dunn writes, it was they who ultimately destroyed the position of the French in Indo-china by occupying the country and successfully forcing their demands on them. When Japan collapsed, she did everything in her power to impede the French reoccupation of Vietnam. The Japanese turned over large stocks of arms, ammunition and money to the Vietnamese revolutionaries, and many Japanese deserters fought beside the Vietnamese rather than sur-render to the Allies.[28]

In June 1940, France fell before the onslaught of Hitler's jugger-naut. The following August, the Japanese government demanded that French authorities in Hanoi grant Japanese troops the right to occupy Vietnam's major cities and strategic points. Japan's aims were, first, to cut off outside aid to Chiang Kai-shek's Nationalist armies and, second, to prepare a springboard for attacks upon other Southeast Asian territories. Without any hope of outside assistance, the French administration in Vietnam had no choice but to accede to Japanese desires. These and subsequent events are absolutely crucial to understanding how a Vietnamese revolution became possible and why it took the form and the course that it did. Without the sweep-ing aside of French power in 1940, without the public humiliation of the once-invincible French authorities, without this stripping from the French of their Mandate of Heaven—and all this at the hands of an Asian people—it is very difficult to imagine how a Vietnamese national revolution would have succeeded, especially one under the leadership of the Communist Party. But the Japanese entrance into the world war, and into Vietnam, gave the small but well-disciplined Vietnamese Communist Party its chance: the Japanese produced the crisis of the French Indochina regime.

The Communists responded to this unforeseen but long-prepared-for opportunity with the Eighth Plenum, which took place at Pac Bo in May 1941. At this crucial assembly, the leaders of Viet-namese Communism made two major decisions, from which much else followed. First, the struggle between classes must be subordi-nated to the struggle for national independence. Second, all anti-Japanese groups and individuals, Communist and non-Communist alike, must unite in a total crusade against the national enemy. As the vehicle for this unity, the Communists established a new front organization called the League for the Independence of Vietnam, or Viet Minh for short.

Exchanging their Communist clothes for the robes of nationalism was perhaps the most important decision Ho and his followers
ever made, because "in terms of revolutionary strategy, Communism has succeeded only when it has been able to co-opt a national
liberation struggle, and has failed whenever it was opposed to or
isolated from a national liberation struggle such as those in Israel,
Algeria, Indonesia, and Burma."[29] In the short run, the substitution
of national independence for class war at the heart of the Communist message brought the party many advantages. The appeal to
nationalism—opposition to the predatory Japanese occupation and
to the French, whose weakness, whose very presence in Vietnam,
made the Japanese occupation possible—helped transcend the many
regional, ethnic, and class divisions among the Vietnamese; without
transcending these divisions, no national revolution could succeed.
The cause of national independence was more attractive to young
intellectuals than class struggle alone had ever been. And most of all,
the promise to get rid of the French and distribute their wealth and
property provided an essential tool whereby the intellectuals who
led the Communist Party could fashion the all-important alliance
with the peasant majority, upon whose shoulders the burden of any
realistic revolutionary strategy would have to be placed.[30]

By creating this Viet Minh front organization, Ho and his followers were pursuing "the primary political tactic of communist revolutionaries since the time of Lenin."[31] The purpose of the Viet Minh,
like the purpose of any Communist front, was to attract, by means of
widely accepted symbols and slogans, non-Communist nationalists
and democratic elements into an alliance that they would not normally wish to enter. Through this alliance, the Communists would
be able to gain favorable attention and access to groups formerly
indifferent to or suspicious of them and thus broaden their support,
not on the basis of Communist goals but of their temporarily adopted
nationalist aims. Once such a front was established, the Communists,
by means of their superior discipline, self-consciousness, and cohe-
sion, their clarity of purpose and ruthlessness of means, would first
manipulate and eventually dominate it.

The front tactic was thus ideally suited to carrying out Lenin's
"Two-Stage Theory" of revolution in colonial areas. Stage one was the
"bourgeois" revolution, by which a broad, interclass coalition (such

as the Viet Minh) came to power. Stage two was the "real" revolution, in which "the workers," led by (or sometimes substituted by) "the vanguard of the proletariat"—that is, the intellectuals who made up the leadership of the party—established their irrevocable control.

In accordance with these tactics, the Communists declared that if Vietnam did not achieve national independence, then no class within it would achieve what it needed or wanted. The salvation of the working class, of the peasantry, and of the bourgeoisie, all depended on national liberation. Class war must be submerged into a "racial patriotism."[32] Thus the Communists dropped their call for general seizure of landed property in favor of the confiscation of French-owned lands only and mere reduced rents for the rest.

With the cities controlled by the Japanese Army, any revolutionary action would necessarily have to take the form of guerrilla warfare in the rural areas. From that circumstance came the Viet Minh promise to distribute foreign-owned lands to the peasants. Thus Ho turned away from the Bolshevik, or Petrograd, model of revolution—the seizure of power in the capital city by a trained force of workers led by intellectuals. In its place Ho adopted what later became known the world over as the Maoist model of revolution. All the elements of that model were taking form: a united national liberation front, guerrilla warfare, the beginnings of a party army, and a secure base area. This decision by Ho to turn away from a metropolitan strategy based on the workers toward a rural strategy based on the peasantry made the Vietnamese revolution possible.[33]

As 1941 drew to a close, the urban areas of Vietnam were fairly tightly in the grip of the Japanese; most nationalist leaders who were not associated with the Viet Minh had fled to China, entered into collaboration with the French, or retired from political life. But persisting in its revolutionary strategy, the Viet Minh grew. Soon it had a monopoly of what noticeable anti-Japanese armed resistance there was, and it reaped rich political rewards for this record. General Vo Nguyen Giap, the schoolteacher turned military commander of Viet Minh forces, had several hundred men in his National Salvation Army by the end of 1943, and he exercised close to undisputed control over the three remote border provinces of Cao Bang, Lang Son, and Bac Kan.[34] As the war entered its final phase, the Americans began parachuting arms to this little Viet Minh army.

Several authorities have noted that the amount of fighting between the Viet Minh and the Japanese was in fact quite minimal. George Kelly states that "actually, there was almost no combat with the Japanese invaders, who were satisfied to leave the countryside to the native guerrilla groups."[35] Joseph Buttinger agrees: "The Viet Minh never dreamed of sacrificing its precious troops in the hopeless and ultimately unnecessary task of fighting the Japanese."[36] Consequently, there is but a single recorded clash between Viet Minh and Japanese forces during all of World War II.[37]

For most of their occupation, the Japanese had been content to rule Vietnam indirectly, using the French as their instruments. On March 9, 1945, however—apparently just two days before the French were prepared to launch a major assault against Giap's guerrillas[38]—they disarmed and locked up all the French forces in the country they could lay hands on. "The psychological effect of this action," writes Dennis J. Duncanson, "was exactly as intended: the peoples of Indochina who witnessed the disarming of French soldiers concluded that French rule was at an end for all time, and with it the whole system of government and apparatus of law and order for which France had stood."[39]

Having thus cast aside the last vestiges of French rule, the Japanese then approached former Annamese emperor Bao Dai and instructed him to declare Vietnam independent under Japanese protection. On March 11, 1945, Bao Dai proclaimed the independence of the empire of Annam and Tonkin, while Cochin China remained under tight Japanese control. These March events broke the spell of French overlordship. French power had disappeared, and defeat was impending for the Japanese; all this created a true political vacuum in Vietnam, a vacuum into which the Viet Minh, with its small but disciplined and devoted numbers, soon marched. For John T. McAlister, "unquestionably the disappearance of its colonial authority in Indochina in the space of a few short days in early March 1945 was for France the gravest consequence of the Japanese intervention."[40]

The seventy thousand Japanese troops in Vietnam were not nearly enough to control both the cities and the countryside, and after March 1945 the Japanese were unconcerned anyway with Viet Minh activities in rural areas. Hence Giap's small armed units were now free to grow at a rapid rate. By the middle of 1945, he commanded five thousand trained men and exercised political control over perhaps 1 million peasants in the border areas. The fact that the Viet Minh actually controlled Vietnamese territory, no matter how small a portion, helped to legitimate it in the popular eye as a true alternative government; this was an enormous advantage for the Viet Minh over the other nationalist groups.[41]

The Japanese occupation produced yet another tremendous, and predictable, windfall for the Viet Minh: famine. The Japanese had been taking rice out of Vietnam for their far-flung wartime purposes and had forced many peasants to produce not rice but jute for Japanese industrial needs. They had also imprisoned the French engineers responsible for the maintenance of the vital dike system in Tonkin. These factors inevitably led to an inadequate rice harvest. With land transport and coastal shipping disrupted by the Pacific war, a serious famine occurred in the northern provinces during the winter of 1944–45. Estimates of the number who died reach 2 million, out of Tonkin's population of perhaps 9 million. The relationship between the shortage of food and the outbreak of revolution in France and Russia is well known, and the Viet Minh would have benefited from this terrible situation even if they had sat still and done nothing. But in many places they led demonstrations in front of government granaries, sometimes seizing the grain and distributing it to the multitudes, in this way winning attention and gratitude. Viet Minh agitation during the famine was a "key to the development of the movement in rural areas throughout the north,"[42] and it provided, along with the front's campaign for national independence, the basis for what popular support it enjoyed in 1945. Nevertheless, by August of that year, the Viet Minh remained a small operation.

The Chinese Nationalists

The contributions of Chiang Kai-shek's Nationalist regime to Viet Minh success were not as decisive as those of the Japanese, but they were quite important.

In accordance with decisions reached during the Potsdam Conference, Japanese units in Vietnam south of the sixteenth parallel were to surrender to British troops, and those north of it to Chinese Nationalist troops. British commanders in southern Vietnam, reflecting policy at the highest levels of government, were sympathetic to the French and sought to aid their return to control. Besides, British forces on the scene tended to view the Viet Minh as Japanese puppets.[43]

In contrast, Chinese forces in northern Vietnam, thoroughly hostile to the French, refused to permit the five thousand French troops who had escaped into China at the time of the March 1945 Japanese coup to return to Tonkin. Instead they had to make an arduous journey via Laos into central Vietnam. At the same time, the Chinese kept those French soldiers who had been disarmed by the Japanese in semiconfinement. These actions by the Chinese proved decisive in allowing the Viet Minh to solidify their control over the Hanoi area and northern Vietnam. French forces did not return to Hanoi until March 1946, more than a half year after the surrender of Japan. And for good measure, hundreds of Viet Minh received training in guerrilla tactics in Nationalist camps inside China.[44]

American Aid and the Viet Minh

From early in World War II, President Roosevelt expressed his disapproval of restoring French control over Indochina and opposed sending French reinforcements there in 1944 (during the war). In Peter M. Dunn's judgment, "Roosevelt's active opposition to the return of the French to Indochina ultimately assured the success of the heralded Communist August Revolution."[45] General Charles de Gaulle, head of the Free French, was deeply offended by this and other Rooseveltian maneuvers (including Roosevelt's recognition, alone among the Allies, of the Vichy regime for almost the entire duration of the war).

The Office of Strategic Services (OSS), the forerunner of today's Central Intelligence Agency, parachuted supplies, weapons, and instructors to Giap's armed bands in northern Vietnam.[46] This aid "did much to transform the Viet Minh from a ragged bunch of irregulars into units that had standardized weapons."[47] Indeed, in Arthur J. Dommen's view, "the arms furnished by the OSS enabled Giap's 'armed propaganda teams' to gain control of the mass rally in Hanoi on August 17 [two days before Ho Chi Minh proclaimed independence under the Viet Minh] and to turn it into a demonstration of support for the Viet Minh, and they [OSS arms] also enabled

them in short order to assassinate the leaders of the nationalist parties."[48] The OSS maintained that aiding the Viet Minh rather than
the French-organized resistance helped save the lives of downed
Allied fliers, but it appears that more of these fliers in fact received
help from the French than from the Viet Minh.[49] Photographs exist
of Giap and OSS officer Archimedes Patti saluting the Viet Minh
flag that flew over the Hanoi citadel, inside of which French soldiers
were imprisoned in grim circumstances. The two men also inspected
the Japanese troops guarding those French prisoners. "France has
never forgotten it."[50] These and similar activities of the OSS in Vietnam allowed many to form the impression that the United States
was backing Ho Chi Minh. At least one authority insists that Ho
Chi Minh's manipulation of the political immaturity of OSS officers
was a major element in his eventual victory.[51] The most authoritative English-speaking student of intelligence has written: "The US
Office of Strategic Services was the most [Communist-]penetrated
intelligence agency in American history."[52]

Adding injury to injury, General Douglas Macarthur forbade Allied landings in Japanese-held territory in Southeast Asia until the
formal Japanese surrender took place, in September. "This directive
[of MacArthur's] had enormous consequences in Indochina, for a
political vacuum was created which was happily filled by Communist leadership. That leadership is still there," wrote Peter Dunn in
1985, as it is at the time of this writing.[53]

In his war memoirs, de Gaulle writes with restrained fury that
these actions of the Allies "had fatally compromised the effect
which the immediate arrival of French troops and officials and the
disarmament of the Japanese by our forces might have produced."[54]
Nevertheless, in spite of all obstacles, "the de Gaulle government
now [1944] installed in Paris was determined to restore French power
over the whole country [of Vietnam]."[55]

The August Revolution

One of the principal theoretician-activists of the Viet Minh, especially in the days during and after World War II, was Truong Chinh
(a pseudonym meaning "Long March"). Of the events known to
history as the August Revolution, he wrote: "World War II created

for the Vietnamese people an extremely favorable opportunity: the enemies of the Vietnamese revolution, the Japanese and the French fascists [of Vichy], had exhausted each other and grown weak. Moreover the Japanese were then defeated by the Soviet army; that was enough for the Vietnamese people to fell them with a single blow and to seize power."[56] It was therefore the policy of the Vietnamese Communists "to lead the masses in insurrection in order to disarm the Japanese before the arrival of the Allied forces in Indochina; to wrest power from the Japanese and their puppet stooges, and finally, as the people's power, to welcome the Allied forces coming to disarm the Japanese troops stationed in Indochina."[57]

In 1945, no Vietnamese revolutionary organization, including the Viet Minh and the VNQDD, had a mass following in Vietnam, or even in Tonkin; consequently, "the events in the August revolution throughout Vietnam were the sphere of a small portion of the total population."[58] At the time, membership in the entire Vietnamese Communist organization was about 5,000, out of a total population of at least 35 million (another way to say this: out of every 7,000 Vietnamese, 1 belonged to the Communist Party).[59] As John T. McAlister succinctly notes, "the quantity of participants in the August Revolution was significant only because of the smallness of their numbers."[60] Even William J. Duiker, who cannot suppress his admiration for Ho Chi Minh, refers to "the shallowness of popular support for the Viet Minh" as late as mid-1946.[61]

But this was no obstacle, or even a problem, for the Communists. For Marxist-Leninists, a revolutionary situation did not necessarily mean that there was great support for the revolutionaries, only that there was little or no support for the government. It was this absence of support that the Communists sought to manipulate, or create. In such conditions, the role of armed forces, those of the government and those of the revolution, became crucial.[62]

The conditions for a Communist seizure of power in Hanoi in August 1945 were extremely propitious. After years of nationalist agitation, the humiliation of the French in 1940, the hardships of the Japanese occupation, and especially the terrible famine, a revolutionary situation was clearly at hand. The revolutionary elite was present in the form of the small but determined forces of the Viet Minh. Now, with the imprisonment of the French in March 1945 and the unexpected surrender of the Japanese Empire on August 15, the revolutionary crisis had appeared. On the night of August 18, Viet Minh troops, about 1,000, moved into Hanoi and the next day proclaimed their control over the city. The police and the 1,500 civil guardsmen of the Japanese-recognized Bao Dai government wavered in the face of the Communists' speed, weapons, and discipline. Most importantly of all, the 30,000 Japanese troops in Hanoi stood indifferently aside as the Viet Minh took over control of government buildings and strategic points around the city. On August 28, Ho Chi Minh announced the Provisional Government of the Democratic Republic of Vietnam. Some Communists had wanted to imitate what Lenin had done in 1917 by setting up an exclusively Communist cabinet; but Ho insisted that some non-Communist members be included, while keeping all key offices safely in the hands of the party. Ho also demanded that Emperor Bao Dai abdicate, and that gentleman complied with his demand. But then, acting on the principle that the front through which the Communists were working must be as broad as possible, Ho immediately appointed Bao Dai "Supreme Political Adviser" to the new regime. At the time, the abdication of Bao Dai made an incalculable impression; in the eyes of many in Vietnam, the Mandate of Heaven seemed to have passed from the emperor to Ho Chi Minh, and the Viet Minh must, apparently, be the only legitimate government.[63] Finally, on September 2, 1945, in an impressive ceremony before a vast Hanoi crowd, Ho proclaimed the independence of Vietnam under the leadership of the Viet Minh.

Two outstanding circumstances permitted the August Revolution and shaped its course. First, the daring takeover of Hanoi resembled a coup much more than the great revolutions in history. It was an elitist movement, with a small number of well-drilled activists grasping the symbols of power amid the confusion of their enemies. Notably absent from these August events, in Hanoi and especially in Saigon, was the participation of middle-class elements. Second, the August Revolution took place thanks to the temporary weakness, or absence, of those who could have opposed it. It was the imprisonment of the French, the neutrality of the Japanese, and the hesitancy of Bao Dai, not the strength of the Viet Minh, that ensured the success of the August takeover.[64] George Modelski summarized that "the major element in this [Viet Minh] success was the weakness of their opponents."[65]

The seizure of Hanoi represented a sudden, if brief, switch back from a rural strategy to the old Bolshevik model of revolution. Indeed, the August Revolution resembled the October 1917 Bolshevik coup in Petrograd in some notable ways. Both occurred during world wars, where military defeat had decisively weakened the regime; in the interval between the collapse of the old order and the Communist takeover, a weak regime tried unsuccessfully to restore stability; and the Communist seizure of power was followed by a civil war. But unlike the revolutionaries in Petrograd in October 1917, the Viet Minh could not hold onto the capital. It was eventually forced back into the jungles and mountains of northern Vietnam, not to reenter Hanoi again until the final capitulation of the French after many years and many deaths. Nevertheless, the August Revolution and the possession of government power in Hanoi, however briefly it all lasted, transformed the image of the Viet Minh from a revolutionary sect to a contender for national power and indeed the embodiment of the national cause. For many Vietnamese, including convinced anti-Communists, the choice now seemed to have narrowed down to a stark one: allow the discredited French to return or join (or at least support) the Viet Minh. At the same time, nobody outside of the Viet Minh, and probably only a handful of people inside it, were aware of the extent to which the Viet Minh was under Communist control. Thus, in those heady and emotional days following the proclamation of independence, many Catholics, including some bishops, offered the Ho regime their tentative support.[66] (Catholics made up about 10 percent of the population of northern Vietnam.)

The attitude of the Japanese Army toward the August Revolution was decisive: "It was the acquiescence of the Japanese rather than Viet Minh strength which ensured Communist predominance over the disoriented Vietnamese caretaker government."[67] After the August Revolution, but before the return of the French, the Viet Minh made good use of the Japanese. Many Japanese officers had viewed World War II in profoundly racial terms as a colossal struggle between the peoples of East Asia and those of the North Atlantic. Imperial Japan had failed in its mighty effort to oust the detestable Caucasians from their Asian colonies, but the struggle might be carried on nonetheless through the agency of local nationalist groups such as the Viet Minh. Hence, all over East Asia in the waning days of summer 1945, the Japanese handed over great quantities of arms and ammunition to such organizations. Japanese troops allowed the Viet Minh to seize the weapons of the French-organized Garde Indochinoise and handed over tons of Japanese Army munitions. In this manner the Viet Minh obtained, among other things, thirty-one thousand rifles and eighteen tanks. In addition, between two thousand and forty-five hundred Japanese soldiers joined the Viet Minh outright; they staffed Giap's training schools and weapons-making facilities or served in guerrilla units. Japanese soldiers also armed and trained units of the Cao Dai religious sect in Cochin China.[68]

As the year 1946 approached, an increasing number of French forces were arriving in southern Vietnam, especially around Saigon. Aware that an open breach with the French would result in the immediate loss of Hanoi (and perhaps much else), Ho decided on compromise. He and French representative Jean Sainteny negotiated the famous agreement of March 6, 1946. By this accord, France recognized the Democratic Republic of Vietnam (DRVN), consisting of at least Tonkin and Annam, as a free state—with an army, a parliament, and a treasury of its own. For his part, Ho accepted the stationing of a modest number of French forces north of the sixteenth parallel for five years, the training of the DRVN troops by French officers, and Vietnamese membership in the French Union (a Gallic version of the British Commonwealth). Ho also conceded that a plebiscite should be held in Cochin China to determine if the people of that area wished to join the DRVN.

The Ho-Sainteny agreement recognized the legitimacy of Ho's government, but it fell short of granting complete independence. There was much opposition to it, even within the Viet Minh. General Giap called the agreement a new Brest-Litovsk (the desperate, time-buying treaty Lenin signed with the German Army in 1918). Aside from the necessity to pursue purely frontist tactics, Ho had appointed non–Viet Minh members to his new February cabinet precisely because he foresaw the opposition that this "surrender" to the French would generate and did not want all the blame to fall on the Viet Minh.[69]

Viet Minh Assassinations

With the signing of the Ho-Sainteny agreement, the triumph of the Communists and their Viet Minh front over the non-Communist nationalists seemed complete. Ho's skilled leadership, the attractiveness of Marxist philosophy to French-educated intellectuals, the temporary submersion of true Communist goals within the vessel of national independence—all had been important factors in this outcome. But so had Communist hostility toward non-Communist nationalists.[70] The Communists had for years been betraying the latter to the French authorities, right up to the outbreak of the real fighting in 1946. This policy had been particularly devastating against the VNQDD.[71] But to consolidate its victory and achieve a total monopoly over the Vietnamese nationalist movement, the Viet Minh increasingly relied on more direct methods. Years ago one often heard the comment that Ho Chi Minh was "a nationalist first and a Communist second." But of course that is a meaningless statement; all Communist revolutionaries in colonial areas had by definition to be nationalists, because only through the expulsion of the colonial authority could they take power. Ho Chi Minh had been a good Communist for decades, indeed as a member of the Comintern he denounced Tito's "betrayal" of Stalin. The simple fact, as Joseph Buttinger notes, was that "Ho had two aims. The first was to achieve independence. . . . But this was not all he wanted. The second aim was that Vietnam, once independent, should be ruled by his party. . . . It had to be a Communist Vietnam." That is, Ho and his fellow Communists had no wish whatsoever to be one component in a Vietnamese national movement and government; they desired an independent Vietnam only if it was completely controlled by them; "indeed the fight for independence was for them only a vehicle for the conquest of power." To this end, they carried out a deliberate campaign to destroy the non-Communist nationalists, murdering rivals or potential rivals by the hundreds: "The elimination of their opponents was one of the most common means the Communists used to establish Viet Minh control over the entire nationalist movement."[72]

This dominance-through-murder policy was quite successful: "The Stalinists [Viet Minh] saw to it that those whose brilliance might have dimmed their own luster were buried in good time."[73] Not only

was the Viet Minh able to establish control of the anti-French movement, but it also severely weakened the future state of South Vietnam.
This "Communist policy of killing all true nationalist opponents of
the Viet Minh" deprived the future South Vietnamese state of the
services of many who might have given it vigor and safety.[74] The Viet
Minh also sought through assassination to decapitate the indigenous
religious sects; it executed the leader of the powerful Hoa Hao, and
corpses of sect members could be viewed floating down the Mekong
River tied together in bundles, like logs.[75] And for good measure the
Communists killed every Trotskyist they could locate.[76] Viet Minh
assassinations soon became "a vice, an intoxication with violence."[77]

The Communist destruction of the leadership of independent
groups was very effective in the short run; in parliamentary elections
conducted by the Viet Minh in January 1946, for example, Ho allegedly received 169,000 votes in Hanoi, whose total population was
supposed to be 119,000.[78] In days to come, the Viet Minh deliberately
tried to provoke French violence against civilians.[79] In light of such
tactics, one authority very friendly to the Viet Minh and bitterly
critical of the French concludes that "the motives of the Communists
in Vietnam were as questionable, and their methods as odious, as
the French."[80] Then and later, in Buttinger's stark comment, "the
measures [Ho Chi Minh] took to achieve a monopoly of power for
the Communist Party divided his people and destroyed his reputation as a man who had devoted his life to making his people free."[81]
During 1946 the Viet Minh massacred thousands of non-Communist
nationalists in Tonkin.[82] These "odious methods" sowed bitter seeds
of uncompromising hostility to the Viet Minh among large sections
of the Vietnamese population, especially in the south.

The Outbreak of Real Fighting

The Ho-Sainteny agreement seemed to promise a peaceful, if not
amicable, short-term settlement to the explosive postwar situation
in Vietnam. Yet even while Ho Chi Minh was in Paris negotiating the
final details of the agreement, French authorities on the scene were
attempting to set up Cochin China as an independent state, separate
from the rest of Vietnam and under French protection. The man behind this provocative move was Admiral Thierry d'Argenlieu, "the

most brilliant mind of the twelfth century," whose appointment as French high commissioner of Indochina has been called "France's major postwar blunder in Southeast Asia."[83] A hastily gathered assembly proclaimed the autonomous republic of Cochin China on June 1, 1946. No Viet Minh government, not even Ho's, could long survive if it recognized such a state of affairs as permanent.

On the other side, the French had little enough reason to have confidence in the Viet Minh. In December 1944 Giap's forces had attacked two remote French outposts. In August of the following year, after the signing of the Ho-Sainteny agreement, Viet Minh forces at Bac Ninh destroyed a French convoy on an authorized mission. Then on November 9, the Viet Minh–controlled Democratic Republic of Vietnam proclaimed a constitution without any mention at all of membership in the French Union. There could be no doubt that a real confrontation was coming, especially since the Viet Minh now had around fifty thousand men under arms (including several thousand Japanese deserters who assisted General Giap with training and arms production). The most dramatic incident took place at Haiphong on November 23. In retaliation for several murderous attacks on French soldiers in Hanoi, the French cruiser *Suffren*, after an ultimatum, opened fire on the Vietnamese quarter of the port of Haiphong. Many, perhaps several thousand Vietnamese, mostly civilians, lost their lives through this barbarous and stupid act; nobody knows how many were wounded. After the Haiphong incident, there could be no more pretense of French paternalism; it was now going to be a naked struggle for power. But however dramatic and regrettable, the shelling of Haiphong has not gone down in the records as the beginning of the war. That event is fixed as the December 19, 1946, attempt by Viet Minh troops to overwhelm Hanoi, with many grisly assaults on French civilians and concerted attacks on French garrisons all over Indochina.[84] The Socialist prime minister of France, Leon Blum, heading an all-Socialist cabinet (he had been prime minister in 1936 when the Popular Front cabinet granted amnesty to revolutionaries in Vietnam) proclaimed a firm policy of military containment of the rebellion. Now the war was really on. At the time, all French political parties, including the Communists, wanted Indochina to remain French. And in May 1947 the Socialist minister of Overseas France, Marius Moutet, called Ho a "war criminal."[85]

The seizure of Hanoi in August 1945 was the Leninist phase of the Viet Minh revolution. The retreat into the countryside, where French control had always been weak, was the beginning of the Maoist phase of the revolution. There were later attempts, in 1968 and 1972, to return to the Leninist mode and provoke the uprising of the vanguard of the oppressed masses in the great cities. But such uprisings somehow repeatedly failed to occur. In the countryside, the Viet Minh forces quickly and easily adopted the time-tested guerrilla tactics of Mao: speed of movement to achieve surprise, never attacking without overwhelming numbers, always planning any military operation with its political effects uppermost in mind. It was a war of attrition against the French authorities, aimed at gaining control over a greater and greater proportion of the civilian population through persuasion or fear. In addition to their guerrilla units, the Viet Minh were building small conventional forces. These troops generally employed tactics very similar to those of the guerrillas (never fight except when the numbers are with you; slip away from superior forces), the principal difference being that guerrilla units attacked to inflict damage, while conventional forces attacked to annihilate.[86]

The Revolution Develops

In the early years of the war, the Viet Minh leadership, faithful to sound frontist tactics, emphasized nationalism and social improvement; it never denied, but also never emphasized, the ultimate program of Communization. The Viet Minh seized the lands not of the well-to-do but only of the French and of Vietnamese collaborators, a policy that had its political costs. Many poorer peasants saw little reason to take risks for the Viet Minh if they were not to be given the land they wanted right away, and this despite the wooing of such persons by the Viet Minh with rent reductions and timely assistance to many during the wartime famine.

Faced with this political dilemma, the Viet Minh concentrated on the skillful indoctrination of those peasants who did join up. In the first years, desertions seem to have been few and morale high.[87] The progression of a recruit through the Viet Minh forces usually consisted of service first in a village unit, then in a provincial unit, with the best going ultimately into the conventional army and also perhaps into Communist Party membership.

The principal military leader of the Viet Minh was Vo Nguyen Giap, whose fame from the First Indochina War is surpassed only by that of Ho Chi Minh. Giap's career, during which he held high positions both in the Viet Minh armed forces and in the Communist Party, illustrates perfectly the Communist insight that military and political considerations are not separate but interpenetrating. Born in 1912 into a mandarin household, Giap studied at the Lycée National at Hue, the same school attended by Ho and Ngo Dinh Diem. He then went to the University of Hanoi, where he took a *license en droit* (law degree) in 1937 and considered going on for a doctorate in political economy. But he left the university after marrying the daughter of a professor there and accepted a position as a history teacher at a private school in Hanoi. The war and the Japanese occupation soon swept him up, and he found himself in command of the tiny military forces of the struggling Viet Minh. Whatever his ideological commitment to the revolutionary cause, Giap had profound personal motives for his hostility to the French; they had guillotined his sister-in-law, an anti-French activist, and his wife died in 1943 after a period of French imprisonment.

Giap often boasted that the only military academy he had ever attended was the bush. As one of his biographers points out, the bush is not a bad military school to attend, but it has the serious disadvantage of lacking a library. Hence, while Giap was learning good tactics, he could not broaden his understanding by reading the works of the great strategists. Time revealed the consequences of this imbalance. Giap had attended guerrilla warfare training in China in 1942. After the August 1945 seizure of Hanoi, Giap the graduate of the Communist bush nevertheless liked to appear in public dandily attired in a white duck suit and striped tie.[88]

The Bao Dai Option

It became clear enough to the French that they could have no hope for a secure victory if the Vietnamese population concluded that the war was about a choice of permanent colonialism under France versus independence under the Viet Minh. Hence they needed a plausible Vietnamese alternative to the Viet Minh, an alternative that would stand for both independence from and close cooperation with France, an alternative that could gather together the disparate but cumulatively numerous elements of the Vietnamese population that looked with distaste or fear upon the prospect of a Viet Minh victory and could also free the French from the stigma of waging a colonial war. To achieve all these ends, France offered independence under Bao Dai.

Born in 1913, Bao Dai was the son of Emperor Khai Din, the twelfth monarch of the Nguyen dynasty.[89] He succeeded to the throne in 1926 and abdicated in the confusion of the August Revolution. As these lines are being written, Bao Dai's image is undoubtedly worse than he deserves. True enough, he became an habitué of French nightclubs and less reputable establishments, but that was after he had endured a long series of sharp rebuffs and profound disappointments at the hands of the French, who would allow him no effective role in the affairs of his own country. Having been raised to be emperor, and being very shy, Bao Dai lacked the common touch, especially compared to Ho Chi Minh (although Bao Dai did marry a commoner). But one noted student of Vietnam has called Bao Dai "an underrated man."[90] According to another authoritative evaluation, Bao Dai "was endowed with intelligence of a high order and possessed a lofty conception of the national destiny. He was also to show a capacity for conducting intricate political negotiations and a shrewd ability to divine the intention of, and on occasion to outwit, both his European and Asian opponents."[91] At any rate, it would be a crude error to dismiss Bao Dai as a French puppet; on the contrary, he was the repository of widespread and well-founded hopes among nationalist, anti-Communist Vietnamese.[92]

However unsuccessfully in the end, Bao Dai undoubtedly worked for what he thought was best for his people. It was he, after all, who appointed the young and intransigent nationalist Ngo Dinh Diem to be his minister of the interior back in the 1930s. And when the Japanese surrendered, Bao Dai sent personal appeals to Charles de Gaulle, President Harry Truman, Chiang Kai-shek, and King George VI, imploring them to recognize the independence of Vietnam under his leadership. One of the main reasons Bao Dai had abdicated as emperor in the face of Ho Chi Minh's demand was his belief that because the U.S. military mission to Vietnam spent most of its time at Ho Chi Minh's headquarters in Hanoi, the U.S. government must have been backing the Viet Minh.[93] In his 1945 abdication message to his people, he had written: "We cannot help but have feelings of regret at the thought of the twenty years of our reign, during which we have not been able to render any appreciable service to our country."[94] Yet Ho himself recognized that Bao Dai enjoyed considerable prestige and popular affection; that is why Ho sought to associate him with the new Viet Minh regime by naming him "Supreme Adviser" and appearing together with him in public.[95] Bao Dai soon realized he was a figurehead for the Communists and, not wishing to be associated with Ho's agreement with the French, went into voluntary exile to China in March 1946.

Now it was the turn of the French to attach him to their cause.[96] Negotiations between the French and the former emperor on the future of Vietnam caused Ho's government to condemn him to death in absentia (December 1947).[97] But in June of the following year, Bao Dai put his signature to a bombshell of a French document that began, "France solemnly recognizes the independence of Vietnam." The chief of state of this independent Vietnam was to be Bao Dai himself, who also persuaded the French government to abandon Admiral d'Argenlieu's project for a separate Republic of Cochin China. (Looking back after all these years, one cannot escape the suspicion that, of all the efforts to prevent a totally Communist Vietnam, this project of d'Argenlieu's was arguably the most likely to have succeeded.)

In any event, as Bernard Fall notes, "Bao Dai had obtained from the French in two years of negotiating what Ho had not been able to obtain in two years of fighting: the word 'independence.'"[98] Even before the Viet Minh leadership had proclaimed its open adherence to Stalinist Communism, news of Bao Dai's triumph rocked the Viet Minh and caused many of its members to defect.[99]

French motives for backing Bao Dai were self-serving, but this should not obscure the fact that a substantial coalition of groups both nationalistic and anti-Communist came together behind Bao Dai. So did persons who had once supported the Viet Minh but had become disenchanted by its increasingly strident Communism. Early in 1948, the indigenous southern religious sects, the Cao Dai and the Hoa Hao, had pledged their support if Bao Dai were to be restored to office, in return for which the French granted the sects virtual autonomy over their local areas in Cochin China. But they undoubtedly would have come along anyway, because both the Cao Dai and the Hoa Hao hated the Viet Minh. By 1954 these sects together commanded at least forty thousand armed men.[100] The small nationalist Dai Viet party in Tonkin also adhered to the Bao Dai coalition, as did disillusioned figures from the Viet Minh. The Catholic minority, perhaps 10 percent of the population in 1945, initially wanted to be on good terms with the Viet Minh, because they knew that, as Catholics, they were widely looked upon as being pro-French. In Donald Lancaster's judgment, "this desire on the part of the Vietnamese hierarchy that the Roman Catholics should redeem their unfortunate [pro-French] reputation deprived the [anti–Viet Minh] nationalist cause of the support of an important minority who were in the last resort irreconcilably opposed to the Communists."[101] But Communist militants could not refrain from attacking Catholic villages and organizations, and so Catholic groups began forming their own armed militias. Toward the end of 1949, the Catholic minority, especially in Tonkin, offered its allegiance to Bao Dai.[102]

Thus, an authentic anti–Viet Minh coalition was emerging. And, in Lancaster's revealing terms,

the prospects for [this] coalition were improved . . . by the fact that many Vietnamese who had been inspired to join the Viet Minh were now dismayed to discover that their desire for national independence was being exploited in order to impose upon the country an alien Communist regime, which was likely to prove more destructive of the national heritage than had been the case with the short-lived French protectorate.[103]

There is no doubt that as time went on, more and more Vietnamese concluded, however sorrowfully, that the nationalism of the Viet Minh stood "revealed as a piece of deception."[104]

President Dwight D. Eisenhower once remarked to Secretary of State John Foster Dulles that "the French could win the war in six months if the people were with them."[105] There is a great deal of truth in that observation, but it is not so easy to know who "the people" actually were supporting (as distinguished from who they were *not* supporting). In their desperation to find additional manpower, the

French set up a separate Vietnamese army owing political allegiance to Bao Dai and his State of Vietnam. By 1952 this army consisted of about 80,000 men, and afterward it grew appreciably. Additional scores of thousands of Vietnamese were serving in the French Union forces. The total number of all Vietnamese in uniform under the command either of the French or of Bao Dai reached 300,000 by 1954. A Vietnamese military academy was opened in 1949, although it produced few officers. Vietnamese units in both the French Union and Bao Dai armies were usually infiltrated by Viet Minh agents; also, the French gave their Vietnamese Army allies secondhand equipment, further undercutting their morale. Nonetheless, between 1946 and 1950, Vietnamese forces fighting against the Viet Minh incurred about 7,500 casualties a year, a very high rate, the proportional equivalent of 75,000 annual American casualties in 2011.[106]

In the south, the French eventually set up a system of warlords, usually local religious sect leaders, to fight the Communists for them; this strategy was not ineffective, but the warlords could flourish only as long as the war went on. Hence they had no real interest in bringing the conflict to a decisive conclusion—an example of the symbiotic relationship between the strength of the Viet Minh and most efforts to destroy them. Moreover, Bao Dai was not unaware that he also had a symbiotic relationship with the Viet Minh; if they were finally defeated, the French would not need him.[107] In any event, the French were grudging and graceless with Bao Dai, always managing to delay granting his government control over defense and foreign policy. And at the Geneva Conference that ended the war, the French shamelessly betrayed him.

Nevertheless, between 1948 and 1954, the Franco–Bao Dai side eventually won the allegiance, or at least the alliance, of the prewar nationalist parties, the Saigon middle class, the great majority of Catholics, and the powerful southern religious sects. On the other side, General Giap's active forces never exceeded three hundred thousand men, less than 1 percent of the Vietnamese population of those days.[108] Fully thirty-five foreign countries maintained diplomatic relations with Bao Dai's state. It seems that, by 1954, when President Eisenhower made his comment about popular support, the situation in Vietnam was something like this: a powerful minority favored the Viet Minh; substantial elements opposed the Viet Minh and hence for the time being cooperated with the French or adhered to Bao Dai; and a third group, probably the largest, desired only to be let alone by both sides.

Why Cochin China Was Different

The French suffered defeat in northern Vietnam but not in the south, especially the populous Mekong Delta region known as Cochin China, with its center in Saigon. Determined resistance to the Communists, moreover, continued in the south for two decades after the final departure of the French.

The factors that contributed to the weak position of the Communists in the south relative to the situation in Tonkin were numerous and revealing. For several centuries before the advent of the French, Vietnam was usually divided into two kingdoms, one based on the Red River Delta, the other on the Mekong Delta, separated from each other by the narrow waist of Annam. Warfare between the kingdoms was not uncommon. The French had established their control over Cochin China earlier than in other areas of Indochina and maintained it as a separate administrative region, a practice the Japanese occupation continued. Distinct regionalism was, and continued to be, a fundamental factor of Vietnamese society.

The famine of 1944, which was of such assistance to the Communists in Tonkin, was hardly felt in Cochin China; Saigon, after all, is almost a thousand miles away from Hanoi, and even farther from the Chinese border. At the time of the Japanese surrender, moreover, Tonkin had been occupied by the Chinese Nationalist armies; deeply anti-French, the Chinese did not permit any significant French reentry in Tonkin until the spring of 1946, thus giving the Viet Minh time to consolidate their position there; in contrast, the French were back in British-occupied Cochin China in strength as early as October 1945.[109]

Most of all, standing in the way of the creation of a powerful Communist organization in the south was the presence of large social groups that were indifferent or hostile to the Viet Minh. The Communists had been bloodily confronting the popular Trotskyists in Cochin China since the 1930s.[110] Saigon (like Hanoi) had only a small Communist organization, due both to effective police surveillance and to the indifference of its relatively sophisticated population to the Viet Minh, who were viewed as bomb-throwing peasants.[111] The half million ethnic Chinese of Cochin China were especially unenthusiastic about the Viet Minh. A consequence of all this was that when the Japanese surrendered, the Communist Party in the south, unlike its counterpart in the north, had hardly any armed units and thus could not control Saigon.

But perhaps the most powerful single source of Communist weakness in the south was the anti-Communist hostility of the sects, principally the Cao Dai and the Hoa Hao. Between them, these religious-economic formations enrolled what may have been close to a majority of Cochin Chinese. The destructiveness of anti-French acts by the Viet Minh at the end of the Pacific war alienated the sects, along with others. Fighting between the well-armed sects and the southern Communists broke out very soon after the August Revolution and continued through the spring of 1947. The Viet Minh assassinated sect leaders and murdered great numbers of rank-and-file members.[112] "Communist terror," notes Buttinger, "gradually drove [the sects] into the French camp."[113]

The French Military Situation

In this chapter, CEF (short for Corps Expéditionnaire Français en Extrême-Orient) refers to all official, regular forces fighting in Vietnam under the French flag, including French, Vietnamese, Foreign Legionnaires, North Africans, West Africans, and sometimes others. In the CEF, the French were a minority, except among the officer corps. It is essential to distinguish the CEF from the scores of thousands of Vietnamese serving in the armed forces of Bao Dai's State of Vietnam, referred to herein as the VNA (Vietnamese National Army).

The French forces sent to Vietnam were unprepared for what they encountered. General Paul Ely wrote, "Our [French] units, organized for warfare in Europe, proved to be ill-suited to a struggle against rebel forces in an Asiatic theatre."[114] The infantry was poorly trained and weighed down by the impedimenta of a Western army. The French Colonial Army, an important element in the CEF, had a venerable tradition of rotating its units among French territories around the globe. Hence there were very few "area specialists" in its ranks, and this shortage of officers and noncommissioned officers familiar with the realities of Vietnam made it very difficult to sustain irregular units and gather intelligence.[115]

In terrain and climate like that of northern Vietnam, "the advantage lies with the well-trained and lightly equipped rifleman accustomed to life in the jungle."[116] And of course, both terrain and climate heavily disfavored the tactics of a conventional army. In a place like Vietnam, a European-type, road-bound military force lost its mobility: "The most significant factor of the physical environment, even more than the exhausting effect of the climate on European troops, was the primitive road network. Historically the geography of Indochina made waterways the most practical means of travel over any distance."[117] The roads that did exist were ideal settings for Viet Minh ambushes, especially roads that led to isolated CEF outposts. Between 1952 and 1954, the CEF lost five hundred armored vehicles, more than 80 percent of them to mines and booby-traps.[118] And one officer's report contained this revealing, and chilling, comment: "Each night the roads were left to the enemy."[119]

From the days of the Japanese occupation, seven provinces in the Viet Bac, the mountainous region north of Hanoi and east of the Red River, made up the stronghold of the Viet Minh.[120] This so-called Free Zone was "the true foundation of [the Viet Minh's] ultimate success" and "made the difference between survival and defeat."[121] The area was too difficult to penetrate and occupy; in much of the terrain, "encirclement" was meaningless, and no roads led into its interior.[122] Besides, large CEF movements could never be secret. And by calculating how many soldiers were needed to protect a given length of road, the Viet Minh could accurately predict at what place an offensive operation would reach its culminating point.[123] Nevertheless, in October 1947, CEF commanding General Jean-Etienne Valluy launched Operation LEA: the aim was to surround the Viet Bac and then capture the Viet Minh Army and political headquarters in the town of Bac Kan. But the guerrillas simply disappeared; the CEF encountered no one. Thus the operation met complete frustration due to the terrain and the enemy refusal to engage. But paratroopers very nearly captured both Ho Chi Minh and General Giap (see below). Had they succeeded in doing so, the war would have come to an end.

The battalions of the Viet Minh fought infrequently, whereas CEF units had to be alert and on patrol every night. Time and again, CEF forces would occupy a village and begin rounding up Viet Minh agents, often with the help of local inhabitants. But then, because of inadequate manpower and supply, they would abandon the place, exposing all the civilians who had assisted them to ghastly reprisals. As the conflict dragged on, CEF infantry units became increasingly dependent on artillery and air support, a sure sign of declining morale.[124]

But above all, the "defining characteristic of the [CEF] was its poverty in trained manpower and in every other necessity, since it had to compete with NATO for every man, gun, truck and litre of petrol," a competition in which it usually came up second best.[125] Before U.S. aid began arriving in quantity in 1951, CEF forces were using weapons from the 1930s, including some of Japanese, German, British, and Chinese manufacture.[126] These conditions were made worse because the supply base of the CEF was in France, while that of the Viet Minh was just over the border in China.

Quite aside from combat and climate, conditions of life for ordinary soldiers were depressing: drinking untreated water accounted for 40 percent of medical cases among European troops in Vietnam, and the daily pay of a French soldier amounted to about nineteen piastres, while a beer in Saigon cost seven piastres.[127]

Consider also that the CEF was fighting to "contain Communism" in Southeast Asia at the very time when fully a quarter of the French Parliament was composed of Communists, the biggest single party in that unlamented body. Liaison with the French Communist Party provided much intelligence to the Viet Minh and helped it cast its propaganda to French prisoners in familiar terms.[128] Ignorance of Vietnamese affairs in French society was profound (no French newspaper had maintained reporters there in the period leading up to the outbreak of war).[129] The French knew very little about disputes and anxieties inside the Vietnamese Communist organization, but the Viet Minh knew all about the disagreements, confusion, and posturing among the French in Paris and even in Hanoi. Communist politicians in France constantly predicted a negotiated settlement in Vietnam or outright defeat of the CEF. Communist mobs stoned trains unloading wounded soldiers in their home towns and abused departing troops at railway stations. Communist factory workers damaged motors and weapons destined for the troops in Vietnam.[130] Pierre Mendès-France, a future prime minister, stated in December 1951 that France could not continue stripping her troops from Europe and sending them to Vietnam. In 1953 the parliamentary leader of the Gaullist party referred to the struggle in Vietnam as "the Fourth Republic's Mexican expedition."[131] One can just imagine the effect of statements like these not only on members of the CEF but also on anti-Communist Vietnamese. And, as a crowning touch, the French government felt it wise to announce that blood donated in France would not be sent to the CEF. These were the conditions in which the army had to recruit volunteers.[132]

It would be an understatement to observe that the conduct of the war by the government in Paris was administratively inept. The Ministry of Defense, the Ministry of Overseas France, and other agencies in Paris all exercised a share of control over military affairs.[133] If unity of administration was poor, continuity of command was nonexistent: from 1945 to 1954, French forces in Vietnam had eight commanders in chief. During that same time, the politicians in Paris, with grotesque frivolity, set up and pulled down no less than sixteen cabinets.[134] The CEF never had enough soldiers from France because the politicians were afraid to send conscripts to Vietnam (thus all French in the CEF were professionals or volunteers).

French Airpower

The French had air supremacy over all Indochina, if only in the sense that the Viet Minh had no air force of its own. But French control of the air was nominal. They never had many more than one hundred modern aircraft (C-47s and C-119s) at any one time, and they did not have those until 1952. By 1953 Chinese antiaircraft were knocking many of those planes out. And as late as 1954, the CEF possessed exactly ten helicopters.[135] Besides, the Viet Minh usually operated at night; and "the Viet Minh made a veritable fetish out of camouflage."[136] Further, the French used what airpower they had in direct support of ground troops, to an extent that many French airmen believed was inefficient. And General Lionel Chassin, when he was the French air commander in Vietnam, remarked that his air force was going to kill water buffalo because they were the "tractors" of the Viet Minh—a comment that should not be overlooked by those seeking the deeper causes of the French failure in Vietnam.[137]

French Numbers

Beset by overlapping authorities and frequent changes of leadership, the French forces also confronted the classic problem of counterguerrilla warfare: how to divide one's forces between static defense and mobile operations. Given enough troops under one's command, this problem is not insuperable. But even with the help of the many Vietnamese enrolled under the French flag or in the forces of Bao Dai, the French never had enough soldiers, mainly because French law forbade the sending of draftees to Indochina.

By 1951, General Giap commanded an estimated 300,000 fighters. According to the commonly used standard of ten counterinsurgents to each insurgent, the French would have needed 3,000,000 troops and police to achieve victory in Vietnam, a quite impossible figure. (Before the Japanese occupation, France had maintained order among the more than 25 million inhabitants of Vietnam with 11,000 French soldiers assisted by 16,000 indigenous auxiliaries.) To reach even a completely insufficient ratio of three-to-one, the French would have needed 900,000. But in fact, by May 1954 the French Expeditionary Corps consisted of 54,000 French soldiers (out of a population of more than 40,000,000), 30,000 colonial troops (mainly North African and "Senegalese," meaning West African), 20,000 Foreign Legionnaires, and 70,000 Vietnamese (in the CEF), along with 15,000 French naval and air personnel. Statistically, the average soldier in the CEF was not a Frenchman. (At its peak strength, the Foreign Legion provided 35 percent of the European manpower in Indochina; perhaps half of the Legionnaires were German, but since their average age was under twenty-three, it is incorrect to label these persons as ex-Nazis trying to escape their condign punishment.) Even after one adds to these the 200,000 men in Bao Dai's army and an additional 60,000 in the sect and Catholic militias, the grand total is at most 450,000—exactly half of the utterly inadequate three-to-one ratio. And of course a very large proportion of these forces were employed in static defense positions.[138]

The solution to the French manpower problem was perfectly, even painfully, obvious: (1) send conscripts from France, or (2) build up a properly equipped and properly trained Vietnamese National Army, or (3) do both. But the French did none of these things.

Border Disasters and French Tactics

A favorite French gambit was to establish outposts far from their base in the Red River Delta (the Hanoi-Haiphong area). Because the French air arm was weak, the outposts had to be supplied by convoys. Of course, the Viet Minh responded by ambushing these convoys. Between 1952 and 1954 alone, the French lost several hundred armored vehicles, mainly in ambushes. To discourage such incidents, the French begin building strongpoints at places where ambushes had previously occurred. These strongpoints, in turn, needed to be supplied by convoy. Hence, convoys went forth to supply outposts that had been erected to protect the convoys; an odd system.[139] In any event, notes George K. Tanham, "the French lived in fear of ambushes to the end of the war."[140] To resupply outlying garrisons was often extremely difficult; consequently, a number of them fell as much from the lack of reliable supplies as from enemy action.[141] From time to time the French decided to simply abandon one of these outposts, thus creating another great convoy begging to be attacked. Such withdrawals produced some of the worst French catastrophes (discussed below).

In 1950 General Giap decided he needed to score some real victories before the anticipated arrival of serious U.S. assistance to the French. He correctly identified the French posts guarding the few usable passages along the eight-hundred-mile, mountainous Sino-Vietnamese border as the easiest pickings. The principal French border strongholds were at Cao Bang and Lang Son. In May 1950 Dong Khe, a strategic point between those two places, fell to the Viet Minh. A dramatic French paratrooper assault soon recaptured it, but the following September, the Viet Minh, with an eight-to-one superiority over its French defenders, retook Dong Khe.

At Cao Bang, the French possessed a good fort with impressive defenses, both natural and manmade. But in October 1950, partly in response to the second fall of Dong Khe, the French high command in

Hanoi ordered Cao Bang to be abandoned. Eventually, sixteen hundred soldiers plus hundreds of civilians left Cao Bang and headed for the city of Lang Son, eighty-five miles to the south. The commander at Cao Bang had received orders to destroy his vehicles and big guns and to evacuate the place on foot. Ignoring or misunderstanding these instructions, the French forces proceeded in the direction of Lang Son with all their vehicles and artillery. Thus the column was road bound, but the "road" was just a miserable track through the majestic forest and was vulnerable to bridge-blowing. The retreat therefore was too slow.[142] At the same time, thirty-five hundred French Moroccan troops were advancing north to meet the column coming from Cao Bang. The two groups eventually linked up, but then the swarming Viet Minh cut them to pieces. In the judgment of Yves Gras, "the disaster was above all a moral one. The essential fact was that French troops—considered the best—had been annihilated in open country by an army of Vietnamese peasants who had up to then been despised."[143] Thus, the affair of Cao Bang constituted "the greatest defeat in the history of French colonial warfare."[144]

The debacle of Cao Bang somehow convinced the French military authorities that they should also abandon Lang Son. This city of one hundred thousand was the main French strongpoint in the entire border region. To avoid alerting the Viet Minh of their departure, on October 18, 1950, the French withdrew from the city without first blowing up their munitions. Thus a rich cornucopia fell to the Viet Minh: ten thousand 75mm shells, gasoline, precious medicines, and much else, all of it truly invaluable. Lang Son was "France's greatest colonial defeat since Montcalm had died at Quebec."[145] Similar disasters resulted from the abandonment of Hoa Binh in 1952 and Sam Neua in 1953. In Bernard Fall's estimation, the capture of Lang Son meant that "for the French, the war was lost then and there."[146]

The French lost at least 6,000 of the 10,000 troops holding the border strongpoints. With sufficient airpower—and perhaps without consistent French underestimation of their enemies—none of these disasters would have occurred. Learning very little from these events, however, in a few years the French set up another outpost battle, at a place called Dien Bien Phu.

The outcome of these border battles strongly suggests, first, that outposts are worse than useless unless they can be reliably supplied and, second, that it is safer for the troops inside a strongpoint to stay there doing their utmost to fight off the enemy than to try to escape that enemy on inadequate roads without air cover. But most of all, the debacles along the northern frontier resulted in giving the Viet Minh unrestricted access to assistance from Mao Tse-tung's newly established regime in China.[147]

Paratroops

The CEF used paratroops extensively throughout the war, partly because of the poor roads and the lack of helicopters. Martin Windrow notes that "the parachute battalions were virtually the only units that could carry the war to the enemy by achieving surprise." Thus, "Indochina was the paratrooper's war par excellence—indeed, it was the only war after 1945 to see large-scale parachute insertions of several thousand troops at a time, as well as numerous small drops by single battalions."[148] In October 1947, during Operation LEA, airborne troops descended on Viet Minh headquarters in the Viet Bac and very nearly captured both Ho and Giap, one of the great what-ifs in modern history.[149] In July 17–20, 1953, paratroopers landed at Lang Son, scene of the 1951 disaster, destroyed much Russian and Chinese equipment, and made it back safely to the De Lattre Line (discussed below). Indochinese, mainly Vietnamese, typically composed 30 to 50 percent of paratroop battalions.[150] Paratroopers, "whose sheer quality tempted commanders to commit them to missions beyond the realistic grasp of such light troops," were often sacrificed in evacuations and lost causes.[151] Thus an entire parachute battalion was annihilated in the effort to save the retreat from Cao Bang in 1951. Others suffered tremendous losses at Dien Bien Phu; the last parachute battalion was dropped there on May 3, five days before the fortress was overrun.

Chinese Communist Assistance

The most serious weakness of the Viet Minh for several years after the beginning of the war was the shortage of modern weapons; they simply could not begin to match the French forces in firepower, and under these circumstances they would never be able to defeat them decisively. This weakness changed when the Chinese Communist armies reached the border of Vietnam in 1949. For the Viet Minh, Mao's victory across the border in China meant the availability of a safe haven, improved training, and most of all, military supplies.

And with the end of the Korean war, President Eisenhower recalled, "the Chinese Communists were now able to spare greatly increased quantities of materiel in the form of guns and ammunition (largely supplied by the Soviets) for use on the Indochinese battle front. More advisers were being sent in, and the Chinese were making available to the Viet Minh logistical experience they had gained in the Korean War." They also provided them with American weapons captured in Korea, superior to those the CEF had. Eventually reaching four thousand tons per month, Chinese supplies to the Viet Minh exceeded French supplies to the CEF. Windrow concurs that "after weapons, munitions, radios and training in their use, the professional education of Vietnamese officers was China's most vital contribution to the transformation of General Giap's guerrillas into an army." Forty thousand Viet Minh received training in China, and Chinese officers and instructors played a vital role at Dien Bien Phu.[152]

Aside from all the materiel and training given to the Viet Minh, the Chinese Communist regime affected the war by casting a dark cloud over French planners in Hanoi and Paris, the cloud of potential Chinese invasion of Tonkin. John Foster Dulles, President Eisenhower's secretary of state, believed that the fear of Chinese intervention sapped the French will to fight in Vietnam.[153]

The arrival of Chinese Communist power on the northern border was also the occasion for Ho and the Viet Minh to proclaim their open and total adhesion to the Communist world under the leadership of Stalin. This act doubtless was encouraged by their Chinese benefactors, and it also won them, for the first time, the open support of the powerful French Communist party (whose chances, however, of coming to power peacefully or otherwise after 1947 were nil). But on balance this ideological confession was a grave error. In throwing off the nationalist mask and revealing the Stalinist face behind it, the Communist directors of the Viet Minh paid a tremendous price: they turned the United States decisively and irrevocably against them.

A struggle that had at least some of the stigmata of a colonial war of independence now became subsumed into the global confrontation between Stalinism and the West. Henceforth, for a quarter of a century, the Americans labored mightily, first by assisting the French, then by helping the southern anti-Communists, and finally by massive intervention of U.S. forces, to prevent the conquest of all Vietnam by the avowedly Communist Viet Minh. In bringing all this upon themselves and their country, "the extremists in the Viet Minh movement incurred a grave responsibility to the Vietnamese people."[154]

And the tide was about to turn against the Communist side.

Giap's 1951 Offensives

In the first half of 1951, emboldened by the fall of the French border posts, General Giap decided to attack the Red River Delta with his conventional forces, supported by Chinese artillery and antiaircraft. His grandiose objective, apparently, was to drive the French from their base in the Hanoi-Haiphong area. For the first time, he deployed his carefully nurtured regular units from the Viet Bac against French prepared positions.

On January 13, 1951, Giap attacked the town of Vinh Yen, located on the northwest edge of the Delta. In this assault, the Viet Minh deployed 22,000 men; Franco-Vietnamese forces numbered 6,000, later increasing to 10,000. The attack was a failure, due in part to good tactics by French aircraft and in part to the fact that Giap developed his attacks in a piecemeal fashion. Incredibly, General Giap publicly blamed the failure of the operation on the cowardice of his troops.[155] Yet the Viet Minh had suffered very heavy casualties, perhaps 6,000 of their best fighters; not for the first or last time, Giap seemed to show "a callous disregard for casualties among his own troops."[156] Fortunately for him, French forces were too numerically weak to pursue their battered enemy. It was this attack, however, that spurred the building of the De Lattre Line (discussed below), still largely in the planning stages at the time of the Vinh Yen battle.

Late in March, Giap launched another major effort, this time against Mao Khe, near the Gulf of Tonkin and only twenty miles north of vital Haiphong. French artillery and aircraft, reinforced by gunfire from navy destroyers, beat back the attacking forces, which advanced in mass waves and sustained heavy losses.

In the last phase of his offensive, on May 29 Giap attacked across the Day River in the southern Delta. The French were taken by surprise because it was the wet season, not good for campaigning. French firepower, supplemented by armed river craft and reinforced by sturdy Catholic village militia, broke up this last effort, and Giap withdrew from the Delta by June 18.

Giap's unsuccessful 1951 Red River Delta offensive brings a number of key aspects of this war into focus. First, Giap was and continued to be outstandingly good at logistics, but his very limited experience in conventional warfare was a handicap to him when commanding large bodies of troops. He had no air or naval forces and consequently underestimated the role these elements played against his Delta campaigns.[157] More than that, Giap was operating on exterior lines (that is, the defenders of the Delta were inside a rough geographic triangle—on "interior lines"). In that position, he needed both to deploy a great superiority of numbers and to keep his enemy from switching troops from an area not under attack to defend another area that was. But in a major error, Giap assaulted the Delta in three separate operations, allowing the French to take full advantage of operating on interior lines.

A second key aspect is that Giap's Delta campaign revealed an important weakness of the Viet Minh, "who were liable to find themselves at a loss when faced with a situation for which no provision had been made in their well-thumbed textbooks on the conduct of guerrilla warfare."[158]

Third, in his offensive operations, Giap's losses approached twenty thousand men. If the French had possessed sufficient numbers of troops, they could then have launched a possibly decisive counteroffensive against the Viet Minh.[159] But General de Lattre lacked the means to follow up his advantage, which soon disappeared. Neither he nor his successors ever possessed the offensive strength to go after Giap in a war-winning campaign. This insufficiency of CEF numbers was "one of the decisive factors in their eventual defeat."[160] At the bottom of the lack of troops were both the unwillingness of the politicians in Paris to send draftees to Vietnam and the reluctance of the French government and military to provide the Vietnamese National Army (the army of Bao Dai's state) with adequate training and equipment. And so the war dragged on, as Giap for the time being pursued more orthodox guerrilla tactics, fighting smaller engagements and watching for an opportunity.

De Lattre and His Line

In December 1950, just before General Giap's offensive against the Red River Delta, a new French commander arrived in Vietnam. His name was Jean de Lattre de Tassigny, a hero of the Free French in World War II and afterward commander in chief of the Western European Union ground forces. In response to the border catastrophes, the French government sent General de Lattre to Hanoi as both commander in chief and high commissioner; like Gerald Templer in Malaya,[161] he thus wielded both supreme military and supreme civilian authority. One U.S. general called him "France's greatest post–World War II soldier"; the French in Hanoi called him Le Roi Jean, "King John," because of both his high offices and his imperious personality.[162]

The fall of Lang Son had led the French to plan for the evacuation of French women and children from the Red River Delta (the area around Hanoi and Haiphong). Almost the first thing de Lattre did in his new command was to order such plans to be scrapped, believing that his soldiers would fight better knowing that they were defending their families. Besides, he had big ideas for dealing with the Viet Minh threat.

In the lurid afterglow of the fall of the border posts and major attacks by General Giap early in 1951, it was clearly necessary to drastically reduce Viet Minh access to the rice and the population of the Red River Delta and also to ensure that French forces had a secure base to fall back on in case of further serious reverses. De Lattre intended to achieve these aims by constructing a great chain of fortifications, eventually known as the De Lattre Line. A fortified line of the sort de Lattre envisioned was a good idea and would have succeeded if—if the French had possessed sufficient numbers to hold the line tightly. But they did not. Thus the Viet Minh were free to raid the Red River Delta at will and withdraw back to their strongholds. Moreover, with the French pursuing their De Lattre Line strategy, the Viet Minh had unimpeded access to their supply sources at the Chinese border.

The fortified line was only one part of de Lattre's great plan to reverse the tide of the war. He also intended to get more men and equipment from France, to appeal to the United States for increased assistance, and—not least—to build up the Vietnamese National Army. By obtaining more troops from France, moving units from Cochin China to Tonkin, and turning over the responsibility for the static defense of the line to this augmented Vietnamese army, de Lattre intended to greatly increase his offensive power.[163]

By the end of 1951, the line consisted of twelve hundred fortified infantry posts, mainly small, but close enough to each other to be mutually supporting. It enclosed seventy-five hundred square miles and 8 million people. But the line was porous, owing to the insufficient numbers of troops under de Lattre's command—hence his desire to raise a proper Vietnamese army. But, while the line immobilized too many troops in static defense, at the same time it failed to protect the Delta from the Viet Minh. Possibly thirty thousand Viet Minh combatants operated *inside* the line, partly or wholly controlling 5,000 of the 7,000 villages enclosed within it. Nights in the Delta resounded with countless small firefights.[164]

In November 1951, as a riposte to Giap's failed offensive, de Lattre launched a paratroop operation against the town of Hoa Binh, twenty miles southwest of the De Lattre Line. On an important north-south Viet Minh supply route, Hoa Binh was also a center of the Hmong people, a minority ethnic group loyal to the French. The operation was supposed to demonstrate that the French could take the offensive outside of the Delta.[165] But Viet Minh forces soon isolated Hoa Binh, which meant that the French had to keep it supplied by air in the teeth of powerful enemy antiaircraft (a foreshadowing of Dien Bien Phu). Viet Minh human wave attacks overwhelmed the small number of tanks the French had at Hoa Binh. In the midst of this struggle, General de Lattre, dying of cancer, returned to France, and was replaced in command by General Raoul Salan (de Lattre died on January 11, 1952, having been created a marshal of France on that day). On February 22, General Salan began the withdrawal from Hoa Binh, a bitter, fighting retreat eventually involving twenty thousand French troops. In the end, the affair of Hoa Binh showed that the French had very little capability for taking offensive action outside the Red River Delta.

Nevertheless, by 1953, several thousand partisans, recruited from among the pro-French minority highland peoples and led by French officers, were operating behind Giap's forces, causing a great deal of trouble. Indeed, in June 1952 the Viet Minh were reduced to asking Mao Tse-tung to send a Chinese division to the Red River around Lao Cai to put down guerrillas of this sort. There were probably as many as fifteen thousand of these pro-French guerrillas in Indochina as a whole, tying down thousands of Viet Minh troops. Many French officers did not like these irregular formations, and so they received little help. But some of them were still active as late as 1959, five years after the French had pulled out of Indochina.[166]

The Vietnamese National Army

As one of the best English-language works on the conflict observes, "today it is little appreciated that the war as a whole, and the battle of Dien Bien Phu itself, were far from being clear-cut confrontations between Europeans and Indochinese, but involved significant numbers of Vietnamese fighting under French command."[167] The conflict was in fact the latest in a long series of Vietnamese civil wars involving foreign powers. This civil war continued long after the French left Vietnam.[168]

In November 1950 the Vietnamese Military Academy opened to train Vietnamese officers, and the following July Bao Dai announced conscription for the newly formed Vietnamese National Army. (Bao Dai thought it would take eight years for the Vietnamese National Army to fully replace the French forces.) The State of Vietnam was devoting 40 percent of its revenue to the war effort. The VNA often drafted university students for officer training. These persons were frequently disdainful of the peasant troops they were supposed to command and also of militia officers who, however skillful at fighting guerrillas, did not have the educational attainments to become regular officers. Whatever its teething pains, at the end of 1953 the VNA enrolled two hundred thousand soldiers, and many young

VNA officers in future years held important posts in the Army of the Republic of Viet Nam (ARVN), the army of South Vietnam.[169]

Were these Vietnamese who fought under the flag of France or of the State of Vietnam traitors to their own nation? Or perhaps they were merely mercenaries? It is true that pay rates in the Vietnamese Army were on a French scale, which means they were high for an Asian country, and they seemed very high indeed to a young peasant boy. But it is inconceivable that only money affected the decision of so many young Vietnamese to openly take sides against the Viet Minh and to maintain the struggle for so many years at the cost of so much danger, bloodshed, and hardship.[170]

Consider that for centuries French civilization attracted admiration and loyalty from inhabitants of many societies, European and non-European, and it still does. It should present no great puzzle or scandal that millions of Vietnamese, especially but not only Catholics and the members of the indigenous sects, saw temporary cooperation with France as at the very minimum the lesser of evils, compared to the permanent triumph of the local representatives of Stalinist totalitarianism. Everyone knew the French would leave someday, but the Viet Minh were hand-in-glove with the Chinese, right across the border. Besides, in the last analysis, France had recognized the independence of the Vietnamese state under Emperor Bao Dai, who received embassies from more than thirty countries, including Australia, Belgium, Britain, Canada, Italy, the Netherlands, Spain, Thailand, Turkey, the United States, and sixteen Latin American states including Brazil. Legally, therefore, the French forces in Vietnam were fighting alongside Bao Dai's army to preserve his sovereign government. The war was thus not about an independent Vietnam but about a Vietnam under Communist control. For many, it was clearly more patriotic—more Vietnamese—to prefer the traditional nationalism of Bao Dai to the Euro-Leninism of Ho Chi Minh, who had lived outside of Vietnam for most of his adult life.[171] In any event, one cannot simply ignore the fact that by spring 1954, as McAlister notes, "nearly 300,000 Vietnamese [were] fighting against the Viet Minh in the CEF, the VNA or local militias. This French capacity to mobilize substantial Vietnamese manpower for military purposes at the beginning as well as at the conclusion of the war is quite revealing of the reality of the situation in Vietnam."[172]

Dien Bien Phu

The Path to Dien Bien Phu

On October 29, 1952, General Salan launched Operation LORRAINE, involving thirty thousand soldiers of the CEF, the largest operation it ever mounted in Vietnam. The objective was to drive deep into Viet Minh country along the line of the Clear River, force the enemy out of his accustomed territory, seize supplies stockpiled at Phu Doan, and damage General Giap's prestige. But Giap declined to offer battle. The CEF forces advanced slowly into a void, ever farther from their base, exposed to unknown dangers, while supply problems multiplied. In mid-November, Salan ordered a withdrawal back to the Delta. The offensive had occupied close to five hundred square miles of enemy-held territory "without having encountered a single Communist unit of any size."[173]

Since 1946, the war had largely been confined to Tonkin and northern Annam. But on April 9, 1953, Giap invaded the Kingdom of Laos, a French protectorate and ally. In response, Salan ordered the evacuation of the Laotian town of Sam Neua, which was held by three battalions, including Laotians. Under furious attack, the retreat turned into a disaster, ranking with Cao Bang: of 2,500 soldiers, only 235 got out alive.[174]

In late 1952 and early 1953, the scales had clearly shifted in favor of the Viet Minh. General Giap now commanded from 100,000 to 125,000 main-force troops, including seven infantry divisions well supplied with Chinese heavy arms, along with 60,000 to 75,000 regional troops of varying quality; these bore much of the fighting, and there were also 120,000 to 200,000 local militia, many of whom were ill equipped and poorly organized. The French Expeditionary Force in the summer of 1952 counted 51,000 French, 18,000 Legionnaires, 25,000 North Africans, and 56,000 Indochinese, mainly Vietnamese, plus about 100,000 in Bao Dai's Vietnamese National Army, which at that time was not a match for Giap's best divisions.[175] Thus, concludes Phillip B. Davidson, "in 1953, the central fact of the Indochina war was that for the conduct of mobile ground operations in the North, the Viet Minh held at least a two-to-one advantage over the French."[176]

In May 1953, Paris replaced General Salan as commander in

Vietnam with General Henri Navarre. Many thought this an odd selection, because Navarre was not a combat commander but an intelligence officer. It was clear to everyone that after almost seven years of fighting, the war had become a stalemate: The French and their allies could not disperse the Viet Minh, and the Viet Minh could not expel the French. The French, with good reason, were getting very tired of this war that nobody could win. In their view, the principal problem was that the Communists rarely engaged in regular battles, in which superior French training and firepower would prove decisive, as in Giap's disaster at Vinh Yen. Instead, the enemy either engaged mainly in guerrilla fighting, in which the CEF was at a serious disadvantage, or simply melted away, as during Operation LORRAINE.

Out of this situation the new French commander developed what became known as the Navarre Plan. Its principal components were (1) to assume the strategic defensive in the north during the 1953–54 campaigning season, (2) to carry out a major pacification effort in the Tonkin Delta, (3) to improve the size and training of the Vietnamese National Army, and (4) to then seek a major battle with the Viet Minh in 1954–55. Then in August 1953, about five thousand CEF troops successfully evacuated their fort at Na Son (not far from Dien Bien Phu), giving General Navarre what proved to be a very misleading idea about the safety of CEF forces in inaccessible strongholds.[177]

Hence, the High Command in Hanoi conceived the idea of building a fortress complex near the Laotian border, in one of the most remote areas of Vietnam. The fortress would serve two purposes: (1) minimally, it would impede easy passage of Viet Minh troops between Vietnam and Laos, and (2) much more importantly, the French hoped that General Giap would find this large but isolated outpost an irresistible temptation to a conventional battle. Taking this bait, the Viet Minh would send in its best conventional units, which would of course be thoroughly chewed up by superior French competence and firepower. That is, the French decided to fight yet another outpost battle, this time at a place, Dien Bien Phu, that they had previously held. On November 20, 1953, six CEF paratroop battalions landed there and began to fortify the area, under the command of Colonel Christian de Castries. Navarre's attention, however, was distracted by his offensive in Annam, called Operation ATLANTE. The offensive began on January 20, 1954; the ground forces were largely drawn from the Vietnamese National Army, and the Viet Minh were able to blunt their attacks.[178] More importantly, ATLANTE subtracted attention and resources from the undertaking at Dien Bien Phu.

But what led General Giap to accept the French challenge and fight a conventional battle around Dien Bien Phu? First of all, Giap had the numbers and the equipment. As 1954 began, the main elements of the Viet Minh Army consisted of the equivalent of fourteen fully armed divisions.[179] In Giap's calculations, the CEF was caught in a dilemma. First of all, the French had to defend militarily or politically crucial areas, including Laos, and areas in Tonkin inhabited by Catholics and loyal ethnic minorities. But secondly, the CEF had little offensive capability beyond the De Lattre Line because of poor roads, jungle terrain, Viet Minh ambushes, inadequate air support, and the CEF's limited numbers of troops (for offensive operations, as opposed to static security, the CEF could muster at most 50,000 men, while Giap could call upon more than 100,000). In addition, at Dien Bien Phu Giap would be relatively close to his base, while the CEF, far from the Red River Delta, would be isolated from its base.

There was, however, another very important reason why Giap accepted the challenge at Dien Bien Phu: like the French, many in the Viet Minh were also becoming dispirited by the war and the huge casualties it was inflicting upon them. A senior Communist Hungarian diplomat remembered this conversation with General Giap: "The battle of Dien Bien Phu, he told us, was the last desperate bid of the Viet Minh Army. Its forces were on the verge of complete exhaustion. The supply of rice was running out. Apathy had spread among the populace to such an extent that it was difficult to draft new fighters. Years of jungle warfare had sent morale in the fighting units plunging to the depths."[180] And indeed in the battle at Dien Bien Phu itself, Viet Minh morale was sorely buffeted because of poor food, heavy casualties, and scanty medical care.[181]

Thus, if fighting a major and perhaps decisive battle violated one fundamental Viet Minh principle of warfare, it accorded well with another principle: military action for political impact. The Viet Minh decided to break the strategic stalemate by attacking public opinion in metropolitan France. That is the fundamental meaning of the battle of Dien Bien Phu.

The Struggle

The site the French had selected for the fortress at Dien Bien Phu was on the floor of a valley; thus the troops, their positions, and the airstrip would all be quite visible to any Viet Minh forces in the surrounding hills. Equally important, perhaps, materials for building a really sound system of fortification had not been available, and in any event the CEF did not possess the air transport to get them there.

What, then, if the Viet Minh placed heavy artillery on the mountains around the valley and pounded Dien Bien Phu to pieces at leisure? Impossible, was the reply: the Viet Minh did not have sufficient artillery or the means to get it into the jungles on the Laotian border. And even if by some miracle they could bring heavy guns into the area and haul them up into the high hills, how could they possibly keep those guns supplied? Besides, let these putative Viet Minh guns fire once, thus revealing their positions, and French counter-battery fire would destroy them quickly and utterly.

French estimates that Viet Minh forces near Dien Bien Phu would run out of proper ammunition for any significant number of artillery pieces were not unreasonable, but in March 1954 Communist China doubled the amount of aid it sent to Giap's forces.[182] The root cause, however, of what was about to happen was that "nobody believed in the strategic mobility and logistics of the Viet Minh."[183]

But again, what if the siege of Dien Bien Phu should go on and on? Wouldn't the French face shortages of ammunition, food, medicines, everything? No. The siege would not last for very long, because the French would quickly maul the attackers. But, for argument's sake, if in fact the battle did become protracted, the fortress's landing strip would allow the CEF to supply its defenders with their basic needs by air.

Thus the French began inserting, by parachute and aircraft, what eventually became a force of sixteen thousand soldiers. Of these defenders of Dien Bien Phu, 36.3 percent were Vietnamese, 26 percent were Foreign Legionnaires, 18.6 percent were French, 17.5 percent were North African, and 1.6 percent were West African.[184]

On March 13, 1954, the siege of Dien Bien Phu began in earnest—with a massive Communist artillery bombardment. The defenders knew immediately that they were in grave and probably fatal trouble.

The Viet Minh eventually deployed three hundred 105mm cannon against the fortress.[185] The French were utterly astounded—that is the right word—that the Viet Minh had been able to haul heavy pieces through roadless jungles and across trackless mountains and, equally important, could keep these weapons supplied with shells. The Viet Minh positioned their artillery and antiaircraft weapons in mountainside caves, so that they were relatively immune to French air strikes and artillery fire. Shortly after the battle began, the French artillery commander inside Dien Bien Phu, believing that what was about to happen to his comrades was his fault, committed suicide.

What defeated the defenders of Dien Bien Phu was artillery, a four-to-one artillery ratio in favor of the besiegers. In the remarkably bland phrase of General Navarre, the artillery and antiaircraft capability of the Viet Minh at Dien Bien Phu was "the principal surprise of the battle."[186] In the perhaps too clinical explanation of General Ely, the last French commander in Hanoi: "The failure at Dien Bien Phu was due to the fact that this isolated base was attacked by an enemy with artillery and antiaircraft."[187]

The Role of Airpower

Dien Bien Phu turned into a battle of supply. "Both Giap and Navarre grasped the fundamental point that whoever won the logistical battle at Dien Bien Phu would win the tactical battle."[188] Throughout the entire eight-year conflict, most Viet Minh victories were "first and foremost logistical victories."[189] Ho Chi Minh had decreed the conscription of all Vietnamese in 1949, and thus General Giap's main force units were supported by literally hordes of civilians, men and women, acting as coolie laborers, using sheer muscle power for transporting food and munitions gathered, sometimes under compulsion, from local populations along the Viet Minh routes, 40,000 porters for every 10,000 soldiers.[190] These persons suffered casualties from French air attacks as well as malaria and other diseases, but this apparently "caused scant concern to the Viet Minh leaders."[191]

It is almost certainly true that the soldiers defending Dien Bien Phu would have been saved by massive air attacks on the besiegers and equally massive air shipments of supplies, as the U.S. Marines and ARVN troops defending Khe Sanh were saved years later. But the most modern French aircraft were too big and too fast for any airfield in Vietnam, and the older types were too few. In addition, weather conditions over northwestern Vietnam, especially during the rainy season, frequently made flying dangerous or even impossible (this was 1954).

Quite aside from meteorological worries, air force commanders in Hanoi warned General Navarre that the distance between Dien Bien Phu and Hanoi—183 miles one way—would place an additional and serious limitation on the help that their planes, only 70 to 120 of them to begin with, could provide. The CEF had been unable to properly fortify Dien Bien Phu to withstand artillery attack in the first place, because the air force had lacked the means to fly in the tons of material necessary. But Navarre silenced all these objections.[192]

It soon turned out that the difficulties of supplying Dien Bien Phu were much worse than anybody had imagined. In March, Viet Minh saboteurs infiltrated the main French air bases in the Tonkin Delta and disabled close to eighty planes, mainly transports. Quite beyond that, and contrary to all expectations, the Viet Minh were able to deploy good-quality Chinese antiaircraft and eventually claimed to have shot down or badly damaged more than eighty French planes at Dien Bien Phu. The antiaircraft fire over Dien Bien Phu proved to be more murderous than that over Nazi Germany during World War II. Many of the Viet Minh antiaircraft units had Chinese advisers with them.[193] (One chronicler of the battle says that the Viet Minh paid for all this assistance through the export of opium, which grew abundantly over the whole area.)[194] Bernard Fall was convinced that "if any particular group of enemy soldiers should be considered indispensable to victory [at Dien Bien Phu], then it must be the Viet Minh anti-aircraft gunners and their Chinese instructors."[195] General Giap himself gave great credit to Chinese assistance for his victory.[196]

Some analysts, moreover, have argued that reliance on airpower to win ground battles is very dangerous and even that "the basic concept of air interdiction is invalid."[197] Whatever the truth of such a statement, "the idea of French strategic mobility through airpower turned out to be a particularly disastrous delusion."[198]

French air assistance sometimes even worked against the defenders: for example, on April 15 a French pilot flying over Dien Bien Phu accidentally dropped out of his cockpit a packet of photographs of the whole battlefield area, including the surviving French positions, photographs that were soon in the hands of General Giap. And on at least one occasion, French pilots dropped their bombs inside the perimeter of the fortress, causing deaths and injuries and blowing up precious artillery ammunition.[199]

And of course, from the beginning of the siege, Viet Minh artillery rendered the Dien Bien Phu airstrip unusable. It was full of shell holes, and even if a plane survived the landing it could be targeted and destroyed either on the ground or during takeoff. Thus, the only way to get vital supplies to the Dien Bien Phu defenders was by parachute—"the most ineffective delivery method in modern war."[200] The besieged troops needed a minimum of 200 tons of supplies per day; French planes were able to drop 120 tons per day, of which only 100 were recovered by the CEF; the rest fell (literally) into the hands of the enemy.[201] Thousands of artillery shells were mistakenly dropped by French planes into enemy lines. This was truly catastrophic, because as Bernard Fall points out, "in the final days of the battle the Viet-minh would have run out of [their] own 105mm ammunition had it not been for the French misdrops."[202]

The CEF inside Dien Bien Phu ran short of ammunition, food, medicine, clean water, clothing, everything. The wastewater pumps broke down, one by one, so that the rains flooded trenches and dugouts. As for the sick and wounded, the original plan called for them to be evacuated by air. This soon became impossible. As the battle raged on, the increasing numbers of sick and wounded had to be cared for in the fortress's small dispensary, which was soon packed to overflowing. Eventually men with quite serious wounds were lying almost everywhere. Many of these helpless persons, despite the heroic efforts of the few and brutally overworked medical personnel, lay for long periods in their own waste, amid scenes of indescribable misery.[203]

At Dien Bien Phu, the Viet Minh had an infantry advantage of at least four to one, they held the high ground, and they had sufficient ammunition (with French help) for their artillery and antiaircraft weapons. General Giap deployed four main force divisions there, including the famous 308th. The fighting took place according to a predictable scenario: the Communist forces formed a noose around the fortress complex, and one by one they overran its strongpoints until nothing was left to the defenders except an area the size of a football field, and then that too was overrun.

The French command in Hanoi did not try to mount a major relief effort on the ground, since in order to assemble sufficient numbers, it would have had to strip or weaken other and more strategic places. But eventually—too late—Navarre did order ground forces about forty miles south of Dien Bien Phu to try to relieve the fortress, a movement called Operation CONDOR. Their advance was so slow and difficult that it was abandoned in early May, about twenty miles away from what was left of Dien Bien Phu. Since the operation deployed only about six thousand men and had no sir support, it is very difficult to see how it could have saved Dien Bien Phu anyway. Navarre then proposed that the fittest remaining men in the fortress, perhaps three thousand, try to break out in three columns and join friendly forces south of them, leaving their wounded behind, but his staff in Hanoi, and General de Castries in Dien Bien Phu (he was promoted on April 16) were all opposed to such a demoralizing and suicidal effort.[204]

Well before the middle of April, all the world knew that the outcome of the battle was foregone. Nevertheless, throughout the contest hundreds of French and Vietnamese soldiers volunteered to be dropped into the doomed fortress. Navarre dispatched the last reinforcements, all volunteers, many of them making their first parachute jump, on May 2. (However questionable the wisdom of Navarre's throwing more troops into a hopeless battle may have been, the sacrificial bravery of those volunteers remains astonishing.) The last strongpoint surrendered on May 8, 1954, the ninth anniversary of VE Day; General de Castries and about eleven thousand of his soldiers became prisoners.[205] Even as Dien Bien Phu was falling, Cao Bang was under siege by anti–Viet Minh ethnic guerrillas. And on June 3, 1954, General Paul Ely replaced Navarre as commander in chief and high commissioner as well, like de Lattre. (In the view of one authority, General Ely was "a willing tool of the politicians in Paris"—bad news for France's Vietnamese allies.)[206]

The Battle of Dien Bien Phu was typical of the entire French effort in Vietnam: flawed strategy, inadequate means, abundant heroism. In a battle of fifty-six days, 16,000 CEF soldiers fought 100,000 Viet

Minh troops. The defenders represented perhaps 5 percent of the French and allied forces in Indochina, while Giap committed nearly 50 percent of his available combat forces to the siege. The CEF lost 7,200 killed, the Viet Minh 20,000.[207] Thousands of CEF prisoners died in captivity or were "unaccounted for"; most of the latter were Vietnamese.

The outcome of Dien Bien Phu tipped the balance in France against continuing a war whose purpose and value the French had never agreed on. Pierre Mendès-France became premier on the pledge to end the fighting in Vietnam within thirty days or resign. Within a few months French forces evacuated northern Vietnam.[208]

The Americans and Dien Bien Phu

In his book *No More Vietnams*, Richard Nixon states that the first critical mistake of the United States in Vietnam was not intervening with sea and airpower to save Dien Bien Phu.[209] The United States had been giving very substantial financial and materiel support to the French war effort in Vietnam for years (many billions in the dollars of 2011) and had fought a major war of its own against two Communist regimes in Korea. On April 5, the French cabinet had requested American air strikes to save Dien Bien Phu.[210] Why, then, did the Eisenhower administration allow the fall of the fortress, with its predictable effects on French public opinion?

Previously, in March, President Eisenhower (who had cautioned the French against the Dien Bien Phu operation in the first place)[211] had told the National Security Council that he would indeed intervene in Vietnam, provided such action enjoyed the support of a bipartisan majority in Congress and the assistance of allies, especially Great Britain and Australia.[212] Some biographers of Eisenhower maintain that he laid down conditions that he knew would not be met.[213] (Eisenhower had written years before: "I'm convinced that no military victory is possible in that kind of theater.")[214] Prime Minister Churchill made it clear that the British were not interested. Even if they had been, leading Republican senators absolutely opposed any U.S. intervention in Vietnam; after all, the GOP had successfully branded the Democrats as the war party in the 1952 campaign and prided itself on ending the stalemated Korean War. Moreover, at the end of April, a National Intelligence Estimate informed President

Eisenhower and the National Security Council that "the fall of Dien Bien Phu would not in itself substantially alter the relative military capabilities of French Union [CEF and VNA] and Viet Minh forces in Indochina during the next two or three months." It was, however, expected to "accelerate the deterioration already evident in the French Union military and political position there. If this trend were not checked, it could bring about a collapse of the French Union position during the latter half of 1954."[215] But the coup de grace to a potential U.S. intervention was administered by several high-ranking army and naval officers who unequivocally recommended against U.S. involvement.[216]

Casualties

The fighting in Vietnam between 1946 and 1954 cost France ten times the value of all its investments there.[217] The price in blood, just to France and its Vietnamese allies, was also enormous. The French Expeditionary Corps suffered 92,000 killed, missing, and unaccounted-for prisoners of war, of whom 40,000 were Vietnamese (43.4 percent of the total), 21,000 were French, and 12,000 were Legionnaires.[218] Just the 21,000 French soldiers lost in Vietnam would equal, relative to the population of the two nations, more than 140,000 Americans in 2011, almost three times the number of American battle fatalities during the U.S. involvement in Vietnam. In proportion to population, well over twice as many French died in Vietnam as Americans in Korea. Thus, as Thomas C. Thayer justly concludes, "the numbers suggest that the French troops fought hard in Indochina."[219]

The war devastated the French officer corps: 1,300 lieutenants, 4 generals, and 21 sons of generals or marshals were lost (including Lieutenant Bernard de Lattre). By 1953 more French officers were dying in Vietnam than were graduating from the national military academy at St. Cyr. Two thousand women served with the French ground forces, and another 150 with air and naval units; of this total, 150 were killed.[220]

Total casualties in Bao Dai's Vietnamese National Army may have reached 45,000. During 1952, 1,860 soldiers from France were killed or missing, compared to 4,049 Legionnaires and North Africans and 7,730 Vietnamese in the CEF and VNA; Vietnamese made up

57 percent of the total number of allied forces killed and missing for that year. More than 14,000 Vietnamese CEF-VNA prisoners of war remained unaccounted for, equal to 63 percent of all unaccounted-for allied prisoners and 91 percent of all Vietnamese prisoners.[221] Since the Viet Minh considered Vietnamese serving in allied units to be traitors, it is not improbable that all these prisoners were killed during or after the war.

No one knows for sure how many Viet Minh died as a result of combat, because they made great efforts to remove their dead and wounded from any battlefield in order to thwart French intelligence. Estimates range from 250,000 to 400,000.

Finally, the death toll among innocent civilians will never be known, but it may have been close to 2 million.[222]

Reflection

Why Did the French Fight?

Some Americans would probably say the French fought for wealth; the French did not want to give up their economic exploitation of the Vietnamese. Even stated so crudely, this answer is not devoid of truth: some French, in Paris and in Hanoi, were indeed making money out of Vietnam, even during the war. But the sums involved, in the great scheme of things, were paltry. For the French economy as a whole, Indochina was a drain, not a source of wealth. Even in 1913, France's trade with all her colonies made up 11 percent of its total external trade, and that total external trade amounted to only 3 percent of the French GNP. With the shadow of Germany growing ever darker over the European continent, the driving force of French imperialism in Southeast Asia and elsewhere was not a quest for wealth but a concern for prestige. And the kaleidoscopic French cabinets spent billions of dollars on the eight-year conflict, more than the aid they received through the Marshall Plan.[223]

The reality was that for a great many French individuals who had, or thought they had, interests in Vietnam, those interests were not primarily, or even partly, financial.[224] Long before the first French flags waved over Vietnam, that country had been the scene of a great missionary effort sustained by the French Catholic Church; by 1660 Tonkin alone was home to four hundred thousand Catho-

lics, and French Jesuit missionaries developed the script in which
the present-day Vietnamese language is written. From time to time
Catholics in Vietnam, native and European alike, were subjected
to grisly attack, often tolerated or even stimulated by Vietnamese
rulers. Napoleon III's interventions in Vietnam, whatever his true
motives, were warmly supported by the church in France, as well
as by those French animated by jealousy of Great Britain or fear of
Germany, especially after 1871.

Many French people saw the war in Vietnam as a fight to maintain France's status in the world, a status brought into sharp and
humiliating question by the disasters of World War II. (Remember
that the serious fighting with the Viet Minh broke out less than
seven years after the fall of France and hardly two years after the
liberation of Paris.) If France abandoned Indochina, how would it be
able to hold onto French North Africa, where 1 million Europeans
lived, many of them born there? This was the region from which the
return to the motherland of General de Gaulle and his Free French
had originated. As General Ely, the last French commander in chief
in Vietnam, stated: "In the Far East, like it or not, our position as a
great power is at stake."[225]

Thus, although the war eventually came to be seen by many, especially in the United States but also in France, as a conflict between
the West (the French, supported by the Americans) and international
Communism (the Viet Minh, backed by the Soviets and the Chinese),
it did not start out that way. In 1946, it was not anti-Communism
but imperialism—grandeur—that fueled the French war machine.
As Bernard Fall wrote, the conflict began as a war of colonial reconquest.[226] The very French leaders—de Gaulle, Jacques-Philippe
Leclerc, d'Argenlieu, and others—who had struggled to end the
German occupation of France would now struggle to maintain the
French occupation of Vietnam.

Why Did the Viet Minh Fight?

Before 1941, three major obstacles had blocked the Viet Minh's path
to power: rival nationalist parties, the French colonial administration,
and then the Japanese occupation. Later, the French police broke up
the non-Communist nationalists (with help from the Viet Minh), the
Japanese thoroughly and irrevocably humiliated the French, and

then the Allies crushed the Japanese. For the Viet Minh, it was all very convenient.

But in 1946, Ho Chi Minh signed an agreement with France, which recognized his regime as merely a "free state" (not an "independent" one) within the French Union, permitted French forces to remain in Vietnam for ten years, and consigned settlement of the exact status of Cochin China to the future. In June 1948 Bao Dai obtained more than that from the French, and full independence would surely have followed in the foreseeable future, peacefully. But Ho Chi Minh now wanted complete independence under the control of his party; the ineluctable result was years of bloody combat. Ho intended, by uniting the Vietnamese in a bitter anti-French struggle, to solidify the control of the Communist party over them. A war against the French would thus have real payoffs for the Viet Minh. Counting on the Soviets and the Chinese to assist him and on the French public to tire of this distant war, Ho was therefore willing to fight on for whatever length of time and at whatever cost in the blood of his countrymen. Even then, when the fighting stopped in 1954, with so many dead or maimed, so much wealth destroyed and so much time wasted, Ho himself had obtained only half a loaf. Was the Viet Minh victory really worth it to them? Eight years of terrible war—a civil war—left them with only the northern part of the country. And then they faced a South Vietnam increasingly supported by the United States.[227]

Why Didn't the French Win?

The demographic, industrial, and financial disparities between France and the Viet Minh suggested—almost demanded—a French victory. What brought the French to the point where they decided to give up Vietnam after paying such a heavy price for so long to hold onto it?

Was Nationalism the Key?

Opinion in the United States tended to blame the loss of Vietnam, and hence the subsequent U.S. involvement, on French failure to recognize the realities of the times and to grant real autonomy, if not immediate and total independence, to Vietnam. In this American

view, the French did not wish to see that World War II had profoundly destabilized, even mortally wounded, colonialism in Asia.
While the British were leaving India and the Dutch Indonesia, the
French battened all the tighter on Indochina. Hence, argues George
K. Tanham, "to have underestimated the force of nationalist feeling
and to have disregarded all opportunities for genuine compromise
may be called the basic French mistakes in Indochina."[228] This is an
overstatement, but it contains elements of truth. French refusal of
even moderate reforms helped stimulate the Viet Minh movement
in the first place.[229] The French then prolonged the war, adding to
the appeal of the Viet Minh, by their self-imposed military limitations and their stubborn refusal to grant true independence to Bao
Dai, although the independence of Vietnam under somebody was
clearly inevitable.

However, this thesis—"French failure to accept the end of colonialism caused the war"—encounters many difficulties. The Viet
Minh became important when it promised (falsely) to distribute the
land to those who tilled it, in the context of the astonishing Japanese
revelation of French weakness. The August Revolution, as we have
seen, was not the result of a popular election or upheaval and could
not have occurred except for the Japanese invasion, followed by its total failure. If it was Vietnamese nationalism that expelled the French,
why did it not expel the Japanese? Moreover, the French could have
undermined the Viet Minh at almost any stage through real rural
reforms. A nationalist revolution meant little to the peasantry, except
as a path to land redistribution. On the contrary, concludes David
W.P. Elliott, both "anticolonialism and landlordism were the elements
that provided the ingredients of a revolutionary movement."[230]

Setting all that aside for the moment, would it not have been
better, smarter, for the French to simply recognize Ho Chi Minh
as head of an independent Vietnam, in exchange for a continuing
French "presence"? No; to have handed control over to the Viet Minh
in 1945–47 would have meant putting into power a relatively small
minority of the population, hated or feared by many. By 1954, more
than three hundred thousand Vietnamese were serving either in the
CEF or in Bao Dai's national army, and scores of thousands of others
were in the Catholic, Cao Dai, or Hoa Hao militias. When Vietnam

was partitioned—by the French and the Communists—1 million people, the equivalent proportionally of 19 million Americans today, fled Viet Minh–controlled North Vietnam. In the years that followed, hundreds and hundreds of thousands of Vietnamese fought against the Vietcong and their Hanoi patrons, and great numbers then fled, or tried to flee, from a conquered South Vietnam. (One still occasionally hears the remarkable comment that the defeat of South Vietnam "proved" that that state had no popular support. Would anyone offer such an observation about republican Spain, or Imperial Japan—or the Confederate States?)

The Maoist Mirage

One distinguished scholar offered quite a different answer to the question of why the French did not prevail: it was because the Vietnamese Communists' version of Maoist revolutionary war was "a strategy for which there is no known, proven counterstrategy."[231] That is, the Viet Minh were victorious in this eight-year conflict because they carried out the invincible Maoist formula for revolutionary war. According to this view, the withdrawal of the French from Vietnam represented an inescapable confirmation of the universal superiority—even invincibility—of Maoist-type guerrilla insurgents over modern armies, especially nonindigenous ones, a superiority that was supposed to have profound implications for U.S. foreign policy all over the globe.

But this is not a tenable position. War is a two-sided affair (at least). Obviously Ho and his colleagues in the Communist leadership usually played the cards dealt to them with impressive skill and ruthlessness. However, it is clear that Ho's victory resulted in great part from the serious shortcomings of his opponents, and most of all from exceptionally favorable circumstances peculiar to the specific time and place.[232]

What were those circumstances? Any reasonable inventory of the factors explaining why the war ended the way it did would surely include the following: the internal political situation of France; the inadequacy of the French military effort; the growing realization that whatever the military outcome of the conflict, France's Vietnamese sun was setting; and last but by no means least, the effect on the war of Chinese aid to the Viet Minh.

France's Internal Politics

At the very beginning of the struggle, and for years thereafter, France was exhausted, morally as well as physically, by World War II, during which it had suffered two invasions in four years, with a predatory, humiliating, and deeply divisive Nazi occupation in between them.

This post–World War II France was the home of one of Europe's largest Communist parties, which eventually collaborated openly with the Viet Minh and physically sabotaged the French war effort. It was mainly because of this large Communist presence in the electorate and the Parliament that France failed to establish stable government, instead of a burlesque succession of weak coalition cabinets (eight of which lasted five months or less) that could not decide on a consistent Vietnam policy, or on much of anything else.[233]

The exhaustion and division within France, originating during World War II and even before that, manifested themselves in the vastly disproportionate psychological effect produced by Dien Bien Phu. Only a small proportion of French forces in Indochina were engaged in that battle. The CEF and its allies had quite sufficient forces left to carry on the struggle, especially if they retrenched around the two deltas. But as General Giap had apparently calculated, to many in France the war now seemed intolerably burdensome. Besides, almost everybody knew that, despite the rhetoric, the possession of Vietnam was not essential to France's well-being; the French could go home, and they did.

French Military Weakness

According to every empirical index, France was much stronger than the Viet Minh, even—or especially—in 1954. But, while the Viet Minh put forth incredible effort and demanded staggering sacrifices, the French fought a limited war (no draftees to Vietnam, for instance). Although the Viet Minh had good leaders, and many of them were dedicated and quite brave, the main reason why the French could not achieve their aims is that they never took the steps that would have amassed sufficient forces to fight a proper counterinsurgent war. Consequently the French were not decisively stronger than their enemies where the fighting was taking place.

It is therefore quite misleading to say "the Viet Minh defeated the French." No Viet Minh forces seized Paris or Toulon—or even

Hanoi and Saigon. The French certainly possessed the physical and financial capability to carry on the war. A more accurate statement of the outcome of the conflict would be this: With the great bulk of the forces France had committed to Vietnam still intact, the cabinet in office in the summer of 1954 decided to abandon a struggle that had come to appear too long and too expensive.[234]

Even without draftees, the French could have overcome their deficit of manpower at least to some degree if they had possessed sufficient mobility. One of the greatest military advantages of modern societies over undeveloped ones is supposed to be airpower, but the weakness of the French air force meant that they were lacking such mobility; the CEF never had, for example, more than ten helicopters at one time.[235] This airpower deficiency is arguably the most important reason for the loss of Dien Bien Phu. Of course, properly training and equipping the Vietnamese National Army would also have significantly strengthened the French effort.

All these situations could have been put right. French industry could have produced the needed planes and helicopters, just as the politicians could have crafted a different conscription law and the French Army could have built up Bao Dai's forces. Why were these things not done? Two reasons immediately stand forth. First, for all seventeen French cabinets presiding over the war, Europe—not Vietnam, on the other side of the world—was the center of foreign policy interest and concern, as it was then and later for the Americans. The politicians of the Fourth Republic in the end chose Europe over Vietnam, as de Gaulle a few years later chose Europe over Algeria, in both instances abandoning to their predictable fate great segments of the indigenous population who had believed in French promises. (The French were not, alas, the last to betray their Vietnamese allies.)

And here is another reason. On June 5, 1948, France "solemnly" recognized the independence of Bao Dai's State of Vietnam.[236] No matter how much the French tried to avoid the consequences of that act, there was no way to put the genie back into the bottle, and the Americans kept pressing for real concessions to the non-Communist nationalists. It became ever clearer that even if France won the war it would lose Vietnam, to one group or the other. As Walter Lippmann pointed out in the *New York Herald Tribune* of April 4, 1950, in the last analysis France would not fight to defeat Ho Chi Minh just to hand the spoils of victory over to Bao Dai.

But in the immediate term the French clearly had somehow to obtain more fighting men. Thus they made deals with warlords, nationalist parties, Catholic dioceses, and indigenous sects,[237] groups interested not in independence but rather in local autonomy, to keep the Viet Minh out of particular provinces or districts. That is, over extensive areas of Vietnam, the French abdicated the most fundamental responsibility of government, the maintenance of order and the protection of life and property, handing this responsibility over to nonofficial groups. But this suspension of legitimate authority provided a vitalizing environment for the revolutionaries. More, these local partners-of-convenience of the French could flourish only as long as the war went on. Hence their relationship to the Viet Minh was symbiotic: if the Viet Minh should collapse, so would the autonomy of France's local armed allies. In a word, "the French were trapped."[238]

Still, all need not have been lost: General Navarre blamed the outcome of the war on "inadequacy of means": he meant that Paris had not given him what he needed. His position is not without merit. But means are inadequate only in respect to particular ends. General Leclerc had written in April 1946: "The ambitions [the ends] of this country in the age in which we live should correspond to available means, or else we will have catastrophe. *Better to hold half or a third of* [Vietnam] *solidly than the whole of it feebly.*"[239] In a word, let the coat be cut to the available cloth. Given that approach, probably the most appropriate French strategy would have been to hold the Red River Delta and Cochin China, build up the National Vietnamese Army, and wait for a favorable turn of events.[240] But to choose this course would have required the correction of "that fundamental failing which plagued all French commanders in Indochina—a gross underestimation of Giap and the Vietminh."[241]

External Influences

After 1939, with war in Europe and war in Asia, the French never again had a free hand in Indochina. With the end of World War II, the efforts at a restoration of French control in Vietnam confronted the extended power vacuum created by first the Japanese and then the Chinese occupation of Vietnam, followed by the arrival of the Chinese Communists on the northern border. All these events had provided tremendous opportunities to the Viet Minh. In fact, Mao Tse-tung had earlier written that it was impossible to make a successful revolution in a colony. But so shattering was the Japanese impact on French prestige and control in Vietnam that he changed his mind and attributed the undeniable success of the Viet Minh to the Japanese occupation.[242] (Who would be more qualified to judge the unintended effects of a Japanese invasion than Mao Tse-tung?)

Moreover, the commitment of military resources to Southeast Asia weakened France's influence in Europe. France's allies there doubted its ability to win in Vietnam and wanted French troops back home.[243]

Finally, something resembling a consensus seems to exist about the role of China. Noted authorities on the Viet Minh war have agreed, over a long period of time and from different perspectives, that the arrival of Maoist forces on the Tonkin border was the primary and decisive factor in the conflict. The following are examples of a broad agreement. Bernard Fall wrote in 1963: "When Red China occupied all the provinces bordering on Tongking [sic], late in 1949, and thus provided the Viet Minh with a 'sanctuary' where its troops could be trained and its supplies stored and replenished, the war had, for all practical purposes, become hopeless for the French."[244] Twenty-five years later, Philip Davidson concluded: "Without a friendly China located adjacent to North[ern] Vietnam, there would have been little chance for a Viet Minh victory against the French, and later against the Americans and South Vietnamese."[245] And a decade after that, Chen Jian concurred:

China's involvement in the First Indo-China War was deep. Beijing provided large quantities of ammunition and military equipment to the Viet Minh, helped the Viet Minh train military commanders and troops, and Chinese advisers participated in the Vietnamese Communist leadership's decision-making processes. Thus, it is fair to say that China's support had played a decisive role in the shaping of a series of Viet Minh victories during the war, such as those in the border campaign, the northwest campaign and, especially, the Dien Bien Phu campaign.[246]

In order to have a serious chance to bring the war to a successful conclusion, the French would have had to decide on some combination of at least two of the following options: (1) send substantial reinforcements from France; (2) build a well-equipped Vietnamese army; (3) establish a truly independent, anti–Viet Minh government in Vietnam; (4) close the border with China, through diplomatic or military means; (5) carry out reforms to separate the peasantry from the Viet Minh hard core; and (6) retrench into super-enclaves in Cochin China and the Hanoi-Haiphong area.[247] Each of these courses of action was feasible, but the French chose none of them, attempting instead to fight on in the accustomed, unsuccessful way in all areas of Vietnam.

Some Consequences

The decision of the French government to pull out of Vietnam of course opened the path for a growing involvement in the region by the United States, which in the last years of the war had been paying 80 percent of the French war costs. But the Americans made little effort to understand what had happened to the French; indeed, "the French experience in Vietnam was almost totally written off and disregarded."[248] At the same time, the Viet Minh rarely, if ever, became a model for insurgent groups in other small countries, especially ones not close to a Communist border.[249] But apparently some North African soldiers who were taken prisoner at Dien Bien Phu were influenced by Viet Minh propaganda, and within a short time they fought against France for Algerian independence. And—not least—in the eyes of many French army officers, the Paris politicians had cravenly forced them to betray their pledges to their Vietnamese allies and abandon them; herein were sown the seeds for the revolt of the French Army four years later in that same Algerian conflict.

Afterword

General Navarre later wrote that his masters in Paris never gave him clear direction and always begrudged him money and reinforcements, especially conscripts, who could have proved decisive at an earlier stage of the war.[250]

And concerning Dien Bien Phu, General Navarre testified, "We were absolutely convinced of our superiority in defensive positions; this was considered in Indochina as a dogma."[251] That and so many other assumptions made by the French military command in Hanoi turned out to be disastrously wrong. It is a duty to record, however, that during French preparations of their stronghold at Dien Bien Phu, none of the foreigners of high rank, including several Americans, who visited the place before the battle, ever questioned the basic strategy. The key, the root mistake of General Navarre was *"his gross underestimation of the Viet Minh and General Giap."*[252] And he was not alone.

The Battle of Dien Bien Phu showed unmistakably that the old war system—the French controlled the cities and towns and defended outposts with artillery and aircraft, while the Viet Minh dominated much of the countryside—was broken. Henceforth the Viet Minh could and would confront and probably defeat substantial CEF formations in set battles. A general CEF pullback followed Dien Bien Phu, abandoning heavily Catholic areas in the Tonkin Delta, home of many of the volunteers in the elite paratroop battalions. (And, not unexpectedly, many non-Communist Vietnamese nationalists were privately elated by the events of Dien Bien Phu, because they seemed to show that Vietnamese troops were no longer inferior to European ones.)[253]

An astute observer of that battle noted that mixed French-Vietnamese units fought better than purely French or purely Vietnamese ones, a lesson (one of several) lost on the Americans.[254]

At about the same time, according to the *Pentagon Papers*, "the Joint Chiefs of Staff desire[d] to point out that, from the point of view of the United States, with reference to the Far East as a whole, Indochina is devoid of decisive military objectives and the allocation of more than token U.S. armed forces in Indochina would be a serious diversion of limited U.S. capabilities."[255] But under President John F. Kennedy, such views were cast aside.

The "Geneva Agreements:" Among Whom, about What?

Early in 1954, a four-power foreign ministers' meeting in Berlin called for a conference later in the year to discuss Korea and Indochina. As it happened, the conference, which included representatives

from the United Kingdom, France, the USSR, and China, with a
Viet Minh delegation under Chinese "sponsorship," convened on
April 26. Dien Bien Phu fell on May 7, and a month after that, Pierre
Mendès-France became prime minister, promising to end the conflict.
The French military forces and the Viet Minh signed the so-called
Geneva Agreements and declared an armistice to be in effect as of
July 21. Events on the ground in Vietnam determined the position
of the delegates in Geneva. Since almost all the serious fighting had
taken place in Tonkin, the stronghold of the Viet Minh (the reader
may wish to review "Why Cochin China Was Different," above),
the conferees agreed to recognize Communist control of northern
Vietnam. The U.S. government silently acquiesced in the partition
of Vietnam into a Communist north and a non-Communist south as
the best option in a bad situation.

Ho Chi Minh was of course opposed to a partition; he wanted
the conference to hand him the whole country. His Chinese and
Soviet mentors, however, feared that conservatives might displace
the Mendès-France cabinet and, with increased U.S. aid, renew the
fighting (Mendès-France himself was already ordering tropical in-
oculations for two French Army divisions stationed in Germany).[256]
So partition it was to be. Ho then demanded that the partition line
be drawn at the thirteenth parallel—in effect, the boundary between
Cochin China and Annam. The conference, however, eventually
settled on the seventeenth parallel, considerably farther to the north.
In retrospect, it is tempting to say that what became known in the
United States as South Vietnam would have been much better off
with the smaller size the Communists wished it to have. The territory between the thirteenth and seventeenth parallels did contain the
ancient and symbolic city of Hue, as well as the ancestral home of
Vietnam's prime minister Diem; but the area was thinly populated,
far from Saigon, and bordered by Laos, through which the notorious and war-winning Ho Chi Minh Trail soon penetrated. Most of
the South Vietnamese and almost all the Americans who died in the
subsequent twenty-year struggle to preserve the South Vietnamese
state died between those two parallels, and it was in this very area
that the South Vietnamese Army suffered the sudden collapse that
brought the final destruction of South Vietnam.[257]

The Bao Dai government, recognized at the time of the Geneva meetings as the legitimate government of all of Vietnam by France, the United States, Britain, and more than thirty other countries, took the unassailable position that neither France nor any other foreign state had the right to cede any Vietnamese territory to anybody or to make any binding agreement regarding the country's future without its consent. Regarding the treatment of Bao Dai's government by the French, one magisterial history of the war asks, "Who had ever heard of the commander [Ely] of an allied [French] army in time of war authorizing the signing of an armistice agreement—much less one that gave away half an ally's territory to the enemy—without so much as consulting the ally? No one, because it had never been done before."[258]

All that aside, it is absolutely essential to note that only the French military and the Viet Minh—no one else—signed the Geneva agreement to end military hostilities, and nobody at all signed the so-called Final Declaration, which called for "free general elections" to settle the future of Vietnam.[259] The wording in the Final Declaration about these elections was remarkably scanty—less than 150 words in the English text—and hence exceedingly vague with regard to the manner of holding them and even about their purpose. The main Geneva document on the ending of hostilities consisted of six chapters and forty-seven articles; the word "elections" appears in it exactly once. The Final Declaration looked forward to "democratic institutions established as a result of free general elections by secret ballot." What does this mean? Would not "democratic institutions" (undefined in the text) have to be already in place in order to carry out "free general elections"? And above all, would a Communist electoral victory indeed have produced "democratic institutions"? The whole Geneva approach to this issue seems either disingenuous or frivolous (or perhaps just ashamed).

Ngo Dinh Diem, constitutionally appointed by Bao Dai as prime minister of the State of Vietnam, made it clear from the start that in the existing circumstances he was opposed to the idea of elections dealing with the question of unification of the two Vietnamese jurisdictions. He and his supporters on both sides of the Pacific maintained that there could be no free elections in a North Vietnam under a Communist regime. This position was, to say the least, based on much concrete experience. (Quite aside from the history of elections in Soviet bloc countries, recall that in January 1946, in elections run by the Viet Minh, Ho Chi Minh allegedly received 169,000 votes in Hanoi, a city whose official population was 119,000.) The Hanoi leaders would almost certainly announce that 98 percent of the northern vote had been cast in favor of whatever position they had endorsed. Since North Vietnam had a greater population than the South, then even if the majority of southern voters should vote against unification under the Viet Minh—a likely outcome, given the combined strength of the Cao Dai, the Hoa Hao, the Catholics, the northern refugees, the CEF and VNA members and veterans, the non-Communist nationalists, the Saigon bourgeoisie, and the substantial Chinese and other ethnic minorities—the South Vietnamese would nonetheless all be handed over to the control of the northern party-state.

In Diem's view, as a result of their military errors the French had cravenly given half of his country to Ho Chi Minh's armed followers through illegal partition and were ready to hand over the other half through phony elections. When the Eisenhower administration became convinced that Diem was able to hold onto power and that he would not cooperate in any rigged election, it supported him in his stance, with bipartisan backing: for example, the junior senator from Massachusetts, John F. Kennedy, declared, "Neither the United States nor Free [South] Vietnam is ever going to be a party to an election obviously stacked and subverted in advance."[260]

During the 1960s the Communist regime in Hanoi propagated with much success in the United States the view that the American involvement in the Vietnam conflict was rooted in Diem's refusal to allow the people of South Vietnam to participate in an honest election as provided by the "agreements" at Geneva. This was a great propaganda victory for the Communist side. But there are good reasons to suspect that informed opinion in neither Hanoi nor Moscow nor Peking nor anyplace else ever expected any elections to take place. To have believed that Diem would take all the pains and risks that he did to set up a government in Saigon, only to hand everything over to the Communists in two years, would have been naive, and nobody ever accused Ho Chi Minh and his entourage of being that. Besides, close to a million northerners fled from Communist control into the welcoming arms of the Diem government, and surely many more would have fled south if the Hanoi regime had not placed numerous obstacles in their path. All this would be inexplicable and even absurd without a deep-seated belief on the part of the refugees, and their supporters and enemies, that their escape would be long-lasting. The authors of the *Pentagon Papers* maintain that setting up two jurisdictions in Vietnam made reunification elections exceedingly improbable. Numerous academic authorities concurred in that view.[261] Most especially, Robert F. Randle, in his impressive study of the Geneva agreements, writes that in light of "the very profound ambiguities in the relevant Geneva documents" and the "ambiguities and incompleteness of the final declaration, it does no justice to the complexities of the Vietnamese situation, either in fact or in legal theory, to speak glibly of 'violations' of the 'Geneva Accords.'"[262]

In any case, when in the summer of 1956 the last possible day to schedule any elections came and went, the Communist world observed this nonevent almost without comment and certainly without action. Indeed, a few months after the election deadline had passed, the Soviet Union proposed that the United Nations admit both North and South Vietnam to membership. As for the French, they continued (according to a logic that escapes the present author) to recognize the Diem government as the only constitutional authority for all Vietnam, not formally opening diplomatic relations with the Hanoi regime until 1973. And the member states of the Colombo Plan—at that time including Australia, Canada, Ceylon, India, New Zealand, and Pakistan—endorsed the legitimacy of the government of the southern Vietnamese state when they chose to hold their 1957 conference in Saigon.

3

Cuba
The House of Cards

When princes think more of luxury than of war, they lose their states.
—Machiavelli

During the Cold War, it was customary in some circles to refer to the seizure of power by Fidel Castro and his followers as the first Communist revolution in the Western Hemisphere. This description was completely misleading. Castro did indeed impose a Communist regime on the Cubans, but he had not led a Communist revolution. Nevertheless, the flight of the dictator Fulgencio Batista out of Havana in the waning hours of the year 1958 signaled not only the complete collapse of his dictatorship but the beginning of a true transformation of the politics of the Western Hemisphere. This transformation had three main aspects. First, contrary to the expectations of many Cubans, including those who had opposed Batista, the triumphant rebels thoroughly dismantled Cuban society, drove out most of the middle class, and created a social upheaval rare in this part of the globe and in some other parts. Second, Cuba soon became that previously most unthinkable entity, a Soviet outpost in the very center of what Americans had long imagined to be their special sphere of influence, a situation that preoccupied Washington administrations (and obsessed one of them) for decades and produced the major American-Soviet confrontation known as the Cuban Missile Crisis. Third, quite a few of those who desired to spread revolution throughout Latin America believed they saw in this Cuban experience a model they could easily imitate. Many

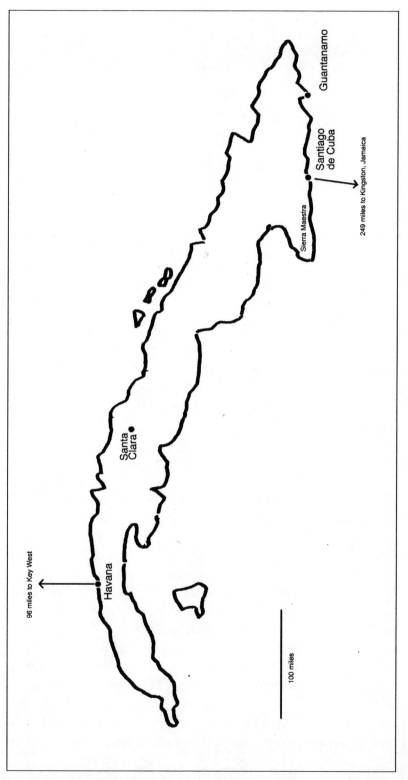

Cuba

years elapsed, much blood was shed, and much egregious nonsense was written before the total absence of success for Cuban-inspired revolts, notably the fatal fiasco of Ernesto Guevara in Bolivia, began to reduce the Cuban Revolution and its leaders to realistic proportions. Another factor in that reevaluation was certain undeniable shortcomings of the Castro regime: for example, Batista's Cuba was a sugar island dominated by a foreign power; after several decades of Castro's totalitarian rule, Cuba was still that.

Before Castro

Bathed by the waves of the Atlantic and the Caribbean, 135 miles from the southern tip of Florida, and forty-four thousand square miles in area (the size of Pennsylvania or Bulgaria), Cuba is the largest and most westerly of the Great Antilles island group. In the age of sail, Cuba was called the Pearl of the Antilles and heavily laden Spanish treasure fleets embarked for Europe from Havana's excellent harbor.

In the last days before the Castro takeover, Cuba had a population of about 6 million, of whom nearly one-quarter lived in greater Havana. The country arguably contained two societies: "one urban, educated, and well-off, the other rural, illiterate and poor."[1] Out of this condition arose one of the most fundamental of the many myths still surrounding and obscuring the reality of the Castro Revolution, the myth that cost Guevara his unhappy life: the myth of a mass rebellion of poor peasants rising in their wrath against intolerable poverty. Quite on the contrary, "the Cuban experience belies the thesis that poverty alone is sufficient to cause revolutionary upheavals."[2] True enough, Cuba's sugar monoculture, the foundation of the island's economic and social life, meant that one out of four employable workers had no job for much of the year. But sugar gave the country one of highest standards of living in the Western hemisphere. Castro himself eventually embraced sugar as the basis of his ongoing revolution, and today, after more than a half century of Castro's rule, Cuba is the world's largest sugar exporter. In any event, it was not from the peasantry but from the urban middle classes that the thrust and leadership of the revolution derived, that is, from that sector of Cuban society that was, by Latin American standards, well advanced economically. In 1958 Cuba was fifth among all Latin American nations in manufacturing, fourth in per capita income, and third in number of physicians; its people were 60 percent urbanized and

75 percent literate. Unions organized a higher percentage of the labor force in Cuba than in the United States; the average wage, allowing for purchasing-power differences, was higher in Cuba than in Belgium or Denmark. Havana had more Cadillacs per capita than any city in the United States, more television sets per capita than any country south of the Rio Grande. But Cuba had reached that most volatile condition for any society: its expectations had outrun its achievements. "The Castro revolution was born not so much out of grinding poverty, racial hatred, economic underdevelopment, or United States imperialism," explains Howard Wiarda, although these factors were certainly present to some degree. More responsible for the revolution was "the fact that the development of a more modern Cuba was not proceeding fast enough to satisfy rising expectations. . . . Revolution came to Cuba not because it was a poverty-ridden, traditional society but because it was a transitional nation which had 'taken off.'"[3]

It was also, for complex reasons, a society that nobody much wanted to defend.

Cuba was the last of the Spanish colonies in the Western Hemisphere to attain its independence (1902). In the nineteenth century, there had been several bloody efforts to end Spanish rule on the island, as well as major slave revolts and race wars (until the later nineteenth century, a majority of Cubans were of African heritage). The Spanish administration, especially in its last years, tended to rely more and more on a system of repression, which was as ineffective as it was provocative. After independence, repression and revolt continued to characterize Cuban politics, with the political arena often resembling a blood-soaked battleground. In perhaps no other Latin American country except Mexico did violence play so prominent a role in political and social life.

Other deeply rooted factors contributed to Cuban instability. Colonial Cuba was almost entirely given over to the cultivation of sugar, and after independence sugar plantation owners were often foreigners and almost always absentee owners. The Roman Catholic Church on the island was served by a clergy totally inadequate in quantity and often in quality; in the days of the Spanish empire, Cuba had been used as a dumping ground for troublesome priests from all over Latin America. Whole districts lacked churches or even temporary chapels. Again, in contrast to other Spanish-speaking republics, Cuba had no heroic traditions embodied in the army; Cuban independence had not been wrested from Spain but received from the United States, and the Cuban national army was created *after* independence, with U.S. assistance. Whatever our evaluation of the historical Latin American ruling trinity—the church, the army, and the landed aristocracy—one can hardly deny that these institutions gave structure, stability, and style to Latin American society, for good and for ill. But in Cuba, these socially and politically defining elements existed in only an attenuated or corrupted form.

Moreover, while the country contained a substantial number of professionals and businessmen, no independent, self-conscious, and politically organized middle class existed as such. "In reality," Ramon Eduardo Ruiz points out, "the infant [post-1898] republic never developed institutions of its own. The laws, the courts, and the government rested on a colonial experience that left the Cubans to rule themselves, and on foreign models ill-suited to domestic conditions. The institutions were victimized by public apathy, corruption, and self-interest."[4]

In addition, with its large African population, the descendants of slaves (27 percent of the population according to the 1953 census, a figure almost certainly lower than the actual percentage), Cuban society was overshadowed by severe racial tensions. Most white Cubans did not support independence until they became a majority of the island's population in the middle of the nineteenth century. A major slave revolt flamed as late as 1879, and a bloody race war raged in Oriente Province as recently as 1912.[5]

In short, Cuba was an artificial and invertebrate society and hence profoundly vulnerable to sudden and radical upheaval.

The Machado Era

Businessman Gerardo Machado won the presidential election of 1924. His program for economic vitalization of Cuba, including construction of a seven-hundred-mile central highway, was at first widely popular. But in 1928 Machado engineered his own reelection, this time for an unprecedented six-year term. Anti-Machado outbreaks in some rural areas were easily suppressed by the army. But violent opposition continued. Elements of the middle class formed the secret society called the ABC (one of its members was a certain Sergeant

Fulgencio Batista). Reacting to terrorism and assassination against the government and the security forces, the Machado regime became ever more repressive. By 1933 it had become painfully obvious that Machado could no longer maintain order. President Roosevelt accordingly sent Ambassador Sumner Welles to Cuba to arrange Machado's peaceful exit. Failing in this, Welles then made it clear that the United States wanted Machado out of power. A general strike broke out in August 1933, Welles threatened to withdraw U.S. recognition of the Cuban government, and the army informed President Machado that he must resign. Thus, in 1933, the United States intervened against a dictatorial regime unable to protect life and property, and it would do so again twenty-five years later.[6]

In this context of upheaval occurred the famous sergeants' mutiny (an episode of the Septembrista revolt). Army officers wanted to repeal the law whereby sergeants and others could become officers. There was also talk of reducing both the size of the armed forces and the pay of sergeants. Hence, in the beginning the sergeants' revolt concerned internal army issues and not national politics. But politicians and student groups soon joined the sergeants. In this chaotic situation, a self-proclaimed government known as the Pentarquía appointed Sergeant Batista, "the outstanding revolutionary of 1933," chief of staff of the army with the rank of colonel, in charge of selecting new officers.[7] Thus a major consequence of the September 1933 revolt was that Batista accelerated promotions for noncommissioned officers, including large numbers of hitherto-excluded Afro-Cubans, and this restructuring remained a source of Batista's popularity for years. At the same time, creating so many new officers drawn from the disadvantaged segments of Cuban society shattered the traditional ties between the army officer corps and the social elites of Cuba. Henceforth, the army was its "own" class.

Who Was Fulgencio Batista?

In the second half of the twentieth century, writing about Fidel Castro became something of an industry in the United States, but until Frank Argote-Freyre's volume appeared in 2006, no scholarly biography of Batista existed. Almost all of the previous writing about Batista, in Cuba and the United States, tends to demonize or to trivialize him, presumably all the better to display the refulgence or mitigate the excesses of his successor. Consequently, notes Argote-Freyre, "much has been written about Cuban decadence and dishonesty, particularly during the Batista dictatorship of the 1950s, but little effort has been made to put that corruption into context. Similar patterns of fraud can be found throughout Latin America, so there is a great need for comparative studies to put the Cuban case in its proper context."[8]

Batista was born in 1901, in Oriente Province, the extreme eastern end of the island. When he was a child, his family inhabited a two-room house with no indoor plumbing and no access to safe drinking water. Fulgencio left school at age eight to join his father as a sugarcane cutter. Years later, he augmented his scanty education by attending a Quaker-run school at night. In the view of some, Batista as an adult was gregarious by nature, a "charming, personable and simpatico" individual who "possessed keen intuition." But he was also "dark, uncomely, and short of stature" and clearly of part-African heritage. Consequently, even after he became president of the republic, Batista was the object of several notable snubs in restaurants and other public places by those Cubans who supposed themselves to be his social superiors.[9]

Swept into prominence by the events of September 1933, Sergeant (now Colonel) Batista helped to craft the broad coalition that elected Havana mayor Miguel Mariano Gómez president in 1936 (the first such election in over eleven years). As head of the army, Batista was in effect copresident with Gómez. According to his biographer, Batista "was never more popular than during the period between 1936 and 1940." The showpiece of Batista's reform agenda was "the rural education program, which was originally envisioned as a campaign against illiteracy. It evolved, however, into a comprehensive educational and health program that reached into virtually every abandoned corner of rural Cuba."[10] Batista employed soldiers to open and staff schools and provide medical care in rural areas, the first time in history most of the rural poor had had access to such benefits. In recognition of his progressive credentials, in 1938 Mexican president Lázaro Cárdenas presented Batista with a national decoration and a thoroughbred horse. Batista also dined with Cárdenas and addressed the Mexican Congress. In further testimony to his leftist sympathies, Batista brought about the legalization of the Cuban Communist party in 1938. Widely seen as a progressive, a populist, a friend of the downtrodden blacks, with many contacts in the army, in 1940 the thirty-nine-year-old Batista ran for president with broad support, including many ex-Machadistas and the Cuban Communist Party. He defeated the veteran liberal politician Ramón Grau San Martín by 800,000 votes to 575,000.[11]

Batista exercised great influence over the apparatus of the state, a fact that might have cast doubt on the validity of the outcome of the voting. Nevertheless, agreement is widespread that the election of 1940 was "reasonably fair by Cuban standards" and "was certainly among the most honest in the nearly four decades of the republic's history," while "impartial observers said there was little evidence of fraud."[12] It is especially notable, in light of subsequent events, that in the election of 1940 Batista received the fervent support of the Cuban Communists. Moreover, he displayed throughout his administration a patent benevolence toward that party, allowing it many privileges, including unlimited authority over the vital Havana dockyards.[13] He also accorded diplomatic recognition to the Soviet Union and appointed Communists to his presidential cabinet.

The Failure of Democratic Government

Being constitutionally unable to succeed himself, in the presidential contest of 1944 Batista supported Carlos Saladrigas against Grau San Martín, the leader of the Autentico Party, who had been his principal opponent in 1940. All Cuba was amazed at the official announcement that Grau won a sweeping victory; it was "the first time in Cuban history that a government-supported candidate had been defeated." The presidential election of 1944 was "probably the cleanest in Cuban history." In any event, "Batista [won] widespread praise for his conduct in holding fair elections."[14] Four years later, outgoing President Grau supported the candidacy of Carlos Prío Socarras, who won with 35.7 percent of the registered vote.

At last, after two generations of turmoil, dictatorship, and incipient civil war, the Cuban republic seemed in the 1940s to be entering a new era of maturity and stability. The administrations of presidents Grau San Martín (1944–48) and Carlos Prío Socarras (1948–52) were the most open and democratic in the island's history. But they were also viewed by middle-class Cubans as among the most brazenly larcenous in the country's experience. One authority has branded the Grau administration as "the most incompetent and corrupt in Cuban history." When President Grau's foreign minister resigned, he used almost identical words, calling the administration "the most corrupt in the history of the republic." Whether those superlatives are completely deserved or not, the Autentico administrations "displayed an almost legendary capacity to steal public funds." Indeed, one noted authority writes that "an estimated 80 per cent of the 1950 budget was used to pay the salaries of public officials."[15]

The corruption might have been bearable, but accompanying it was an unprecedented level of organized partisan violence. The notorious *pistoleros*, mainly Grau's hired gunmen, fought each other and the police on the streets of Havana. President Prío subsidized them from public funds. As a result, "violence and terror became the extensions of party politics and the hallmark of Autentico rule."[16]

Autentico leadership between 1944 and 1952 discredited civilian administration. Embezzlement, fraud, and the rapacity of public officials permeated virtually every branch of national, provincial, and municipal government. The word *gangsterismo* entered the Cuban lexicon to describe the tenor of the national political order, a climate characterized by kidnappings, assassinations, violence on university campuses, and running gun battles in Havana streets.[17] Political instability and personal insecurity overshadowed the island.

Young army officers disgusted with Prío's graft and gangsterism approached Batista and suggested that he lead a coup d'état.[18] Rumors of an Autentico plot to prevent the election of 1952 and thus forestall an opposition victory (not a victory of Batista, although he was a candidate) persuaded him to lead the coup, which took place on March 10, 1952. An army junta declared itself the interim government and appointed Batista chief of state and head of the armed forces. So unpopular were the Autenticos, so disillusioned was popular opinion, that the army's seizure of power encountered no visible resistance from any quarter. After the Batista coup, a young law-school graduate named Fidel Castro, who was a candidate for Congress in the aborted 1952 election and had advocated armed rebellion against the Autenticos, publicly referred to the Prío regime as "a government of murderers and thieves."[19] As Howard Wiarda observes, it is "indicative of the failure of liberal, pluralist democracy in Cuba that at least initially the bulk of the population welcomed Batista back [to the presidency] with a sense of general relief."[20] It would be well to keep that point in mind.

In November 1954, Batista was elected president without serious opposition, after former president Grau withdrew—twice—from the contest. But not long after his return to power in 1952, Batista began to gather more and more control into his own hands, while allowing the already corrupted state to devolve into a sort of full-time extortion racket. These trends stirred up opposition and criticism, which Batista met with a harshness previously uncharacteristic of him, provoking more opposition and requiring more repression, in a vicious circle. Within a few years of Batista's initially popular (or at least not un-popular) coup, many Cubans were longing for a new leader. Among those who were preparing to assume this role was Fidel Castro.

The Early Days of the Castro Rebellion

Fidel Alejandro Castro Ruz was born in 1926 in Oriente Province, which was Batista's birthplace as well.[21] But the childhoods of the two men could hardly have contrasted more. Castro was born on his father's estate, a plantation that employed hundreds of sugar workers. Educated in Jesuit schools, young Castro received a law degree in 1950 from the University of Havana. Like almost all well-to-do Cubans, he was intensely interested in politics from a very early age. He was known at the university as a critic of Batista. Indeed, so passionate was the youthful Fidel about politics that on July 26, 1953, quite a while be-fore the Batista "tyranny" really got started, he and some companions staged an armed attack on the Moncada Barracks in Santiago, Oriente Province.[22] Government forces crushed this amateurish effort in a few hours, and Castro went to prison. But in May 1955 a broad amnesty proclamation by President Batista set him at liberty.

Shortly after his release, Castro arrived in Mexico, where he was joined by some of his friends and other Cuban revolutionaries. The little band studied political philosophy, along with the rudiments of irregular warfare, under Colonel Alberto Bayo, a guerrilla leader in the Spanish Civil War.[23] They soon attracted the attention of the Mexican government and found it prudent to return home. Thus, on December 2, 1956, Castro landed in Cuba aboard the *Granma*, accompanied by about eighty armed followers. They chose Oriente

Province as the site of their invasion, in conscious imitation of the 1895 arrival in that province of the revered Cuban patriot José Martí. This landing was so poorly planned and executed that security forces rounded up almost the entire *Granma* complement; fewer than twenty managed to escape with Castro into the mountains of the Sierra Maestra in the extreme southeastern section of the island.

In those days, Castro had not proclaimed, or even hinted, that he was a Communist; not until much later did he decide that "a select core of intellectually superior and proven revolutionaries has to lead the masses."[24] The Cuban Communist Party, moreover, did not believe in Castro or his methods; in its view, what Cuba needed was not another revolution but free elections. Hence the party did not commit itself to helping the rebels until the summer of 1958, after it became clear that Batista was going to lose. No, Castro did not proclaim a Communist revolution: on the contrary, the aims he announced in the Sierra were the overthrow of Batista and the restoration of free and democratic elections.

Castro first came to the attention of the U.S. public through a series of articles by Herbert Matthews in the *New York Times*. When read today, these stories seem incredibly, almost willfully, naive. After visiting Castro in the Sierra, Matthews wrote that Castro was "an idealistic reformer intent on restoring the democratic Cuban constitution of 1940";[25] moreover, explained Matthews, "in the end, General Batista cannot possibly hope to suppress the Castro revolt."[26] In his remote mountain fastness, without power and without responsibility, the youthful Castro quickly became the symbol of resistance to tyranny, the embodiment of all virtues, and the repository of all hopes. In contrast to this, the aging and prosaically larcenous Batista made a poor show indeed. Favorable press articles helped to bring Castro much-needed money and arms from American sympathizers. U.S. ambassador to Cuba Arthur Gardner, in contrast, told the State Department that Matthews had overstated Batista's weaknesses and Castro's strength.[27]

In the initial stages of the rebellion, Castro and his men would attack small patrols and isolated army outposts, withdrawing immediately to prepared positions from which they could ambush their pursuers. Besides the "propaganda of the deed," the main purpose of these early raids was to procure weapons. Eventually businessmen began making protection payments to Castro, so money for arms was not lacking. While it is clear that weapons reached Castro from outside Cuba, how many they were and who sent them has been a disputed question. One author estimated the proportion of these outside weapons to be as low as 18 percent of the insurgents' total. But U.S. ambassador Earl Smith later wrote that "the revolutionaries were continuing to receive shipments of arms from the United States, Venezuela, Mexico and other nations." Speedboats carried weapons from Miami to the Bahamas and thence to Pinar del Rio Province, west of Havana. Herbert Matthews told the State Department that Castro was receiving weapons from Mexico. Former president Prío sent planeloads of arms, money, and men from airports in Central America; so did Costa Rican president Jose Figueres. Tad Szulc, a *New York Times* correspondent, later wrote that President Wolfgang Larrazabal of Venezuela sent Castro arms and ammunition; Szulc even claimed that the CIA provided Castro with thousands of dollars and also flew arms to him.[28]

Batista's Army

According to the *Statesman's Yearbook* for 1958, the army that defended the Batista regime was quite small: 946 officers and 14,000 enlisted men, one-quarter of 1 percent of the total Cuban population. Nevertheless, such a force should have been more than adequate to deal with Castro's challenge. But predictably, inevitably, this army revealed grave and diverse handicaps. To begin with, its artillery was like that which had defended Verdun in 1916; many of its rifles were 1903 models. A more difficult problem than that of armaments, which would have been relatively easy to resolve, was the grave deficiencies in its personnel. Batista's army was no fighting force: Hugh Thomas explains that "the Cuban army, after all, had no experience, and therefore no traditions of combat; the wars of independence had been fought by amateurs before the army was founded. No regiments had battle-honours, none had captured flags to flaunt in regimental chapels."[29] In a word, "the Cuban military was not accustomed to real war."[30]

Most crucially, the officer corps was in serious disarray. Partisan considerations had determined appointments and commands in the Cuban Army at least since the Liberal Party victory of 1908; thus the Cuban Army "had very early acquired the character of an armed adjunct of the incumbent political party."[31] When Batista came back into power, he began revamping the entire armed forces hierarchy. In Louis A. Perez's words, "political credentials and nepotism governed promotions and commands in the early 1950s, Batista virtually dismantling the professional officer corps." All this "produced widespread demoralization among younger commanders who were proud of their academy training and took umbrage at appointments that made a mockery of professional standards and placed the old sergeants [of 1933] in positions of command."[32] The return of Septembristas (men of the 1933 mutiny) offended the younger academy-trained officers, who deeply disapproved of the practice of appointing commanders for political loyalty. Nevertheless, "in the space of twenty-four months the Batista government had counteracted twelve years of professional development [in the army]."[33]

Even worse than their lack of professionalism, as Hugh Thomas writes, under the Batista regime "officers regarded commands merely as means of enrichment by the use of intimidation. The army was rotten and became more so as time went on." In a word, according to Thomas, Batista's army was led by "a demoralized gaggle of corrupt, cruel, and lazy officers without combat experience."[34] Predictably, while many officers used their army commands to obtain wealth, the ordinary soldier was ill-paid.[35] It had been by understanding and manipulating the nature of the army that Batista had come to power, but it turned out that even Batista did not understand his army well enough.

Because of the poor condition of the national army and the small size of Castro's forces, which could disperse and hide easily, the regime did not mount any serious efforts in the Sierra that sheltered the rebels for a long time; Batista evidently hoped they would go away or give up. Thus, Castro was given invaluable time in which to build up a good base area. Eventually, Batista realized he had a serious challenge on his hands and ordered the Sierra to be cordoned off. But the mountains ran 100 miles east-to-west and from 15 to 25 miles north-to-south. The area contained no major paved road, and the dirt roads became sodden in the rain. Thus the Sierra, the most formidable mountain range on the island, was excellent guerrilla territory; it had in fact been the locus of several historic guerrilla conflicts. But very few in the Cuban Army had ever had any anti-guerrilla training. The five thousand troops assigned to cordon the more than two-thousand-square-mile area (one soldier for every eighty-eight yards of perimeter) therefore faced an impossible task, quite aside from their previously mentioned debilities.[36]

The Antiguerrilla Effort

Castro's forces continued to attack only small and isolated government posts; in response, the Batista troops fell back to larger and more consolidated posts and fortifications, abandoning the countryside and undermining their own morale. When the army tried to make thrusts against the rebels, the rapacity and inefficiency of the troops alienated increasing numbers of initially neutral civilians. Batista and his commanders never grasped that guerrilla war is at least as much a political as a military phenomenon and that therefore counterguerrilla war must be political as well. When the army preys upon the civilians among whom it operates, treating them like enemies, the civilians become just that. Soldiers of the Soviet Army in Afghanistan who were fighting against an alien, primitive people ignored by the outside world, by the United Nations, by the "peace movement," even by most of their Third World fellow Muslims, and who were under orders to win the struggle at any cost, even if it meant turning the country into a depopulated desert—those soldiers may have believed (erroneously) that they were free to forget the political dimensions of counterguerrilla warfare. But Batista, waging a campaign in his own country, less than 150 miles from Florida and under the hostile eyes of the *New York Times*, committed a costly error (if only by omission) in allowing his soldiers to behave badly, even if they did so on a comparatively restricted scale.

Thus the Castro rebellion took root and grew. In September 1957, some young naval officers engaged in a brief but violent pro-Castro rising at the Cienfuegos base, an event that should have alarmed and galvanized the regime but did not. Then on February 16, 1958, Castro forces destroyed the small garrison at Pino del Agua. Notes Hugh Thomas, "after this date it began to be evident to all the people of the hills that Castro and his men were there to stay and that therefore they had nothing to gain in the long run from working with Batista's army."[37] Displaying increasing confidence and boldness, Castro decreed from the Sierra that after April 1, 1958, Cubans should cease to pay their provincial and municipal taxes, because they would only have to be paid again as soon as the revolution triumphed. Anyone serving in the executive branch of the government after April 5 would be guilty of "treason"; anyone who joined the armed forces after that date would be considered a "criminal." Judges must resign their posts if they wished to be able to continue practicing law after the revolution, and so on.[38]

The Cuban Army had mastered the techniques necessary to suppress violence in urban areas (metropolitan Havana contained a quarter of the country's population); but it had never developed any capacity to wage war against rural guerrillas. For years, U.S. advisers and equipment had primed the Cuban Army to act as an element in the defense of the Western Hemisphere in the Cold War. Testifying before a congressional committee, former U.S. ambassador Arthur Gardner said that "fighting in the mountains was not what the Cuban troops were ever taught." U.S. ambassador Smith explained what he saw as the consequence: "It appears that the Cuban Government has been unable to liquidate the Sierra Maestra rebellion, that there is little possibility that it can do so in the near future, and that the operation will continue to plague Cuban armed forces, with possibly serious effects on their morale."[39]

The Rebellion Spreads

The guerrillas of Oriente Province were not the only violent anti-Batista element. In Havana and other cities, activists threw or planted bombs in nightclubs, restaurants, theaters, parks, and buses. Assassinations of army officers, police chiefs, and even common patrolmen became usual occurrences. On March 13, 1957, a largely student group attacked the presidential palace, seeking to kill Batista. Some of the would-be assassins actually made it to the second floor of the palace, but they failed to kill the president, who was on the third floor. From the Sierra, Castro condemned the attack.[40]

In the following summer, an attempted anti-Batista general strike in Havana quickly collapsed. The U.S. Embassy in Havana informed the State Department that the strike failed because of the "general disorganization among opposition groups."[41] A more serious general strike began on April 9, 1958. But that effort also failed, in large part because the student activists of the anti-Batista Directorio revolucionario in Havana did not support the strike. Neither did the Communist Party or the Havana labor unions (Batista kept the loyalty of the leaders of the Cuban Confederation of Labor—the CTC—until quite near the end). Popular interest in the strike was minimal.[42] According to Hugh Thomas, "the failure of the strike reduced Castro's prestige considerably."[43] It also put an end to any serious attempt to use the cities as a base from which to overthrow Batista; the so-called urban underground had shown itself unable either to murder Batista or to organize a serious strike in the capital.

The failure of the 1958 general strike in Havana made it inevitable that the regime would launch a military offensive against the guerrillas in Oriente. The original plan for the offensive called for deploying twenty-four army battalions, but Batista reduced the number to fourteen because he could not spare so many soldiers from security duties throughout the island. He issued a call for volunteers, and many responded to that call, including even peasants from Oriente Province, the alleged epicenter of mass Castro popularity. The fact was that in the summer of 1958 support for Batista among the black population and sugarcane cutters remained far from negligible, largely owing to the president's persisting image as a man of power who was concerned about the poor. But a portentous consequence of the influx of volunteers to the army was that of the 12,000 troops involved in the offensive against the guerrillas, many were raw recruits. (Later, Castro claimed that at the time of the offensive he commanded a mere 180 men.)[44]

The rebels were burning sugar fields and mills all over Cuba, and Batista had to assign large numbers of soldiers to protect the sugar harvest. Consequently, the offensive had to take place between June and December, the rainy season. Motorized detachments became bogged down, weather hampered communications between units and between them and the capital, and the rain and mud caused the curtailment of patrols. Batista's officers, without combat experience or even simple esprit de corps, also lacked accurate information on the numbers and location of the rebels; one consequence was that in June the Eleventh Battalion was badly cut up by a much smaller force of Fidelistas. At the same time, Castro possessed the Cuban Army code. He could therefore send false information to the Batista air force, which then dropped napalm more often on Batista's men than on Castro's. Nor did the government have any helicopter gun ships, vehicles that might have turned the tide in the mountain war.

The principal army generals did not go to Oriente but remained in Havana; perhaps worst of all, command of the troops in Oriente Province was divided among several officers.

Nevertheless, the offensive was having an effect on Castro's forces. Hence, in June and July 1958, at the height of the army's campaign, the rebels kidnapped scores of Americans and Canadians working on the island in order to compel Batista's air force to stop bombing rebel sites. The cessation of bombing attacks gave great relief to Castro's units, and the kidnappings also seemed to underline the regime's inability to maintain order.

Alarming signs of discontent were surfacing within the army itself. The discovery of alleged plotting by elements of the officer corps, in cooperation with armed Autenticos, led Batista to carry out sweeping purges of some of the most qualified officers, just when the Castro challenge was becoming serious. Fear of further conspiracies caused Batista to keep his most trusted officers and best-trained troops in Havana, not in the Sierra. Younger officers, not sure they should be fighting to protect an increasingly unpopular regime anyway, became highly susceptible to Castro's Radio Rebelde propaganda promising the restoration of civil liberties and free elections.

Simultaneously, the offensive began to fail badly. Thousands of young draftees, trained in thirty days instead of the normal six months, were sent into the mountains against hardened guerrillas. The almost instantaneous collapse of such poorly prepared units further weakened the army's resolve to fight. Retreating troops left behind a great deal of valuable equipment and ammunition for the rebels. Through bribery, an entire armored train was betrayed to insurgent forces under Guevara. Batista noted that "other units had been needlessly surrendered without combat through the strange conduct of their chiefs, who let themselves be cut off so easily."[45] One result of these conditions was that possibly 85 percent of the weapons now possessed by the rebels had originally belonged to the regular army. Batista later complained bitterly, "How strange it was that military units were being continually surrendered without combat to an enemy who, in number and military capacity, could not possibly possess the strength necessary to immobilize the army." With the failure of the 1958 offensive, many officers gave up trying to uproot the guerrillas. (And all this time, the second in command of

Batista's military intelligence was—but of course!—a Castro agent.)[46] Moreover, by the fall of 1958 a new guerrilla campaign was taking shape in the Escambray Mountains of central Cuba.

The Arms Embargo

But a real thunderbolt struck the Batista regime on March 14, 1958, when the Eisenhower administration announced an embargo on arms shipments to Cuba and the Department of State requested that other countries not sell arms to Batista.[47] Arms embargoes, like that of the Roosevelt administration during the Spanish Civil War, by forbidding transfers of arms to either side in an insurrection or civil conflict, work in fact against the incumbent government, placing it on a moral level with the insurgents and preventing it from strengthening its armed forces. Hugh Thomas writes that "no step by Castro could have so disheartened Batista." The arms embargo, along with restrictions on credit and discouragement of investment in Cuba, "put a severe strain on the regime and [caused] gradually a failure of nerve within the administration that spread to the military and made it practically impotent long before most of the troops had ever heard a rifle shot."[48] Before the embargo, "Batista could suggest in a hundred small ways that behind him stood if need be the armed might of the world's most powerful country." Now Batista and his regime were isolated. In the dictator's own words: "The prohibition of the sale of arms to the Cuban government weakened the faith and the will to fight in many of our men." In U.S. ambassador Smith's view, the embargo had "a devastating psychological effect upon the armed forces." He continued: "There can be no doubt that the decision by the State Department to suspend the shipment of arms to Cuba was the most effective step taken by the Department of State in bringing about the downfall of Batista."[49]

The Collapse of the Regime

In part the accelerating disintegration of the Batista regime resulted from sending inadequately trained draftees into combat while elite units were kept in Havana.[50] But the truth was even simpler than that; as one of Batista's own officers told him during the offensive, "the soldiers are tired and the officers do not want to fight."[51] Many of these officers were receiving letters from brother officers who had gone over to Castro, urging them to defect. In August, therefore, the high command ordered a general retreat.[52] As the meaning of all this began to sink in, Castro carried out a move reminiscent of Maoist tactics during the Chinese civil war: he released four hundred Batista prisoners taken during the offensive. Predictably, "many soldiers concluded that it was far wiser to fall prisoner than to risk their lives resisting insurgent advances."[53] Raul Castro said to one group of captured Batista soldiers: "We took you this time. We can take you again. And when we do we will not frighten or torture or kill you, anymore than we are doing to you at this moment. If you are captured a second time or even a third time by us, we will again return you exactly as we are doing now." Such "expression[s] of utter contempt for the fighting potential of the defeated" weakened even further the self-confidence both of the army and the regime.[54]

Castro's propaganda proclaimed that it was not the soldier who was the enemy, but rather the Batista regime, which exploited him and everyone else; Castro said, "We do not fight against the army, only against Batista." Shortly after the failure of the 1958 offensive, Castro made a radio broadcast in which he appealed to the younger officers to forsake the regime: "We are at war with the tyranny, not with the armed forces."[55] This supremely clever effort to convince lower-ranking officers that they might have a future separate from that of a sinking Batista had a powerful effect.[56] Numerous officers began making plans to remove Batista, plans that were supposed to ripen around mid or late December. The fighting qualities of the troops deteriorated even further; one high-ranking officer wrote later: "Our army, tired and decimated by two years of fighting without relief had completely lost its combat power. Desertion to the enemy increased daily. We lacked reserves and a great part of the officers confined to barracks were in contact with the enemy."[57]

Meanwhile, by late summer Castro was levying and collecting a tax on each bag of sugar milled, including that milled by U.S.-owned firms. In the autumn, the United States evacuated fifty-five of its citizens from the town of Nicaro, a sure sign of disbelief in Batista's ability to win.[58]

Yet even now, according to Hugh Thomas, "the civil war was far from lost, if only Batista could have brought himself to admit that a civil war, properly speaking, was in existence." Batista still had cards to play, the area of Cuba under control of the rebels was quite small, the bulk of the population still lived in government-held areas, and certainly "Castro did not expect Batista to collapse as fast as he now did."[59] But Batista did not want to exert the effort required, assuming that he knew what was required, which would have included (1) cleaning out all the decayed wood from the top of the army down, men such as General Francisco Tabernilla, "the real author of the army's defeat," who was preparing to enter negotiations with Castro, and (2) playing his remaining really big card: the election and installation of an anti-Castro reformer as his successor.[60]

The 1958 Election

A presidential election was due in 1958. Under the prevailing circumstances, it would have been exceedingly difficult to hold one that would be satisfactory to most parties. Still, if a reasonably free election had taken place, it would have been a grave strategic defeat for Castro. The U.S. State Department urged Batista to restore constitutional guarantees and then hold an election. If the principal opposition groups nevertheless refused to participate in the election, the United States would encourage Batista to hold it anyway. In the department's view, "if a sizeable vote could be polled and a respectable man elected to the Presidency by the Government, there would remain the possibility that he might provide a transition towards a more democratic form of government."[61] But Batista would not restore constitutional guarantees while Castroite violence was rampant, and the non-Castroite opposition disingenuously refused to participate in any election without those guarantees. But beyond that, Castro proclaimed that anyone who stood as a candidate in the presidential election would be executed and voters would be machine-gunned at the polling places. To give point to his admonitions, Castro caused a prominent politician to be murdered. Fear consequently persuaded many potential voters to stay away from polls.[62]

In the event, the Batista candidate Andrés Rivero Agüero was declared the overwhelming victor against the main opposition candidate, Carlos Marquez Sterling. Former president Grau San Martín, the Autentico candidate, placed third. (Note that even at that point the opposition could not agree to back one anti-Batista candidate.) President Batista had requested, in vain, international observers, especially from the United Nations, to be present in Cuba for the elections. Ambassador Smith believed that the victory of an opposition candidate would have greatly reduced the chances of Castro's coming to power. But since the Batista-endorsed candidate won, everyone believed—or said they believed—that the election must have been fraudulent. And now, with Batista clearly on his way out to make room for his successor, his whole remaining support system began to crumble. At the same time, plans for the Organization of American States, in union with Cuban church and business groups, to bring about a negotiated settlement or ceasefire collapsed.[63]

Now, recall that for many years before and after 1958, various U.S. administrations accepted the officially declared outcomes of Mexican presidential elections, even though the most politically innocent person could see that they were the results of ballot fraud on a truly Herculean scale. Nevertheless, on December 10, Ambassador Smith informed Batista that the United States would not recognize the incoming administration of Rivero. In effect the United States was withdrawing its recognition from Batista's government. This move drastically undermined Batista's remaining support in the army. Late in November, the State Department considered a plan whereby Batista would appoint a caretaker government unfriendly to him and then resign. The United States would in turn recognize this government and send arms to it, in order to keep Castro from seizing power. That did not work either; the State Department position was that the Cuban situation could not be stabilized until Batista left; Batista maintained that he could not leave until the situation was stabilized.[64]

On December 23, 1958, Acting Secretary of State Christian Herter told President Eisenhower: "Above all else, we want to help avoid the appalling mob violence which attended the fall of Machado in 1933, and which Cubans fatalistically expect to occur again."[65] At about the same time, high-ranking officers in the army were getting in touch with Castro, proposing the installation of a military junta with which Castro would then negotiate.[66]

Undoubtedly, Batista was badly shaken by the arms embargo, and so were many of his followers. It seemed to mean that the United States was betting against him, perhaps even siding against him. This suspicion, combined with the increasing defection of most people of the upper and middle classes, caused the leadership to have serious doubts about the long-term chances of the regime to endure, and these doubts infected the army. When the offensive failed and the United

States withdrew its recognition, panic began to set in all around. The city of Santa Clara, astride the Central Highway, fell to the rebels, and Santiago was besieged. Accordingly, on New Year's Eve, 1958, Batista fled the country and went to the Dominican Republic.[67] The war, if that is the correct word, was over. The upheaval was about to begin.

Reflection

However doubtful, insecure, and badly led an army may be, it must be defeated by *somebody*. Clearly, the rebels were generally both brave and intelligent. Nevertheless, the scope and scale of the fighting during the rebellion was embarrassingly small. The only serious encounters were the 1958 summer offensive and the battle of Santa Clara in December, during which the rebels suffered six fatalities. Throughout the two-year conflict, the Batista forces probably lost no more than three hundred men, fewer than three per week, about the same number that could have been expected to be killed in vehicular accidents and barroom brawls. Most soldiers knew, of course, that if they became prisoners the guerrillas would not kill them. On the day that Batista fled his country, whole units of the Cuban Army had not yet fired a shot in anger, indeed had not even glimpsed the enemy. Rather than a bloody death struggle, "the Cuban civil war had really been a political campaign in a tyranny, with the campaigner [Castro] being defended by armed men."[68]

The higher officer corps was not loyal to Batista. On the contrary, it was riddled with his would-be successors and their shortsighted schemes and inept plots. And the willingness of Batista commanders to make deals with the enemy, so that Castroites could go almost anywhere they wished whenever they wished, rivals the most egregious episodes of betrayal from the history of classical Greece or Renaissance Italy. The U.S. arms embargo was undeniably a severe blow, and Castro played his cards very well. But in the last analysis the Cuban Army did not suffer a defeat but experienced a collapse, the result of "its own weaknesses, divisions, jealousies, and errors."[69]

All of this, of course, indicates a profound and protracted failure of leadership at the top. The army could never have been so ineffective, so disinclined to any physical activity whatsoever, if the highest political levels had not been complaisant. The defects of the army reflected those of the regime. How could it have been otherwise? If Cuba had possessed an efficient, well-turned-out army with at least a minimum of professional pride and ideological coherence, no one like Batista could have come to power in the first place. Well beyond the activities of Castro's miniscule bands, "Batista's laziness and weakness damaged morale more than anything else; the president played canasta when he should have been making war plans; as his press secretary put it in exile, 'Canasta was a great ally of Fidel Castro.'" Many would agree with the succinct summation of the fall of Batista offered by one distinguished student of Latin American affairs: "He was not forced out—he simply abdicated."[70]

Therefore, the well-known and widely accepted principle that a regime defended by an intact army cannot be overthrown by makeshift forces has been severely tested but not clearly refuted by the Cuban case.[71] Batista fled the stage well before the last curtain. Besides, one might argue with only slight hyperbole, Batista did not possess an army, as the term is commonly understood, but rather a sort of uniformed collection agency.

Almost from the first hours of his regime, Castro repudiated his promises of free elections and other reforms. The fate of Cuba was to become a Communist one-party dictatorship. Accordingly, Castro restored the death penalty, which had been illegal under Batista. Even today, no one knows for sure how many hundreds of soldiers, especially officers, of the old army the Castro regime executed after hasty trials by kangaroo courts. Certainly far more members of the army were executed after the conflict than had been killed during it. Had the army been able in 1957 or 1958 to glimpse its future, it would undoubtedly have fought with much more determination.

Clearly, there would have been no Castro regime in 1959 without the Batista coup in 1952. But that coup, in turn, would hardly have been conceivable without the dismal record of the Autenticos during the preceding eight years. Moreover, the Batista regime was not a foreign occupation, and Batista himself, in origin and appearance, was obviously much more a man of the common people than Castro. Hence there are those who argue that Batista's "principal weakness was a reluctance to be sufficiently ruthless [against Castro] under conditions of extreme provocation, out of an excessive desire to achieve and hold popularity with the masses."[72] Recall that Batista pardoned Castro after the latter's ludicrous fiasco at Moncada in 1953.

And there is of course the major and perhaps decisive role in these events played by Washington, and especially the State Department. True enough, military and other dictatorships were collapsing across Latin America in the late 1950s: Argentina's Juan Perón in 1955, Peru's Manuel Odría in 1956, Colombia's Gustavo Rojas Pinilla in 1957, and Venezuela's Marcos Pérez Jiménez in 1958. Not one of them, however, was succeeded by a Leninist dictatorship: that happened only in Cuba. On August 30, 1960, Ambassador Smith stated before a subcommittee of the U.S. Senate, "Without the United States, Castro would not be in power today." More specifically, said Smith, "by no longer supporting the existing government of Cuba, the United States helped Castro rise to power in preference to a number of politically sound and friendly leaders we might have supported."[73] According to one of the most exhaustive studies of these events, "the reasons for Batista's fall did not lie in the Sierra [that is, in the guerrilla conflict]. The field of struggle was in Havana and in Santiago, and in Washington as well." Moreover, the U.S. government's role had been both "ambivalent and extraordinary, even if in the end unsatisfactory to Batista and to Castro." In short, "American political intervention had delivered Cuba to Communism."[74]

The withdrawal of U.S. support to Batista was in part due to his inability to maintain the appearance of control. But that inability in turn was in part related to the gradual but public withdrawal of U.S. support. In short, between 1957 and 1959, the United States helped mightily to replace a dictator friendly to it with a dictator hostile to it, who soon began to align his country with the Soviet Union. Among the costs the United States eventually paid for that policy were the Bay of Pigs and the Cuban Missile Crisis.

If our analysis of these Cuban events is at least relatively valid, it follows that any attempt to export the Castro revolution to Latin American countries possessing real armies and the serious support of the United States should have met with failure. In several countries, including Venezuela, and above all Guevara's fatal foray into Bolivia, the utter defeat of Cuban-inspired rebellions is exactly what we encounter.[75] In contrast, as of this writing there is not one clear-cut, unambiguous case of the Castro experience's being successfully imitated anywhere in Latin America. The main reason for this across-the-board failure to replicate the Cuban revolution is that Castro's self-proclaimed imitators were not in fact imitating his revolution at all. The essential combination of conditions that allowed Castro to come to power—an isolated ruling clique representing no one but themselves, disdained by substantial elements of the middle and upper classes, the Church, and the U.S. government, and reliant on an incompetent army—have been found nowhere else in Latin America. Indeed, the slaughter of army officers, the imposition of a Leninist regime, and the mass emigration of the Cuban middle class to Florida alarmed and galvanized Latin American governments, as well as Washington. Of course, the final nail in the coffin of these efforts to export the Cuban revolution was that his admirers forgot—perhaps—that when Castro was in the Sierra, he was promising democracy, whereas his would-be imitators promised Leninist dictatorship, confrontation with the United States, and alignment with the Soviet Union.

Thus the Castro regime, the first Communist dictatorship in the New World, eventually became one of the very last Communist dictatorships anywhere at all.

Castro undoubtedly has always had a large measure of popular support, and perhaps at times even majority support, but one can make the same observation about Hitler. Yet, what if the Cuban people had been able in 1958 to look into the future and see themselves in 1968—or 2008? What if they could have foreseen that Castro would betray the promises he made while in the Sierra, with consequent violations of individual and communal liberty far more drastic and systematic than anything under Batista? What if they had been able to foresee the mass exodus to Florida of Cubans who otherwise would have wound up in concentration camps; fifty years of economic deprivation and decay; or the unknown number of young Cubans sent away to die or be maimed or contract AIDS in proxy wars in Africa to pay for Soviet subsidies? Had they been able to foresee such a future, one wonders how many Cubans would have thought that replacing Batista with Castro would be worth it.

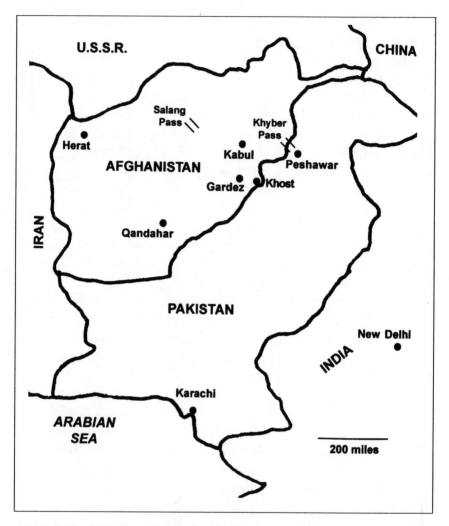

Afghanistan, 1980. From Anthony James Joes, *America and Guerrilla Warfare*
(Lexington: Univ. Press of Kentucky, 2000).

4

Afghanistan
End of the Red Empire

In 2001, U.S. and allied troops entered Afghanistan and overthrew the grotesque Taliban regime that had long terrorized that country. The Taliban had taken power in the aftermath of the protracted and savage conflict between Soviet armed forces and most of the people of Afghanistan. Any description of that Soviet-Afghan struggle generates a string of superlatives. For example, the popular resistance to the Soviet invasion constituted "the largest single national rising in the twentieth century."[1] The Afghan war was the longest military conflict in Soviet history: direct Soviet involvement extended from December 1979 to mid-1988. During the conflict Soviet forces reached the city of Qandahar, the southernmost penetration by Russian power since the days of Peter the Great. The Soviets pursued one of the most destructive counterinsurgency campaigns ever seen, and one of the least successful, providing a textbook example of how a major power—or any power—should not wage a counterinsurgency. The Soviet armed forces suffered their clearest reversal since the fall of Nazi Berlin, the first time a Russian army had been decisively checked by insurgents in modern history. The war provided the arena for the biggest CIA clandestine operation in that organization's history. It was perhaps the most satisfying experience the Americans ever had with guerrilla warfare. The Afghan insurgents received material help from an exceedingly heterogeneous group of states. All of these circumstances helped to stimulate forces that exerted the most profound effects on the Soviet empire and indeed the entire global configuration. In the end, the Soviets withdrew their troops from Afghanistan, but that turned out to be only the first of such withdrawals.

The Country

When the author of these pages was a boy, "Afghanistan" was a word, like "Timbuktu," used to denote unimaginable remoteness. But the historian Arnold Toynbee described Afghanistan as one of the two great crossroads of cultural dispersion from prehistory to the Renaissance. Lying astride the principal trade routes between Persia and India, Afghanistan links the Middle East and South Asia. It also constitutes the intersection of Central Asia and the Indian subcontinent. The country is roughly the combined size of France, Belgium, the Netherlands, and Switzerland, or Illinois, Indiana, Michigan, Wisconsin, and Ohio. Stupendous mountain ranges fanning out from the towering Hindu Kush are interspersed with fertile valleys. At the time of the invasion there were no railways and few real roads; Norway, another mountainous country, with half the area of Afghanistan, had about twenty times the paved road mileage. The population is highly diverse ethnically and linguistically, speaking perhaps thirty languages and dialects; Dari, the Afghan version of the Persian tongue, has long served as a lingua franca. Before the Soviet invasion, the Afghans numbered about 15.5 million, of whom the 6 million Pushtuns were numerically and politically the most important. From very early times, "the Pushtoons [sic] have been characterized as turbulent, warlike, predatory and revengeful."[2] Yet the leader of the first official British mission to Afghanistan found them "fond of liberty, faithful to their friends, kind to their dependants, hospitable, brave, hardy, frugal, laborious and prudent" as well as "less disposed than the nations in their neighborhood to falsehood, intrigue, and deceit." Prostitution was almost unknown "until the arrival of the free-spending [British]."[3] The "ideal male personality type in Afghan society [was] the warrior-poet." The Pushtun moral code included a prohibition on killing women or children or musicians, or anyone who had asked for mercy or was found in a mosque. In the view of at least one visitor, "quite possibly the Afghans [were] the most hospitable people in the world."[4]

During World War II, Afghanistan provided a refuge for numerous Jews seeking to escape the European holocaust.

Persian-speaking Tajiks composed about one-fifth of the population. In the center of the country there were at least 1 million Hazaras; Mongolian in origin and Shiite in faith, these have often been slaves or servants. Many other ethnolinguistic groups were present as well. Kabul, the capital, with about nine hundred thousand inhabitants, was by far the largest city.

Preinvasion Afghan society was overwhelmingly rural, made up in large part of independent farmers. Great landholdings were relatively rare. Afghanistan was a poor country: per capita income on the eve of the Soviet invasion was about $168, and the literacy rate was 10 percent (much lower for women). But by most Asian standards, the people were well fed. Everyday life revolved around local affairs and religion. Indeed, among the fiercely independent Afghans, the basic unifying social force had been the adherence of 90 percent of the population to Sunni Islam.

Before the Soviet Invasion

The written history of Afghanistan begins in 329 B.C. with the arrival of Alexander the Great, who found a bride, Roxanne, for himself there. Islam reached Afghanistan after A.D. 600, although it took several hundred years to establish its dominance. In 1219, Genghis Khan invaded and conquered the area. This was a true catastrophe: the conquerors systematically destroyed irrigation systems, turning much good land to desert. More Mongol invasions occurred between 1370 and 1500. By the end of this period, Afghanistan was prostrate. Its only hope of recovery lay in the revival of trade, but new sea routes had opened up between Europe and the East, and thus Afghanistan sank into the status of a remote and uninviting territory.

Afghanistan's present borders were gradually established during the nineteenth century. This was the era of the Great Game between the czarist and the British empires for control of the Indian frontier regions. Afghanistan was able to establish and maintain what independence it possessed in part because it provided a convenient buffer between the two contending empires. But being a buffer meant that its borders were artificial, embracing a hodgepodge of tribes, religions, and tongues. As a result, most Afghan peoples have ethnic brethren across the borders, in former Soviet Central Asia or in Pakistan. The mountainous terrain, poor communications, and linguistic diversity kept Afghanistan administratively decentralized, with little national consciousness. Arguably, Afghanistan was a "nation only in its xenophobic perception of outsiders."[5] Presiding over this diverse population was a monarchy with hardly any bureaucratic apparatus and usually no real program except survival. Political life was mainly local.

The Victorian world burst in upon Afghanistan in the form of a British invasion during the First Afghan War (1839–42). That conflict showed, not for the last time, how much easier it was to overrun Afghanistan than to control it. The principal event of this incursion was the annihilation of the British garrison at Kabul, the greatest British defeat in modern history until the fall of Singapore.[6] It is important to note, in light of contemporary events, that the Afghanistan that inflicted this bloody repulse on a waxing British imperialism lacked both the structure of a modern state and access to modern weapons. Alas, their success at resisting British control meant that in the twentieth century the Afghans never attained the efficient railway system, trained civil service, professional judiciary, and modern armed forces that India and Pakistan inherited upon independence.[7]

The conclusion of World War II was the beginning of the British retreat from empire. Thus the traditional counterweight to Russian domination of Afghanistan disappeared; India, successor to the British Raj, was too weak, and the United States was too preoccupied elsewhere, to replace the British in the Great Game. The United States did not extend diplomatic recognition to Afghanistan until 1934 and did not send a U.S. representative to Kabul until 1942.

The Saur Revolution

The Afghan constitution of 1964 placed almost all power in the hands of the king, the diffident Zahir, born in 1915. Zahir ruled with the support of a conservative parliament. During the 1960s the Afghans held national parliamentary elections, with secret ballots and woman suffrage. But on July 17, 1973, while the king was in Italy, a bloodless coup in Kabul proclaimed his rule at an end and a republican regime in force. Mohammed Daoud, a cousin and brother-in-law of the king, had been prime minister from 1953 to 1963. He was the instigator of the coup and proclaimed himself both president and prime minister. This first Afghan experiment with republicanism, a political form unfamiliar to the people and their leaders, was not off to a propitious start. Thus Daoud set the stage for his own personal tragedy.

The 1973 coup was not a Communist enterprise, although the Afghan Communists were no doubt glad to see the end of the monarchy, one unifying institution in a multilingual, multiethnic society. In reclusive exile in Rome, Zahir proclaimed his intention to return to his country as king only if a plebiscite called him back. Some Afghans later blamed Zahir for all their subsequent sufferings, saying that the Communists were able to take over the country because Zahir had done nothing to move it out of its backwardness.[8]

Daoud had some big ideas about bringing the country toward the modern era. In need of large-scale financial assistance for economic and military development, he looked to the United States, but Washington expressed no interest in Afghanistan. Daoud then turned to the Soviet Union, which was more receptive. By 1976, however, Daoud apparently had come to regret his dependence on the Soviets; he sought to counterbalance their influence by turning more closely to India (a pale reflection of the old Anglo-Russian Great Game). In the beginning of his rule, Daoud had the support of the Afghan Communists, called the People's Democratic Party of Afghanistan (PDPA), and its numerous members and sympathizers in the army officer corps. His attempts to edge away from the USSR antagonized these groups. In April 1978, the PDPA organized a large demonstration in Kabul. Alarmed, Daoud ordered the arrest of the principal party leaders—but not their friends in the army. This turned out to be a literally fatal mistake. Communist elements in the armed forces apparently feared that after he had arrested and perhaps killed the leadership of the PDPA, Daoud would turn on them. Leftist officers thereupon organized a coup against Daoud. After some bitter fighting with Daoud's guards on April 27–28, they killed him, as well as all the members of his family they could get their hands on.

The Afghan Communist party mythologized the murder of Daoud as "the Great Saur [April] Revolution," but it was in fact "an urban coup d'état against an unpopular, autocratic government" carried out by a relative handful of military officers.[9] The coup, however, was shortly followed by the installation of a completely PDPA cabinet. How the miniscule PDPA managed to take over so quickly and easily is still not entirely clear.[10] Neither is it clear to what degree the 1978 coup was Communist-engineered from the beginning. Certainly the timing of the move against Daoud itself was fortuitous, being triggered by Daoud's orders to arrest leaders of the PDPA. The Soviet Union apparently knew about, and approved, the coup and supported the new PDPA cabinet. But Soviet participation in the coup, both the instigation and the actual deed, seems to have been minimal. Part of the explanation for the PDPA takeover of power from Daoud lies in the fact that for years he had allowed its members to infiltrate the officer corps and the bureaucracy; indeed Daoud himself had appointed many PDPA members and sympathizers to office.

At any rate, former U.S. ambassador Robert Neumann advised the Jimmy Carter administration to cut off all U.S. aid to the new PDPA regime. Neumann later stated that the mild American reaction to the killing of Daoud contributed to the subsequent Soviet invasion. President Carter's national security adviser Zbigniew Brzezinski agreed with this assessment.[11]

The PDPA Regime

Properly speaking, the Afghan Communist party had existed only since January 1965. All the founding members of the organization were from the educated elite of Afghan society; it had no worker or peasant members, and the party won only two parliamentary seats (out of more than two hundred) in the 1969 elections. There is some evidence that PDPA founding father Babrak Karmal, who later played a leading role in the tragedy that engulfed his country, was as early as 1965 an agent of the KGB. The party soon split into irreconcilably hostile factions, the Parcham ("Banner") and the Khalq ("the masses"). Ideological differences seem to have been less important than sociological and personal ones. Members of the Parcham were overwhelmingly Kabulis, relatively sophisticated and Persian-speaking and thoroughly subservient to the Soviets. Khalq supporters tended to be from the provinces and heavily Pushtun. Khalqis predominated in the army officer corps, while Parchamis eventually controlled KHAD (the acronym for the East German–trained "State Information Services," the security police). KHAD provided its members with good salaries, housing, medical care, and trips to the Soviet Union; it also possessed heavily armed paramilitary units. Its membership averaged perhaps twenty thousand; it was reputedly "the largest known sponsor of terrorism in the world."[12]

After the killing of President Daoud, the new PDPA government included Nur Mohammed Taraki as president, Hafizullah Amin as foreign minister and the most important figure in the cabinet, and Babrak Karmal as deputy prime minister. All had been founders of the PDPA, and they later became, respectively, the first, second, and third presidents of "Communist" Afghanistan.

Nur Mohammed Taraki was the first known member of the Afghan Communist Party. He studied English in Bombay, where he allegedly joined the Indian Communist Party in 1937. He worked in the U.S. aid mission in Kabul and in the U.S. Embassy in the 1950s and 1960s. By the time of his selection as president, he was an alcoholic. Hafizullah Amin was the son of a government employee and a graduate of Kabul University. He earned an M.A. in education at Teachers College of Columbia University in the 1950s and unsuccessfully sought a Columbia Ph.D. Babrak Karmal, founder of the Parcham faction of the PDPA, was born in 1929, the son of an army general. He attended Kabul University in the early 1950s after having previously failed his entrance examinations.

The new Taraki-Amin dictatorship first purged followers of Daoud from the bureaucracy, then turned against members of the Parcham faction. One result of this intraparty strife was that young and inexperienced Khalqis were put into sensitive offices, where they soon made a mess of government programs. The regime also turned its wrath against the non-Communist intelligentsia and the religious leadership. During 1978 and 1979, the new government admitted killing twelve thousand political prisoners. Some estimates run much higher. The Taraki-Amin regime encouraged factionalism within the PDPA and ignored political organization within the army. Most of all, the regime alienated vast strata of the population with a program badly conceived and even worse administered. For example, Khalqi reforms required that women achieve equality with men, and doing so meant first of all making women literate. Hence, women would be dragged out of their homes and made to sit in literacy classes, where the lessons often consisted of attacks against religion. Mullahs (Islamic religious teachers) who opposed such practices were often simply shot by enlightened young Kabuli PDPA types, with no trial or other ceremony. In 1978 there were perhaps 320,000 mullahs in the country, and the regime thoroughly alienated this strategic group. Growing numbers of Afghans viewed the policies of the clique in Kabul as "repulsively anti-Islamic."[13]

The Kabul regime also pursued land redistribution, masking its eventual Communist aim of rural collectivization. Nobody in the Afghan government seemed to know how much land would be available for or distributed by government land reforms. In the villages, land was taken away from arbitrarily defined "rich landlords" and handed over to "poor peasants" on the Leninist model. Such reforms both cut tenant farmers off from the age-old village social security system provided by patronage from larger landowners and offended traditional Islamic ideas of legal propriety.[14] As one careful study concluded, "the hastily conceived and partially implemented land reform program was an economic disaster that brought chaos to all levels of society."[15]

Many adherents of the PDPA regime undoubtedly wanted to raise the status of women in Afghan society; they also viewed literacy as a great boon that they would bestow on the population. Undoubtedly, Westerners would find these ideas laudable. But the tiny PDPA and a somewhat larger circle of sympathizers provided a very slender political base for the new and illegitimate regime. When, therefore, the government launched headlong attacks on the whole Afghan way of life, treating any who resisted such attacks (eventually the majority of Afghans) as enemies to be crushed, it was provoking disaster. The whole PDPA approach to governing suggests not naive sympathy but profound hostility toward the peasantry. It was not liberation but modernization that the PDPA intended to impose, modernization at any cost, no matter how destructive: a true Central Asian Stalinism, in essence an "attempt by a minority regime to drastically alter the existing Afghan value system and social structure, and the brutality associated with this attempt, that finally provoked large-scale resistance."[16] Thus this tiny minority—city-dwelling, peasant-despising, religion-hating, and teacher-killing (reminiscent of the Greek Communists)—kindled the wrath of the population against it. In March 1979, nearly a year before the Soviet invasion, furious crowds demonstrated in the streets of Herat, the country's third-largest city, killing hundreds of Afghan Communists and scores of the numerous Soviet personnel in their city. Many Kabul soldiers in the city joined in the antiregime and anti-Soviet explosion. The regime restored its control in Herat at the cost of between 3,000 and 5,000 civilian deaths. On the eve of the Soviet invasion, perhaps as many as twenty-three of the country's twenty-eight provinces were under antiregime guerrilla control.[17]

The leaders in Moscow became alarmed at the egregious incompetence displayed by their protégés in Kabul. President Taraki, who found himself more and more pushed into a figurehead role, journeyed to the Kremlin, where he apparently received orders to get rid of Amin, the radical force in the Kabul regime. In September 1979, Taraki attempted to arrest or kill Amin at government headquarters, whereupon an authentic shoot-out occurred. The unexpected result of this palace gunfight was that Amin threw Taraki into prison and took the presidency for himself. A few weeks later the regime announced that ex-president Taraki had "died of a serious illness."

The Soviet Invasion

As early as the spring of 1979, the Kremlin was showing signs that it had decided an invasion might be necessary. Among these signs were the visits to Kabul by numerous high-ranking Soviet officers, including General Ivan Pavlovskii, who had commanded the invasion of Czechoslovakia in 1968. Indeed the move into Afghanistan was modeled upon that Prague scenario: subversion of an unreliable Communist regime and its replacement by pliant stooges, after Soviet troops had taken control of the capital city in a lightning move.

During the last weeks of December 1979, in preparation for the coming invasion, Soviet advisers began removing the batteries from Afghan army tanks for "winterization" and gathering up antitank ammunition for "inventory." Afghan army officers invited to a Soviet reception got drunk and found themselves locked up. On December 24, flight after flight of Soviet airborne troops began to descend upon Kabul, occupying key positions and buildings. At the same time ground troops poured across the border, heading for Kabul and Herat. On December 27, special Soviet units attacked the palace where Amin was living; after a fierce fight, during which they sustained numerous casualties, Soviet troops killed Amin and members of his family.

The Kremlin brazenly explained to the world that the Afghan government had requested Soviet aid. A request for assistance (i.e., invasion) was in fact made, but by Babrak Karmal; this Central Asian quisling asked, from a radio station inside the Soviet border, that Moscow send assistance to his country—after twenty thousand Soviet troops had already crossed the frontier. No invitation ever came from Amin, an invitation that would have given the Soviet invasion the figleaf of legality; Amin was dead, killed by his erstwhile Soviet patrons who had come to "assist" him. Indeed, the Soviets later claimed that Amin was a CIA agent.[18] In return for Babrak Karmal's services, the Soviets installed him as president.

The Soviet coup was a masterpiece of its kind, better planned and executed even than the Czech invasion and incomparably superior to the monstrous and bungled assault on Hungary in 1956; after all, practice makes perfect. Conceivably, Amin could have organized resistance around Kabul, called for a popular rising, or requested foreign assistance. But he did none of these things, "because the first move of the Soviet invasion was an airborne coup de main [by elite Soviet airborne troops] which suppressed any attempt at resistance."[19] The timing seemed good, too: the Carter administration was reeling from both foreign and domestic setbacks; the American polity was still punch-drunk from Vietnam and Watergate and distracted by the upcoming presidential election and the hostage crisis in Iran. But the invasion, technically a success, did not work out as it was intended. Instead of quenching popular resistance to the puppet regime in Kabul, it enflamed it. Seizing the capital city was the easy part; enforcing the authority of Karmal and the PDPA over the rest of the country was a greater challenge.

The Invasion: Why?

Since the first days of the invasion, observers have expressed the belief that the Soviets entered Afghanistan in order to enforce the Brezhnev Doctrine; that is, to prevent the overthrow of a Communist regime, an event that would have endangered Communist rule everywhere. "The Afghan intervention," wrote Martin Malia, "was not dictated by geopolitical considerations, such as advancing a salient toward Middle East oil, as the West thought at the time, but by a senescent ideological concern for the inviolability of the frontiers of socialism."[20]

But this explanation needs to be supplemented by other considerations. From an ideological standpoint, the Afghanistan that the Soviets invaded in 1979 was not a Communist or even a socialist state; it was merely a state ruled by Communists.[21] Clearly, permitting the overthrow of a pro-Soviet regime, especially one on the very borders of the USSR, would hardly enhance the prestige or the security of the leaders in the Kremlin, but there are additional, more historically rooted explanations available.[22]

Afghanistan's geography, including its thousand-mile border with the Soviet Union, made it inescapably interesting to its northern neighbor. Czarist Russia had long cherished ambitions to move toward the shores of the Indian Ocean. Recall Leon Trotsky's 1919 dictum that "the road to Paris and Berlin lies through the towns of the Punjab and Afghanistan."[23] (Of course, history has shown that in this, as in so many other things, Trotsky was wrong—dead wrong, so to speak—but that is beside the point: he and other Communist leaders probably wished to believe it.) In the infamous Hitler-Stalin Pact of 1939, the region of future Soviet territorial loot was identified as being "south of the Soviet Union in the direction of the Indian Ocean" and "in the general direction of the Persian Gulf."[24]

Occupied as he was with digesting and imposing socialism on his new eastern European subjects, Stalin displayed little interest in the Third World. But Khrushchev, who had emerged as supreme leader by 1957 at the latest, had another view. His neo-Trotskyist interest in the underdeveloped world as the weak link in the defenses against Soviet expansionism manifested itself partly in the attention he gave to neighboring Afghanistan. (Martin Malia wrote: "For the world's premier socialist state, and a superpower to boot, to be rummaging in the Third World wreckage of European 'imperialism' for such prizes as Angola and Afghanistan would be farcical were it not so tragic.")[25]

There was a great deal of ethnic overlap between then-Soviet Central Asia and Afghanistan's northern, Soviet-contiguous provinces. Thousands of Tajiks and Uzbeks in those northern provinces were descendants of people who had fled or were driven from the USSR in the 1920s. These areas also contain most of Afghanistan's natural resources. Impressive mountain chains divide the northern provinces from the rest of the country, and for decades there has been sentiment in favor of at least regional autonomy for the area.[26]

Besides, a Sovietized Afghanistan would have made a perfect base from which to propagate the independence of "Baluchistan" and "Pushtunistan." The success of this policy would have achieved the dismemberment of Pakistan, ally of the United States and China, and the establishment of a group of pseudoindependent Soviet protectorates stretching from the Soviet border down to the Indian Ocean.

Beginning in the 1950s, therefore, the Soviet Union lent Afghanistan money, delivered MiG-15 fighters, and built three air bases in the country. Many Afghan army and air force officers and cadets went to the Soviet Union for training.[27] Most of these officers who had been exposed to the Soviet Union came back to Afghanistan profoundly impressed with the military might of their northern neighbor. The king, suspicious of the returnees, would not let them rise to the highest ranks. Here was one of the roots of the coup that destroyed the monarchy and eventually brought the country to its subsequent catastrophe. Another was that the educational reforms of the 1950s began to produce an element in the population cut off from both the traditional power wielders and the conservative masses. Embarrassed by their country's position in the world and their own position within their country, these new would-be elites turned to the Soviet Union for inspiration. Thus, the Brezhnev Doctrine quite aside, "the invasion appears as the logical culmination of decades of Soviet [and czarist] policies aimed at achieving ever-greater control of Afghanistan."[28] However, if the Soviets had not invaded in 1979, and the result had been the overthrow of a friendly regime in Kabul and its replacement by a militantly anti-Communist and Islamic Afghanistan, the effects on the millions of Muslims living in Soviet Central Asia could have been very serious.[29] Soviet leaders feared that the fall of the PDPA would produce a new regime in Kabul hostile to them. Even if the PDPA had been able to survive and contain the insurgency, the Soviets had to consider the possibility that Amin would imitate Egypt's Sadat: that is, expel the Soviets and turn to the West. It had long been Soviet policy to keep unfriendly powers out of Afghan territory, but some in the Kremlin suspected that the United States wanted Afghanistan as a substitute for that valuable listening post on the Soviet border it had once had in Iran. We need to recall as well that the Afghanistan invasion occurred in a context of increasingly bold Soviet international behavior.[30] Article 28 of the Brezhnev constitution of 1976 proclaimed, "The foreign policy of the USSR shall aim at . . . supporting the struggle of peoples for national liberation." Soviet submarines were making repeated incursions into Swedish waters; Soviet aircraft wantonly shot down a civilian Korean airliner in 1983, and so on.[31] According to Edward Luttwak, the invasion of Afghanistan merely underlined in red that the world was "confronted by clear evidence of an utterly novel boldness on the part of the Soviet military leaders, and of an equally new confidence on the part of the Kremlin leaders in the professional competence of their military colleagues."[32]

In the end, whether the Soviet invasion of Afghanistan was objectively offensive or objectively defensive is irrelevant. Empires seek border security; hence the bolstering of a friendly government in Kabul would have been defensive in the Kremlin's view.[33]

The Uprising

Not long after the April (Saur) coup, armed risings occurred in several provinces. These were revolts against government policies but were not necessarily intended to precipitate or end in the fall of the government itself; armed resistance to unpopular Kabul policies was a venerable exercise. But the PDPA in Kabul responded with such violence that it drove the resisters to real civil war.[34] Then came the Soviet invasion, the first true foreign occupation of Afghanistan in modern times. Now dissatisfaction with government policies was overshadowed by the explosive, elemental power of outraged religion. In Mark Urban's view, "more than any other factor, the arrival of this foreign [Soviet] army had galvanized the resistance and brought it as many new recruits as it could arm."[35]

The Afghan freedom fighters, as President Ronald Reagan and others called them, faced truly tremendous odds. These included the enormous disparity in size, wealth, population, and technological capacity between Afghanistan and the Soviet Union, the proximity of the invading power, the geographic and political isolation of Afghanistan, a widespread tendency in world capitals to write off Afghanistan as being "within the Soviet sphere of influence," and finally, but not least, internal disunity within the insurgent ranks approaching fragmentation. As one keen observer put it, "the Afghan Resistance [was] not an army but rather a people in arms; its strengths and weaknesses [were] those of Afghan society."[36]

Traditionally, local leadership had been independent of national or even provincial control; accordingly, in this conflict, the first loyalty of a guerrilla in Afghanistan was usually to his commander, often a tribal or provincial figure of importance. The localism, individualism, and readiness to defend one's honor so characteristic of the Afghan people made them excellent prospects for guerrilla war but also worked against unity within the resistance. For one thing, most mujahideen ("warriors of God") were quite reluctant to fight outside their home province. And potentially explosive rivalries riddled the insurgency: among the various religious, regional, and tribal groups inside Afghanistan; among the exiled party politicians in Pakistan; between these politicians and the guerrilla commanders inside Afghanistan; and among the guerrilla commanders themselves.

Tribal and ethnic divisions made it possible here and there for the Kabul regime to recruit local militias, composed of tribes or clans different from those in the area that supported the resistance.[37] Most of these militias appear to have been "simply mercenaries attracted by the substantial pay (about £30 per month)," and "throughout the war, the militias' willingness to take Communist money . . . far exceeded their willingness to fight."[38]

When Gerard Chaliand visited Afghanistan in 1980, he observed that the resistance was vastly popular but structurally weak. Unlike many other post–World War II guerrilla movements, the Afghan resistance was overwhelmingly conservative in its political orientation, resembling the Spanish guerrillas that fought Napoleon's occupation. But unlike the Spanish case, the old precoup establishment was largely absent from the leadership of the resistance; this was especially true of army officers and professional politicians of the old regime. The former, pre-Saur political structure of Afghanistan appears to have been completely shattered. In its place a new leadership group was rising, including many non-Pushtun elements. But the lack of unity (and worse) within this leadership presented an unattractive picture to the outside world. The resistance movement rapidly divided into many different parties, each with its headquarters in Pakistan. These parties funneled supplies to particular guerrilla bands associated with them inside Afghanistan. They also sought to represent the resistance to the outside world.

Some students of the war saw tribal divisions or the influence of some outstanding personality as much more important than ideology as an explanation for fragmentation within the resistance.[39] There was undoubtedly much truth in this view. Nevertheless, the parties can be usefully, if untidily, divided into two main groups. The moderates, friendly to the West, professed to seek a new government based on democratic elections, possibly with former King Zahir playing an important if symbolic role. The so-called fundamentalists, often devoted to the Iranian Ayatollah Khomeini, wished to establish a post-Soviet Islamic republic and expressed profound hostility to King Zahir and the West as well. Some elements in the Hazara area of central Afghanistan actually declared that they were fighting for eventual incorporation into a "Greater Iran." As a result of all these centrifugal forces, during the anti-Soviet conflict the Afghan resistance never established a true governmental infrastructure, like that of Unita in Angola. The resistance movement produced no Ho Chi Minh, not even a Grivas or a Ben Bella.[40] The insurgency had no central coordination, and thus there was never a general strategy. This state of affairs allowed the Soviets to operate against one resistance group at a time.

A principal and unresolved source of friction within the resistance was the disposition of supplies coming across the Pakistan border, because "Mujahideen groups located well within Afghanistan were at the end of the pipeline and found that perhaps 40% of their material had gone to other Mujahideen groups between issue and final receipt."[41] Often mujahideen commanders would not allow supplies for other parties to pass through their territory.[42] "Much to the annoyance of the CIA," the Islamic fundamentalists commanded by Gulbuddin Hekmatyar (who became well known in the West during the latter part of the conflict) received more equipment than some other groups in part because they were more effective.[43]

Predictably, armed clashes between rival resistance groups were not rare occurrences.[44] "At its worst [this] feuding [amounted to] civil war between the Mujahideen. During the eleven years of the [war] hundreds of Mujahideen . . . died at the hands of their comrades-in-arms in different Parties, or under rival commanders." A Pakistani authority understandably complained of "the amount of time and effort that was wasted trying to sort out Mujahideen feuds" and not devoted to the fighting.[45]

After 1984, the disarray inside the resistance ranks abated to a degree. Significant moves toward at least formal unity among most of the different groups made it possible for them to send a unified delegation to the fortieth anniversary celebration at the United Nations. In January 1987, leaders of the resistance parties in Peshawar proclaimed a united program consisting mainly of two points: (1) complete Soviet withdrawal from Afghanistan and (2) mujahideen government of the country until free nationwide elections. Early in 1988, resistance leaders established a provisional government, with a supreme council including the leaders of the seven main parties.[46]

Besides lacking unity, the resistance lacked modern weapons. For years Afghan guerrillas were poorly equipped, much more so than their contemporaries in El Salvador or Angola. Most guerrilla units were self-supporting; they captured their guns from Soviet and Kabul forces. Defectors from the Kabul army and from ostensibly pro-Kabul local militias were another major source of weapons and ammunition. Foreign arms shipments did not assume any importance until well after the Soviet invasion.[47] Pakistan, Egypt, Saudi Arabia, China, and Kuwait sent arms, while certain particular types of modern weapons supplied by the United States became especially crucial in the mid-1980s.

In the early years, nothing seemed to be going well for the resistance. The dominant theory of guerrilla warfare holds that as the fish move in the water, so the guerrillas move among the civilian population, receiving life-giving sustenance and life-saving intelligence from it. But in fact, by 1984, because of the dreadful depredations of the Soviet invaders and their murderous marionettes in Kabul, the impoverished civilians in many areas were not able to provide the guerrillas with food, so that the freedom fighters had to carry their own. In many instances the guerrillas provided food for starving villagers.[48]

Infiltration by the enemy also afflicted the resistance. Both the KGB and KHAD penetrated the various insurgent groups inside Afghanistan, in Pakistan, and also in Europe. That some KGB agents were from Soviet Central Asia facilitated the infiltration. This is one area where the fragmentation within the resistance did not have entirely negative consequences, because it limited what KHAD and the KGB could discover. KHAD operated with some effect in the refugee camps in Pakistan, spreading rumors and dissension and occasionally killing a resistance leader. These refugee camps (one sheltered 125,000 persons) were havens for families of mujahideen fighters, and they were places where mujahideen could come for rest. But the camps aroused understandable resentment from Pakistanis who lived in their vicinity.[49]

KHAD and the KGB also took Afghan children to the Soviet Union, where they were trained in the use of explosives and sabotage and then sent back to infiltrate resistance units.[50] These activities bore fruit. There were a few spectacular defections from the resistance to the Kabul-Soviet side, most notably that of Ismatullah Achekzai, who took more than one hundred guerrillas with him. The regime also sought to win over tribes and clans with cash donations and privileges such as exemption from the draft. These overtures were not always rejected, although most such alliances between local leaders and Kabul turned out to be tactical and temporary.

The Resistance: Resources, Tactics, and Strategy

Clearly, the resistance ledger was not all debits, or the war would have come to an end in a few years with a Soviet victory. The fragmented nature of Afghan society made resistance unity impossible, especially since no truly charismatic leader appeared who could transcend tribal, regional, and religious divisions among the freedom fighters. But it also deprived the Soviets of a decisive target, a true center of gravity, against which to launch a major, decisive attack. The resistance was amorphous and therefore almost impossible to destroy. (Recall that it was a loosely organized, multilingual Afghan society that inflicted a serious defeat upon the mighty British Empire in the First Afghan War.)

The rugged mountainous terrain of most of Afghanistan is well suited to guerrilla warfare. Medical care for mujahideen inside Afghanistan was poor, but most of the guerrillas possessed hardy physiques and stoic attitudes, bequeathed to them by many centuries of spartan living. The resistance also enjoyed the truly priceless asset of a sanctuary in Pakistan. That country served not only as an area in which guerrillas could leave their families in relative safety; it was also an irreplaceable conduit for outside assistance, especially sophisticated American weapons. The years of combat against the Soviets also helped forge a new sense of Afghan nationality.[51]

But above all, the strength and basis of the resistance was Islam. The mujahid was "fighting for his faith, his freedom, and his family, which [gave] him an enormous moral ascendancy."[52] Some Western analysts, uncomfortable with the subject of religion, tended to ignore the decisive influence of Islam in the resistance movement. But from the first days of the Soviet invasion, the guerrillas were fighting not only for national (or more accurately, provincial) freedom but also—and most especially—for the true religion. The one weapon, therefore, that was never lacking to the resistance, the most important weapon in any army, was high morale; after all, as freedom fighters would ask, if God is with us, who shall prevail against us?

The exact number of active guerrillas at any one time is difficult to determine. Estimates vary from 80,000 to 150,000, but the latter figure is probably much too high. Arrayed against these were, by 1985, 115,000 Soviet troops, backed up by 30,000 regular Afghan army troops (down from a preinvasion force of 80,000–100,000), and perhaps 50,000 in other Kabul units. From the beginning the Communist forces controlled the cities and large towns, and the resistance controlled the countryside. The basic insurgent tactics were mining roads and ambushing convoys and patrols. These were quite effective, especially given the mountainous terrain and the great length of Soviet supply lines. Surprise moves by Soviet ground units were close to impossible, because the country's few roads were easily watched by the mujahideen. They liked to carry out ambushes in the evening, when their targets would be tired and less alert and the gathering darkness would allow them to break off contact and escape countermoves and air attacks. As in almost all such conflicts, "the ambush [was] a favorite tactic of the guerrilla since it allow[ed] him to mass forces covertly, attack the enemy, seize needed supplies and retreat before the enemy [could] effectively react."[53] Such spoils were essential for maintaining the mujahideen in the field.

The paucity of good roads magnified the effects of mujahideen tactics, so that sending supplies to and maintaining communications between regime-held urban centers became especially difficult and dangerous. From time to time the resistance would succeed in literally isolating a city or regime fortress, which would have to be supplied by aircraft, sometimes for years. The mujahideen were most active at night, attacking small fortified posts, blowing up bridges, and launching rocket attacks. Soviet soldiers particularly feared insurgents' sniper fire.[54] (Consequently, "the Kalashnikov assault rifle was not always better than the World War I–design bolt-action British Enfield rifle. The Enfield shot farther accurately and would penetrate flak jackets designed to stop Kalashnikov bullets.") Nevertheless, "although the popular conception of the Mujahideen combatant is a hardened warrior clutching a Kalashnikov rifle, the most important Mujahideen weapon was the RPG-7 anti-tank grenade launcher. This Soviet-manufactured, short-range weapon allowed the Mujahideen to knock out tanks, trucks, and occasionally helicopters."[55] The mujahideen also carried out 107mm rocket attacks, "by far the most common Mujahideen tactic in Afghanistan."[56] In 1984 the Soviet and Kabul forces lost two hundred helicopters and other aircraft, mostly destroyed on the ground, plus two thousand vehicles, including tanks. One authority estimates that during the length of the conflict, the resistance destroyed eleven thousand Soviet trucks, with even higher losses among the Kabul army.[57] The insurgents also increasingly carried out assassinations of government figures, notorious collaborators, and Soviet officials and soldiers.

During the first five years of the war, Soviet and Kabul forces would emerge from the cities to carry out extensive "sweeps" of the surrounding guerrilla-held territory. In the face of these major efforts, the resistance fighters often simply faded into the hills. Villagers would also disappear, abandoning their homes and their scanty possessions. The troops would arrive in a designated area and find no one to kill, little to loot, and nothing to eat. Unable therefore to live off the land, they would have to bring in supplies by convoy, always a dangerous undertaking, or else retreat back to their strongholds. When the troops went away, the villagers would return. This was the general pattern of repeated Soviet-Kabul campaigns in the strategic, seventy-mile-long Panjshir Valley, some sixty miles to the northeast of Kabul. Sometimes, however, the insurgents would not retreat in the face of an attack. These attacks would usually have Kabul troops in the lead, with Soviet soldiers behind them. Typical insurgent tactics let the Kabul forces pass and then concentrated fire on the Russians. In the meantime, many of the Kabul soldiers would have run away or defected to the insurgents. Sometimes a freedom fighter would strap a homemade gasoline bomb to his body and leap onto a Russian tank.[58] Neither side took many prisoners.

On the tactical level, the mujahideen were prepared for a long war. Their goal was to hit, survive, and fight again. Thus, the mujahideen could not exploit success. After a victory, they went home (much like the patriot guerrillas led by the Swamp Fox in the American War of Independence). Even group leaders, let alone loose coalitions, could not hold a force together for long after a fight. A century earlier, British soldiers noted that the mountain warriors could not stay together in victory or defeat. Thus, "tactical victory could not be converted into operational gain."[59] Nor did the mujahideen commanders create specialized forces, such as sappers or antiaircraft units, with the very notable exception of the celebrated leader Ahmed Shah Massoud. A Tajik and a onetime engineering student in France, still fluent in French, who now led the resistance in the Panjshir Valley, Massoud was "certainly the finest of the rebel commanders."[60] Besides, "most

Afghans hibernate[d] in winter," because the weather was "an infi-
nitely tougher opponent than the Soviets."[61] Therefore, there was no
Tet Offensive in Afghanistan, because mujahideen commanders were
unable, until very late in the war, to combine the followers in big
numbers. Nevertheless, large resistance operations did occur in 1983
against the cities of Urgun and Khost, close to the Pakistan border.
But when Massoud's followers captured the fortress at Pechgur, in
the Panjshir Valley, in June 1985, with a good haul of prisoners and
weapons, his men numbered no more than the five hundred Kabul
troops inside the place.

In sum, according to two keen observers, "the Mujahideen understood that guerrilla war is a contest of endurance and national
will. Battlefield victory is almost irrelevant."[62] The basic strategy of
the insurgents was not to *defeat* the Soviets, whose superior firepower
and discipline would have made such a task impossible. It was instead to make the war so costly for them that they would eventually
negotiate or just get out altogether. Stalemate was the objective of the
resistance, and stalemate was what it achieved before the end of 1985.

The Kabul Regime

Most PDPA leaders, activists, and members were urban or urban-
oriented, eager to imitate as far as possible Soviet experience and
policies and therefore full of impatient and embarrassed contempt
for traditional Afghan society. In no area of state activity did these
characteristics show as clearly, or with such disastrous consequences,
as in the approach of the Kabul regime to the Afghan peasantry, the
overwhelming majority of the population the PDPA claimed to rule.
There is no doubt that many small farmers and landless peasants
were poor and could have benefited from land reform, a principal
plank in the PDPA program. But countless country people were reluctant to participate in land-reform programs that seemed to them
unnecessarily punitive and confiscatory, violating local custom and
Islamic law. PDPA activists sent to stir up class feeling in the rural
areas made the peasants march together in formation through the
streets of their villages, shouting strange slogans and denouncing
unknown enemies ("American imperialists"). Ordinary Afghans
considered this kind of behavior to be immodest and demeaning.

It seems that no opportunity was lost to dismay, insult, or shock the peasants. For example, PDPA activists in rural areas often forbade dancing at weddings and set very low maximums for how much food could be served at these celebrations, all of which offended peasant ideas of propriety and hospitality. In addition, the PDPA anti-Islam campaign forced young army conscripts to drink alcohol.[63]

Since a Marxist-Leninist revolution requires a proletariat, and since such a class was hardly visible in Afghanistan, the PDPA conceived the idea of creating a "Proletariat of Women," who presumably would be glad to support radical social change. As anybody but PDPA zealots could have predicted, village women were not interested in fulfilling the role of historic substitute for the Petrograd proletariat; besides, the government made few efforts to follow up on this idea, since it faced more explosive problems. The whole project collapsed, but not before additional strata of the Afghan rural population had been alienated. Things were not much better in Kabul itself. Many reports described government or party agents' entering a private home on the pretext of searching for rebels and weapons and then simply looting the place.[64]

Because the PDPA and its programs attracted few supporters (party membership probably never exceeded fifty thousand),[65] the party eventually resorted to the time-tested Leninist expedient of the front organization. The National Fatherland Front was supposed to provide an umbrella group for people who would not join the PDPA but might be induced to support the government because they disliked or feared the resistance. This front, like all the other programs of the PDPA, had little effect.

Meanwhile, Parcham-Khalq hostility within the PDPA continued and even increased, even though the party-regime was fighting for its very survival. After the murder of Amin, President Babrak Karmal freed his fellow Parchamis from prison. They immediately turned on their Khalqi persecutors, humiliating or even killing many. The split within the party was beginning to take on aspects of a traditional Afghan blood feud, but it also reflected some serious policy differences. The Parcham side was totally pro-Soviet and therefore in favor of "softening" the PDPA revolutionary program in order to attract more support or at least calm some of its opponents. The Khalqis, however, grew ever more bitter and intransigent toward the resistance, indeed toward the whole Afghan population: many of them insisted on a total, immediate revolutionizing of all Afghan society. Correctly perceiving the Kremlin as being in favor of a "soft" policy, the Khalqis, many of them, displayed increasing suspicion and hostility toward their Russian mentors.

Afghan civil society had begun to crumble even before the Soviet invasion, and the process accelerated over the years. During the first year of Soviet occupation, many among the Afghan elites either defected to the resistance or escaped to foreign countries: diplomats, athletes, airline crews, almost everybody who was in a position to get out.

The Afghan educational system suffered mortal wounds. The PDPA put intense pressure on schoolteachers to join the party; those who refused lost their jobs, often their freedom, and sometimes their lives. Higher education was totally disrupted: almost the entire preinvasion faculty of Kabul University had been purged or had fled by the end of 1981; their posts were filled by Russians or unqualified PDPA members. One authority estimates that by 1985 from 50 to 70 percent of the preinvasion university faculties had been driven into exile, thrown into prison, or killed.[66]

Despairing of finding sufficient support for Communism in a country like Afghanistan, the Soviets took ten thousand Afghan children to the Soviet Union to form them into the nucleus of a new Communist state. In November 1984 alone, nearly nine hundred Afghan children under ten years of age were sent to the Soviet Union for ten years of schooling. But the principal result of the PDPA's war against Afghan civil society and the Soviet invasion and campaign to destroy the resistance was depopulation. Eventually, close to 2 million civilians lost their lives, out of a preinvasion population of 16 million; other millions fled across provincial or national lines, so that whole areas of the country became in effect uninhabited.[67] By 1989, "every ninth Afghan had died, every seventh had been disabled, and every third had fled [from home]."[68] It was an unparalleled catastrophe.

PDPA activists were not upset by these disasters, this massive killing and destruction. On the contrary, one official announced that even if only 1 million Afghans were in the end left alive, that would be sufficient to build a new socialist society.[69]

The Kabul Army

As the Soviets were invading Afghanistan, most of the Afghan army allowed itself to be disarmed by Russian advisers and troops. There were exceptions: the Afghan Eighth Division put up very stiff resistance and suffered heavy casualties as a consequence. Predictably, the postinvasion military performance of Kabul troops was so miserable that the Soviets, to their dismay, found themselves assuming a greater and greater share of the fighting.[70]

A major contributing factor in the poor showing by the regime army was the condition of the officer corps. The postinvasion officer corps consisted mostly of new men. What had happened to the eight thousand officers of the pre-1978 army? The Taraki-Amin government had killed great numbers of experienced officers because they were not Communists or because they belonged to the wrong PDPA faction. (Even as late as September 1982, General Wodud, commander of the Central Corps, was found shot dead in his office.) Many of the rest had gone into exile, accepted work in other government agencies, or joined the resistance.[71] Political interference with promotions and assignments also weakened and demoralized the officer corps. Most of the officers who belonged to the PDPA were Khalqis; hence the Babrak Karmal regime, as well as the Russians, distrusted them and gave them politically less critical assignments wherever possible.

As the fighting escalated, the standard training period for officers was cut from three years to two. The training period in the Kabul Military Academy was cut from five years to three months. Some officers who deserted to the resistance claimed that they had had only three months of training. Conditions among enlisted men were comparably bad. Aside from poor preparation and humiliating subservience to the Russian invaders, the Kabul troops were often improperly used. The 444th Commando Brigade, perhaps the best of the regime units, was decimated when it parachuted into the Panjshir Valley in the summer of 1985, in one of the numerous efforts to sweep the area.[72]

Above all, the army of the Kabul regime was being destroyed by the unwillingness of its members to remain in its ranks. Most of those who deserted just went home, but significant numbers wound up in the ranks of the resistance, often bringing their invaluable weapons with them. Of the eighty thousand men in the Afghan army on the eve of the invasion, more than half either deserted or defected to the resistance.[73]

The unreliability of the Kabul forces assumed alarming proportions even before the Soviet occupation. In May 1979, on the road between Gardez and Khost, the motorized brigade of the Afghan Seventh Division—the whole unit, two thousand officers and men, with their armored vehicles and heavy weapons—surrendered to the guerrillas without a fight. Mutinies among Kabul units, including the killing of officers, were common. Outside the defense perimeter of the capital city, Kabul troops during most of the war were completely unpredictable.

Soviet officers planned most, if not all, operations by Kabul forces. Suspecting members even of the highest ranks of the Kabul army of collaboration with the insurgents, the Soviets forced any Afghan, even a general officer, to submit to a search before entering the precincts of the Ministry of Defense. They eventually deprived their allies of what tanks and heavy weapons the resistance had not destroyed, for fear that these also would eventually fall into insurgent hands. So great became the distrust on the part of the Russians for the Kabul forces that the latter were not allowed to have on hand at any one time more than a week's supply of materiel. Conditions within the Kabul army eventually sank to such depths that the soldiers were required to turn in their weapons when not fighting. The Russians tried to increase the reliability of the Afghan army by training officers in the Soviet Union, but many of those so trained also deserted or defected.[74]

The PDPA regime used several methods to induce men to join its forces and to stay, rather than to desert or join the resistance. It sent conscripts to serve away from their home areas. The minefields that surrounded regime garrisons and forts served both to keep the mujahideen out and the troops in. Another method was accelerated promotion: one defecting officer told the mujahideen that of four hundred men in his unit, no less than twenty were brigadier generals. Army pay for officers was much higher than for comparable civilian jobs. Young men who joined the Kabul paramilitary forces were paid more than what a deputy minister received before the 1978 coup. Any tenth-grader who volunteered for the army would receive a twelfth-grade diploma after completion of his military service. Any eleventh-grader who volunteered would be guaranteed admission to any institution of higher education without having to take entrance examinations.[75]

These inducements were not enough. So the draft age was lowered to sixteen in 1984, and eventually the government declared that all males between the ages of fourteen and fifty were liable to conscription. These moves by the regime, as well as an increase in the duration of conscripted service from three years to four, contributed to mutinies and defections even in the Kabul area.[76] When the insurgents captured young regime conscripts, they usually either paroled them to their homes or incorporated them into the ranks of the resistance.

By the end of 1986, the Kabul armed forces consisted of about 30,000 regular troops, with 10,000 in the air force and perhaps another 40,000 in paramilitary units, secret police, and militia organizations. Relatively few new officers joined the PDPA, and often they did so because the resistance had asked them to infiltrate the party. And in the midst of all these perils and calamities, hostility between Khalq and Parcham raged unabated. Indeed, units commanded by Parchami officers sometimes clashed bloodily with units commanded by Khalqis.[77]

Overall, the army and the paramilitary units of the Kabul regime were "ill-treated, ill-led, unreliable, untrustworthy, riven with factionalism, and uncommitted to the regime in the rank and file."[78] Nevertheless, as Soviet troops began withdrawing, the willingness of some regime units to fight noticeably increased, for reasons to be discussed shortly.

Russian Wars in Central Asia

The Afghanistan imbroglio was of course not the first (or last) time that Russians found themselves fighting a determined Islamic foe in mountainous terrain. The conquest of the Caucasus between 1820 and 1860 offers a similar scenario, allowing an opportunity to study the classic Russian manner of dealing with this kind of military challenge.

Like Afghanistan, the Caucasus was inhabited by many different tribes. The mountains provided excellent possibilities both for guerrilla warfare and for guerrilla disunity. European visitors to the area described the inhabitants as brave, handsome, deeply religious, and punctiliously hospitable: "every man was a born rider, a keen swordsman, a good shot."[79]

The Russian method for defeating Central Asian peoples was perfected in these struggles. It had three components: (1) isolate the insurgent region, (2) destroy the insurgent leadership, and (3) devastate the local economy so that it could not sustain the guerrillas. To these ends, the Russians advanced slowly into the Caucasus, building roads and bridges before them, constructing lines of forts, laying waste to settlements, driving off or killing cattle, and—most important of all—bringing in enough troops to make all of these policies effective. Even so, from time to time forts in the Russian line would be overrun with heavy losses: for example in 1845, near the village of Dargo, on the border of Chechnya and Daghestan, insurgents killed or captured four thousand Russian soldiers, including three generals.[80]

The internal and external dimensions of the struggle to subdue the Caucasus grew complex. In later phases of the conflict, Christian populations in Georgia and Armenia supported the Russians against Muslim guerrillas. However, the resistance received encouragement and sometimes weapons from the Turks and the British.[81]

During the 1920s and 1930s the Soviet regime faced a serious rising in its Central Asian provinces, the so-called Basmachi Revolt. This was in essence an outright struggle between Russian Communism and Central Asian Islam. Predictably, tribal rivalries weakened the Basmachi insurgents, but their revolt was protracted, in part because the kingdom of Afghanistan allowed them to cross the border at will. Soviet troops also crossed into Afghanistan several times.[82]

The Russians sought with some success to further the fragmentation of their Central Asian subjects by encouraging the cultivation of local languages and dialects, with Russian as the sole lingua franca. The czarist army would normally not accept Central Asians for service. But the huge losses suffered by that army in World War I led to the imposition of the draft in Central Asia, a move that provoked massive and persistent riots. During World War II, the Germans were able to recruit many soldiers from the ranks of their Central Asian prisoners.

In the 1980s, most Central Asian subjects of the Soviet Union had inferior educations and hence were found in the lower ranks of the Soviet Army and in the less technical and noncombat branches of the service. This situation encouraged many ethnic Russians to believe that the blood cost of the war inside Afghanistan was being borne in undue proportion by young Russians.[83]

Soviet Strategy in Afghanistan

From one perspective, the invasion of Afghanistan by the Soviets was a great success and an operational model. But the Soviets were surprised and dismayed by two factors on which they had not counted: one was the widespread and determined internal opposition to their occupation of the country; the other was the amount of foreign help to this resistance.

When the Soviets invaded their southern neighbor, they expected that Kabul forces would do most of what fighting needed to be done. (Brezhnev had said, "It'll be over in three or four weeks.")[84] By January 1980 there were only about fifty thousand Soviet troops in Afghanistan, many of them Central Asian reservists recently mobilized; the invasion of Czechoslovakia a decade earlier had been on a much larger scale. But the intensity of popular resistance, as well as the reluctance to fight and the tendency to desert or defect on the part of the Kabul troops, made it clear that the Soviets were going to have to carry a very much bigger burden of combat than originally planned. Scott McMichael writes that "in what must be considered a gross failure of intelligence and strategic assessment, the Soviets completely underestimated the strength, vitality and resilience of the resistance and vastly overestimated the feasibility of regenerating the Afghan [PDPA regime] armed forces."[85] (The Russian Army fell victim to incredibly poor intelligence again in 1994, in the invasion of Chechnya.) The Soviets were never able to adjust to the Afghan situation effectively because Moscow, for reasons that have not become completely clear (at least not to this author), never committed enough troops to Afghanistan to do the job.

By the end of 1984, the Soviets had 115,000 military personnel in Afghanistan; this number was raised to 120,000 by 1987, with perhaps 30,000 immediately over the Soviet border in support. Some 22,000 of these troops were holding down Kabul. These numbers amounted to a mere 4 percent of the total Soviet ground forces. Only perhaps 6 of 194 Soviet combat divisions were in Afghanistan on a full-time basis. Admittedly, more than 50 percent of these forces were combat troops, a much higher ratio than the Americans ever reached in Vietnam. But after subtracting garrison security forces, the Soviets were left with only about one battalion in each province for offensive operations—that is, going hunting for guerrillas. Even with their Kabul allies, the Soviets never remotely approached the ten-to-one ratio of government troops to insurgents that many students of guerrilla warfare have believed is a necessary condition for victory. According to the new *U.S. Army/Marine Corps Counterinsurgency Field Manual*, instead of the classic ten-to-one ratio, "a better force requirement gauge is troop density, the ratio of security forces including the host nation's military and police forces as well as foreign counterinsurgents to inhabitants. Most density recommendations fall within a range of 20 to 25 counterinsurgents for every 1000 residents in an [Area of Operations]." To reach even this relatively modest standard, Soviet and Kabul forces would have had to number between 325,000 and 375,000.[86]

The Soviets consequently had to adopt a strategy dictated by the inadequate number of their troops in the field. They eventually settled on a modified enclave strategy. In essence it consisted of five elements:

1. Holding Kabul and other main cities in sufficient force to prevent expulsion.
2. Protecting communications between these cities. Soviet supply lines were long: Kabul is well over 250 miles from the Soviet border; Qandahar is 370 miles away from Herat. Control of the roads was so tenuous that Soviet bases and even the garrisons in big towns had to be supplied mainly and sometimes exclusively by aircraft.
3. Clearing the northern Afghan provinces of guerrillas in order

to safeguard supply routes to Soviet forces in Kabul and to prevent any spillover of fighting from northern Afghanistan into the Muslim provinces of the USSR.

4. Launching periodic sweeps to break up mujahideen concentrations or seize their strongholds.
5. Interdicting supplies and infiltrators from Pakistan and Iran.

As the conflict dragged on, Soviet strategy expanded to include:

6. Building up a Sovietized Afghan elite that was expected to eventually take over the war and run the country and
7. Destroying systematically the economy of those provinces that the Soviets did not control.[87]

The main mujahideen supply source was Peshawar, capital of Pakistan's North-West Frontier Province, located at one end of the storied Khyber Pass. The U.S. Central Intelligence Agency bought Soviet-made weapons from the Egyptians and sent them to Pakistan. For the soldiers to block these supplies was close to impossible: "Soviet border strategy was based on maintaining a multitude of posts, large and small, close to Pakistan. They were intended to seal the border and interdict our [Pakistani] supply routes. It was rather like a person trying to shut off a large tap by putting his hand over it."[88] The Soviets also tried, unsuccessfully, to close mountain passes with aerial mines. During its engagement in Vietnam, the United States sent forces into Laos and Cambodia to destroy sanctuaries and supply lines for its enemies, but Soviet ground forces did not make any serious move into Pakistan, however great the temptation must have been.

Soviet Counterinsurgency

No doubt to the surprise of many—very many—the conflict in Afghanistan turned into a cruel and reputation-wrecking experience for the Soviet armed forces. Why did that happen?

Before the invasion of Afghanistan, the Soviet Army possessed a widespread image as a fearsome fighting force, mainly because of its size but also because of its undeniably impressive achievements against Germany in World War II. But in that conflict, the Russian soldier was defending his home against a brutal invader; in Afghanistan he was the invader. Moreover, between the surrender of Nazi Germany in May 1945 and the invasion of Afghanistan in December 1979, the Soviet Army had had less combat experience than the armies of Britain, China, Egypt, France, India, Israel, Pakistan, Portugal, South Vietnam, or the United States. Probably for this reason, the Soviet Army sought to give as many of its officers as possible a "turn" at the Afghanistan combat; it was a policy similar to that pursued by the United States in Vietnam and presumably with a similar negative impact on army effectiveness. The so-called Afghan Brotherhood within the Soviet Army might eventually have replaced the dominance of those who served in "the West" (World War II) with those who served in "the South."[89]

Not only was the Soviet Army that invaded Afghanistan a force untested in major combat for decades, but it had been built, much like the American army, to wage World War III, to fight NATO in Central Europe, not mountaineers in Central Asia.[90] In Soviet military planning, "future war was seen as a lethal, high tempo event where forces and firepower were carefully choreographed. Consequently, Soviet tactics were simple. They were designed to be implemented rapidly by conscripts and reservists."[91] This is a real clue as to why Soviet forces did well in the actual invasion itself but not well at all in the long campaign to subdue the recalcitrant rural population.

Before Afghanistan, Soviet armed forces had actually accumulated a fairly wide range of experience with counterinsurgency. In the 1940s and early 1950s they had waged a fierce campaign to exterminate guerrillas in the Ukraine. But since that grim struggle was officially a secret, even a nonevent, there were no serious studies on the topic for wide use by the army. Later, the Soviets assisted friendly Third World governments fighting against guerrillas. Almost everywhere—in Angola, Cambodia, Ethiopia, and Mozambique—Soviet assistance produced disappointing results. The lackluster Soviet record on counterinsurgency in the Third World had several causes.

In the first place, no Soviet doctrine for waging a counterinsurgency existed. For this grave deficiency, Marxist-Leninist ideology as interpreted by the Soviets must receive its share of blame. According to that worldview, rebellions were by definition waged by the oppressed against capitalist exploitation. Hence, there was no need for a Soviet doctrine about fighting against rebellions. Even after nine years of war in Afghanistan, the Soviet Union had not produced a single manual for counterinsurgency. Second, the Soviets were generally unsuccessful in denying the guerrillas outside assistance and sanctuaries. Third, they sought to have the army of the local regime that they were assisting do most if not all of the real fighting. This was a good idea, but Soviet efforts to create or expand indigenous forces capable of carrying out such a responsibility were largely unsuccessful, Afghanistan being merely the most egregious case. Finally, but by no means least in importance, the Soviets, and the states they controlled or influenced, would not address the root causes of the local insurgencies they faced, namely unpopular (often disastrous) government policies. The Soviet method for dealing with Third World societies (or any society in their grip) consisted of centralized political control, suppression of criticism, and a bureaucratized, collectivized economy, including agriculture. Predictably, these policies aggravated rather than alleviated the conditions that produce the insurgency. Thus, modern Soviet counterinsurgency doctrine was woefully underdeveloped.[92]

The Condition of the Soviet Army

The army that the Kremlin sent into Afghanistan of course reflected in many ways the larger society from which it was drawn. Soviet forces were supposed to be a paradigm of an idealized Soviet society: "disciplined, effective, loyal, and wholly at the disposal of the elite who alone had the facts and the authority to be able to judge the best course of action to take."[93] Accordingly, centralization, rigidity, and punishment for failure discouraged initiative among the junior officers, a really fatal handicap in fighting guerrillas, where so much depends on small-unit action and local decision making. (A U.S. Marine Corps study advised, "Subordinate commanders must make decisions on their own initiative, based on their understanding of their seniors' intent, rather than passing information up the chain of command and waiting for the decision to be passed down.")[94]

Moreover, explains Mark Galeotti,

the [Soviet] army's training program . . . presupposed a draft intake [of young men] thoroughly prepared for military discipline, physically fit and already possessing basic military skills courtesy of an interlocking trinity of programs developed for this purpose: the Party's youth movements, schooltime basic military training, and voluntary military sports . . . but this whole edifice was manifestly crumbling and in disrepair.[95]

When young Soviet draftees arrived at their military camp, it looked more like a labor camp, a place where "frightened, half-trained boys [were] kept behind barbed wire, pacified with vodka, until the armed military policemen came to herd them to their plane like convicts."[96] Beatings, rape, actual murders of younger soldiers, even of noncommissioned officers, by older ones were everyday occurrences.[97] Hundreds of young conscripts perished annually from physical or nervous exhaustion or from suicide.[98]

After surviving such ordeals, many Soviet privates arrived in Afghanistan with less than a month's training.[99] In their classic study *Afghanistan: The Bear Trap*, Yousaf and Adkin wrote:

What puzzled me as a professional soldier was the almost total lack of even basic training given to men who were posted to operational [fighting] units in the early days of the war. It was quite normal for a recruit to go on operations with only three weeks training behind him. Even worse was the prisoner who described how, during his first six weeks in the Army, he was merely given food and a uniform, no weapon and no training at all. Then he was posted to Afghanistan . . . where he was immediately sent on village clearing and house-to-house searches, looking for Chinese, American or Pakistani mercenaries. Initially, this man explained, he had to rely on his lessons on the AK-47 that he had received as a twelve-year-old school boy.[100]

Even noncommissioned officers often had little experience or training.

In Afghanistan, the Soviet Army hurled into mountain warfare thousands of youths who had probably never even seen a real mountain; indeed, "it is hard to imagine a war to which Russia's conscript army would be less well-suited than a counter-insurgency in mountainous Afghanistan." Among many other disadvantages it imposes on attacking forces, mountainous terrain compels them to break down into smaller components that may not be in contact with one another and hence cannot support one another, exposing them to the danger of being destroyed piecemeal. Thus, to their profound dismay, "the Soviets came to realize that terrain and climate [occupied] first place above all other factors in terms of their influence on destroying the enemy."[101]

Unsurprisingly, such troops often underperformed in the real or supposed presence of the enemy. Poor tactics became worse: "Many times [Soviet soldiers] would not leave their armored vehicles. Or at the last moment [would not] push forward an assault to clinch a victory. They were also scared of night operations. Everything stopped at night. There were no convoys, no movements, no attacks, and very few patrols during darkness." These conditions of course did not prevail among the elite Special Purpose Forces–the "Spetsnaz"—but as late as 1986, "the performance of the average conscripted Soviet soldier remained unimpressive."[102]

Efficient tactical communications, especially by radio, are of the essence in counterinsurgency, but deficiencies in this area plagued the Soviets throughout their experience in Afghanistan. The problem stemmed from faulty and inadequate equipment and methods, and poor training as well. One author concludes that "the widespread deficiencies in tactical communications [were] fully reflective of endemic Soviet inflexibility, lack of imagination, . . . and reluctance to depart from rote, textbook procedures, even when they [did not] work."[103]

Quite apart from combat, for all too many of the rank and file, everyday life in the Soviet Army was totally miserable: "Living conditions were harsh. Even in Kabul camps were often tented, with forty men living in each throughout the winter, packed around a single stove in the center. In the field, the soldiers received sleeping bags that were made of cotton, and not waterproof."[104] Poor diet and worse hygiene gravely lessened the efficiency of the troops. Many soldiers were hungry much of the time. Their rations were insufficient in quantity and lacked both variety and vitamins; they rarely consumed fruit or vegetables.[105] The Soviet soldiers' poor food harmed them in other ways as well: "Soviet field rations came in shiny cans. Digging in the mountains was difficult, so the Soviet soldier threw his empty ration cans around his fighting or ambush position, easy to spot by Mujahideen reconnaissance."[106] And there was more: "Soldiers would often go a month without a shower, and water—especially drinking water—was universally scarce. Not surprisingly, the primitive conditions and the (especially at first) cavalier attitude of the army toward hygiene favoured the spread of a variety of infectious diseases, gastric disorders, lice and parasites."[107] In effect, the Soviet Army was its own worst enemy: "Disease cut into units' present-for-duty strength in Afghanistan as poor field sanitation practices and poor diet contributed to the spread of [sickness]. From one-quarter to one-third of a unit's strength was normally sick with hepatitis, typhus, malaria, amoebic dysentery, and meningitis."[108]

The effects of all this neglect were predictable but nonetheless staggering. Colonel David M. Glantz writes:

Soviet dead and missing in Afghanistan amounted to almost 15,000 troops, a modest percent of the 642,000 Soviets who served during the ten year war. And the dead tell no tales at home. Far more telling were the 469,685 casualties, fully 73% of the overall force, who ultimately returned home to the Soviet Union. Even more appalling were the numbers of troops who fell victim to disease (415,932), of which 115,308 suffered from infectious hepatitis and 31,080 from typhoid fever. Beyond the sheer magnitude of these numbers is what these figures say about Soviet military hygiene and the conditions surrounding troop life. *These numbers are unheard of in modern armies and modern medicine.*[109]

Even if Soviet soldiers returned to Russia unwounded or relatively healthy, the Afghan conflict followed them. An English visitor to Moscow recorded this incident: "I can still squirm at the memory of eating in a restaurant as two perfectly sober and polite young army officers with combat decorations were chased off. The solicitous maitre d'hôtel rushed back to reassure us that this was not the sort of establishment where 'that sort' could be expected to eat."[110]

In the early months of the conflict, most of the Soviet Muslim troops originally sent into Afghanistan had to be withdrawn because of indiscipline and unwillingness to fight, as well as inability to speak Russian well or at all.[111] Russian civilians at home resentfully concluded from events like this that the miserable Afghanistan conflict was a "Slav war" that fell disproportionately on ethnic Russians. But in fact, according to one acerbic commentator, "the burden rested where it always has, whether in a capitalist society or the self-proclaimed 'proletarian state,' on the poor, the ill-educated, the un-streetwise, the workers; the same victims of the system who were to serve out their lives in the cheerless drudgery of the machine shop or the farm, raising a new generation of disenfranchised underclass to fill their shoes in turn."[112]

The Soviet Army against Guerrillas

A standard Western method of fighting guerrillas, as set forth in the manuals, is to try to separate them from the civilian population and to gain the goodwill of the latter. That was not the Soviet way. At certain points in the war in Afghanistan, they made some efforts at winning over the religious leaders (mullahs) by preaching the compatibility of Marxism and Islam, by helping to repair mosques, and so forth. But this was not their dominant approach. Winning hearts and minds was not their style, "but rather wholesale destruction, the killing of civilians, or the driving of them into exile." In summary, "often, Soviet actions seemed deliberately designed to harden the resolve of the resistance."[113]

The Soviets' overall strategy was to drain the water in which the guerrillas might swim: to remove or destroy any civilian population friendly to, or even close by, the guerrillas.[114] To this end the Soviets sought, with much success, to empty the provinces along both the Soviet and the Pakistan borders by forced migration. But since virtually the whole country rose against the Soviets and their Kabul puppets, this policy of devastation was eventually employed in almost every province.

According to the report of the human-rights organization Helsinki Watch, the Soviets waged a campaign of deliberate terror against the civilian population. They systematically bombed villages, attacked columns of refugees, chopped down orchards, and killed or maimed animals.[115] In the presence of Kabul troops, the Soviets were usually more restrained. In October 1981, when the resistance captured a noted Soviet geologist and offered him in exchange for fifty Afghan hostages, the Soviets simply killed all the hostages. A report issued by the United Nations in the fall of 1982 indicated that the Soviets had used chemical weapons, and they apparently employed poison gas while campaigning in the Panjshir Valley in the spring of 1984. They trained children to act as saboteurs and even assassins. Responsible observers have accused them of the deliberate and repeated bombings of hospitals.[116] Finally, numerous witnesses have testified that Soviet aircraft often dropped explosive devices in the shape of toys and pens. Dr. Claude Malhuret, executive director of Médecins sans Frontières, wrote, "Their main targets are children, whose hands and arms are blown off."[117]

By the first anniversary of the invasion, Soviet policies had created 1.5 million Afghan refugees. After a few more years, that number had risen to more than 4 million Afghan men, women, and children; nobody knows how many died or were simply killed. In 1985, perhaps one Afghan in three was an internal or external refugee.[118] One result of Soviet devastation was that Kabul's population doubled, from nine hundred thousand to more than 2 million. As a percentage of the total population, more Afghans perished at the hands of the Soviets than Russians had at the hands of the Nazis. Soviet claims that this disaster, what the anthropologist Louis Dupree has called "migratory genocide,"[119] resulted from the machinations of native reactionaries and CIA troublemakers were grotesque. The outside world, for the most part, tried with varying degrees of success to ignore the Soviets' crimes.[120] But justice—elementary justice—demands recognition that the refugees, inside Afghanistan, in Pakistan, and in Iran, were not an accidental or unavoidable consequence of war; they were an intended, engineered result, "a part of Soviet warfare strategy."[121]

By dispersing the population, the Soviet scorched-earth policy seriously damaged the infrastructure of the resistance. Nevertheless, the mujahideen were not defeated, because they continued to receive supplies from outside, as well as intelligence from both Pakistani agencies and sympathizers within the Kabul government.[122]

Young Soviet conscripts had been told that they were in Afghanistan to save the people. What they actually encountered severely shook many of them. In Mark Galeotti's stark terms, "when Soviet soldiers could crouch down in their foxholes and read in their newspapers that they were distributing loaves of bread and medicine to happy Afghan peasants, the whole episode was a case study in duplicity, the moral bankruptcy and the practical failings of the Brezhnevian order."[123] Until 1988 military tombstones were not permitted to say that the soldier had died in Afghanistan.[124] Lying about the war only opened floodgates of rumor about how many were being killed, discrimination against Baltic and Caucasian peoples, and so forth. One Russian journalist, insisting that the regime greatly under-reported troop losses, estimated that twenty thousand Soviet troops had lost their lives in Afghanistan by May 1981. The wide perception of blatant official mendacity, along with the barbarous treatment of civilians and the harsh living conditions, go far to account for the increasing incidents of theft and sale of military equipment by Soviet soldiers to the resistance in return for drugs, including heroin.[125]

As a general statement, counterinsurgency is a light infantry-man's war, but "throughout the [Afghanistan] war, the Soviets were hampered by lack of sufficient infantry forces."[126] The mujahideen, in contrast, "were natural light infantry."[127] Thus, the Soviet insuf-ficiency of training and inadequacy of numbers magnified each other. These factors, considered together with the difficult terrain and mujahideen familiarity with Soviet tactics, explain why Soviet encirclement operations so often failed.

But if "the Soviet Army never had enough forces in Afghanistan to win," why didn't it?[128] Why didn't Moscow send enough troops into Afghanistan? Apparently, because "enough" might well have been far more than the regime could afford, logistically or financially or politically. Besides, a major escalation of numbers would not necessarily have guaranteed victory but might well have led to a major incursion into Pakistan, with unpredictable and possibly quite disastrous consequences. From these circumstances arose the Soviet reliance on special forces. But the elite airborne and air assault units, while often quite effective, were not very abundant, and even these were often understrength.[129]

In spite of this deplorable array of daunting handicaps, the So-viet Army did learn, slowly, in combat, a very expensive education indeed. Eventually the Soviets gave up their costly and generally ineffective valley sweep operations. They placed more emphasis on such classic counterinsurgency tactics as using ambushes against the guerrillas, preceding convoys by tanks without turrets and with mine-detecting rollers on the front, and rapidly airlifting small, well-trained detachments of Spetsnaz troops, of which perhaps five thousand were in Afghanistan in 1986.[130] Nevertheless, at the end of the fighting as at the beginning, the bulk of Soviet forces—motorized rifle units—were road-bound.

The Stinger

Things would certainly have been much worse for the Soviets had it not been for their helicopter gunships. In February 1980, and again in April, antiregime and anti-Soviet riots gripped Kabul. The Soviets strafed the crowds with these gunships, killing hundreds. But it was against guerrillas, not against civilian rioters, that the Soviets found the best use for the helicopter. Indeed, it proved to be their most effective weapon. The number of helicopters in use in Afghanistan rose from 60 in mid-1980 to more than 300 by the end of 1981. Helicopter gunships provided the Russians with the kind of firepower normally obtainable only from tanks—in the mountains, where tanks cannot operate effectively. Gunships escorted convoys passing along especially vulnerable sections of mountain roads. But helicopters are relatively slow and not very maneuverable, and they can be easily hurt, especially their rotor blades, as the Americans learned to their great cost in Vietnam. In January 1982, mujahideen in Paktia Province were able to down a helicopter whose crash resulted in the death of a Soviet lieutenant general.[131] Nevertheless, until the resistance was able to obtain heavy machine guns in 1983, there was little defense against the gunships. In 1986 the Russians introduced new helicopters with armored bottoms almost totally immune to machine-gun fire; consequently, the "lack of an effective and suitable anti-aircraft weapon was the most serious defect in the Mujahideen armoury."[132]

Nevertheless, the period of nearly complete Soviet domination of the battlefield through the helicopter was coming to an end. In 1983, using surface-to-air missiles (SAMs), resistance fighters shot down several helicopters near Khost. The introduction of SAMs sent waves of panic throughout the Soviet establishment in Afghanistan. Nobody knew how many of these SAMs the freedom fighters had, but knowledge that any at all were in hostile hands persuaded all pilots to fly higher than was effective. Then, toward the latter half of 1986, the United States began providing the resistance with the excellent Stinger missile, a one-man, easy-to-use, surface-to-air missile launcher.

Pakistan's president Zia had initially opposed the introduction of Stingers into Afghanistan. If one of the weapons fell into Soviet hands, how could Pakistan continue to deny it was allowing direct U.S. support to the mujahideen? And besides, terrorists might use captured or stolen Stingers against Zia's own personal airplane.[133]

Along the same lines, the U.S. Army and the CIA opposed providing Stingers to the resistance for fear that the technology would be obtained by the Soviets or by terrorists (one resistance chief sold eighteen Stingers to Iran). Another reason for CIA opposition was that the Stingers would make the conflict look like one between the USSR and the United States instead of between the USSR and the Afghan people. The State Department also opposed sending Stingers, mainly because such a move would escalate tensions with the USSR.[134]

During 1986, the Soviets were mounting much more aggressive attacks against the mujahideen, whose morale and effectiveness were noticeably diminishing. Hence, objections to delivering Stingers to the insurgents were overcome, and these priceless weapons began to reach the mujahideen by the fall of 1986. (Unaccountably, Shah Massoud, probably the best of all the insurgent leaders, received none of these weapons.)[135] It had always been very dangerous for the resistance to stand and fight against Soviet and Kabul forces because of the probability of air attacks. The Soviets had been relying more and more on their total control of the air to surprise mujahideen units and devastate civilian villages. But the Stinger went far to neutralize the effectiveness of the helicopter gunship: painfully aware that the resistance possessed these weapons, Soviet and Kabul pilots flew at inefficiently high altitudes, while daylight airlifts of supplies and troops became rare. The Stinger missile was a war-altering weapon; it "robbed the Soviet forces of their command of the air."[136] Indeed, "the [mujahideen's] acquisition of surface-to-air missiles was critical to their ability to counter . . . Soviet tactics. Since late 1986, when SAMs were used in significant numbers, the Mujahideen were able to move without constant fear of Soviet helicopter attacks."[137] Late in 1986 the Soviets launched a major offensive based on air mobility and Spetsnaz units, but the Stinger noticeably limited the success of the operation. By sharply diminishing the value of Soviet airpower, the Stinger truly changed the course of the war.[138] In one authority's judgment, the Stinger "convinced the Soviet command that the war was not winnable for them, neither then nor later."[139]

The vigor of the resistance and the inadequacy of Soviet and Kabul force levels led inexorably to the most appalling aspect of the entire war: the Soviet policy of depopulating the main insurgent areas. But the resulting destruction, extensive and systematic, was in vain. The mujahideen held on until the Soviets finally returned to their own country in a state of total frustration and deep humiliation.

Their lack of good counterguerrilla doctrine, which led to employing systematic brutality toward the civilian population, made the Soviets' experience in Afghanistan far different from what they had expected at the time of the invasion. Indeed, for one authoritative observer, "the most significant effect of the war in Afghanistan was the loss of the Soviet military's image of invincibility."[140] And even after so many defects and shortcomings of the Soviet Army had become glaringly apparent in Afghanistan, little had been done to correct the situation by the time Russian forces attacked Chechnya.

The Course of the War

The revolt against the Kabul regime began in October 1978, more than a year before the Soviet invasion. In the following March, serious fighting in Herat, the country's third-largest city, took the lives of hundreds of Afghan Communists and Soviet personnel. Thousands of civilians died during the restoration of regime control in that city.[141] By November 1979, a month before the Soviet invasion, insurgent forces dominated Badakhshan Province (the link with China) and most of the Hazarajat, in the center of the country.

During 1980, demonstrations and strikes rocked Kabul. Because Afghan soldiers often refused to fire on student demonstrators, Soviet troops were called in and did much killing. Because of the Soviets' very conservative strategy—holding key cities and the roads between them—and their lack of confidence in the Kabul army, there were few sizable operations during the first year of Soviet occupation and for much of 1981. The road-bound, mountain-hating Soviet Army thus failed to take advantage of mujahideen disunity, lack of equipment, and inexperience with up-to-date guerrilla techniques. More than half of the country was under insurgent control by the end of 1980.[142] In April 1981, mujahideen killed the deputy head of KHAD in Kabul. That same month and again in September, insurgents briefly overran Qandahar, the country's second-largest city (named after Alexander the Great). By the end of 1981, every single Afghan province was experiencing some form of armed resistance.

Pacification efforts were much more elaborate during 1982. The Panjshir Valley lies about sixty miles northeast of Kabul; in resistance hands it would threaten the capital, the vital Bagram air base, and road communications between Kabul and the Soviet Union. About 14,000 Soviet and Kabul troops attacked the 5,000 insurgents in the valley under Massoud. After campaigning hard for six weeks and suffering 3,000 casualties and 2,000 defections, the Soviet-Kabul forces withdrew.[143] Increased Soviet combat activity after 1982 of course meant increased casualties.

By the end of 1983, the insurgents had extended their control to about two-thirds of the territory and three-quarters of the population. The Soviets again bombed the city of Herat, killing several thousand civilians. The insurgents in turn carried out increasingly frequent and deadly attacks inside Kabul; they hit the Soviet Embassy with mortar shells and assassinated numerous Kabul-regime officials and collaborators. As the fourth year of the Soviet occupation drew to a close, resistance casualties probably totaled between 50,000 and 100,000, and regime casualties between 50,000 and 60,000.[144]

During 1984, the Soviets greatly increased their operations. For big offensive movements, they no longer used mainly conscripted units but instead deployed trained mountain fighters. They again attacked the Panjshir Valley, this time with 20,000 Soviet troops, five hundred armored vehicles, and thousands of Kabul soldiers—and again they failed. The Soviets could not sustain these conventional offensives for more than a few weeks, because of manpower and logistic problems. In June the Soviets launched a massive effort around Herat, forcing some insurgent groups to retreat into Iran. High-altitude saturation bombing was a common feature of these campaigns, and Soviet forces also looted the city of Qandahar twice during the month of October.[145] Concerted efforts were made to assassinate key insurgent leaders. Radio Kabul announced the death of Ahmed Shah Massoud, the

"Lion of the Panjshir," but the announcement turned out to be quite premature. Many of these antimujahideen assassination attempts, especially by KHAD, failed because the targets of the attacks were tipped off in time. Massoud and his forces survived no less than nine Soviet-directed offensives against them.

After five years of occupation, close to ten thousand Soviets and their wives (no children) lived in a specially constructed ghetto in Kabul, surrounded by barbed wire, armed guards, and intense danger.[146] Life in Kabul had never been secure, but during 1984 conditions deteriorated. In March alone, fifteen PDPA officials were killed by the resistance in just one area of the city.[147] On August 31, a bomb was set off at Kabul International Airport; less than a month later another action inside the capital destroyed a dozen Soviet armored vehicles and killed numerous Kabul-regime troops.[148]

The year 1985 opened with the disruption of the PDPA's anniversary celebration by a mujahideen rocket barrage. The arrival of a new Soviet commander, General Mikhail Zaitsev, heralded a series of major offensives in Kunar and Paktia provinces and the much-fought-over Panjshir Valley. The Paktia operation, employing fifteen thousand Communist troops, including at least three Soviet regiments, ended in defeat. By destroying bridges and making many roads impossibly dangerous, the insurgents were thwarting the basic Soviet strategy of maintaining communications between the occupied cities. The insurgents were now acquiring heavy weapons; above all, they improved their air defense. With Soviet airpower reduced, ambushes of convoys increased in effectiveness.[149] The resistance enjoyed some less strategic but quite spectacular successes in 1985; in June, for instance, under the leadership of Massoud, they attacked the five-hundred-man, tank-defended fort at Pechgur, capturing almost all the troops and many weapons. Life in the capital became even more dangerous, with attacks on the airport and the Soviet Embassy, even stabbings of Soviet officials in the streets. At the end of the sixth year of Soviet occupation, the war in Afghanistan, at a higher level of fighting than ever before, had clearly become a stalemate.

In January 1986, the Kabul regime proclaimed a six-month cease-fire, but neither that regime's troops nor the Soviets reduced their operations against the resistance under this or subsequent so-called cease-fires. Looking for a scapegoat, the Soviets dumped their puppet

Babrak Karmal and replaced him as boss of the PDPA with the head of the secret police, the Pushtun Mohammed Najibullah, a onetime physician. The Soviets were improving their tactics; in the spring they occupied and destroyed the resistance complex at Zhawar, a grave blow.[150] By now, mass defections by Kabul troops had practically ceased; sometimes they would actually stand and fight and even win an engagement. The insurgents still had not learned to specialize (for example, after all these years there were still no skilled sappers among them); they had not yet held an entire provincial capital for any length of time; and KHAD agents had penetrated their organizations.

But the guerrillas had even more thoroughly penetrated the regime: it was very difficult for Kabul or the Soviets to mount surprise attacks because of the omnipresence of resistance agents and sympathizers. A regime fort at Ferkhar fell to the resistance in September, with three hundred of its defenders killed or captured. The security situation in Kabul continued to deteriorate.[151] Very significantly, Massoud was now deploying units of up to 120 men who were willing to fight anywhere in the entire north, not just in their local areas. This development greatly increased the ability of the guerrillas to concentrate against sizable targets.

By 1987, Kabul and the Soviets controlled about 35 percent of the country's territory, with about another 20 percent in dispute (of course any precise definition of "control" would be difficult to arrive at). At the same time, the insurgents were receiving better equipment from abroad, they now had permanent bases in strongly defended mountain areas, and their various leaders were cooperating more closely. In Paktia Province (a key area on the Pakistan border), a major Soviet-Kabul operation, including air strikes, heavy artillery, and assaults by Spetsnaz commandos, was repulsed with heavy casualties; the cooperation of several different resistance groups, enhanced by good logistics and buoyed by the participation of political leaders from Peshawar, made the difference. A major Soviet effort to open the road between Gardez and Khost, closed by the guerrillas since 1979, also failed. The resistance demonstrated increasing willingness to target Soviet forces and operate in Soviet-controlled areas during 1987. Mortar shells continued to hit the Soviet Embassy in Kabul and rockets often fell on the Bagram air base (north of the capital, the most important Soviet installation in the country).[152] Insurgent forces often disrupted oil supplies and electricity to Kabul; as a result, in the capital, "winters were bleak, cold and lightless."[153]

Because the resistance increasingly used long-range artillery, the Soviets had to expand and multiply the security perimeters around Kabul. But the insurgents easily penetrated these defensive rings around the capital and other occupied cities. For one thing, the Soviet troops were reluctant to come out of their posts at night. Insurgents sometimes slipped through by disguising themselves as regime troops. Often they bribed Afghan guards, or the latter simply let them pass through to avoid the inevitable consequences of refusal.[154]

During the summer, Soviet garrisons abandoned several outlying posts, leaving most of the country without any Soviet presence at all. In July insurgent units stormed Kalafgan, less than fifty miles from the Soviet border, seizing priceless artillery. For the first time the Soviets acknowledged that the resistance had raided the territory of the Soviet Union itself, although reports of such forays into the USSR had appeared in the Western press years earlier.[155] *Izvestia* provided an interesting indicator of the growing power of the resistance by charging that the mujahideen were being trained by instructors from Pakistan, France, Saudi Arabia, the United States, China, Egypt, Iran, and Britain—even Japan.[156]

The World Watches the War

Late in 1988, diplomats and international relief workers estimated that 3 million Afghan men, women, and children had died as a direct result of the war. Three-quarters of Afghanistan's villages were destroyed or abandoned. Tens of thousands of inhabitants had been maimed for life. One-third of the prewar population of 16 million had fled across one or another border, producing the world's largest refugee mass. "Moscow," said the *Washington Post*, was "committing one of the world's great crimes."[157]

Yet the response to this genocide by what some people actually refer to as the "international community" was shockingly low-key: "The discrepancy between the magnitude of the tragedy and the paucity of the international attention it received worked very much to Moscow's advantage."[158] The Soviets counted on being able to carry out this genocide in relative secrecy, with the world simply pretending to forget about Afghanistan. The Soviets from time to time issued threats against foreign journalists who might be captured in the company of mujahideen,[159] but the lack of concern on the part of the world's press greatly assisted Moscow in its actions.[160]

But help was coming. The most essential foreign supporter of the freedom fighters was Pakistan. That neighboring country provided a home to millions of Afghan victims of war, and all the important Afghan political parties made their headquarters in the city of Peshawar, at the Pakistan end of the Khyber Pass. Most of all, Pakistan allowed its territory to be used for transshipment of aid into Afghanistan. The fourteen-hundred-mile-long Afghanistan-Pakistan border, with its countless mountain passes, was the lifeline of the resistance. Corrupt Pakistani officials siphoned off some of the aid flowing through Pakistan from the outside world, and sometimes old weapons replaced new ones. Yet without the support of the Pakistani government, it is not easy to see how the Afghan resistance would have survived. Pakistan took big risks to assist the mujahideen. Many ethnic groups overlap the border between Pakistan and Afghanistan, and the Soviets promised to punish Pakistan by stirring up Baluchi and Pushtun nationalism, a menace to the country's very survival.[161] If the Soviet leaders had decided to make an all-out effort against the huge resistance infrastructure across Afghanistan's eastern border, Pakistan would have been in mortal peril. But the Soviets held back from a major blow, no doubt influenced by the official hostility toward its Afghanistan policy of all the world's other great powers, from the United States to China, from West Germany to Japan. In January 1980, China's foreign minister visited Pakistan's President Zia; President Carter's national security adviser Brzezinski arrived in February. In June 1981, the Chinese premier paid a well-publicized visit to a refugee camp near Peshawar. Two years later, U.S. secretary of state George Shultz told refugees in Pakistan, "We are with you." Even so, many in Pakistan paid with their lives for the policy of assisting the insurgency: in 1984 alone, Soviet air and artillery "errors" killed at least two hundred Pakistanis.[162]

Other Muslim states also supported the resistance. In January and again in May 1980, conferences of foreign ministers of Islamic countries condemned the Soviet invasion. Aside from Pakistan,

Saudi Arabia was the first and for a while the only country to give aid to the mujahideen. President Anwar Sadat of Egypt supplied weapons that he had received from the Soviets before his break with them in 1972.[163] Resistance leaders were invited to various world Islamic conferences. On the other hand, in 1987 the infamous Saddam Hussein received the Kabul prime minister in Baghdad; it was the highest-level reception up to that point for a member of the puppet government outside the Soviet bloc.[164] Soviet clients and semiclients such as Syria, South Yemen, and the PLO gave at least verbal support to the Kabul regime. And the noisy and ludicrously named Non-Aligned Movement accomplished absolutely nothing for the suffering millions of Afghanistan.

In Iran, the postrevolutionary leadership was more bitter against the United States than against the Russians. Even after the Soviet genocide in Afghanistan became well known, the Iranians gave most of their attention after September 1980 to their murderous conflict with neighboring Iraq. Nevertheless, Teheran included mujahideen leaders in its own delegation to the May 1980 Islamic Conference (from which Kabul's representatives were banned) and supplied arms to particular resistance groups, almost exclusively drawn from Afghanistan's Shia minority. More than once Soviet units in pursuit of fleeing insurgents crossed into Iran.[165]

China steadfastly supported Pakistan, its only friend in the region. The leadership in Beijing saw the Soviet occupation of Afghanistan as another move in a gigantic Soviet encirclement of China that included Vietnam, India, and Mongolia. Beijing repeatedly declared the withdrawal of all Soviet forces from Afghanistan to be a precondition for improved relations between the two Communist behemoths.[166] The Chinese sent rocket launchers, heavy artillery, and assault rifles into Afghanistan, but no one outside the Chinese government knows the quantities.

Various European governments, parties, and private groups reacted with hostility to the invasion. Italian Communist Party leaders were so publicly bitter about events in Afghanistan that they were not permitted to address the Twenty-sixth Soviet Party Congress in Moscow in 1981. But of all the Europeans, the French were probably the most interested in and sympathetic to the Afghan resistance. French medical personnel provided significant help, often at the peril of their lives. French groups helped found Radio Free Kabul in 1981 (which the Kabul regime identified as "a Jewish radio station").[167] And in 1987 the French foreign minister met with resistance leaders in Pakistan.

Soon after the invasion, the United Nations began voting year after year by big margins that all "foreign troops" should leave Afghanistan. In 1986, the vote was 122 to 20; it is not clear exactly how these votes assisted the Afghan people, whose villages and whose society were being destroyed. Meanwhile UNICEF—in September 1986—presented an award to the puppet regime in Kabul for its literacy campaign, a campaign that helped spark the insurgency in the first place because women were forced to attend classes during which their religion was ridiculed.[168]

And then there was India. At the Emergency Session of the United Nations General Assembly in January 1980, the Indian representative criticized the General Assembly for presuming even to discuss the Soviet invasion of Afghanistan. India consistently refused to condemn the Russian occupation and recognized the Kabul regime and extended aid to it. In 1987, when the United Nations voted 123 to 19 that "foreign troops" should leave Afghanistan, India abstained. On May 3, 1988, the head of the Kabul regime visited New Delhi, the only non-Communist capital that accorded him full honors as head of state.

The Americans and the Afghans

In 1953, the Joint Chiefs of Staff informed President Dwight Eisenhower, "Afghanistan is of little or no strategic importance to the United States." This statement encapsulates the traditional American approach to that country. The United States refused Afghan requests for military aid in 1948 and 1951 (under President Truman) and in 1954 (under President Eisenhower). Policymakers in Washington did not view Soviet moves to increase their influence in Afghanistan as a threat to the United States, and besides there was little the United States could do about the situation. The Americans looked upon Afghanistan as being in the "Soviet sphere of influence," believing that no matter how much aid they might give to Afghanistan, nothing would ever be able to pull that country out of the Soviet orbit. In

1956 the National Security Council determined that arms transfers to Afghanistan might provoke the Soviet Union into strong counter-measures. Besides, Pakistan would have objected to any plans for American assistance to Afghanistan in view of their age-old border dispute, and Pakistan was Washington's ally in the Baghdad Pact, which Afghanistan had declined to join. Most of the time the U.S. Embassy in Kabul contained nobody who could speak Dari adequately.[169] Hence, it may be distressing but not surprising that the word "Afghanistan" does not appear even one time in the index of the first volume of President Eisenhower's memoirs. For that matter, it does not appear at all in the memoirs of President Truman, or Secretary of State Dean Acheson, or the theorist of containment George F. Kennan.

Faced with Secretary of State Dulles's support for Pakistan in its border disagreements with Afghanistan, Daoud turned to the Soviets. The Russians built the Bagram airport north of Kabul. In the 1960s they also constructed the Salang Highway, as well as the Salang Tunnel through the Hindu Kush mountains, eighty miles north of Kabul, a "masterpiece of engineering" and, at eleven thousand feet, the second-highest tunnel in the world. All these projects proved extremely useful for the invasion of 1979. From 1980 to 1989, 8 million tons of Soviet weapons and supplies moved through this famous tunnel.[170]

It appears almost certain that Moscow expected little trouble with the United States over its invasion of Afghanistan. The Americans in the end had done nothing about the Soviet invasions of Hungary (1956) and Czechoslovakia (1968). Still wallowing in its "Vietnam syndrome," the United States did not try to block Soviet activities in Angola and Ethiopia. By 1979, the Carter administration was in an obvious and apparently irreversible downward spiral. More importantly, the Kremlin expected no effective response from the Americans because it expected no effective response from the Afghans.[171]

In fact, however, the invasion thoroughly alarmed the Carter administration. With impressive hyperbole, the excited American president called the Soviet move "the greatest threat to peace since the Second World War."[172] Washington viewed the invasion as extremely ominous: it was not only the first-ever Soviet military movement outside the Soviet bloc, but it also carried Soviet armed forces perilously close to the source of major Western and Japanese oil supplies. "If the Soviets could consolidate their hold on Afghanistan," Carter wrote later, "the balance of power in the entire region would be drastically modified in their favor, and they might be tempted toward further aggression."[173]

President Carter's response to the invasion was wide-ranging. He postponed consideration of the Salt II treaty by the Senate (where in light of the invasion it was doomed anyway). He proclaimed a U.S. boycott of the 1980 Moscow Olympics, in which he was joined by China, Japan, West Germany, and fifty other countries. He imposed an embargo on wheat sales to the Soviet Union, sought a condemnation of the invasion by the United Nations, and initiated legislation aimed at a reintroduction of the draft. Most importantly from the Soviet view, perhaps, Carter called for greatly increased aid to Pakistan, Secretary of Defense Harold Brown journeyed to Beijing, and military and financial assistance began to flow to the mujahideen.[174] And, in case the Soviets should have ideas about further advances toward the Persian Gulf, President Carter in his State of the Union message on January 23, 1980, issued this warning: "Let our position be absolutely clear: An attempt by any outside force to gain control of the Persian Gulf region will be regarded as an assault on the vital interests of the United States of America, and such an assault will be repelled by any means necessary, including military force."[175]

Nevertheless, in the early years of the conflict, even into the first Reagan administration, the movement of American arms to the resistance was not great. There was no large Afghan ethnic element in the United States to put pressure on Congress to act, and U.S. news media coverage of the fighting and destruction inside Afghanistan was scanty. One observer wrote that only about 20 percent of resistance weapons came from foreign sources.[176] Nevertheless, as the brutality of the Soviets and the determination of the mujahideen to resist became ever clearer, American interest in and commitment to the resistance deepened.

At the time of the Greek Civil War, President Truman declared it to be the policy of the United States to render assistance to "free peoples" resisting subversion or subjugation by Communist forces; this declaration, the essence of the Cold War Containment Policy, came to be called the Truman Doctrine. As the war in Afghanistan grew ever more desperate, President Reagan enunciated what became known as the Reagan Doctrine: this extended the principle of assistance to include not only free peoples resisting the Communist yoke but also "subjugated peoples" seeking to escape from it. Observers at the time viewed the Reagan Doctrine as a repudiation of and challenge to the so-called Brezhnev Doctrine, which declared that once Communists had taken governmental power in a country, by whatever means, the Soviet Union and other fraternal socialist states would never permit that country to have any other kind of government. (This of course had been the doctrinal basis for the Warsaw Pact invasion of Czechoslovakia in 1968.) To give point to his attitude, President Reagan received a delegation of mujahideen leaders in the Oval Office in May 1986.[177]

By the end of 1984, the United States was providing perhaps only $80 million worth of aid to the resistance. This amount expanded to something like $470 million in 1986 and $700 million in 1988. A great deal of this aid never made it through Pakistan into Afghanistan, a fact that American policymakers will wish to reflect on in any similar future conflict. The Central Intelligence Agency was given charge of assistance to Afghan insurgents, and this turned out to be the largest covert (so to speak) CIA operation since Vietnam. Fearing that too-open provision of U.S. aid would provide a good excuse for serious Soviet retaliation against Pakistan, the CIA supplied the insurgents with many Soviet weapons (often purchased from onetime Soviet ally Egypt) to mask (or figleaf) their source.[178]

The Departure of the Soviets

By mid-1987 at the latest, from the Soviet point of view the military situation was a stalemate at best. On the one hand, the mujahideen could not capture the big cities because they could not overcome the combination of Soviet air and firepower, plus fortifications and the mines that defended them; the Soviets in fact laid down between 10 and 16 million mines in Afghanistan, which served to keep mujahideen out—and Kabul soldiers in.[179] On the other hand, the Soviets and their Kabul allies had lost their complete air supremacy and controlled little of the countryside; they held only the larger cities, the key airports, and the vital north-south highway to Kabul.

Nothing the Soviets had done in Afghanistan seemed to work. On the contrary, after seven years of savage conflict, the insurgents were better armed and more determined than ever before. Soviet efforts on the political and diplomatic fronts had failed as well. As a U.S. State Department paper summarized the situation, "by 1987 the Mujahideen had fought the Soviet and regime forces to a stalemate: Moscow's Afghan policy had alienated it from the Islamic, Western and non-aligned countries; and the Soviets failed to find a client leader in Kabul who could capture the loyalty of the Afghan people."[180]

In the first eight years of the war, official Soviet sources placed the number of Soviet casualties between 48,000 and 52,000, including 13,000 to 15,000 deaths. Some commentators on the war believe that the actual numbers, especially deaths, were twice the official figures. But if one accepts those official figures, Soviet forces suffered approximately 35 deaths per week between December 1979 and December 1987. In view of the fact that the Soviets were combating a resistance force of between 80,000 and 150,000, this was hardly a shocking number. But it was certainly far more than anybody in the Kremlin was predicting in January 1980. The same was true of the number of aircraft, including helicopters, downed by the resistance: something like 1,000, with possibly 500 lost in 1987 alone (the Stinger effect). The insurgents had also destroyed roughly 600 tanks, 800 armored personnel carriers, and thousands of trucks and other military vehicles; the handful of Western correspondents sometimes in the country reported seeing dozens of Soviet and Kabul army vehicles destroyed in just a single engagement.[181] And there was no end in sight.

By 1984, the war was costing the Soviet Union around 3 billion dollars a year. The Russians were recovering much of this expense through exploitation of Afghanistan's mineral resources. The Soviets took vast quantities of natural gas out of Afghanistan by agreement with Kabul but paid only a fraction of the world market price for it; in summary, "robber and plantation economies [would have been] clearly indicated for Afghanistan's future if Soviet control there [had been] consolidated."[182]

But the Afghan war, begun under Leonid Brezhnev, was imposing many other costs on Mikhail Gorbachev's Russia. It had wrecked détente; provided a lever President Reagan used to pry huge defense budgets out of his Congresses; brought Washington and Beijing closer together; created profound hostility among Islamic nations; dissipated the mystique of the invincible Soviet Army; resolidified the ring of hostile states around the USSR, from Norway and Turkey to China and Japan; and severely damaged the prestige of the USSR in the Third World, partly because of the invasion's imperialist aspects, but perhaps most of all because of its lack of military success.[183] And, on the other side of the Soviet empire, the people of Poland were assuming an alarming posture of defiance to the puppet regime in Warsaw and its masters in Moscow. The war in Afghanistan was having the same effect on the Europe of Gorbachev as the war in Spain had on the Europe of Napoleon: "The willingness of the Poles to fight the Soviet army juggernaut might have been less if the Afghans had not been showing that it could be done." There are many imponderables in the ultimate decision against sending the Red army into Poland, but as one observer expressed it, "there can be little question that the old men in the Kremlin would have been far more willing to risk an invasion of Poland if the Afghan albatross had not already been weighing them down."[184] In all these ways, the effort in Afghanistan, instead of enhancing Soviet security, was undermining it.

Arguably the most menacing consequence of the war was a Soviet variation of the venerable Domino Principle: the long-term effects of the endless Afghanistan campaign on the Soviet Union's Muslim population, 50 million strong and rapidly increasing. The Muslims of Soviet Central Asia inhabited territories the Russians had acquired by conquest, and relatively recently. These peoples were held inside the Soviet Union not by the appeal of Marxism—"perceived not as an internationalist philosophy but as a technique devised by the Russians to protect their colonial rule"—but by the power of the Soviet Army.[185] There was practically no intermarriage at all with ethnic Russians. In the British and French empires, the subject populations had shown relatively little inclination to challenge their imperial overlords until they saw these masters defeated at the hands of an Asian people in World War II. What did Russia's Central Asian Muslims make of the events in Afghanistan, where the all-conquering Red Army had for years been badly mauled by the warriors of God, the Red Star eclipsed by the Crescent, Leninism tamed by Islam, an Islam resurgent all over the world and nowhere more vigorously than on the southern borders of the Soviet empire? What if the international response to the war in Afghanistan taught them that there was indeed a Muslim world community that stretched far beyond the borders of their less-than-invincible utopia?[186]

How had the Soviets become entangled in this dread predicament?

What happened to the Soviets in Afghanistan can perhaps be best understood as the mutually aggravating effects of four basic circumstances. First, their invasion confronted the Soviets with a forbidding terrain inhabited by hardy and high-spirited people who saw themselves as intolerably provoked into a defense of both their independence and their religion. In a word, Afghanistan was no Czechoslovakia.

Second, from the beginning the Soviets had greatly overestimated their ability to cut off supplies to the guerrillas by using modern weapons technology. Munitions got in from Pakistan, from America, from Iran and China and Egypt and Saudi Arabia—surely one of the most heterogeneous coalitions ever seen, and daunting indeed in its implications for Moscow. The Soviets thus learned how very difficult it is to defeat a popular insurgency possessing secure sources of outside aid.[187] And very late in the war, but not too late, the foreign supporters of the mujahideen provided them with weapons that came close to driving the vaunted Red air force from the daytime skies. In analyzing the war, it would be impossible to overestimate the importance either of the willingness of foreign powers to assist the insurgents with modern weapons or the failure of the Soviets to isolate the country from this assistance.

Third, the numbers of troops the Soviet Union committed to the conflict proved totally inadequate for the subjugation of the country, or even for the secure possession of major parts of it. This was the root of the Soviet terror campaign against the civilian population: lacking the manpower for pacification, they turned to depopulation. But the tremendous firepower of the Soviet armed forces, with apparently no limitations whatsoever on its use and enhanced by incursions into Pakistan and assassinations of resistance leaders in Peshawar, did not silence the insurgents. Instead, the Soviet terror policy actually constructed, among the millions of Afghans who fled across the borders into Pakistan and Iran, a vast support system and recruiting ground for the resistance. Thus had depopulation fatally backfired.

Fourth, by no means least, the various political formulas advanced by Moscow to solve the Afghanistan problem had all failed. In response to initial armed resistance in 1978–79, the Soviets and their mannequins in Kabul had pursued policies that only made their opponents more determined. Attempts to reverse these blunders, including crudely engineering major leadership changes and launching a "national conciliation government," achieved nothing. The goal of establishing a pro-Soviet government in Kabul that would be popular and legitimate, or at least tolerated by the Afghan people, was revealed as an illusion. Truly, it is nothing less than astonishing that in a country with such deep racial, ethnic, religious, linguistic, and tribal fissures, the Soviets should have proved incapable of developing effective divide-and-rule policies. In a profound sense, the Soviet political failure produced the military failure.[188]

One possible response to all these negatives would have been to decide finally to win the war, but as a State Department study concluded, "the Soviet leadership recognized that there could be no military solution in Afghanistan without a massive increase in their military commitment."[189] There may have been approximately 200,000 mujahideen in 1987, and perhaps 100,000 of these were active fighters. To reach the standard ten-to-one ratio of soldiers to insurgents generally believed necessary to wage conclusive counterguerrilla warfare, and assuming the ineffective Kabul forces remained at around 80,000 (an optimistic assessment), the Soviets would have had to put more than 900,000 troops into Afghanistan at the same time—eight times their actual commitment. The logistic challenges of supplying such a force in the Afghan terrain were staggering, unimaginable. And by the middle of the 1980s the Kremlin leaders had ceased trying to hide the fact that the Soviet Union was facing a systemic economic crisis with the most profound and alarming political implications.

But even if the Soviet Union had bitten the bullet and decided on a massive increase of its troop levels in Afghanistan, that would not have guaranteed quick or even complete success. Consider that South Vietnam was one-quarter the size of Afghanistan; the populations of the two countries at the time of the main American and Soviet interventions were roughly equal. Yet the number of U.S. military personnel in South Vietnam at its peak was nearly five times the size of the Soviet forces in Afghanistan. Moreover, these U.S. forces were assisted by fully 1 million South Vietnamese soldiers and militia. Besides, even if the Soviets had decided to pour hundreds of thousands of additional troops into Afghanistan, the United States and China could have easily increased the assistance they were giving to the mujahideen; and all the while the Reagan administration was applying powerful pressures on more vital Soviet interests. Thus, although the Kremlin had not suffered clear defeat in Afghanistan, it faced either endless conflict or an escalation that was unacceptably costly and perhaps impossible.

Against precisely what danger, for precisely what gain, and at precisely what internal and international costs was Gorbachev obligated to continue and perhaps greatly escalate the conflict? This Afghanistan mess was not even his creation; it was Brezhnev's. By 1988, Brezhnev was quite dead, and most of the members of the politburo that had supported his invasion were also dead or dying. Unsurprisingly, therefore, "in the final analysis, [Gorbachev's] Moscow deemed the overall costs of pursuing a military solution to be too high." And so it chose the policy of withdrawal. On April 14, 1988, Pakistan and the PDPA regime signed the Geneva Accords, to become effective May 15; the United States and the Soviet Union were guarantors of the pact. On May 15, 1988, the Soviet forces began their withdrawal from Afghanistan, monitored by the United Nations Good Offices Mission in Afghanistan and Pakistan (UNGOMAP).[190] By February 1989, all or almost all Soviet troops had left Afghanistan, but substantial numbers of advisers and KGB personnel remained in the country.[191]

From Insurgency to Civil War

By the middle of 1988, the mujahideen controlled more than three-quarters of the national territory. Notably, they held the capitals of several provinces in the strategic northern and eastern parts of the country. The Soviets, who had directed the war, occupied some key cities, policed the highways, provided air mobility to the Kabul army, and sent special forces to interrupt insurgent supplies, were leaving. The Americans therefore believed that the PDPA would soon find itself presiding over "Socialism in One City," and Kabul itself would quickly fall.[192] But as the conflict reached the decade mark, these expectations of Kabul's capture proved overly optimistic, for several reasons.

Effective enough in guerrilla warfare, the organization and tactics of the insurgents proved less successful in the siege of cities. The level of cooperation among the various mujahideen fighting groups had improved since the early days. Nevertheless, internecine rivalries and jealousies within the resistance—including the assassination of proven leaders and even occasional open combat between various groups—continued to impede mujahideen success.[193]

At the end of 1988, the Kabul regime maintained armed forces equal, at least numerically, to those of the active mujahideen. These included about 40,000 regular army troops, often unreliable; 35,000 better-quality KHAD and Sarandoy (Interior Ministry paramilitary police); and about 25,000 tribal militia, composed of men from ethnic groups different from that of the local mujahideen. They were highly paid, of questionable loyalty, and only nominally under the control of Kabul; nevertheless in their own areas the militias usually kept the insurgents out and the roads open.[194]

As the Russians withdrew, the minority of Afghans, mainly urban, who had for one reason or another supported the Kabul regime increasingly fought with an intensity born of desperation. With their Soviet allies leaving, they feared that the collapse of the regime would mean widespread massacres. Such fear was well founded. Certain foreign volunteers among the insurgents, especially Saudis, were accused of real brutality toward the civilian population, including rape and enslavement. Moreover, as the day of victory seemed to grow nearer, some insurgents sought vengeance for so many years of untold suffering. The *Far Eastern Economic Review* reported, "Atrocities and revenge killings by the guerrillas after capturing small provincial capitals have not enhanced their reputation among civilians in the large Afghan cities." In June 1988, the garrison of the capital of Badakhshan Province (in the far northeast) handed the city over to the resistance, but after that the frequent massacres of Kabul soldiers who had surrendered to the mujahideen brought defection by regime troops to an almost complete halt.[195]

The consequences of the increased willingness to fight on the part of the Kabul forces were quite serious. In March 1989, in contrast to their previously successful guerrilla tactics, the insurgents launched a major conventional attack on the city of Jalalabad, chosen in part because of its proximity to the Pakistan border and in part because it was large enough for the Afghan Interim Government (AIG), the leaders of the seven largest parties, to move in and proclaim it the capital of a liberated state. But the expected defection of the garrison did not occur; on the contrary, the Kabul troops at Jalalabad fought tenaciously, because of earlier prisoner killings by mujahideen. Moreover, the garrison possessed massive amounts of Soviet supplies, plenty of Soviet Army advisers, abundant firepower, good defensive positions, and numbers equal to those of the attackers. The insurgents assaulted the place in broad daylight, thus abandoning any hope of surprise, failed to coordinate their movements, and took a tremendous mauling from regime air and artillery units. Worst of all, according to Pakistani intelligence, "a decisive factor in the attackers' failure [at Jalalabad] was lack of cooperation between the Commanders." Indeed, during the Jalalabad operation, Hekmatyar's fundamentalist followers attacked some of Massoud's units in Takhar Province, on the Soviet border. (Massoud, the most successful and popular of the mujahideen leaders, was treacherously assassinated by al-Qaida in 2001.) According to one well-informed Pakistani observer, the mujahideen "never recovered from Jalalabad."[196] In any event, the failure of the mujahideen effort against that city greatly increased the morale of the Kabul forces.

The successful defense of Jalalabad showed that the city of Kabul itself was safe, at least for a while. Within the capital, many who would never have joined the PDPA nevertheless supported the city's defense, because of what seemed to them the needlessly indiscriminate shelling of Kabul by the insurgents, or because the growing influence of Pakistan and Saudi Arabia over the mujahideen was accentuating the radical Islamic flavor of the resistance, or for both reasons. Something like 60 percent of PDPA members were by now in the security forces. The ranks of the party had expanded considerably during the conflict, mainly in the cities; urban women were even joining militia units. By that point, members of the PDPA and its various political front groups, plus the security forces, and all the dependents of these, must have totaled close to 1 million persons. And the Kabul air force was developing tactics to lessen the effect of Stingers.[197]

But most important of all to Kabul's survival was aid from the Soviet Union. The Soviets were indeed leaving the territory of Afghanistan. But unlike the Americans in South Vietnam, the Soviets were not simply abandoning their allies to their fate. The Soviets left behind $1 billion worth of equipment and supplies, and "substantial deliveries of military equipment—including tanks, armored personnel carriers, and aircraft—continued unabated through 1988."[198] American aid to the mujahideen for all of 1989 amounted to about $600 million, an amount matched by Saudi Arabia. In comparison, the Soviets were giving the Kabul regime $250 million a month.[199] This Soviet cornucopia of weapons, fuel, and food "played a determining role in sustaining the Afghan economy."[200] Soviet military advisers and Soviet-supplied aircraft were decisive in the defense of Kabul. Notably, much of the Soviet military equipment going to Kabul came from Soviet forces leaving central Europe.

Few realized it at the time, but the Soviet withdrawal from Afghanistan was the overture to the disintegration of the Soviet state itself. Through December 1989 Communist puppet regimes collapsed all over central Europe. In September 1991 the Congress of People's Deputies declared the USSR dissolved. In April 1992, twenty thousand mujahideen entered Kabul. In September 1996 the Taliban took over the capital, invaded the UN compound where Najib (Najibullah), head of KHAD and the puppet state, had taken refuge, and lynched him.

The Soviet Union's Vietnam?

By the mid-1980s it had become fashionable to refer to Afghanistan as "Russia's Vietnam," and that phrase is still heard today. Such a comparison is valid to a limited degree: "the Soviet forces in Afghanistan," writes one analyst, "repeated the U.S. experience in Vietnam, in that they did not lose but could not win at a politically acceptable cost."[201]

But, while all would readily admit that no two wars can ever be exactly the same, the contrasts between the American and the Soviet conflicts in Asia are of such magnitude that we ought to be very wary of facile comparisons. Among the principal differences between the Soviet experience in Afghanistan and the American experience in Vietnam are their geographic dimensions, the nature of the two governments, the composition of their opponents, the levels of force commitment, and the indigenous support for their respective counterinsurgent efforts.

In the first place, Afghanistan is just across the border from the Soviet Union, as are Czechoslovakia and Hungary. In contrast, Washington is closer to the South Pole than to Saigon. It would therefore be less misleading to compare the Soviet withdrawal from Afghanistan to an American withdrawal not from Vietnam but from northern Mexico.

Second, the nature of the Soviet polity was much better suited to suppressing a foreign insurgency. American forces in Vietnam, like the French before them, only occasionally and in violation of their own laws committed the kinds of actions that for the Soviet forces in Afghanistan were standing policy, and the French and the Americans were under the scrutiny of increasingly hostile and sensationalist news media.

Third, although in area Afghanistan is three and a half times the size of South Vietnam, the U.S. forces in South Vietnam at their peak were five times as numerous as Soviet forces in Afghanistan. The Kremlin committed to Afghanistan less than one soldier per five square kilometers. It sent approximately 800,000 soldiers into the Afghan conflict at one time or another, equivalent to roughly one-quarter of 1 percent of the total Soviet population, or 3.4 percent of males reaching military age, during the war years. Officially, something like 15,000 Soviet soldiers perished in Afghanistan between 1980 and 1989—undoubtedly a figure much lower than the actual number. During that same period, 65,000 people in the USSR died in road accidents, and between 35,000 and 75,000 Soviet soldiers died from bullying, suicide, and carelessness. During Stalin's four-month war against Finland in 1940, the Soviet armies had suffered at least 200,000 casualties.[202]

A fourth major contrast is that the Americans and the Soviets faced far different opponents. Although American casualties in Vietnam were much higher than Soviet casualties in Afghanistan, the disparity was by no means solely due to the much smaller Soviet troop commitment. The mujahideen were brave and resilient, but in Vietnam the Americans faced opponents much better trained, organized, and equipped than the Soviets encountered in Afghanistan. The politburo in Hanoi, having developed its military and political techniques during long years of struggle against the French, gave the Viet Cong unity, discipline, and direction. Hanoi also sent into the south a constant and increasing flow of well-trained combatants and effective weapons. The mujahideen had nothing like this; thus the Afghan struggle had no remote equivalent of a Tet or an Easter Offensive.

In a fifth difference, indigenous support for a non-Communist South Vietnam was incomparably greater than that for a Soviet-dominated Afghanistan. In any given year in the early 1970s, more than 1 million persons served in the South Vietnamese Army or in the militia, out of a population of 17 million. Fatalities in the regular South Vietnamese Army (ARVN)—*excluding* figures from the militia—were the proportional equivalent of 2.6 million American military deaths. To those numbers must be contrasted the barely 100,000 men and boys the Kabul regime scraped together from a population of 16 million. That is why, even after the United States completely abandoned its Vietnamese allies, it required a conventional invasion by the regular North Vietnamese Army, the largest cross-border assault in Asia since the Korean War, to finally destroy the South Vietnamese state.

Sixth, soon after completing their military withdrawal from South Vietnam, the Americans began slashing their assistance, even medical supplies, to their erstwhile allies. In contrast, the Soviets poured food, weapons, and ammunition into Kabul, supplies that enabled the regime there to go on fighting. The Soviets had pursued a more conservative military strategy than the Americans in Vietnam and had decided to get out before the strains of the war had become too severe; nevertheless, their leaders were determined that their investment in Afghanistan should not be allowed simply to go down the drain. The collapse of the Soviet system a short time after the withdrawal and the consequent cessation of Soviet aid do not mean that Moscow's commitment to sustaining the Kabul regime was insincere or unsustainable.

The Meaning of the Soviet-Afghan War

During the decade of the 1980s, the Soviets unleashed upon the poor and simple people of Afghanistan the full horror of a deliberate campaign of devastation. By 1988, according to one authority, roughly 1.25 million Afghans "had died as a result of aerial bombing raids, shootings, artillery shelling, antipersonnel mines, exhaustion and other war-related conditions."[203] (In proportion to population, the equivalent in American deaths in 2011 would be more than 24 million.) Yet the fearsome technology of the Soviet armed forces, wielded with utter indifference to questions of legality or humanity, proved insufficient for victory. At a truly frightful price and with good help from their well-wishers in the outside world, the Afghan people fought to a stalemate the forces of a superpower on their very border. Afghanistan provides an exceedingly rare example of a struggle in which guerrillas were successful by themselves, unsupported by the proximity of friendly conventional forces.

But the Afghan struggle was more than an embarrassing colonial defeat for the world's last multinational empire. By successfully refusing to be bullied into a Central Asian imitation of Ceausescu's Romania, the Afghan freedom fighters inflicted the first (but not the last) indisputable reverse on the "historical inevitability of Marxism-Leninism" in which Brezhnev had so devoutly believed. This double defeat helped stimulate the profound pressures for change that were already building inside the Soviet empire, hastening its process of decomposition. The full consequences of that decomposition are not yet clear. What is all too clear is that the war against the Soviets left Afghanistan physically and morally devastated, abandoned by the United States, and hence vulnerable to the gathering forces of international terrorism. But indisputably, by their resistance to the Soviet invasion, the brave, sorrowful, martyred people of Afghanistan helped to alter the course of world politics. Thus Trotsky's aphorism about the connection between Central Asia and Europe was vindicated with supreme irony: the cries of battle in the Afghan mountains found an echo in the shouts of freedom at the Berlin Wall.

5

Lessons Learned—or Not

Now let us review the most salient features of the conflicts we have analyzed and see what useful lessons we can find.

China

In seeking to explain the victory of Mao Tse-tung and the Communists over Chiang Kai-shek and the Nationalists, one cannot ignore, of course, the multifaceted and deeply rooted socioeconomic backwardness of twentieth-century China. Nevertheless, that consideration does not explain why the Communist victory occurred in 1949, instead of 1939 or 1959—or occurred at all. Any effort to offer a full explanation of the final victory of Maoist Communism needs to give due weight to key political and military conditions in which that victory took place. Those conditions include the nature of the international system of the 1930s, Mao's grasp of certain military realities of the time, major errors by Mao's opponents, including at least some that were certainly avoidable, and the effect of cataclysmic but unpredictable international events, including Pearl Harbor and Hiroshima.

In the first place, Japanese forces sent to subdue Kuomintang China were far fewer than were needed and by no means of uniformly high quality. Their equipment, moreover, even if superior to that of the KMT, was inadequate. Consequently, these forces pushed the Nationalist armies deep into southwestern China but were not able to overcome them, even before Japan hurled itself into a war against the United States. Between these two armies—one unable to protect the country and the other unable to conquer it—Mao Tse-tung found the space to make his reputation and his revolution.

In failing both to defeat the Nationalists and to annihilate the Communists, the Japanese played a determining role in the coming Communist revolution. They badly damaged the armed forces and the prestige of Chiang Kai-shek's government. At the same time, unable to pacify the vast countryside, and committing the most appalling atrocities, the Japanese in effect acted as recruiting agents for Chinese Communist Party guerrilla bands. Finally, at the end of World War II, they supplied the CCP with great quantities of weapons, as well as numerous volunteers and valuable instructors.

As for the Nationalists, their exhaustion at the end of World War II, the huge size of China, its primitive communications systems, and above all a lack of airpower severely handicapped the KMT on the eve of their final confrontation with Mao's forces. Those Communist forces, moreover, had to a large degree evolved from the status of guerrillas to that of relatively well-equipped conventional armies. Then Chiang's fateful decision to overextend his strength by occupying Manchuria, the mistreatment of Chinese collaborationist forces, the sudden demobilization of great numbers of Nationalist troops, the neglect of basic political education for KMT soldiers, and indeed the scandalously inadequate attention to the most elementary needs of those same soldiers—all of these factors opened the door wide for the deficiencies of the Nationalist high command to have their effect. Those deficiencies included notably the destructive rivalries among KMT generals, widespread and corrosive corruption, and arguably above all the habit of fighting a static, defensive war against Mao's forces, enabling him to destroy his enemies segment by segment. As the war progressed, an increasing tendency for KMT commanders to defect made it seem all the more necessary for Chiang to appoint his generals on the basis of political reliability rather than military prowess. All, or almost all, of these weaknesses were correctable in principle; if the Nationalists had corrected at least a few of them, the outcome of the conflict would surely have been quite different.

A distinguished student of these events once wrote: "Agonizing as the [problems of China] were, there would have been no revolution but for the existence of an organized revolutionary movement armed with a doctrine, long-term objectives and a clear political strategy susceptible to common-sense adjustments in a time of crisis."[1] True enough, but this same movement was on the edge of annihilation in 1936. It was not Mao or Stalin but the Japanese who saved Chinese Communism. After the surrender of Japan, Mao came to power not through a proletarian revolution, or even a peasant uprising, but through conventional military conquest. There could have been no such conquest, no numerous and well-armed People's Liberation Army—arguably no PLA at all—without the Japanese invasion. The Japanese contribution aside, the blunders and defects of the Nationalist forces after World War II played at least as great a role in their defeat as did Communist prowess. Hence, we need to firmly resist the temptation—to which more than a few have succumbed—to erect Maoist revolutionary techniques into some sort of irresistible metaphysical blueprint for victory. Mao himself never claimed universal applicability for his type of warfare.[2] If our analysis of the Maoist victory is valid, then later efforts to imitate it in different environments and time periods should have been unsuccessful—and they were.[3]

The Ch'ing dynasty failed to modernize China; so did Chiang Kai-shek. Unable to protect China from foreign depredations, both regimes were swept away. But Mao Tse-tung also failed to make China a modern, prosperous, orderly country. Indeed, from the Korean War through the Great Leap Forward into the Cultural Revolution, he brought a series of unparalleled disasters upon the Chinese people. Nor, notably, was he able to conclude the great civil war with the KMT. After more than eight decades this conflict remains unresolved and may yet one day help trigger a Sino-American confrontation of massive proportions and unpredictable consequences.

French Vietnam

This is the only one of our four cases in which the counterinsurgent forces had to wage their campaign far from home, actually halfway around the globe. The others were fighting either in their own country or in a neighboring one. In the end, proximity in itself, or the lack of it, did not make much difference for the outcome.

From the beginning, French efforts in Vietnam encountered severe obstacles, both internal and external. The most obvious of

France's internal weaknesses was the extraordinary discontinuity of government leadership: between September 1944 and September 1954, four national parliamentary elections took place. No fewer than twenty-one cabinets took office and then (usually after a few months, or even less time) collapsed. And during those years, at least another dozen efforts to install a cabinet failed. The main causes of this kaleidoscopic politics lay in the divisive and humiliating experiences of defeat and occupation by the Nazis and the emergence (closely related to those experiences) of the Communists as the country's largest single party. In 1951 that party received more than 26 percent of the first-ballot votes and elected one-sixth of the members of the National Assembly.[4]

The French military forces stationed in Vietnam were (like the Japanese in China before them and the Soviets in Afghanistan after them) quite inadequate numerically. There were two main reasons for this. First, it was illegal to send conscripts to Indochina. That was why the war could go on for so long: French casualties in Vietnam were not draftees but professional soldiers, many of whom were not even French. Nevertheless, France had used conscripts for its wars beginning in the 1790s, from Egypt to Moscow, and used them abundantly and victoriously in Algeria in the 1950s. The absence of conscripts in Vietnam, a signal that the country was not considered essential to France, was also a harbinger of Vietnam's eventual abandonment.

The other main reason for French numerical inadequacy in Vietnam was France's failure to build up properly trained and equipped indigenous forces. Quite substantial elements of the Vietnamese population opposed the Viet Minh and, if properly organized, could have had a decisive effect on the war. (Even under the actual unpropitious circumstances, the Vietnamese who fought on the French side were at least as numerous as those who followed the Viet Minh.) But the French recognized, at least implicitly, that an indigenous Vietnamese army strong enough to defeat the Viet Minh would have been strong enough one day to challenge continued French domination of the country. Along the same lines, why should France make sacrifices for victory in Vietnam at all if, as the United States urged, it was to become independent?

Quite aside from insufficient numbers, other serious weaknesses hobbled the French military effort. From beginning to end, the bulk of the French forces were not trained and equipped to wage a large-scale counterinsurgency, especially in a place like Vietnam. The small size of their air arm in Vietnam placed severe limitations on French offensive power, but the French military command never employed its limited forces to the best effect, which would have meant concentrating on the defense of strategic areas. Last—certainly not least—the French never lost the habit of underestimating their opponents. (Robert E. Lee said that one should always expect the opponent to do what he should do, but who bothers to read Lee anyway?)

All of these internal factors by themselves should have been quite enough to predict an eventual French defeat, or at best an intolerable stalemate.

But external factors played their part as well. Why were the Vietnamese Communists so weak in 1938 and so strong in 1945? Because during World War II the Japanese destroyed French control and French prestige in Vietnam, made no effort to hinder Viet Minh organization, and at the end provided the Viet Minh with weapons and numerous volunteers. The Japanese occupation of Vietnam was the death warrant of French dominion there.

Upon Japan's surrender, a true politico-military vacuum developed in Vietnam. The so-called August Revolution took place in this vacuum. Subsequently, the Nationalist Chinese prevented the French from returning to northern Vietnam for an extended period and provided guerrilla training for Viet Minh units inside China. During the war, the OSS had parachuted weapons to the Viet Minh; afterward, members of the OSS appeared in public with Ho Chi Minh, allowing the Communists to spread the impression that Ho had the backing of the United States.

Second in importance to the Japanese invasion, and a consequence of it, was the effect of the establishment of Mao's regime across Vietnam's northern border. Newly Communist China provided the Viet Minh with training, supplies, and sanctuary. It would be difficult to exaggerate the importance of this assistance. One contemporary and influential student of insurgency asserts that "unless governments are utterly incompetent, devoid of political will, and lacking resources, insurgent organizations normally must obtain outside assistance if they are to succeed." In the view of another, "external assistance appears to be the most common enabler of insurgent success."[5]

At the same time, hovering darkly over the Vietnamese battle area, the possibility of an inundation of Red Chinese troops into Tonkin deeply disheartened the French.

The withdrawal of the French from Vietnam occasioned by the tactical—not strategic—defeat at Dien Bien Phu suggests the reasonable hypothesis that democracies are disinclined, or perhaps unable, to fight a protracted war in circumstances where their interests are not clearly engaged or threatened. Dien Bien Phu provided the opportunity for the French to get out of a war whose purpose or value they had never agreed upon. Hence in 1954 the French abandoned their numerous non-Communist allies in Vietnam; less than twenty years later, the Americans did the same thing.

Cuba

Cuba is something of a control case for some of the views set forth in this book: in the other cases examined here, the counterinsurgents were foreigners; only the Cuban insurgents fought against an indigenous regime and army. In addition, the Cuban conflict was relatively brief, and it developed in a country one-sixth the size of Afghanistan.

In explaining the fall of the Batista regime, two factors are preeminent: the actions of the U.S. government and the condition of the Cuban Army.

Fidel Castro managed to win over, or at least disarm, influential strata of American opinion by presenting himself as a democratic reformist who promised free elections. It was partly as a result of this calculated deception that the United States imposed an arms embargo on Batista's Cuba and later refused to recognize his successor—in effect handing the island over to Castro.

The United States could have made a Castro victory quite impossible by publicly backing Batista while simultaneously insisting that he carry out sensible reforms (the policy followed later in El Salvador). The United States could also have imposed a true arms embargo by cutting off Castro from outside aid. To say the least, one may well question the wisdom of a Washington policy that resulted in the Castro regime. Almost overnight it became the focus, symbol, and stimulus for anti-U.S. sentiment and activity throughout the Western Hemisphere (and beyond), continuing so for a half century, and it provided the occasion for the Cuban Missile Crisis, the most dangerous great-power confrontation of the entire Cold War.

But the true essence of the revolutionary situation was the inability of the Cuban Army to fight effectively. In this fact above all, one sees the real nature of the Batista regime: incompetence masquerading as frivolity. If there was anything Batista absolutely needed to do, it was to be attentive to his army, the institution that enabled him—the true son of the common people—to rise to power. That army greatly outnumbered Castro's bands, but in the beginning of the struggle Batista all but ignored Castro, thus giving the rebels time to establish themselves. Besides, the Sierra was excellent country for guerrilla operations, and hardly anyone in the Cuban Army had counterinsurgency skills. Furthermore, that army had neither a fighting tradition nor real combat experience, and promotion and command, as in KMT China, depended more on political connections than leadership abilities.

When it became undeniably clear that his army could not extirpate, or even contain, the Castro guerrilla bands, Batista could have ordered the selection and training of a competent counterinsurgent force, even if only a few battalions, he could have chosen as his successor someone who would have been acceptable to the United States, or he could have taken both actions. But of course nothing so sensible was done. The number of Castro's active combatants was risibly small, many units of Batista's army had not even been in action when he fled the island, and those units that had been engaged suffered relatively few casualties.[6] Hence, the end of the Batista government truly was a collapse, not an overthrow. As evidence of the incomprehensible inadequacies of the Batista regime, consider the fate of Che Guevara. Less than a decade after marching with Castro into Havana, he decided to ignite an insurgency in Bolivia, one of the most remote and underdeveloped countries in the Western Hemisphere, one of those places whose mountainous topography seems designed by nature for guerrillas. After a brief and semifarcical "campaign" there, Guevara met his death at the hands of a regime and an army with not much more than the will to fight. And as with the case of Maoism, if this analysis is basically correct, it ineluctably follows that efforts to implant self-proclaimed Castroite regimes elsewhere had to fail—which has been the case.

The fact that Castro and his followers did not come to power through a popular upheaval, but rather picked up the power that had been abandoned by their feckless enemies, goes far to explain why the Castro regime had to set up the Western Hemisphere's sole totalitarian dictatorship.

Afghanistan

In the quarter century preceding their intervention in Afghanistan, the Soviets had invaded two other countries along their borders: Hungary in 1956 and Czechoslovakia in 1968. The Czechs chose not to resist; the Hungarians put up a tremendous fight for weeks against massive Soviet armored forces. In the end the outcome was the same: the reimposition on both countries of a foreign domination as harsh as it was detested.

On the surface, these two cases strongly suggested to many that a Soviet intervention must be as irresistible as a tsunami. But both Hungary and Czechoslovakia shared a border not only with the USSR but also with other Communist states. Both countries were small, Hungary being less than one-seventh the size of Afghanistan (about the size of Indiana) and largely a plain. Hence it was relatively easy for Soviet forces to overrun both countries and shut them off from the outside world. In contrast, two-thirds of Afghanistan's extensive borders were with Muslim states, and its peoples had a long tradition of vigorous guerrilla resistance to invaders, defending home and religion in a mountainous country ideal for that kind of fighting.

Mujahideen guerrilla tactics had changed little since the First Afghan War (1838–42), during which the British had developed some effective counterinsurgency methods. The Soviets, of course, had not bothered to study that conflict.[7] But in addition, the Soviets' intelligence failure with regard to the struggle they were about to embark upon was truly impressive. Even though Afghanistan was their neighbor, and even though they had had intimate contacts with the Afghan regime, the Soviets gravely underestimated the fighting will of the insurgents and also wildly overestimated the reliability of the Afghan regular army. These two really remarkable errors account for the utterly inadequate numbers of troops the Kremlin wished to believe would be sufficient to accomplish their purposes in Afghanistan.

But it was not only Soviet numbers that were inadequate. The Red Army had not fought a real war in three and a half decades; it had spent its time and energy practicing to fight against NATO. Its units were unprepared for any sort of counterinsurgency, most especially in one of the most rugged, roadless areas on the planet. Inside this Soviet Army, conditions were appalling: training was rudimentary, rations were not nutritious, drinking water was often unobtainable, sanitation was primitive, sleeping bags were not waterproof, and rape of and suicide by young conscripts were commonplace—the unconscionable litany goes on and on. The quantitative and qualitative shortcomings of the Soviet forces in Afghanistan resulted in the policy of trying to stamp out the insurgency by devastating the civilian population, a course that not only failed to discourage the resistance but justified and enflamed it, while simultaneously stirring up dismay and anger across great swaths of the Islamic world.

And since, in Soviet calculations, any fighting in postinvasion Afghanistan would be brief and carried out mostly by the Kabul army, little consideration was given to controlling the country's borders. But soon inestimably valuable aid began flowing to the insurgents, mainly across the Pakistan border, from an unusual coalition of countries—the United States, China, Iran, several Arab states—that alarmed and astounded the Kremlin. Thus, like the Japanese in China and the French in Vietnam, the Soviets committed insufficient numbers to the Afghanistan conflict, and again like the French in Vietnam, they failed to seal off the country from decisive quantities of outside aid (two conditions that are of course closely related).

Nevertheless, the Soviets might have salvaged all, or at least much, by effective manipulation of the numerous rifts among the Afghan resistance elements. The gross political failure here was as remarkable as it was unpredictable. The Soviets' policy and behavior was so uninspired that even the very badly fractured Afghan insurgent leadership could outlast them.

In these circumstances, the prestige of the invincible Red Army quickly evaporated. And simultaneously with this endless and embarrassing Afghan disaster, the Kremlin was distracted and dismayed both by the escalating crisis of the Communist regime in Poland and the global strategic challenge to the very continuation of the Soviet empire mounted by the Reagan administration.

Soviet failure in Afghanistan was one of the greatest surprises of the century up to that time, a harbinger, and a cause, of an even bigger surprise, the implosion of the Soviet system. Clearly, long before Afghanistan, the Soviet Army had been suffering from unimaginative and even incompetent leadership at many levels. The Soviets/ Russians were reluctant or unable to translate their Afghanistan experience into new doctrine and practices.[8] Hence the further embarrassments of the war in Chechnya. Russia's operations against the little neighboring country of Georgia (one-250th of the size of Russia) in 2008 did not eliminate serious questions about the state of Russian military effectiveness.

Common Weaknesses and Failures

The same significant and perhaps surprising errors show up time after time in the counterinsurgencies we have examined. These include failure to provide adequate military leadership, to offer the adversary a peaceful path to change, to cut the insurgents off from outside help, and, arguably most consequential of all, to commit numerically sufficient forces to the conflicts.

The *quality of military leadership* among the counterinsurgents was inadequate. This is no mere tautology. The Japanese, the French, and the Soviets were guilty of arguably the most grievous error any military leadership can commit: underestimating the enemy. When the Japanese realized they had a serious guerrilla problem on their hands, they could come up with nothing better than the "three alls" policy. The heterogeneous nature of the coalition led by Chiang Kai-shek required him (as he thought) to appoint commanders for their political reliability, not their military skills. The French replaced their military commanders in Hanoi with the same dismaying frequency that they replaced their government leaders in Paris. In Cuba, from the beginning of that relatively brief struggle there, it was apparent that the army command was unable to organize even the semblance of a competent campaign against Castro's followers. But perhaps the most surprising deficit of military leadership was among the Soviets in Afghanistan: the vaunted conquerors of Hitler turned out to be ghosts. More will be said about this shortly, but for just one notable instance, the indifference and incompetence of the Soviet high command regarding the most fundamental aspects of logistics—the most elementary physical needs of their soldiers—is astonishing.

None of the counterinsurgencies examined in this book provided their adversaries a *peaceful road to change,* that is, a recognized, nonviolent method for redressing grievances. The often systematic violations of rectitude on the part of counterinsurgent forces of course both reflected and aggravated this situation. Accordingly, the insurgents could rightly claim that they had no recourse except arms. Now elections, however free and democratic, are clearly not a panacea for political violence, and they may actually provoke or worsen such violence. Besides, most cultures have long experience with other methods for settling disputes or patching together something roughly resembling a consensus. Nevertheless, many have rightly called the ballot box the coffin of insurgency, and one can make the case that internationally observed elections in Cuba in 1956 or even 1958 might well have kept Castro from power. True, none of the leading figures in the Cuban, Chinese, Vietnamese, or Afghan conflicts had any intention of submitting the fate of their power and ambitions to honest elections. But this attitude certainly would not have characterized all, or probably most, of their followers at all times in those conflicts.

Not one of the counterinsurgents succeeded in *preventing vital outside direct assistance* from reaching their adversaries. Quite possibly, Mao would have won his conflict even without Soviet help after 1944, but no one denies that Chinese aid turned the tide in French Vietnam (just as it did years later in South Vietnam). External assistance, both direct and indirect, to Castro helped convince everyone that the Batista regime was on its way out, while the multinational cornucopia of munitions and money to the Afghan mujahideen increased casualties and undermined morale among the Soviet forces and arguably made their war unwinnable.[9] (It is true that, even though they failed to close the Ho Chi Minh Trail, the Americans and their numerous allies defeated the Viet Cong; but that case hardly proves that isolating the battlefield is less than vitally important to the counterinsurgents.)

But arguably the primary and decisive failure, especially in the Japanese, French, and Soviet cases, was *to commit woefully insufficient forces to the conflict.*[10] The definition of insufficient forces is that the counterinsurgents cannot simultaneously isolate the battle area, defend what must be defended, and carry out disruptive operations against the guerrillas. (Batista had more than enough troops on paper, but few of these were prepared to fight insurgents, or perhaps to fight anybody at all.)

Inadequate counterinsurgent numbers of course resulted from several factors. One was the aforementioned failure, notably in French Vietnam and Soviet Afghanistan, to cut off outside aid to the insurgents, while in turn inadequate numbers made it all the more impossible to cut off or limit that outside aid.

A further major contributing factor to the force-level problem was the inability of the counterinsurgent power to *devote full attention* to the conflict at hand, a consequence of *indirect aid* to their enemies. This is not a recent phenomenon. During the American War of Independence, the British became fearful of a French invasion of the home islands and consequently neglected the campaigns in North America. At the same time that the French Revolution faced major insurgencies in western and southern France, it was waging war against all of Europe. Napoleon's endless wars, and above all his Russian expedition, made it easier for guerrillas in Spain to establish their control over most of that country, providing a base and a stage for the man who one day became known to the world as the Duke of Wellington. In like manner, the Japanese invasion distracted Chiang Kai-shek from the final extermination of the Chinese Communist Party; the American onslaught across the Pacific took Japanese attention away from counterinsurgency in China; German rearmament seemed to necessitate the stationing of the bulk of the French Army in Europe, not Vietnam (where French prestige had already been fatally damaged by the Japanese occupation); and the Soviet effort in Afghanistan languished in the face of growing instability in eastern Europe and the strategic challenge mounted by the United States.

Nevertheless, the complexities of international politics do not fully account for inadequate counterinsurgent numbers. Both the French and the Soviets, for example, could have compensated for their numerical limitations to a very large degree at the least by raising many more indigenous armed units than they did. The French feared a well-trained and well-armed anti–Viet Minh Vietnamese army only less than they feared the Viet Minh itself; but recall that after Vietnam, the French in Algeria recruited and armed more indigenous personnel than the insurgents did. Of course, the barbarity of the Japanese in China and the Soviets in Afghanistan not only made recruitment of substantial and reliable indigenous forces almost impossible but also greatly increased the numbers and determination of their opponents. Thus, the thickest roots of force-level inadequacy are found in the political field. Truly, when one considers how ethnically and religiously fragmented the population of Afghanistan was, the inability of the Soviets to win or buy the support of a larger proportion of the Afghan peoples, or at least not to outrage almost everybody, remains an impressive monument—a tombstone—to their political ineptitude.

But even if the counterinsurgent side was unable or unwilling to raise, train, and properly arm large numbers of local allies, all need not have been lost: the counterinsurgents could have adjusted their ends to their means—that is, they could have determined their objectives in light of the forces available. Recall the words of General Leclerc in 1946: Better to hold half or a third of Vietnam solidly than the whole of it feebly.

In the end, the Japanese, the French, and the Soviets abandoned their counterinsurgencies and went home. But that course of action did not solve their more fundamental problems. Four years after France deserted its Vietnamese allies, the entire Fourth French Republic circus was swept away (the consequence of another counterinsurgency, this time successful, in Algeria). Three years after it stalked out of Afghanistan, the Soviet Union ceased to exist. And even a complete withdrawal from China would not have averted the devastation and occupation of Japan.

Some Considerations for Americans

To what extent can the cases examined in this volume offer instruction with regard to U.S. counterinsurgency policy in the twenty-first century?

In the first place, compared to the forces of countries that have waged unsuccessful counterinsurgencies in the past, today's U.S. armed forces possess great and possibly decisive advantages. U.S. forces are vastly superior to those of Imperial Japan or Nationalist China or Fourth Republican France, most especially in airpower. American officer selection and training far outstrips that of the Nationalist Chinese and the Soviets in Afghanistan, to take only two examples. U.S. logistics are incomparably better than those of the Soviets in the 1980s or of any other country today. In contrast to the systematic assaults on the civilian population carried out by the Japanese in China or the Soviets in Afghanistan, American measures against insurgency, from the Philippines to Iraq, have consistently included the construction of a peaceful road to change and the establishment of indigenous armed units. By no means least, one can hardly imagine the U.S. government suffering the spectacular instability that characterized the French Fourth Republic. And one could clearly extend this list.

Furthermore, from the cases here considered, it is clear—though perhaps counterintuitive—that being a dictatorship does not necessarily confer any special advantage upon a country battling insurgents. In fact, democratic polities have achieved some notable successes in this kind of war: recall the British in Malaya; the French in Algeria;[11] and the Americans in the Philippines (twice, post-1898 and post-1945), in Greece, in South Vietnam, and in El Salvador. It is but one measure among many of how poorly the Americans are served by their schools and universities and their news industry that most of them are greatly surprised to discover that South Vietnam fell not to Viet Cong guerrillas but to the regular North Vietnamese Army, years after U.S. combat units had left.

Nevertheless, some powerful countervailing considerations arise. In the first place, the frustrating Vietnam experience of the Americans was by no means unique in the modern era; on the contrary, counterinsurgency has presented a major challenge to all militarily powerful states. We recall once again the ominous warning of a close student of guerrilla war at the beginning of the twentieth century: "Guerrilla warfare is what regular armies always have most to dread, and when this is directed by a leader with a genius for war, an effective campaign becomes well-nigh impossible."[12]

It has hardly been a secret, furthermore, that fighting irregular forces is far from the kind of war-making important elements of the U.S. military wish to be involved in.[13] There is no intention here to disparage the primacy of U.S. conventional forces. Those forces defeated Nazi Germany and Imperial Japan and deterred the Soviet Union until it imploded—accomplishments that spared the Americans and indeed the human race incalculable calamities. There can be little doubt, though, that engaging in irregular warfare throws away or at least limits some of the principal American war-making advantages.

The enduring institutional distaste for waging counterinsurgency is not the only structural problem for the U.S. Army. Counterinsurgency is mainly an infantry effort. Like the Japanese in China, the French in Vietnam, and the Soviets in Afghanistan, the Americans both in Vietnam and in Iraq never had enough combat infantry on the ground to cope with the multiple challenges of even poorly directed insurgencies. Indeed, the effort to wage or support counterinsurgencies simultaneously in Iraq and Afghanistan overstretched U.S. forces to a dangerous degree. Inadequate numbers of combat infantry may well prove to be a persisting feature of the U.S. armed forces. Moreover, insufficient numbers of infantry have been in large part a consequence of failure to isolate the theater of combat. This was clearly the case with the French in Vietnam, the Soviets in Afghanistan, and the Americans in Vietnam, where the purely political decision not to shut down the Ho Chi Minh Trail had the most profound consequences.

Quite aside from the widespread distaste within the U.S. military for counterinsurgency operations, Americans—both military and civilian—are notoriously disinclined to master foreign languages and acquire familiarity with foreign cultures. These regrettable weaknesses can be serious handicaps in any counterinsurgent endeavor and can undermine the best efforts of even the most courageous, dedicated, and well-equipped U.S. military personnel.[14] They can, among other effects, dangerously reduce the quality, quantity, and understanding of the intelligence available to American troops in a combat area. It appears, moreover, that most Americans, even highly placed Washington policymakers, are not completely aware of the depth of their own cultural self-absorption and the consequences of it. In Jeffrey Record's pungent formulation, "the United States is probably the only modern country in the world where a person who speaks no foreign language can be considered well-educated."[15]

But the most important consideration of all for Americans may be this one: the counterinsurgency experiences of neither dictatorships nor democracies are encouraging for those who desire quick victory at modest cost. An insurgency is always a limited war for the counterinsurgents, and notably for the United States—but it is always an all-out war on the part of the insurgents. This imbalance can wear down the patience of even the strongest power. Andrew Mack, in his seminal study, offered this essential insight: "The military defeat of the metropolis [colonial or occupying state] itself was impossible since the insurgents lacked an invasion capability. In every case, success for the insurgents arose not from a military victory on the ground—though military success may have been a contributory cause—but rather from the progressive attrition of their opponents' *political* capability to wage war. In such asymmetric conflicts, insurgents may gain political victory from a situation of military stalemate or *even defeat.*"[16] Victims of this phenomenon include the French in Algeria and the Americans in Vietnam. The Romans knew that counterinsurgents' most telling weapon is perseverance. But the protracted nature of guerrilla insurgency and the moral ambiguities that arise in any war present American politicians with apparently irresistible temptations to score short-term political advantage by attacking the conduct of and even the motives for the conflict. In this destructive work, the politicians receive powerful assistance from the sensationalism and superficiality that characterize much of the American news industry.[17] Consider the ultimately successful British counterinsurgency in Malaya. That country was smaller in area than Alabama. The British were intimately familiar with Malaya and had long exercised complete administrative control there. The insurgents were grossly outnumbered, possessed no foreign sanctuary, received hardly any outside aid, and bore the hostility of great sections of the civilian population. Nevertheless, it took a dozen years for the counterinsurgency to attain final success. It is possible, but not easy, to imagine the American electorate consenting to a major overseas commitment of such duration.

And, like the Japanese, the French, and the Soviets, the Americans always have the option to leave the locus of a protracted counterinsurgency. Enemies of the United States all over the world know this, or at least they ought to.

Given this less-than-auspicious combination of factors, it should be comforting to reflect that one can hardly identify territory outside the immediate Western Hemisphere where truly vital U.S. interests could be irredeemably threatened by guerrillas alone. If this view is sound, and if the foregoing analysis has merit, then one could argue that American policymakers should consider involving this country against insurgents, if that becomes clearly necessary, only according to the model set by the Truman administration during the Philippine Huk insurgency and the Greek Civil War and by the Carter and Reagan administrations in El Salvador: that is, through limited support to indigenous counterinsurgent forces. In such circumstances, leaders of the U.S. government would need to understand thoroughly, and be able to explain clearly, why the insurgency against which they wish to intervene is going on and why the United States should oppose it. Outside of the most unusual contingencies, U.S. ground combat units should not become involved, indeed should not set foot in the affected country, especially if they would have to confront elements of a warrior society in a state of religious exaltation or undertake operations in urban areas.[18] On the contrary, one might continue to argue, in almost every case the Americans would do better to limit their involvement mainly to interdicting outside aid to the guerrillas and sending carefully selected and well-prepared U.S. military personnel into the host country principally as advisers. Beyond that, important American contributions to the counterinsurgency would take the form of intelligence, logistics, and financial help. Finally, it would be essential that the United States make it clear to the host government that all such assistance was contingent upon its maintaining or instituting a peaceful path to change and eliminating or ameliorating abuses that may have contributed to the outbreak of the insurgency.[19] Above all, the United States would need to require of the host government that its soldiers display right conduct toward both civilians and prisoners. If there is anything like an incontrovertible lesson that emerges from a comparative study of counterinsurgencies, especially unsuccessful ones, it is that right strategy is indissolubly linked to right conduct. Rectitude is worth many battalions.

Postscript: The Soviets and the Americans in Afghanistan

In December 2009, in a move that reminded many of the "surge" ordered by President George W. Bush in Iraq in 2007, President Barack Obama announced a substantial increase in the number of U.S. combat forces in Afghanistan, intending to bring the total there to almost 100,000 (at their height, U.S. forces in Vietnam numbered close to 600,000). President Obama thus became, to the deep dismay of some of his original supporters, the first Democratic president since Lyndon Johnson to deploy significant numbers of American combat troops into a war zone. The destination of these troops was a land devastated by armed conflict for more than thirty years, where U.S. forces had been fighting for close to a decade. (At the time of the president's announcement, the total number of U.S. military fatalities in Afghanistan in the previous eight years was well below one thousand, equivalent to the number of motor vehicle deaths in Michigan in 2009.) President Obama pledged to disrupt the Taliban strongholds in southern and eastern Afghanistan, increase civilian security, offer amnesty to disaffected elements of the Taliban, build up effective indigenous security forces, and maintain a peaceful path to change, in the form of reasonably presentable elections.

A disturbing question: can the Americans succeed in Afghanistan, where the Soviets failed? After all, the Soviet Army, the vaunted conquerors of the Third Reich, had at least as many troops in the country and fewer inhibitions on their actions than the Americans would have. Notably, they were fighting in a land right across the border of the Soviet Union, whereas Washington is on the other side of the globe from Kabul. In some ways, American soldiers are at least as foreign to Afghans as the Soviets were. In addition, polls indicated that substantial sections of the U.S. electorate were unenthusiastic about the president's new departure, and leaders of the Taliban could note with interest that he had promised to begin the withdrawal of U.S. forces from Afghanistan within eighteen months (by July 2011).

But the question needs refinement: what was it that the Soviets failed to do in Afghanistan, and what is it that the Americans hope to achieve there? The Soviets intended to impose and maintain by blunt military force a regime that had no chance of attaining legitimacy or even popularity. In this project the Soviets carried many burdens, mostly self-inflicted. Their systematic brutality created a hostile Afghan majority willing and able to offer serious and sustained armed resistance. The army of the Soviets was not, to say the least, what it had been in earlier decades. Not surprisingly, they failed utterly to organize an Afghan army that could take the pressure off Soviet forces or even effectively assist them. In addition—for what it was worth—the United Nations annually condemned the Soviet occupation by lopsided votes. Worst of all, the USSR's move into Afghanistan soon faced a hostile coalition of impressive diversity that delivered an ever-increasing flow of weapons and money to the insurgents. Nevertheless, it is essential to remember that the Soviets were not defeated in Afghanistan. The insurgents had captured no Soviet city, or even Kabul. Only a small fraction of the Soviet Army had been involved in the fighting. The Soviets left Afghanistan because the Gorbachev leadership decided the enterprise was not worth the cost. A different politburo might have reached a different estimate.

In contrast, the American aim is not the subjugation of the country but the establishment of a stable, indigenous, democratically elected government. At the time President Obama announced his decision to send more troops, the United States confronted only a minority of the Afghan population; had many allies in the country, including both Afghan and NATO forces; and enjoyed the blessing of the United Nations. Moreover, for years the Iraqi conflicts distracted American attention from Afghanistan, but the situation in Iraq had stabilized to a degree few would have predicted in 2005 or 2006. And the armed forces of the United States in 2010 were incomparably more capable in almost every way than those of the Soviet Union in 1985.

A central concern involved the security of the border between Afghanistan and Pakistan. The loss of control of the frontier with China destroyed whatever chances the French had of holding onto Vietnam. Later, failure to stem the massive violations of its western borders was decisive in the fall of South Vietnam. In the 1940s Greek guerrilla units were often able to escape the pursuing Greek Army by crossing unopposed into Communist Albania, Yugoslavia, and Bulgaria, and later returning to Greece. To their great cost, the Soviets were unable to seal off Afghanistan's border with Pakistan, which enjoyed the full backing of the United States. Would Pakistan, with that same support, be able—and willing—to control that same border? If the answer turned out to be "yes, mainly," then the resulting relative isolation of the Taliban insurgents, plus an approximation of free elections and the fielding of reasonably effective Afghan security forces would constitute key and very probably decisive differences between the Soviet and American involvements in Afghanistan.

As Winston Churchill remarked on the eve of World War I, "it would be a pity to be wrong."

Notes

Introduction

1. C.E. Callwell, *Small Wars: Their Principles and Practices* (1906; Wakefield, England: EP, 1976), 126.

2. See Anthony James Joes, *Resisting Rebellion: The History and Politics of Counterinsurgency* (Lexington: Univ. Press of Kentucky, 2004), 278, 146n.

3. At one time most American schoolchildren knew that the climactic event of the American War of Independence was the surrender of General Cornwallis at Yorktown; few, however, knew that Cornwallis had retreated to Yorktown largely to escape American guerrillas.

4. *The U.S. Army/Marine Corps Counterinsurgency Field Manual* (Chicago: Univ. of Chicago Press, 2007). For just two examples of such criticism, see Edward Luttwak, "Dead End: Counterinsurgency Warfare as Military Malpractice," *Harper's* (Feb. 2007); and Gian P. Gentile, "The Selective Use of History in the Development of American Counterinsurgency Doctrine," *Army History* 72 (Summer 2009).

5. C.H.V. Sutherland, *The Romans in Spain* (1939; Westport, CT: Greenwood, 1982).

6. Bernard Brodie, "The Continuing Relevance of *On War*," in Carl von Clausewitz, *On War*, ed. and trans. Michael Howard and Peter Paret (Princeton, NJ: Princeton Univ. Press, 1976), 54; Ian F.W. Beckett, *Modern Insurgencies and Counter-Insurgencies: Guerrillas and Their Opponents since 1750* (London: Routledge, 2001), 249–50.

7. Austin Long, *The 'Other War': Lessons from Five Decades of RAND Counterinsurgency Research* (Santa Monica, CA: RAND, 2006), 15; Lesley Anne Warner, "Conclusions: Lessons Learned for Future Counterinsurgencies," in *Money in the Bank: Lessons Learned from Past Counterinsurgency* (Santa Monica, CA: RAND, 2007), 69 (my italics).

8. *The U.S. Army/Marine Corps Counterinsurgency Field Manual* (Chicago: Univ. of Chicago Press, 2007), li–liii. See also Ian F.W. Beckett, *Insurgency in Iraq: An Historical Perspective* (Carlisle, PA: Strategic Studies Institute, 2005); Colin S. Gray, *Irregular Enemies and the Essence of Strategy: Can the American Way of War Adapt?* (Carlisle, PA: Strategic Studies Institute, 2006). Certainly, insurgents learn, or try to learn, from past insurgencies; see Christopher C. Harmon, "Illustrations of 'Learning' in Counterinsurgency," *Comparative Strategy* 11 (1992).

9. William Rosenau, "Counterinsurgency: Lessons from Iraq and Afghanistan," *Harvard International Review* 31 (Spring 2009): n.p.

10. Aristotle, *The Politics,* book 5, chap. 6; Vladimir I. Lenin, "Left-Wing Communism: An Infantile Disorder," in *Collected Works of V.I. Lenin* (Moscow: Progress, 1964), 31:17–118; Crane Brinton, *Anatomy of Revolution* (1936; New York: Vintage, 1965); Chorley, *Armies;* and see also Anthony James Joes, *From the Barrel of a Gun: Armies and Revolution* (Washington, DC: Pergamon-Brassey's, 1986).

11. Niccolò Machiavelli, *The Prince;* Skocpol, *States and Revolutions;* Record, *Beating Goliath;* O'Neill, *Insurgency and Terrorism.*

1. China

1. Pye, "China: Erratic State," 58.

2. Fairbank, "Reunification of China," 14; in the original, the entire sentence is in italics.

3. The Great Taiping Rebellion (1850–64), one of the major wars of the century, was both nationalist (against the Manchu dynasty) and egalitarian (against the Confucian elites); Fairbank, *Great Chinese Revolution,* 73. The rebels actually captured and held Nanking for years, and no one knows for sure how many millions perished in the upheaval. See the excellent study by Wright, *Last Stand of Chinese Conservatism.* For the Nien conflict, see Chiang, *Nien Rebellion;* and Teng, *Nien Army.*

4. Fairbank, *Great Chinese Revolution,* 81.

5. One very notable exception to this statement is the extraordinary story of Matteo Ricci (1552–1610). An Italian Jesuit, Ricci entered China in 1582, became accepted as a member of the literati, and eventually served as mathematician and astronomer at the Imperial court. He sent to Europe its first modern detailed report on China. See Vincent Cronin, *The Wise Man from the West* (New York: Dutton, 1955); and Spence, *Memory Palace of Ricci.*

6. Zarrow, *China in War and Revolution,* 7. "In a sense the whole history of modern China can be seen as a reaction to imperialism, an outside force that threatened the country's very existence." Bianco, *Origins of the Chinese Revolution,* 140.

7. Young, *Presidency of Yuan,* 254.

8. Fairbank, *Great Chinese Revolution*, 161.

9. Young, *Presidency of Yuan*, esp. chap. 8.

10. See Pye, *Warlord Politics*; McCord, *Power of the Gun*; Ch'i, *Warlord Politics*.

11. Zarrow, *China in War and Revolution*, 86.

12. Johnson, *Autopsy on People's War*, 13.

13. Studies of Sun abound. See Bergère, *Sun Yat-sen*; Linebarger, *Sun Yat-sen*.

14. See Fairbank, "Maritime and Continental."

15. Sheridan, *China in Disintegration*.

16. Ibid., 230. Canton was the first Chinese port regularly visited by Europeans; the far-sailing Portuguese secured a foreign trade monopoly there in 1511. Canton is ninety miles from Hong Kong and sixty-five miles from Macau. The overseas Chinese, very numerous in Singapore, Indonesia, the Philippines, and elsewhere, wanted a strong Chinese state to protect them from persecution and exploitation in the lands of their residence.

17. Sheridan, "Warlord Era."

18. Of a prominent Mandarin family, educated at an American school in China and later in Japan, Chou (1898–1976) served for many years as premier or foreign minister (or both) of the People's Republic.

19. F.F. Liu, *A Military History of Modern China, 1924–1949* (Princeton, NJ: Princeton Univ. Press, 1956), 11.

20. Liu, *Military History*, 7. Michael Borodin (Mihail Gruzenberg) was sent by the Comintern to help reorganize the KMT and simultaneously build up the Chinese Communist Party. See Holubnychy, *Borodin and the Chinese Revolution*.

21. Clubb, *Twentieth Century China*, 122.

22. Chiang, *China's Destiny*.

23. Ibid., 20, 111, 83, 84.

24. Ibid., 78; see also 111 and 179. On this intriguing subject of warlordism, see Sheridan, *Chinese Warlord*; Pye, *Warlord Politics*; Ch'i, *Warlord Politics*; Sutton, *Provincial Militarism*.

25. Sheridan, "Warlord Era," 288–89. See also Pye, *Warlord Politics*. On the value of mercenary troops, see Machiavelli's *Prince*, chap. 12.

26. Jordan, *Northern Expedition*, 231, 234, and passim, quotation on 234.

27. Ibid., 277. See also Hu, *Brief History*.

28. Marks, *Counterrevolution in China*, 80. Chiang of course had quite given up trying to convert the members of the CCP.

29. Zhang, *Chinese Communist Party*, 1:580–81.

30. Taylor, *Generalissimo*, 66.

31. See Whiting, *Soviet Policies in China*; Brandt, *Stalin's Failure in China*; Isaacs, *Tragedy of the Chinese Revolution*; Roy, *Revolution and Counterrevolution*; and the novel by André Malraux, *Man's Fate* (New York: Modern Library, 1936).

32. Taylor, *Generalissimo*, 85.

33. Wilbur, "Nationalist Revolution," 720.

34. Eastman, "Nationalist China," 163; see Eastman, *Abortive Revolution*; and Hung-Mao, *Government and Politics*, chap. 1; Shieh, *Kuomintang*; Wakeman and Edmonds, *Reappraising Republican China*.

35. See Young, *China and the Helping Hand*.

36. MacAleavy, *Modern History of China*, 267; see also Wilbur, *Nationalist Revolution*.

37. Linebarger, *China of Chiang Kai-shek*, 274.

38. Bedeski, *State-Building in Modern China*, ix. See also Jordan, *Northern Expedition*, 67 and passim.

39. Born in Hunan Province in 1893, Mao Tse-tung was the son of a prosperous farmer, graduated from the provincial teachers college, was one of the original members of the Chinese Communist Party, and emerged as supreme leader of the CCP during the Long March. The literature on Mao is voluminous. See Mao's semiautobiography produced by Snow, *Red Star over China*, and subsequent editions.

40. Actually, it was inappropriate for Russia too, as any honest and well-instructed Marxist would have acknowledged in 1917.

41. Gray, *Modern Strategy*, 292–93.

42. Mao, *Selected Military Writings*, 14.

43. Mao, "On Protracted War," 2:172 (my italics).

44. Mao, *Basic Tactics*, 81.

45. Mao, *Selected Military Writings*, 274.

46. For a brief analysis of Trotsky's construction of the Red Army, including his use of political commissars, see Anthony James Joes, *From the Barrel of a Gun: Armies and Revolutions* (Washington, DC: Pergamon-Brassey's, 1986), 43–47.

47. Mao, "On Protracted War," 144.

48. Luis Taruc, chief military leader of the Huk rebellion, once wrote: "Sickness was our worst enemy and accounted for many times the casualties inflicted by the Japanese and their puppets. It was the one problem we were never quite able to overcome. Malaria was the worst cause of death. Our squadrons were often forced to live in the swamps, which were thickly infested with malarial mosquitoes. . . . Dysentery and stomach ulcers from inadequate food were often serious afflictions." Taruc, *Born of the People*, 139. And a young Boer guerrilla left this image, based on his experience one night: "Our guide lost his way; we were floundering ankle-deep in mud and water, our poor weakened horses stumbling and slipping at every turn; the rain beat down on us and the cold was awful. Toward midnight it began to sleet. The grain bag which I wore [from lack of other clothing] froze solid on my body like a coat of mail, and

I believe that if we had not kept moving every one of us would have died." Reitz, *Commando*, 223.

49. Mao, *Basic Tactics*, 130.

50. Johnson, *Peasant Nationalism*, 82–83.

51. Mao, *Selected Military Writings*, 33.

52. Mao, "Strategy in Guerrilla War," 85.

53. Mao, *Basic Tactics*, 56. Confer: "We should resolutely fight a decisive engagement in every campaign or battle in which we are sure of victory; we should avoid a decisive engagement in every campaign or battle in which we are not sure of victory; and we should absolutely avoid a strategically decisive engagement on which the fate of the whole nation is staked," because "we are not gamblers who risk everything on a single throw." Mao, *Selected Military Writings*, 254, 257.

54. Mao, "On Protracted War," 180; "Strategy in China's Revolutionary War," 237.

55. Mao, *Selected Military Writings*, 72.

56. Mao, *Basic Tactics*, 86, 73.

57. "Strategy in Guerrilla War," 84; *Basic Tactics*, 102.

58. Liu, *Military History*, 250.

59. See Huntington, *Political Order*, chap. 5.

60. Mao, "Strategy in Guerrilla War," 94.

61. Ibid., 99. Of course, later events in Palestine, Cyprus, Chechnya, Northern Ireland, and other constricted territories showed that even Mao had not thought of everything.

62. Fairbairn, *Revolutionary Guerrilla Warfare*, 298. It is true that those who allow themselves to be taken prisoner might not be a random sample of the guerrilla movement as a whole.

63. Johnson, *Revolutionary Change*, 163.

64. See Pye, "Roots of Insurgency," 159–60.

65. Sun, *Long March*. See also Wilson, *Long March*.

66. See Wu, *Sian Incident*.

67. Mao, "Strategy in China's Revolutionary War," 266, 213.

68. Mao, "Strategy in Guerrilla War," 104.

69. Whitson, *Lessons from China*, 7.

70. Leung, *Dictionary of Revolutionary China*, 122.

71. Wei, *Counterrevolution*, 121.

72. See Michael, *Taiping Rebellion*; and Wright, *Last Stand of Chinese Conservatism*.

73. See Whitson, *Lessons from China*.

74. Credit for this new tactic should go to the KMT itself, not to visiting German officers, as is sometimes alleged. See Wei, *Counterrevolution*, 108ff.

75. The British had used blockhouse lines very effectively against Boer guerrillas in the South African War; by 1902 eight thousand blockhouses extended for thirty-seven hundred miles, manned by 50,000 white troops and 16,000 Africans. The typical earth-and-iron blockhouse cost only £16 to construct. Each blockhouse was connected to its neighbors by telephone lines; between them stretched barbed wire, as well as trip-wires laden with pebble-filled tin cans. Armored patrol trains protected and were protected by them in turn. The Japanese employed a similar technique after their 1937 invasion of China, building thirty thousand strongpoints, intended mainly as a protection against small-arms fire, since Chinese guerrillas rarely possessed artillery. In the 1950s the French built a highly effective modification of the blockhouse idea—the famous Morice Line—along hundreds of miles between Algeria and Tunisia.

76. Concerning the Fifth Encirclement Campaign, Mao wrote: "The Red Army was greatly weakened, and all the base areas in the south were lost." *Selected Military Writings*, 98. See also Mao Tse-tung, *Selected Works* (New York: International, 1957), vol. 1, chaps. 4 and 5, 198–254.

77. Van Slyke, *Chinese Communist Movement*, 33.

78. On the Sian Incident, see pages 24–25.

79. Hillam, "Counterinsurgency," 231ff.

80. David Lu, introduction to Morley, *China Quagmire*, 291.

81. James, "American and Japanese Strategies," 706 (my italics); Crowley, *Japan's Quest for Autonomy*, xvi. See also Barnhart, *Japan Prepares*; Iriye, *Origins of the Second World War*; and Sun, *Origins of the Pacific War*.

82. Crowley, introduction to Morley, *China Quagmire*, 9.

83. James, "American and Japanese Strategies," 705.

84. Pyle, *Japan Rising*, 62; Jansen, *Japan and China*.

85. Coox, "Pacific War," 315; quotation in Lu, introduction to Morley, *China Quagmire*, 290.

86. Coox, "Pacific War," 323. See Grew, *Turbulent Era*, vol. 2, chap. 34, "Pearl Harbor: from the Perspective of Ten Years."

87. Maki, *Conflict and Tension*, 105. And see Morton, "Japan's Decision."

88. Julian Jackson, *The Fall of France: The Nazi Invasion of 1940* (New York: Oxford Univ. Press, 2003), chap. 6; David Reynolds, "Fulcrum of the Twentieth Century?" *International Affairs* 66 (1990).

89. James, "American and Japanese Strategies," 706; Hata, "Continental Expansion," 309, 313, Chiang quoted on 313.

90. Morison, *History of Naval Operations*, 3:63; quotation in Geoffrey Blainey, *The Causes of War*, 3rd ed. (New York: Free Press, 1978), 251. On this complex and controversial subject, see Scott D. Sagan, "From Deterrence to Coercion to War:

The Road to Pearl Harbor," in *The Limits of Coercive Diplomacy*, ed. Alexander L. George and William E. Simons (Boulder, CO: Westview, 1994); and Frederick W. Marks III, *Wind over Sand: The Diplomacy of Franklin Roosevelt* (Athens: Univ. of Georgia Press, 1988); Hata, "Continental Expansion," 310.

91. See Lloyd Eastman, "Relations between Chiang Kai-shek and Wang Jing-wei during the War against Japan," *Republican China* 14 (1989).

92. Johnson, *Peasant Nationalism*, chap. 2; Barrett, "Wang Jingwei Regime"; see also Linebarger, *China of Chiang Kai-shek*, 197–211.

93. Boyle, *China and Japan at War*, 6.

94. Chu Teh, *On the Battlefronts*.

95. On this subject see also Ch'i, *Nationalist China at War*; and Bunker, *Peace Conspiracy*.

96. See Boyle, *China and Japan at War*; also Brook, *Collaboration*; F.C. Jones, *Japan's New Order in East Asia: Its Rise and Fall, 1937–1945* (London: Oxford Univ. Press, 1954).

97. Crowley, *Japan's Quest for Autonomy*, 398.

98. Eastman, "Nationalist China," 590.

99. Chou, *Chinese Inflation*, 258; Pepper, "KMT-CCP Conflict," 741. In postwar Shanghai, the government tied working-class wages to an inflation index; hence that group was relatively shielded, at least for a while, from the ravages of superinflation; but the salaries and savings of the middle classes were devastated. Barnett, *China on the Eve*, 19ff.

100. Mao, "Strategy in Guerrilla War," 23.

101. Hata, "Continental Expansion," 307.

102. Liu, *Military History*, 205. Lincoln Li believes there were only 770,000 Japanese troops in China in 1940 and that the stalemate that characterized most of the Sino-Japanese War was due to the inadequate numbers of the Japanese; see *Japanese Army*, 6, 12, 220.

103. Colin S. Gray, *The Leverage of Seapower: The Strategic Advantage of Navies in War* (New York: Free Press, 1992), 256; *The Statesman's Yearbook, 1944* (New York: St. Martin's, 1944), 1067; van Slyke, "China Incident," 232–33. See Li, *Japanese Army*, 12; and Wheal et al., *Dictionary of the Second World War*, 244.

104. The 1943 estimate is in Coox, "Pacific War," 320; for the 1944 estimate, see Van Slyke, "Chinese Communist Movement," 708.

105. See Hsu and Chang, *Sino-Japanese War*, 565; Kirby, *War against Japan*, 196; Chu Teh, *On the Battlefronts*, 35.

106. Spoken Japanese and spoken Chinese are nearly as different from each other as English is from either of those languages. Johnson, *Peasant Nationalism*, chap. 2; Harries and Harries, *Soldiers of the Sun*. See also Dear, *Oxford Companion*, 221; and Carlson, *Chinese Army*, 27–28.

107. Van Slyke, "Chinese Communist Movement," 682; Mao, "On Protracted War," 158; Mao, "Strategy in Guerrilla War," 86.

108. See Samuel B. Griffith, *Mao Tse-tung: On Guerrilla Warfare* (New York: Praeger, 1961), 67, 94. See also Harries and Harries, *Soldiers of the Sun,* 260–62, 320–21, 348. In July 1939 a substantial Japanese force entered the Soviet puppet state of Outer Mongolia from Manchukuo. After receiving powerful reinforcements, Soviet troops counterattacked. They surrounded and wiped out the Twenty-third Division of the Japanese Kwantung Army. Nomonhan was the name of the border post where the Soviet Army crossed into western Manchukuo. See Coox, *Nomonhan;* and P. Snow, "Nomonhan—the Unknown Victory," *History Today,* July 1990.

109. Harries and Harries, *Soldiers of the Sun,* 348–54; Overy, *Why the Allies Won,* 222. See also Li, *Japanese Army;* quotation in Overy, *Why the Allies Won,* 221. In fact, the German army was not what many later imagined it to be, either: The 3 million German soldiers who invaded the USSR in June 1941 were accompanied by 3,500 tanks and 700,000 horses. During 1942 another 400,000 horses were brought into the service of the German armies.

110. Overy, *Why the Allies Won,* 221.

111. Barnhart, "Japanese Intelligence," 432, 424.

112. Harries and Harries, *Soldiers of the Sun,* 253–54. By 1940 the IJA had severely defeated Communist guerrillas in Manchukuo; see Lee, *Counterinsurgency in Manchuria,* 65 and passim; see also Hanrahan, *Japanese Operations,* 8; and De Lee, "Far Eastern Experience."

113. Johnson, *Peasant Nationalism,* 72–73, 94, 69, quotation on 94.

114. Li, *Japanese Army,* 227; Lee, *Counterinsurgency in Manchuria.*

115. Johnson, *Peasant Nationalism,* 59.

116. Fairbairn, *Revolutionary Guerrilla Warfare,* 118.

117. Johnson, *Peasant Nationalism,* 16.

118. Mao, "On Protracted War," 122.

119. Johnson, *Peasant Nationalism,* 4.

120. Griffith, *Mao Tse-tung,* 69. "In terms of revolutionary strategy, Communism has succeeded only when it has been able to co-opt a national liberation struggle, and has failed whenever it was opposed to or isolated from a national liberation struggle." Johnson, *Autopsy on People's War,* 12, 10, quotation on 12. This was a venerable as well as effective Communist stratagem. The willingness of the Bolsheviks to don the garments, however incongruous, of Russian nationalism against Polish, French, and Japanese interventionists helped save them during the civil war that followed the Leninist coup of October 1917.

121. Mao, "Strategy in China's Revolutionary War," 200.

122. Emerson, *Empire to Nation,* 89.

123. Huntington, *Political Order,* chap. 5.

124. Johnson, *Autopsy on People's War*, 12 (my italics).

125. Johnson, *Revolutionary Change*, 161; Johnson, *Peasant Nationalism*, 4.

126. Lenin, "Left-Wing Communism," 602–3 (my italics).

127. Hofheinz "Chinese Communist Success," 72–77.

128. Mao, *Selected Military Writings*, 210–11. "The second stage may be termed one of strategic stalemate" (212).

129. Van Slyke, *Chinese Communist Movement*, 111–12.

130. Marks, *Counterrevolution in China*, 83.

131. Odd Arne Westad, *Decisive Encounters: The Chinese Civil War, 1946–1950* (Stanford, CA: Stanford Univ. Press, 2003), 30.

132. Van Slyke, *Chinese Communist Movement*, 6, 104, 120–21.

133. Pye, *Warlord Politics*, 3.

134. Liu, *Military History*, 105.

135. Ibid., 104. See also Sutton, "German Advice."

136. Chung, *Rape of Nanking*.

137. Coox, "Pacific War," 320.

138. Liu, *Military History*, 148; Eastman, "Nationalist China," 572; Van Slyke, "China Incident," 221.

139. Chassin, *Communist Conquest*, 45; Sun, *Art of War*, xi, 29.

140. Ch'i, "Military Dimension," 175, 176, 173.

141. Liu, *Military History*, 136.

142. Ibid., 139; Eastman, "Nationalist China," 574.

143. Sun, *Art of War*, xi, 32.

144. Liu, *Military History*, 138.

145. Eastman, "Nationalist China," 573.

146. Ibid.

147. Clubb, *Twentieth Century China*, 234.

148. Liu, *Military History*, 138.

149. Ch'i, "Military Dimension," 171; Eastman, *Seeds of Destruction*, 210.

150. Eastman, *Seeds of Destruction*, 220–21.

151. Eastman, "Nationalist China," 576.

152. Ibid., 577.

153. Ch'i, "Military Dimension," 169.

154. See Taylor, *Generalissimo*, esp. chap. 6. See also White, *Stilwell Papers*.

155. Ch'i, "Military Dimension," 168.

156. Ibid., 169.

157. Ibid., 170.

158. Eastman, "Nationalist China," 569.

159. See esp. Liu, *Military History*, 266–67. The Communists were aware of the disorder within the Nationalist chain of command. See Chu Teh, *On the Battlefronts*.

160. Eastman, "Nationalist China," 571.

161. Tang, *America's Failure*, 50.

162. Ch'i, *Nationalist China at War*, 80–81.

163. Liu, *Military History*, 219; Eastman, "Nationalist China," 581. Van Slyke estimates 300,000; see his "Chinese Communist Movement," 706.

164. Skocpol, *States and Social Revolutions*, 32.

165. Eastman, "Nationalist China," 583.

166. *FRUS*, 1947, 7:178–79. General Barr identified the defense of isolated cities from inside the walls as a major Nationalist tactical defect. Van Slyke, *China White Paper*, Aug. 1949, 2:337. One should note that (1) the *White Paper* makes hardly any mention at all of the role that Soviet assistance to the CCP played in the fall of the KMT regime, and (2) Secretary of Defense Louis A. Johnson refused to have his department identified in any way with the publication.

167. Pepper, "KMT-CCP Conflict," 781; O. Edmund Clubb, in *FRUS*, 1947, 181.

168. Eastman, *Seeds of Destruction*, 205, 204, 209.

169. Forrest C. Pogue, *George C. Marshall: Statesman, 1949–1959* (New York: Viking, 1987). For General Marshall's almost willful naïveté toward the CCP, see Taylor, *Generalissimo*, chap. 8, "Chimera of Victory." But see also Bland, *Marshall's Mediation Mission*; and Beal, *Marshall in China*.

170. Pepper, *Civil War in China*, chap. 1.

171. The dynasty established its rule over the Malay-Polynesian inhabitants of Taiwan (called Formosa–"beautiful"—by Portuguese explorers) in 1683, made it a province in 1886, and lost it to the Japanese in 1895. The population in 1940 was 6 million. An actual armed rebellion broke out on Taiwan in 1947 against the KMT, which had never in fact ruled over the island, and was repressed with needless ferocity. Many Taiwanese had long adapted themselves to Japanese ways and came to regret the passing of Japanese rule, which had been characterized by arrogance but also by efficiency and honesty. See Linebarger, *China of Chiang Kai-shek*, 187.

172. Schram, *Mao Tse-tung*, 242.

173. Liu, *Military History*, 243–44.

174. Ibid., 250.

175. Levine, *Anvil of Victory*, 238; Westad, *Decisive Encounters*, 83.

176. Liu, *Military History*, 239; see the general's book, *Wedemeyer Reports!*

177. See, for example, Taylor, *Generalissimo*, esp. chaps. 5 and 8.

178. Gillin and Etter, "Staying On," 511 and passim; Wedemeyer, *Wedemeyer Reports*, 347.

179. *FRUS*, 1947, 7:212; Levine, *Anvil of Victory*, 245; Liu, *Military History*, 229.

180. Liu, *Military History*, 229.

181. Pepper, *Civil War in China*, 242–43; Mao, "Strategy in Guerrilla War," 104; *FRUS*, 1947, 7:214, 215.

182. *FRUS*, 1947, 7:210. See also Rea and Brewer, *Forgotten Ambassador;* and see a summary of his views in Van Slyke, *China White Paper,* August 1949, 240–42. The official reference for the *White Paper* was U.S. Department of State, *United States Relations with China.*

183. See Wedemeyer, *Wedemeyer Reports,* 397–98.

184. Regarding the American equipment, General Barr later wrote: "I pointed out that a large amount of the arms and ammunition in the hands of the Communists was captured Nationalist equipment and the practice of permitting such material to fall into the hands of the Communists was prolonging the war. Although I stressed this point many times after that, it was of little avail. The Chinese seemed inherently unable to destroy anything of value." Van Slyke, *China White Paper,* 326.

185. Clubb, *Twentieth Century China,* 289–90; Liu, *Military History,* 260; Pepper, "KMT-CCP Conflict," 766, 774, 777. Perhaps as few as 20,000 KMT troops escaped from the Manchurian disaster. Spence, *Search for Modern China,* 507. Despite the huge numbers of soldiers involved, the great majority of Chinese were passive onlookers, desiring only to stay out of the path of war. Westad, *Decisive Encounters,* 69.

186. Pepper, "KMT-CCP Conflict," 768.

187. Van Slyke, *China White Paper,* 338.

188. Tang, *America's Failure,* 483.

189. Clubb, *Twentieth Century China,* 291; *FRUS*, 1947, 7:166, 167.

190. Clubb, *Twentieth Century China,* 291. A message from the U.S. Embassy stated: "The ridiculously easy Communist crossing of the Yangtze was made possible by defections at key points, disagreements in the [Nationalist] High Command, and the failure of the Air Force to give effective support." Van Slyke, *China White Paper,* 305.

191. An important Red Army commander in the civil war, Lin eventually became defense minister under Mao and later his heir apparent. He died in a mysterious airplane crash in Mongolia in 1971.

192. Liu, *Military History,* 263–64, 245, 267.

193. Liu, *Military History,* 268–69; Pepper, "KMT-CCP Conflict."

194. Liu, *Military History,* 266.

195. Pepper, "KMT-CCP Conflict," 738; Wright, "Revolution to Restoration"; Taylor, *Generalissimo,* 592.

196. Chassin, *Communist Conquest,* 50.

197. Ibid., 249.

198. Li, *Japanese Army,* 209.

199. Chassin, *Communist Conquest,* 258.

200. Liu, *Military History,* 270.

201. See Joes, *From the Barrel of a Gun,* chap. 3, "The Hungarian Revolu-

tion"; and Anthony James Joes, *Urban Guerrilla Warfare* (Lexington: Univ. Press of Kentucky, 2007), chap. 2, "Budapest 1956."

202. Hillam, "Counterinsurgency."

203. Mao's comment in 1936: "Our political power exists in scattered and isolated mountainous or remote regions and receives no outside help whatsoever." Mao, "Strategy in China's Revolutionary War," 198.

204. Eastman, "Nationalist China," 547; Spence, *Search for Modern China*, 437; Laqueur, *Guerrilla*, 259; Johnson, *Peasant Nationalism*, 49, 155; Sih, introduction to Sih, *Strenuous Decade*, xx; Fairbank, "Reunification of China," 44; Li, *Japanese Army*, 11, 231; O'Neill, *Insurgency and Terrorism*, 35; Fairbairn, *Revolutionary Guerrilla Warfare*, 118.

205. Tang, *America's Failure*, 51; Van Slyke, "Chinese Communist Movement," 613, 620.

206. "Chiang had never stolen from the state and he did not have his own private cache of gold," writes Taylor, *Generalissimo*, 401; Pepper, "KMT-CCP Conflict," 751.

207. Ch'i, "Military Dimension," 174. For a completely hostile portrait of Chiang Kai-shek, see Tuchman, *Stilwell and the American Experience in China*.

208. Churchill, *Second World War*, 4:92.

209. Eastman, "Nationalist China," 583.

210. Taylor, *Generalissimo*, 194–95.

211. See, for example, Pike, *PAVN*, 213.

212. "In truth, the Tet Offensive for all practical purposes destroyed the Viet Cong." Davidson, *Vietnam at War*, 475. "Tet was the end of People's War, and essentially of any strategy built on guerrilla warfare and a politically inspired insurgency." Timothy J. Lomperis, *From People's War to People's Rule: Insurgency, Intervention, and the Lessons of Viet Nam* (Chapel Hill: Univ. of North Carolina Press, 1996), 341. "Never again was the Tet strategy repeated." Gabriel Kolko, *Anatomy of a War: Viet Nam, the United States, and the Modern Historical Experience* (New York: Pantheon, 1985), 334. And see also Johnson, *Autopsy on People's War*. Lenin's statement was written in 1920 in criticism of the egregious Hungarian Communist leader Bela Kun. V.I. Lenin, *Collected Works* (Moscow: Progress, 1965), 31:166.

213. Mao, "Strategy in China's Revolutionary War," 180.

214. On unintentional or indirect aid to insurgent forces, see Record, *Beating Goliath*, 44.

215. Fairbank, *Great Chinese Revolution*, 296 (my italics). The vagueness of the numbers is so revealing. "The famine that ensued was one of the greatest human tragedies of the twentieth century. According to recent demographic analyses, around 20 million people died directly or indirectly from starvation between 1959 and 1962." Richard Madsen, "The Countryside under Commu-

nism," in *The Cambridge History of China,* vol. 15, *The People's Republic, Part 2: Revolutions within the Chinese Revolution, 1966–1982,* ed. Denis Twitchett and John K. Fairbank (New York: Cambridge Univ. Press, 1992), 642. See also Nicholas P. Lardy, "The Chinese Economy under Stress, 1958–1965," in *Cambridge History of China,* vol. 14, *The People's Republic, Part 1, The Emergence of Revolutionary China, 1949–1965* (New York: Cambridge Univ. Press, 1987), 371, 380, 395.

216. Pye, *China,* 250. Mao caused the deaths of more people than Stalin and Hitler combined. Short, *Mao,* 631.

217. The "undeniable madness" assessment is from Pye, *China,* 307; Whyte, "Urban Life," 734. "In his last years Mao was as much a wreck as the country and party he had twice led to disaster. The GPCR is now seen, especially by its many victims, as ten lost years in China's modern development." Fairbank, *Great Chinese Revolution,* 335. See also Harding, "Chinese State," 107, 211.

218. Pye, *China,* 271.

219. Ibid., chap. 17.

2. French Vietnam

1. One of the critics of that approach is David W.P. Elliott; see his *Vietnamese War,* 1:3.

2. Duncanson, *Government and Revolution,* 19, 39; Truong, *Vietcong Memoir,* 283. "The Vietnamese are as conscious of region as the Indians are of caste." Douglas Pike, *Viet Cong* (Cambridge, MA: MIT Press, 1966), 6.

3. Arendt, *On Revolution.*

4. "In fact, during the first three decades of the [twentieth] century, French administration of Indo-China was as well run and as efficiently organized as the best colonial governments and created a vast system of roads, railways and other communication facilities, provided the public with the full apparatus of a modern government, and undertook economic measures meant to benefit large numbers. It also showed a great interest in the history and culture of Indo-China, preserving with care the monuments of the past and maintaining a famous institute of Oriental studies." Panikkar, *Asia and Western Dominance,* 221.

5. Fall, *Two Vietnams,* 35; Duncanson, *Government and Revolution,* 193, 100; Hammer, *Struggle,* 73.

6. McAlister, *Vietnam,* 300–301.

7. See Bui Tin, *Following Ho,* 6–9.

8. McAlister, *Vietnam,* 74.

9. Duncanson, *Government and Revolution,* 128; Lancaster, *Emancipation,* 78–79.

10. Hammer, *Struggle,* 79.

11. Besides Ho Chi Minh, alumni of the school include Ngo Dinh Diem

(son of the school's founder), Vo Nguyen Giap, and Pham Van Dong; Fall, *Two Vietnams*, 92.

12. Stafford Cripps (1889–1952) served as ambassador to the USSR and chancellor of the exchequer, among other posts.

13. Truong, *Vietcong Memoir*, 190.

14. Deutscher, *Trotsky*, 456–59.

15. Turner, *Vietnamese Communism*, 5; Duiker, *Communist Road*, 16. Ho, "Path to Leninism."

16. Hammer, *Struggle*, 75.

17. Blum, *Drawing the Line*, 218.

18. On the subject of Communist betrayals, and Ho's part in them, see Hoang, *Colonialism to Communism*, 18, 44; Pike, *History*, 29; Turner, *Vietnamese Communism*, 8, 9, 11; Dunn, *First Vietnam War*, 4; Fall, *Two Vietnams*, 99; Duncanson, *Government and Revolution*, 143; Lancaster, *Emancipation*, 183ff.; see also William J. Duiker, *Ho Chi Minh* (New York: Hyperion, 2000).

19. Fall, *Two Vietnams*, 83.

20. Duncanson, *Government and Revolution*, 144; Democratic Republic of Vietnam, *Thirty Years*.

21. Pike, *History*, 20.

22. Duncanson, *Government and Revolution*, 140.

23. Duiker, *Communist Road*, 45.

24. Buttinger, *Dragon Defiant*, 72.

25. Duiker, *Communist Road*, 26.

26. Among the fifty Communists guillotined in the aftermath of the revolt was the sister-in-law of Vo Nguyen Giap.

27. Duiker, *Communist Road*, 58–59.

28. Dunn, *First Vietnam War*, 52.

29. Johnson, *Autopsy on People's War*, 10.

30. Popkin, *Rational Peasant*, 218; on the essential nature of the "revolutionary alliance" of the intelligentsia and peasantry, and the role nationalism plays in this alliance, see Huntington, *Political Order*, chap. 5.

31. Johnson, *Autopsy on People's War*, 12.

32. This is very much like the program of the Fascist revolutionary Mussolini after World War I, except that his conversion to nationalism was not merely tactical. See Anthony James Joes, *Mussolini: A Political Portrait* (New York: Franklin Watts, 1982); quoted phrase in Popkin, *Rational Peasant*, 218; Ely, *Lessons of the War*, 32.

33. Duiker, *Communist Road*, 70–71; Woodside, *Community and Revolution*.

34. O'Neill, *General Giap*, 29.

35. Kelly, *Lost Soldiers*, 38.

36. Buttinger, *Dragon Embattled*, 1:299.

37. O'Ballance, *Indo-China War,* 49.

38. Dunn, *First Vietnam War,* 67.

39. Duncanson, *Government and Revolution,* 155.

40. McAlister, *Vietnam,* 105.

41. Lancaster, *Emancipation,* 116; McAlister, *Vietnam,* 318.

42. Duiker, *Communist Road,* 103.

43. The Labour government, and Foreign Minister Bevin in particular, did not share U.S. hostility to colonialism in general and French colonialism in Vietnam in particular. Bevin's successor, Antony Eden, was convinced that Britain would need France's aid in controlling Germany and hence must not oppose French reassertion of power in Southeast Asia. Dunn, *First Vietnam War.* But see Hughes, "'Post-war' War."

44. McAlister, *Vietnam,* 211; on Chinese Nationalist hostility to the French, inherited from the Manchu dynasty, see Duncanson, *Government and Revolution,* 128; Buttinger, *Dragon Embattled,* 1:338–39 and passim; Devillers, *Histoire,* 104.

45. Dunn, *First Vietnam War,* 69.

46. O'Ballance, *Indo-China War,* 48.

47. McAlister, *Vietnam,* 148.

48. Dommen, *Indochinese Experience,* 98.

49. Dunn, *First Vietnam War,* 34.

50. Ibid., 4, 43, 50.

51. Ibid., 14. Dommen writes, "The presence of OSS men at the side of Viet Minh leaders such as Ho and Giap created the impression in the eyes of the Vietnamese population that the United States was supporting the revolution, an impression the Viet Minh leaders were happy to promote. *Indochinese Experience,* 122; on 96 Dommen accuses the OSS in Vietnam of "astounding naiveté." And see the stiff protest General Leclerc sent to the French Foreign Ministry on September 27, 1945, in Bodinier, *La guerre d'Indochine,* 1:193. Also see Bartholomew-Feis, *OSS and Ho.*

52. Andrew, *Defend the Realm,* 368.

53. Dunn, *First Vietnam War,* 112.

54. De Gaulle, *War Memoirs,* 260. In the same volume, de Gaulle writes of "the hostility of the Allies—particularly the Americans—in regard to our Far Eastern position" (187).

55. Windrow, *Last Valley,* 84.

56. Truong, "August Revolution," 18.

57. Ibid., 14.

58. McAlister, *Vietnam,* 192, 318, and passim, quotation on 192.

59. Duncanson, *Government and Revolution,* 161; Dunn, *First Vietnam War,* 23.

60. McAlister, *Vietnam,* 128.

61. Duiker, *Communist Road,* 118.

62. See Anthony James Joes, *From the Barrel of a Gun: Armies and Revolution* (Washington, DC: Pergamon-Brassey's, 1986).

63. McAlister, *Vietnam*, 151; Dunn, *First Vietnam War*, 18.

64. Duiker, *Communist Road*, 107; McAlister, *Vietnam*, 149; Hammer, *Struggle*, 101.

65. Modelski, "Viet Minh Complex," 201; this is a truly brilliant essay. For a more leisurely account of the August events, see Marr, *Vietnam*.

66. Modelski, "Viet Minh Complex," 206n; Duiker, *Communist Road*, 107; Buttinger, *Dragon Embattled*, 1:292–300; Devillers, *Histoire*, 186.

67. McAlister, *Vietnam*, 149.

68. Fall, *Two Vietnams*, 65; see also Lebra, *Japanese-Trained Armies;* and O'Ballance, *Indo-China War*, 55, 56; McAlister, *Vietnam*, 233; Lancaster, *Emancipation*, 88. For more about Cao Dai, see the section of this chapter titled "Why Cochin China Was Different."

69. Buttinger, *Dragon Defiant*, 85.

70. From Ellen Hammer's *The Struggle for Indochina* and Marguerite Higgins's *Our Vietnam Nightmare* through Joseph Buttinger's *Vietnam: A Dragon Embattled* and Dennis Duncanson's *Government and Revolution in Vietnam,* Arthur Dommen's *The Indochinese Experience of the French and the Americans,* and Mark Moyar's *Triumph Forsaken: The Vietnam War, 1954–1965* (New York: Cambridge Univ. Press, 2006)—for just a few examples—serious students of Vietnamese events have always distinguished Ho and his Communists from authentic Vietnamese nationalists.

71. Hoang, *Colonialism to Communism*, 44; Buttinger, *Dragon Embattled*, 1:86.

72. Buttinger, *Dragon Embattled*, 1:379, 1:399, 1:408; see Marr, *Vietnam*, 519.

73. Buttinger, *Dragon Embattled*, 1:409; for more on this issue, see Truong, "August Revolution," 24; Fall, *Two Vietnams*, 101; McAlister, *Vietnam*, 190–92; Bodard, *Quicksand War*, 208–9; Hammer, *Struggle*, 110, 158, 176, 215, 240.

74. Buttinger, *Dragon Embattled*, 1:412.

75. Fall, *Two Vietnams*, 101. See the Communist condemnation and announcement of the execution of the head of the Hoa Hao on April 1, 1947, in Bodinier, *La guerre d'Indochine*, 2:467.

76. McAlister, *Vietnam*, 192.

77. Modelski, "Viet Minh Complex," 210. And see MacDonald, *Giap*, 82.

78. Devillers, *Histoire*, 201; Turner, *Vietnamese Communism*, 48; McAlister, *Vietnam*, 221.

79. Windrow, *Last Valley*, 102.

80. Buttinger, *Dragon Embattled*, 1:435.

81. Ibid., 1:379.

82. Dommen, *Indochinese Experience*, 154.

83. Fall, *Two Vietnams*, 72–73; Devillers, *Histoire*, 248–71.

84. O'Neill, *General Giap*, 31; McAlister, *Vietnam*, 233. By the summer of 1946, Giap may have had 60,000 soldiers, including three regiments of artillery. Gras, *Histoire de la guerre*, 126; Buttinger, *Dragon Embattled*, 1:428; Fall, *Two Vietnams*, 76, 77. "Each side could claim with some justification that the beginning of the conflict was the other side's fault." Gras, *Histoire de la guerre*, 155.

85. Kelly, *Lost Soldiers*, 59.

86. Tanham, *Communist Revolutionary Warfare*, 84.

87. Ibid., 64.

88. O'Neill, *General Giap*, 45.

89. There is no biography of Bao Dai in English. Bao Dai's *Dragon d'Annam* contains subtle and interesting interpretations of events. But see Chapuis, *Last Emperors*.

90. Pike, *Viet Cong*, 48.

91. Lancaster, *Emancipation*, 182.

92. Dommen's authoritative *Indochinese Experience* treats Bao Dai's national vision and political skill very seriously indeed; see, for example, 184.

93. Bao Dai's letter of August 18 to de Gaulle and the people of France said, in part: "I beg you to understand that the only means of safeguarding French interests and the spiritual influence of France in Indochina is to recognize unreservedly the independence of Vietnam and to renounce any idea of re-establishing French sovereignty or French administration here in any form." De Gaulle never replied. See Cameron, *Viet-Nam Crisis*, 49; Fall, *Two Vietnams*, 101.

94. Fall, *Two Vietnams*, 203; see the full (French) text in Bao Dai, *Dragon d'Annam*, 120–21.

95. See the description of a September 1945 dinner in Hanoi including Bao Dai, Ho Chi Minh, and Vo Nguyen Giap, in Bao Dai, *Dragon d'Annam*, 127–29.

96. Nevertheless, Bao Dai was not "invented" by the French; he had real appeal to many non-Communist nationalists. See Dommen, *Indochinese Experience*, 184.

97. See Bao Dai's statement of September 18, 1947, to the people of Vietnam that he was ready to resume power if they wanted him. Bao Dai, *Dragon d'Annam*, 184–85.

98. Fall, *Two Vietnams*, 212; U.S. Department of Defense, *Pentagon Papers*, 57–67. This agreement was reconfirmed by the Elysée Treaty of March 1949.

99. Fall, *Two Vietnams*, 213.

100. Hammer, *Struggle*, 211, 47. On the Cao Dai, see Werner, *Peasant Politics*. On the Hoa Hao, see Hue, *Millenarianism*. Warner, *Last Confucian*, 77.

101. Lancaster, *Emancipation*, 196; Bernard Fall, *The Viet-Minh Regime: Government and Administration in the Democratic Republic of Vietnam* (Ithaca, NY: Cornell Univ. Press, 1954), 69–72.

102. Lancaster, *Emancipation*, 196.

103. Ibid., 175.

104. Modelski, "Viet Minh Complex," 212.

105. Spector, *Advice and Support*, 203.

106. Navarre, *Agonie*, 46; Ely, *Lessons of the War*, 59; Fall, *Two Vietnams*, 220; Carver, *War since 1945*, 112.

107. Duncanson, *Government and Revolution*, 189; Lancaster, *Emancipation*, 194. In the same way, de Lattre's emphasis on building up Bao Dai's military forces antagonized the Hoa Hao, because they knew they would eventually lose most, if not all, of their autonomy. Elliott, *Vietnamese War*, 1:145–46.

108. "Taken together, the forces lined up against the Viet Minh were quite significant but badly divided internally," and too dependent on outside support. Elliott, *Vietnamese War*, 1:148, 2:1390, quotation on 1:148; O'Neill, *General Giap*, 69. It is not clear that Giap's logistic system could have handled a larger number of troops.

109. See the comments on this subject by Truong in "August Revolution," 36; the arrival in Saigon of the Second Armored Division, under the famous General Leclerc, increased French forces in southern Vietnam to about 25,000.

110. The Trotskyists had been winning 80 percent of the vote in Cochin Chinese elections before the Pacific War.

111. Duiker, *Communist Road*, 152.

112. Lancaster, *Emancipation*, 136–37; Fall, *Two Vietnams*, 101.

113. Buttinger, *Dragon Embattled*, 1:410; for French negotiations with the Hoa Hao and also the Binh Xuyen, see Dommen, *Indochinese Experience*, 194–95; and Bodinier, *La guerre d'Indochine*, 2:463–67.

114. Ely, *Lessons of the War*, 193.

115. Ibid., 217, 158.

116. Ibid., 162.

117. Windrow, *Last Valley*, 96.

118. Fall, *Street without Joy*, 354.

119. Ely, *Lessons of the War*, 76.

120. The provinces of Cao Bang, Ha Giang, Tuyen Quang, Bac Kan, Tai Nguyen, Bac Giang, and Lang Son.

121. Modelski, "Viet Minh Complex," 194, 208.

122. Fall, *Street without Joy*, 30.

123. Ibid., 78n.

124. Ely, *Lessons of the War*, 93, 216, 200.

125. Windrow, *Last Valley*, 172.

126. Ibid., 179.

127. Ibid., 183.

128. Kelly, *Lost Soldiers*, 89.

129. Devillers, *Histoire*, 358.

130. Lancaster, *Emancipation*, 267; Fall, *Street without Joy*, 257.

131. Williams, *Crisis and Compromise*, 144; this was of course a disparaging reference to Napoleon III's unsuccessful effort in the 1860s to keep Maximilian of Austria on the throne of Mexico.

132. Windrow, *Last Valley*, 172.

133. Fall, *Two Vietnams*.

134. For disunity, lack of direction, and domination of foreign policy by domestic and tactical-electoral concerns, see Williams, *Crisis and Compromise*.

135. Fall, *Street without Joy*, 242.

136. Ibid., 65.

137. Tanham, *Communist Revolutionary Warfare*, 107–10; Fall, *Street without Joy*, 242; Warner, *Certain Victory*, 89.

138. McAlister, *Vietnam*, 47, 106; Pimlott, "Ho Chi Minh's Triumph," 67. O'Ballance presents similar figures in *Indo-China War*, 174. These figures approximate those presented in Navarre, *Agonie*, 22. The French relied heavily on their Vietnamese troops, who were not at all difficult to recruit. Elliott, *Vietnamese War*, 1:133, 147; Windrow, *Last Valley*, 198; Hammer, *Struggle*, 287; Navarre, *Agonie*, 22; Lacouture and Devillers, *La fin d'une guerre*, 36.

139. Fall, *Street without Joy*, 354; Bodard, *Quicksand War*, 239.

140. Tanham, *Communist Revolutionary Warfare*, 90.

141. Pimlott, "Ho Chi Minh's Triumph," 79.

142. Fall, *Two Vietnams*, 110.

143. Gras, *Histoire de la guerre*, 354.

144. Lancaster, *Emancipation*, 218.

145. Fall, *Street without Joy*, 30.

146. Fall, *Two Vietnams*, 111.

147. During the war China supplied scores of thousands of rifles along with great quantities of mortars and machine guns. See, among others, Gras, *Histoire de la guerre*, 315. Dean Rusk reported that 30,000 Viet Minh were training in China. *FRUS, 1950*, 6:878.

148. Windrow, *Last Valley*, 194, 193.

149. Davidson, *Vietnam at War*, 49; Tanham, *Communist Revolutionary Warfare*, 9; Bodard, *Quicksand War*, 13; Fall, *Street without Joy*, 127.

150. Lancaster, *Emancipation*, 284; Windrow, *Last Valley*, 196.

151. Windrow, *Last Valley*, 226.

152. Eisenhower, *White House Years*, 338; O'Ballance, *Indo-China War*, 162, 262; Windrow, *Last Valley*, 157; Duncanson, *Government and Revolution*, 177.

153. *FRUS, 1952–1954*, 13:782. See also references to a Chinese invasion in the National Intelligence Estimate of December 29, 1950, in *FRUS, 1950*, 6:959.

154. Hammer, *Struggle*, 248.

155. O'Ballance, *Indo-China War*, 127; O'Neill, *General Giap*, 90.

156. Davidson, *Vietnam at War,* 13.

157. Ibid., 123–27.

158. Quotation in Lancaster, *Emancipation,* 226n; Davidson, *Vietnam at War,* 135.

159. Davidson, *Vietnam at War,* 110–21; Fall, *Street without Joy,* 39; O'Neill, *General Giap,* 90–99.

160. Davidson, *Vietnam at War,* 114.

161. Cloake, *Templer.*

162. Davidson, *Vietnam at War,* 101. De Gaulle wrote that de Lattre's faults "were rather the excesses of his virtues." De Gaulle, *War Memoirs,* 38.

163. Concerning the galvanizing effect on the French forces exerted by de Lattre, whom Liddell Hart compared to Turenne, see Gras, *Histoire de la guerre,* 367–70, 427.

164. Buttinger, *Dragon Embattled,* 2:757; Fall, *Street without Joy,* 180; O'Ballance, *Indo-China War,* 194.

165. Lancaster, *Emancipation,* 239.

166. Windrow, *Last Valley,* 219, 218, and passim; O'Ballance, *Indo-China War,* 202.

167. Windrow, *Last Valley,* 188. General Navarre wrote that 300,000 Vietnamese were fighting against the Viet Minh and 400,000 for it. Navarre, *Agonie,* 46. General Navarre was very ungenerous in his remarks about the quality of the NVA, many of whose principal deficiencies were the fault of the French themselves.

168. "The Vietnamese civil war and the East-West conflict were merely suspended." Gras, *Histoire de la guerre,* 583.

169. Bao Dai, *Dragon d'Annam,* 252; Lancaster, *Emancipation,* 249n, 248–49; Hammer, *Struggle,* 287. By the beginning of 1954, the Vietnamese National Army counted 200,000, with another 50,000 special contract soldiers; close to 80,000 belonged to local militia and police forces; an additional 100,000 Vietnamese were in the French forces. *FRUS, 1952–1954,* vol. 13, part 1, 908.

170. For insights into who these Vietnamese were, see Wiest, *Vietnam's Forgotten Army;* and Lam, *Twenty-Five Year Century.*

171. See Lam, *Twenty-Five Year Century;* Hammer, *Struggle,* 321; see the full list of states in Dommen, *Indochinese Experience,* 1036n; see Bui Tin, *Jaws of History.*

172. McAlister, *Vietnam,* 281.

173. Fall, *Street without Joy,* 89.

174. Davidson, *Vietnam at War,* 150.

175. Ibid., 162; Buttinger, *Dragon Embattled,* 1:759; O'Ballance, *Indo-China War,* 174.

176. Davidson, *Vietnam at War,* 163.

177. O'Ballance, *Indo-China War,* 201.

178. Later, General Navarre defended the idea of viewing Dien Bien Phu as a means of protecting Laos from invasion by Giap's forces; he stated that he had not envisioned a battle to "smash" the Viet Minh. Navarre, *Agonie*, 199–200. See also Rocolle, *Pourquoi Dien Bien Phu?* Davidson, *Vietnam at War*, 211–13.

179. Kelly, *Lost Soldiers*, 78.

180. Radvanyi, *Delusions and Reality*, 8.

181. Fall, *Hell in a Very Small Place*, 237–38.

182. Lancaster, *Emancipation*, 297.

183. Roy, *Battle for Dien Bien Phu*, 60. Fall disputes Roy's statement in *Hell in a Very Small Place*, 471n.

184. Windrow, *Last Valley*, 647; O'Ballance, *Indo-China War*, 237. And see figures in Fall, *Hell in a Very Small Place*, 481.

185. Pimlott, "Ho Chi Minh's Triumph," 76.

186. Navarre, *Agonie*, 218–19.

187. Ely, *Lessons of the War*, 154.

188. Davidson, *Vietnam at War*, 213.

189. Fall, *Viet Minh Regime*, 76.

190. O'Ballance, *Indo-China War*, 172; Windrow, *Last Valley*, 153.

191. Lancaster, *Emancipation*, 246.

192. Davidson, *Vietnam at War*, 175, 188.

193. Ibid., 219; O'Ballance, *Indo-China War*, 225; Fall, *Hell in a Very Small Place*, 237, 266. The Chinese provided one hundred artillery pieces, sixty thousand shells, and 2.4 million rounds of ammunition for the battle at Dien Bien Phu. Chen, "China and the First Indochina War, 1950–1954." Further, from 1956 to 1963, Chinese aid to North Vietnam included ten thousand artillery pieces and twenty-eight naval vessels. Chinese antiaircraft troops defended important sites in the North. A total of 320,000 Chinese engineers and other troops served in North Vietnam. "Without that support, the history, even the outcome, of the Vietnam war might have been different." Chen Jian, "China's Involvement in the Vietnam War, 1964–1969," *China Quarterly* 142 (June 1995), 380.

194. From a story in *Le Monde*, quoted in Fall, *Hell in a Very Small Place*, 20–21.

195. Fall, *Hell in a Very Small Place*, 455.

196. Giap, *Dien Bien Phu*, 146–47.

197. "The simple historical truth is that no air interdiction campaign has prevented an enemy from moving adequate supplies to its front-line troops. The Germans moved supplies in World War II, the [North] Koreans and Chinese did it in the Korean War, the Viet Minh did it in [Indochina], and the North Vietnamese did it [in later years]." Davidson, *Vietnam at War*, 216–17.

198. Ibid., 164.

199. Fall, *Hell in a Very Small Place*, 255; Windrow, *Last Valley*, 508.

200. Davidson, *Vietnam at War*, 237.

201. Ibid., 219.

202. Fall, *Hell in a Very Small Place*, 473n.

203. Quite aside from the crucial problem of supplying the soldiers inside Dien Bien Phu with tolerably sufficient quantities of food was the question of kinds of food. The defenders of Dien Bien Phu came from many nations and cultures. Six different types of food rations were required: European, North African, West African, Vietnamese, T'ai, and "prisoners of war." Muslims of course could not eat the standard canned pork of the French (actually, the Americans); Europeans could not subsist mainly on rice for very long, but all the Vietnamese wanted rice with every meal. And of course French aircraft parachuted 50,000 gallons of wine and 7,000 gallons of "wine concentrate" into the besieged fortress. See Fall, *Hell in a Very Small Place*; see also Paul Grauwin, *J'etais médecin à Dien Bien Phu* (Paris: Editions France-Empire, 1956); and Genevieve de Galard, *Une femme à Dien Bien Phu* (Paris: Arenes, 2003).

204. Davidson, *Vietnam at War*, 268–69; Navarre, *Agonie*, 246ff.; Windrow, *Last Valley*, 571–75, 586–88.

205. The last radio message to Hanoi from de Castries' headquarters: "In five minutes everything will be blown up here. The Viets are only a few metres away. Good luck to everybody." Windrow, *Last Valley*, 616.

206. Dommen, *Indochinese Experience*, 247.

207. Fall, *Hell in a Very Small Place*, 225; Pimlott, "Ho Chi Minh's Triumph," 77.

208. Keegan, *Dien Bien Phu*; Pouget, *Nous étions à Dien Bien Phu*; Simpson, *Dien Bien Phu*; Langlais, *Dien Bien Phu*.

209. Nixon, *No More Vietnams*, 31. On the U.S. decision not to intervene at Dien Bien Phu, see Eisenhower, *White House Years*, 332–56; Nixon, *RN*, 150–55; U.S. Department of Defense, *Pentagon Papers*, 97–106; Ambrose, *Eisenhower*, 173–86; Billings-Yun, *Decision against War*; Divine, *Eisenhower*, 39–55; and see Fred I. Greenstein, *The Hidden-Hand Presidency: Eisenhower as Leader* (New York: Basic Books, 1982).

210. U.S. Department of Defense, *Pentagon Papers*, 461–62.

211. Eisenhower, *White House Years*, 350–51.

212. Eisenhower later wrote that he had "no intention of using United States forces in any limited action when the forces employed would probably not be decisively effective." *White House Years*, 341.

213. Ambrose, *Eisenhower*, 77. See also Divine, *Eisenhower*, 41–44.

214. Robert H. Ferrell, ed., *Eisenhower Diaries* (New York: Norton, 1981), entry for March 7, 1951, 190.

215. "National Intelligence Estimate, April 30, 1954," in *FRUS, 1952–1954*, 13:1451, 1455.

216. U.S. Department of Defense, *Pentagon Papers*, 89, 443.

217. Fall, *Two Vietnams*, 223.

218. Windrow, *Last Valley*, 694n. Numbers of course vary. O'Ballance wrote that 23,000 Vietnamese in CEF units were never accounted for. *Indo-China War*, 249. See Fall, *Street without Joy*; Thayer, *War without Fronts*, 9; Pike, *Viet Cong*, 49n. See also Clayton, *French Decolonization*.

219. Thayer, *War without Fronts*, 9.

220. Fall, *Street without Joy*, 45, 136; "National Intelligence Estimate, December 29, 1950," in *FRUS, 1950*, 6:959.

221. Lancaster, *Emancipation*, 281, 251n; Windrow, *Last Valley*, 648.

222. See *Agence France Press*, April 3, 1995. "The war had cost the French Expeditionary Corps 59,745 dead and missing in action, of which 26,923 were [Vietnamese] serving in the Corps. The Vietnamese National Army had lost 58,877 dead and missing in action. But the main casualties had been the civilians . . . of which an estimated 100,000 to 150,000 had been assassinated by the Viet Minh." Dommen, *Indochinese Experience*, 252.

223. Fall, *Two Vietnams*, 28; *Street without Joy*, 314n.

224. Duncanson, *Government and Revolution*, 132. John Cady writes:

The taproot of French imperialism in the Far East from first to last was national pride—pride of culture, reputation, prestige and influence. This was the constant factor which ran through the kaleidoscope of episodes of missionary dedication and daring, of naval coups, and of private adventures. . . . One need not discount the genuineness of the religious zeal which sustained the program of the Société des Missions Etrangères over two centuries or challenge the vitality of the liberal religious revival under Louis Philippe to see in both of them an expression of supreme confidence in the superiority of French spirit and culture. Christian missions were supported in large measure because they were French.

Politically, French imperialism expressed itself most frequently in eastern Asia in terms of perennial rivalry with Great Britain. British pretensions of superiority were unendurable and therefore to be opposed, whenever and wherever possible. The basic considerations behind French policy in the Far East from the time of Louis XIV to that of Louis Napoleon and Jules Ferry were more political than economic.

Cady, *Roots of French Imperialism*, 294–95.

225. Kelly, *Lost Soldiers*, 63. "To many Frenchmen it seemed that if France did not stand firm in one part of the empire, she might lose it all." Hammer, *Struggle*, 209. See Cady, *Roots of French Imperialism*.

226. Fall, *Street without Joy*, 16.

227. Modelski, "Viet Minh Complex," 202.

228. Tanham, *Communist Revolutionary Warfare,* 7.

229. Buttinger, *Dragon Embattled,* 1:202–3.

230. Elliott, *Vietnamese War,* 2:1388.

231. Pike, *PAVN,* 213. But see Anthony James Joes, *Resisting Rebellion: The History and Politics of Counterinsurgency* (Lexington, KY: Univ. Press of Kentucky, 2004), chap. 14, "The Myth of Maoist People's War."

232. This is Buttinger's verdict, in *Dragon Embattled,* 1:267. See also Johnson, *Autopsy on People's War.*

233. See the data in Williams, *Crisis and Compromise,* appendix 2, 494–95.

234. On this important point, see the groundbreaking essay by Mack, "Why Big Nations Lose Small Wars"; but see also Record, *Beating Goliath,* a slender volume bristling with provocative insights. Other studies of this subject are Arreguin-Toft, *How the Weak Win Wars;* and Gil Merom, *How Democracies Lose Small Wars: State, Society, and the Failures of France in Algeria, Israel in Lebanon, and the United States in Vietnam* (New York: Cambridge Univ. Press, 2003); both these studies are erudite and vigorous but offer very controversial conclusions.

235. Fall, *Street without Joy,* 242.

236. See the text of the declaration in Bao Dai, *Dragon d'Annam,* 368–69.

237. In some provinces Catholics made up 50 percent of the population. Duncanson, *Government and Revolution,* 103; Bodinier, *La guerre d'Indochine,* 2:463–66.

238. Duncanson, *Government and Revolution,* 189.

239. Dinfreville, *L'opération Indochine,* quoted in Kelly, *Lost Soldiers,* 33n. Leclerc had never believed in the possibility of a strictly military French reconquest of all of Vietnam; see Dansette, *Leclerc.*

240. See Davidson, *Vietnam at War,* 275.

241. Ibid., 172. "The supercilious rejection by the [French] general staff of unpopular facts reported to them by the fighting men in the field was to remain a constant factor in the Vietnamese situation." Fall, *Hell in a Very Small Place,* 50.

242. Mao, *Selected Military Writings,* 17. Duncanson, *Government and Revolution,* 155, agrees with Mao's judgment.

243. O'Ballance, *Indo-China War,* 254.

244. Fall, *Two Vietnams,* 108.

245. Davidson, *Vietnam at War,* 35–36; see also 59–60, 71.

246. Chen Jian, "China and the Vietnam Wars," in Lowe, *Vietnam War,* 158. See also Chen, "China and the First Indochina War"; and Qiang, *China and the Vietnam Wars.*

247. General Leclerc suggested something along these lines in the spring of 1946.

248. Thompson, *No Exit from Vietnam,* 133.

249. Modelski, "Viet Minh Complex," 211, 213.

250. Lancaster, *Emancipation*, 311.

251. Windrow, *Last Valley*, 222.

252. Davidson, *Vietnam at War*, 275 (italics in original).

253. Lancaster, *Emancipation*, 310n, 311n, 304; Fall, *Two Vietnams*, 105.

254. Fall, *Hell in a Very Small Place*, 8.

255. U.S. Department of Defense, *Pentagon Papers*, 1:511.

256. Fall, *Two Vietnams*, 229.

257. Thayer, *War without Fronts*.

258. Dommen, *Indochinese Experience*, 248.

259. See the relevant Geneva documents in Randle, *Geneva 1954*, 569–607; and in Turner, *Vietnamese Communism*, 365–81.

260. Fishel, *Vietnam*, 147; U.S. Department of Defense, *Pentagon Papers*, 1:245.

261. U.S. Department of Defense, *Pentagon Papers*, 1:161–66; see Bator, *Vietnam*; McAlister, *Vietnam*, esp. 325–26; Smith, *International History*, esp. 20, 30; and Davidson, *Vietnam at War*, 843.

262. Randle, *Geneva 1954*, 444–45.

3. Cuba

1. Wiarda, "Cuba," 241, 214.

2. Ibid., 233; see also Draper, *Castroism*.

3. Lazo, *Dagger in the Heart*, 83; Ruiz, *Cuba*, 9–10; Wiarda, "Cuba," 235. Leon Trotsky, who presumably knew a couple of things about revolution, wrote: "In reality the mere existence of privation is not enough to cause an insurrection. If it were, the masses would always be in revolt." *History of the Russian Revolution* (Ann Arbor: Univ. of Michigan Press, 1960), 2:vii.

4. Ruiz, *Cuba*, 153.

5. Ibid., 149–53. Slavery was not abolished until 1886.

6. Good treatments of these events include Beals, *Crime of Cuba*; and Aguilar, *Cuba*.

7. Quoted phrase in Thomas, *Cuban Revolution*, 263.

8. Argote-Freyre, *Fulgencio Batista*, 242.

9. Quotations in Ruiz, *Cuba*, 88. On one notable occasion, long before anybody heard of Fidel Castro, President Batista, partly and unmistakably of African heritage, entered an exclusive Havana restaurant, whereupon every other customer got up and walked out. See, for example, Argote-Freyre, *Fulgencio Batista*, 124–25.

10. Argote-Freyre, *Fulgencio Batista*, 214, 215.

11. Perez, "Cuba," 439.

12. Halperin, *Castro's Road to Power*, 24; Perez, "Cuba," 77; Hargrove, "Fulgencio Batista," 137; see also Lazo, *Dagger in the Heart*, 61.

13. Ruiz, *Cuba*, 127 and passim.

14. Lazo, *Dagger in the Heart*, 64; Halperin, *Castro's Road to Power*, 26; Gellman, *Roosevelt and Batista*, 213. See also Farber, *Revolution and Reaction*, 108.

15. Lazo, *Dagger in the Heart*, 65; Ameringer, *Cuban Democratic Experience*, 41; Aguilar, *Cuba*, 241; Perez, "Cuba," 442.

16. Perez, "Cuba," 442.

17. Perez, *Army Politics*, 124.

18. Ameringer, *Cuban Democratic Experience*, 179.

19. Ibid., 88, 183, quotation on 88. Castro was running on the ticket of the Ortodoxos, a secession from the Autenticos.

20. Wiarda, "Cuba," 239.

21. The regime divided historic Oriente, home of the U.S. base at Guantanamo, into several smaller units in 1976.

22. "The assailants selected Moncada . . . largely because of the Oriente post's notorious military weakness and lax discipline." Perez, *Army Politics*, 138.

23. Russell, *Rebellion, Revolution, and Armed Forces*, 116.

24. Kline, "Cuba," 452.

25. *New York Times*, Feb. 24, 25, 26, 1957; quotation in Feb. 24 issue. Matthews, whose profound naïveté was paralleled by an incredible egotism, declared that his interviews with Castro constituted "the biggest scoop of our times" and had changed the United States and Cuba forever; see his *Cuban Story*, 45 and passim. See also DePalma, *Man Who Invented Fidel*.

26. Matthews, quoted in Szulc, *Fidel*, 410.

27. *FRUS, 1955–1957*, 841. In April 1958, the intelligence arm of the State Department said that the evidence suggested that Castro was "immature and irresponsible." *FRUS, 1958–1960*, 77.

28. Chappelle, "How Castro Won," 334; Smith, *Fourth Floor*, 97; Bonachea and San Martín, *Cuban Insurrection*, 237, 66, 205, 240; *FRUS, 1958–1960*, April 3, 1958, 79; see also 265; *FRUS, 1955–1957*, 859–60; and see Szulc, *Fidel*, esp. 427ff., 442, 456.

29. Thomas, *Cuban Revolution*, 258, quotation on 259.

30. Bonachea and San Martín, *Cuban Insurrection*, 260.

31. Perez, *Army Politics*, 29, 34, 168, quotation on 29.

32. Perez, "Cuba," 448.

33. Perez, *Army Politics*, 145.

34. Thomas, *Cuban Revolution*, 257, 215.

35. Ibid., 258.

36. Taber, *War of the Flea*, 39.

37. Thomas, *Cuban Revolution*, 196.

38. Ibid., 202.

39. Perez, *Army Politics*, 157; message to the Department of State, Sept. 16, 1957, *FRUS, 1955–1957,* 847.

40. Bonachea and San Martín, *Cuban Insurrection,* 75, 130, and passim; Smith, *Fourth Floor,* 76; Perez, *Army Politics,* 143–44.

41. Aug. 5, 1957, in *FRUS 1955–1957,* 843.

42. Some members of the Cuban Communist Party served as informers against the strike organizers. See Bonachea and San Martín, *Cuban Insurrection,* 212–13 and passim.

43. Thomas, *Cuban Revolution,* 208. For the Department of State analysis of the strike's failure, see *FRUS, 1958–1960,* 81–83.

44. Bonachea and San Martín, *Cuban Insurrection,* 230, 130, 229; Lazo, *Dagger in the Heart,* 152.

45. Batista, *Cuba Betrayed,* 101n, 89.

46. Thomas, *Cuban Revolution,* 261; Batista, *Cuba Betrayed,* 102; "Local military commanders surrendered, often without firing a shot." Perez, "Cuba," 453; Smith, *Fourth Floor,* 202.

47. Smith, *Fourth Floor,* 100. See *FRUS, 1958–1960,* 60–68.

48. Thomas, *Cuban Revolution,* 203; Taber, *War of the Flea,* 38.

49. Thomas, *Cuban Revolution,* 258; Batista, *Cuba Betrayed,* 43; Smith, *Fourth Floor,* 48, 107.

50. Perez, *Army Politics,* 155–58.

51. Batista, *Cuba Betrayed,* 99.

52. Brennan, *Castro, Cuba, and Justice,* 232–33; Thomas, *Cuban Revolution,* 215.

53. Perez, *Army Politics,* 154.

54. Thomas, *Cuban Revolution,* 217.

55. Ibid., 218.

56. Batista, *Cuba Betrayed,* 107n.

57. Ibid., 105n.

58. Thomas, *Cuban Revolution,* 228.

59. Ibid., 240, 241.

60. Among other things, in December 1958 Tabernilla told Batista, "The soldiers are tired and the officers do not want to fight." He also told the U.S. ambassador that the regime was finished and the army could not save it. Batista, *Cuba Betrayed,* 99, 122.

61. *FRUS 1955–1957,* 876 (Dec. 19, 1957).

62. In December 1957, the U.S. Department of State recommended "a quiet removal, transfer or retirement of those military and police officers who [had] been notorious for their excessive brutalities in the past." Ambassador Smith

proposed that the rebels renounce their threats against Batista and other key officials. But in the atmosphere created by Castroite threats against ordinary citizens standing in voting lines, such efforts were useless. *FRUS 1955–1957*, 869, 875. Lazo, *Dagger in the Heart*, 156; Thomas, *Cuban Revolution*, 229; Smith, *Fourth Floor*, 76; Bonsal, *Cuba, Castro, and the United States*.

63. Lazo, *Dagger in the Heart*, 155; Smith, *Fourth Floor*, 174.

64. Smith, *Fourth Floor*, 169–74, 164–65, 181; Thomas, *Cuban Revolution*, 236; *FRUS, 1958–1960*, 271 (around Nov. 27, 1958); Lazo, *Dagger in the Heart*, 157–58.

65. *FRUS, 1958–1960*, 307. In his memoirs, President Eisenhower devoted exactly two pages to his administration's policy toward the Batista regime; see Dwight D. Eisenhower, *The White House Years: Waging Peace, 1956–1961* (Garden City, NY: Doubleday, 1965), 520–21.

66. Batista, *Cuba Betrayed*, 110ff.; Bonachea and San Martín, *Cuban Insurrection*, 307–11.

67. Edward Gonzalez, *Cuba under Castro: The Limits of Charisma* (Boston: Houghton Mifflin, 1974), 91. Batista died in Spain in 1973.

68. Thomas, *Cuban Revolution*, 256, 258, quotation on 256.

69. Ibid., 258.

70. Ibid., 259; Wiarda, "Cuba," 244.

71. See the excellent studies by Chorley, *Armies*; and Andreski, *Military Organization and Society*. See also Anthony James Joes, *From the Barrel of a Gun: Armies and Revolution* (Washington, DC: Pergamon-Brassey's, 1986).

72. See, for example, Lazo, *Dagger in the Heart*, 42.

73. Smith, *Fourth Floor*, 49, 134.

74. Thomas, *Cuban Revolution*, 157; Lazo, *Dagger in the Heart*, 404.

75. Ryan, *Fall of Che Guevara*; Daniel James, ed., *The Complete Bolivian Diaries of Che Guevara and Other Captured Documents* (New York: Cooper Square Press, 2000); James, *Che Guevara*.

4. Afghanistan

1. Isby, "Soviet Strategy and Tactics."

2. Fletcher, *Highway*, 13.

3. Ibid., 14, 100.

4. Dupree, "Post-Withdrawal Afghanistan," 31; Fletcher, *Highway*, 25.

5. Urban, *War in Afghanistan*, 204.

6. Sale, *First Afghan War*, 9; "The chief cause of the disaster that ensued was the extraordinary ineptness of the British leadership, particularly among the military." Fletcher, *Highway*, 110. See also Patrick Macrory, *Retreat from Kabul: The Catastrophic British Defeat in Afghanistan, 1842* (Guilford, CT: Lyons, 2007).

7. Urban, *War in Afghanistan*, 3–4.

8. Poullada, "Road to Crisis," 54; Amstutz, *Afghanistan*, 103.

9. Collins, *Soviet Invasion of Afghanistan*, 50.

10. Bradsher, *Afghanistan and the Soviet Union*, 80.

11. Hammond, *Red Flag over Afghanistan*, 63.

12. Arnold and Klass, "Divided Communist Party," 141; Kaplan, *Soldiers of God*, 12. McMichael, *Stumbling Bear*, 49.

13. Saikal and Maley, introduction to Saikal and Maley, *Soviet Withdrawal*, 5.

14. Bradsher, *Afghanistan and the Soviet Union*, chap. 5. Land reform meant "soldiers breaking into houses, raping or trying to rape the women, defecating on the [sacred] dishes, executing the local mullah and headman, and confiscating land in a haphazard manner that enraged everyone, benefited no one, and reduced food production." Kaplan, *Soldiers of God*, 116.

15. Magnus and Naby, *Afghanistan*, 77.

16. Krakowski, "Soviet Global Interests," 164.

17. Tahir, "Afghan Resistance," 380.

18. Karmal can be compared to the traitor Kadar in Hungary. Urban, *War in Afghanistan*, 47; Arnold, *Afghanistan*, 95; Collins, *Soviet Invasion of Afghanistan*, 100; Amin, "Sovietization," 306.

19. Luttwak, *Grand Strategy*, 58.

20. Malia, *Soviet Tragedy*, 379; Mark Galeotti also believed that the Brezhnev Doctrine was the main motive for the invasion. See his *Afghanistan*, 11.

21. Arnold, *Afghanistan*, 133.

22. Dobrynin, *In Confidence*, 442–47.

23. The more pithy but less accurate version is "The Road to Paris lies through Peking."

24. Raymond J. Sontag and James S. Beddie, eds., *Nazi-Soviet Relations, 1939–1941: Documents from the Archives of the German Foreign Office* (Washington, DC: Department of State, 1948), 259.

25. Malia, *Soviet Tragedy*, 381.

26. On the planned incorporation of northern Afghanistan into the Soviet Union, see Bodansky, "Soviet Military Operations."

27. Collins, *Soviet Invasion of Afghanistan*, 26.

28. Krakowski, "Soviet Global Interests," 162.

29. Bradsher, *Afghanistan and the Soviet Union*, 156.

30. Cordovez and Harrison, *Out of Afghanistan*, 47; see also Litwak, "Soviet Union in Afghanistan." See, among others, Porter, *USSR in Third World Conflicts*.

31. Krakowski, "Soviet Global Interests," 167.

32. Luttwak, *Grand Strategy*, 60.

33. See Luttwak, *Grand Strategy*; see also Urban, *War in Afghanistan*, 205.

34. Dupree, "Post-Withdrawal Afghanistan," 31.

35. Urban, *War in Afghanistan*, 72.

36. Isby, *War in a Distant Country*, 93.

37. Karp, *Seven Years*, 9.

38. Brigot and Roy, *War in Afghanistan*, 74; Isby, *War in a Distant Country*, 62; McMichael, *Stumbling Bear*, 49–50.

39. Bradsher, *Afghanistan and the Soviet Union*, 294.

40. Girardet, *Afghanistan*, 201; Urban, *War in Afghanistan*, 215.

41. Jalali and Grau, *Other Side of the Mountain*, 403. See also Jalali and Grau, *Afghan Guerrilla Warfare*.

42. Yousaf and Adkin, *Bear Trap*, 71.

43. Ibid., 119.

44. Amstutz, *Afghanistan*, 122.

45. Yousaf and Adkin, *Bear Trap*, 129, 135.

46. Karp, *Eight Years*, 8; U.S. Department of State, *Afghanistan*.

47. Amstutz, *Afghanistan*, 204.

48. Trottier and Karp, *Afghanistan*, 6.

49. Yousaf and Adkin, *Bear Trap*, 138.

50. Amin, "Sovietization," 325.

51. Chaliand, "Bargain War," 330.

52. Yousaf and Adkin, *Bear Trap*, 35.

53. McMichael, *Stumbling Bear*, 23; Jalali and Grau, *Other Side of the Mountain*, 3; also see 65.

54. Amstutz, *Afghanistan*, 152.

55. Jalali and Grau, *Other Side of the Mountain*, 400, 66.

56. Yousaf and Adkin, *Bear Trap*, 126.

57. Ibid., 128; Jalali and Grau, *Other Side of the Mountain*, 148.

58. Arnold, *Afghanistan*, 98; Malhuret, "Report."

59. Jalali and Grau, *Other Side of the Mountain*, 401.

60. Galeotti, *Afghanistan*, 28.

61. Yousaf and Adkin, *Bear Trap*, 154, 156.

62. Jalali and Grau, *Other Side of the Mountain*, 399.

63. Yousaf and Adkin, *Bear Trap*, 145.

64. Edwards, "Origins of the Anti-Soviet Jihad," 24; Amstutz, *Afghanistan*, 142.

65. McMichael, *Stumbling Bear*, 53.

66. Girardet, *Afghanistan*, 125; Rubin, "Human Rights," 343.

67. Girardet, *Afghanistan*, 63; Trottier and Karp, *Afghanistan*, 5; Noorzoy, "Long-Term Soviet Interests," 91.

68. Kakar, *Afghanistan*, 254.

69. Amstutz, *Afghanistan*, 145.

70. Ibid., 150.

71. Van Hollen, *Afghanistan*, 5; Amstutz, *Afghanistan*, 124.

72. Urban, *War in Afghanistan*, 69; Amstutz, *Afghanistan*, 186–87; Urban, *War in Afghanistan*, 69; Karp, *Six Years*, 7.

73. Chaliand, "Bargain War," 335.

74. Amstutz, *Afghanistan*, 166, 184; van Hollen, *Afghanistan*, 5.

75. Amstutz, *Afghanistan*, 183, 189.

76. Girardet, *Afghanistan*, 141. McMichael writes, in *Stumbling Bear*, 47, that the Soviets forced children aged thirteen to fourteen into the Afghan army; *New York Times*, March 21, 1984, 7.

77. Karp, *Seven Years*, 9; Arnold, *Afghanistan*, 102; van Hollen, *Afghanistan*, 7; McMichael, *Stumbling Bear*, 46.

78. McMichael, *Stumbling Bear*, 50.

79. Baddeley, *Russian Conquest*, xxxvi.

80. Bodansky, "Soviet Military Operations," 234; Allen and Muratoff, *Caucasian Battlefields*, chap. 3.

81. Allen and Muratoff, *Caucasian Battlefields*, chap. 3.

82. Bauman, "Russian-Soviet Unconventional Wars."

83. Jukes, "Soviet Armed Forces," 88.

84. Dobrynin, *In Confidence*, 445.

85. McMichael, *Stumbling Bear*, 10.

86. Karp, *Eight Years*, 2. "Most Western estimates put Soviet troop strength at about 120,000 men." U.S. Department of State, *Afghanistan*, 5. Amstutz, *Afghanistan*, 168, 196; *U.S. Army/Marine Corps Counterinsurgency Field Manual* (Chicago, IL: Univ. of Chicago Press, 2007), 23.

87. Karp, *Six Years*, 7.

88. Yousaf and Adkin, *Bear Trap*, 159.

89. Urban, *War in Afghanistan*, 176.

90. Bradsher, *Afghanistan and the Soviet Union*, 210.

91. Grau, *Bear Went over the Mountain*, 201. But see also Feifer, *Great Gamble*.

92. McMichael, *Stumbling Bear*, 40; Hosmer, "How Successful"; Jukes, "Soviet Armed Forces," 84.

93. Galeotti, *Afghanistan*, 200.

94. U.S. Marine Corps, *Warfighting* (Washington, DC, 1997), 78.

95. Galeotti, *Afghanistan*, 33.

96. Ibid., 33–34.

97. Urban, *War in Afghanistan*, 127.

98. Anthony James Joes, *Urban Guerrilla Warfare* (Lexington: Univ. Press of Kentucky, 2007), 136.

99. Urban, *War in Afghanistan*, 129.

100. Yousaf and Adkin, *Bear Trap*, 54–55. Mark Urban also found that many conscripts arrived in Afghanistan with only three weeks' training. *War in Afghanistan*, 129.

101. Urban, *War in Afghanistan*, 213; McMichael, *Stumbling Bear*, 63.

102. Yousaf and Adkin, *Bear Trap*, 76; Karp, *Eight Years*, 9.

103. McMichael, *Stumbling Bear*, 103.

104. Grau, *Bear Went over the Mountain*, 205.

105. Yusaf and Adkin, *Bear Trap*, 55; for more on the poor food, hygiene, and shelter of Soviet troops, see Alexiev, *Inside the Soviet Army*.

106. Grau, *Bear Went over the Mountain*, 206.

107. Galeotti, *Afghanistan*, 35.

108. Grau, *Bear Went over the Mountain*, 202. Nevertheless, Galeotti writes that "93% of the wounded troops received medical aid within 30 minutes and the attention of a specialized doctor within six hours." *Afghanistan*, 67.

109. Glantz, introduction to Grau, *Bear Went over the Mountain*, xiv (my italics); General William Odom writes that more than 400,000 Soviet soldiers contracted serious illnesses in Afghanistan. *Collapse of the Soviet Military*, 249.

110. Galeotti, *Afghanistan*, 152.

111. Alexiev, *Inside the Soviet Army*, 42.

112. Galeotti, *Afghanistan*, 228.

113. Yousaf and Adkin, *Bear Trap*, 180; Grau, *Bear Went over the Mountain*, 208.

114. Bodansky, "Soviet Military Operations," 259.

115. *New York Times*, Dec. 17, 1984, 1. See also a report by Amnesty International, *Afghanistan*; Girardet, *Afghanistan*. This method, "perfected" in Afghanistan, has been used also in Ethiopia and Cambodia. See Malhuret, "Report," 427ff.

116. Yousaf and Adkin, *Bear Trap*, 180; Girardet, *Afghanistan*, 228; Amstutz, *Afghanistan*, 175–76, 188; *Christian Science Monitor*, Oct. 26, 1988, 11; Girardet, *Afghanistan*, 219–20; Malhuret, "Report."

117. Malhuret, "Report," 430; on this revolting topic of toy bombs, see also Girardet, *Afghanistan*, 213; Amstutz, *Afghanistan*, 145; Arnold, *Afghanistan*, 99; Bradsher, *Afghanistan and the Soviet Union*, 211; McMichael, *Stumbling Bear*, 104; *New York Times*, editorial, Dec. 10, 1985, 30.

118. Bradsher, *Afghanistan and the Soviet Union*, 279.

119. Karp, *Eight Years*, 9. "The Soviet command found itself facing one of the fundamental problems of any counter-insurgency: how to separate the guerrilla from the environment which shelters him. The solution devised by the Soviets can only be described as genocide." McMichael, *Stumbling Bear*, 53.

120. Just one example is that during 1987 the Soviets carpet-bombed Qan-

dahar, Afghanistan's second-largest city, for months. "By 1988, the population of [Q]andahar, about 200,000 before the war, amounted to, by one estimate, no more than 25,000 inhabitants. . . . The American media not only ignored the [Q]andahar story but in most cases were probably not even aware of it. The grinding, piecemeal destruction of Afghanistan's second-largest city constituted an enormous black hole in foreign news coverage in our time." Kaplan, *Soldiers of God*, 188. This remarkable little volume is well worth reading.

121. Malhuret, "Report," 430; see also Ermacora's "Report on the Situation of Human Rights in Afghanistan."

122. For the argument that insurgents who have access to outside aid and intelligence sources are immune to attack and a counterinsurgency will not be effective, see Arreguin-Toft, *How the Weak Win Wars*, 198.

123. Galeotti, *Afghanistan*, 44.

124. Ibid., 85.

125. Borovik, *Hidden War*, 281; Karp, *Six Years*, 8. Selling anything—everything—including ammunition and weapons, for drugs, became a common occurrence; see Alexiev, *Inside the Soviet Army*, 54–55; Yousaf and Adkin, *Bear Trap*, 55–56; and McMichael, *Stumbling Bear*, 124. These practices became even worse in Chechnya; see Joes, *Urban Guerrilla Warfare*, chap. 7.

126. Jalali and Grau, *Other Side of the Mountain*, 340; "Afghanistan was a light infantryman's war—and the Soviets did not have light infantry." Grau, *Bear Went over the Mountain*, 205.

127. Jalali and Grau, *Other Side of the Mountain*, 404.

128. Grau, *Bear Went over the Mountain*, 202.

129. Litwak, "Soviet Union in Afghanistan"; Grau, *Bear Went over the Mountain*, 204.

130. Karp, *Seven Years*, 11.

131. Collins, *Soviet Invasion of Afghanistan*, 85; Girardet, *Afghanistan*, 42; Amstutz, *Afghanistan*, 149; Urban, *War in Afghanistan*, 68; van Hollen, *Afghanistan*, 9.

132. Yousaf and Adkin, *Bear Trap*, 59.

133. Ibid., 181.

134. Harrison, "Soviet Occupation," 198 and passim; Shultz, *Turmoil and Triumph*, 692, echoes all this.

135. McMichael, *Stumbling Bear*, 91.

136. Brigot and Roy, *War in Afghanistan*, 151.

137. U.S. Department of State, *Afghanistan*, 5.

138. "Soviet counterinsurgency effectiveness began to deteriorate rapidly after Stinger missiles were introduced in the mujahideen arsenal in late 1986," and again, "As resistance military skills and weapons . . . improved, especially [after] the introduction of effective anti-aircraft missiles in late 1986, Soviet

performance . . . actually declined." Alexiev, *Inside the Soviet Army,* 63, 61 But Galeotti is less impressed with the role of the Stinger; see, for example, *Afghanistan,* 196. Grau and Gress wrote, in Russian General Staff, *Soviet-Afghan War,* 222:

Much has been written in the western press about how the introduction of the U.S. "Stinger" shoulder-fired air defense missile "won the war" for the Mujahideen. The Stinger is an effective system, but an examination of Soviet aircraft losses shows no appreciable rise in the number of aircraft shot down after the introduction of the Stinger. Stinger [*sic*] did not shoot down that many aircraft. What Stinger did was cause a complete revision of Soviet aerial tactics. Once Stinger was in theater, helicopters stayed over friendly forces and limited daytime flights, jet aircraft flew much higher. . . . Stinger was effective—not by the number of aircraft that it downed, but by the change in [Soviet] tactics it engendered. Stinger made the pilots cautious and less of a threat to the Mujahideen.

In stunning contradiction, Scott McMichael asserts that up to the summer of 1986, the Soviets lost about 600 aircraft of all types. After that time, aircraft losses ballooned to between 400 and 540 annually. McMichael, *Stumbling Bear,* 91.

    139. McMichael, *Stumbling Bear,* 62.

    140. Odom, *Collapse of the Soviet Military,* 247.

    141. Collins, *Soviet Invasion of Afghanistan,* 59.

    142. Amstutz, *Afghanistan,* 132.

    143. Ibid.

    144. Ibid., 135, 128, 181; Bureau of Intelligence and Research, "Afghanistan," 2.

    145. McMichael, *Stumbling Bear,* 126–27; Trottier and Karp, *Afghanistan,* 4; *New York Times,* Oct. 24, 1984, 1.

    146. Amstutz, *Afghanistan,* 140.

    147. Arnold, *Afghanistan,* 98.

    148. Trottier and Karp, *Afghanistan,* 2.

    149. Karp, *Six Years,* 2.

    150. Karp, *Eight Years,* 12; Bodansky, "Soviet Military Operations," 261.

    151. Urban, *War in Afghanistan,* 200; Karp, *Seven Years,* 1.

    152. Urban, *War in Afghanistan,* 214; Karp, *Eight Years,* 6, 3.

    153. McMichael, *Stumbling Bear,* 35.

    154. Ibid., 59.

    155. Karp, *Eight Years,* 5; see, for example. *New York Times,* Jan. 25, 1984, 1.

    156. Bradsher, *Afghanistan and the Soviet Union,* 276. "Let me abolish a myth that has been built up by Soviet propaganda and many journalists. Up to the Soviet withdrawal from Afghanistan in early 1989, no American or Chinese instructor was ever involved in giving training or any kind of weapon or equipment [directly] to the Mujahideen." Americans helped train certain Pakistanis

who trained the Mujahideen, however. From 1983 to 1987, 80,000 Mujahideen had received training in Pakistan and many thousands more in Afghanistan. Yousaf and Adkin, *Bear Trap*, 115, 117.

157. *Christian Science Monitor*, Oct. 24, 1988; *Washington Post*, Dec. 15, 1985.

158. Van Hollen, *Afghanistan*, 11.

159. Girardet, *Afghanistan*, 248.

160. Malhuret, "Report." Robert D. Kaplan, in his article "Afghanistan: Postmortem" in the April 1989 *Atlantic*, wrote that foreign newsmen gave poor coverage to the Afghan war partly because there were no modern cities with good hotels close at hand.

161. Girardet, *Afghanistan*, 67; Farr and Merriam, *Afghan Resistance*, xii; Amin Saikal, "The Regional Politics of the Afghan Crisis," in *The Soviet Withdrawal from Afghanistan*, ed. Amin Saikal and William Maley (New York: Cambridge Univ. Press, 1989), 54.

162. Collins, *Soviet Invasion of Afghanistan*, 153; on continuation of bombings of villages inside Pakistan, see, for example, *New York Times*, Jan. 29, 1984, 1; and *New York Times*, March 25, 1987, 1.

163. Bradsher, *Afghanistan and the Soviet Union*, 222.

164. Karp, *Eight Years*, 22.

165. Urban, *War in Afghanistan*, 97.

166. See Vertzberger, "Afghanistan in China's Policy," 1–24; Holmes, "Afghanistan and Sino-Soviet Relations," 122–42.

167. Amstutz, *Afghanistan*, 216.

168. Amin, "Sovietization of Afghanistan," 322.

169. Poullada, "Road to Crisis," 48, 44; Collins, *Soviet Invasion of Afghanistan*, 19; Hammond, *Red Flag over Afghanistan*, 26–28; Collins, *Soviet Invasion of Afghanistan*, 20, 170. Yousaf and Adkin, *Bear Trap*, 74; Galeotti, *Afghanistan*, 197.

171. Arnold, *Afghanistan*, xii; Collins, *Soviet Invasion of Afghanistan*, 134.

172. Long-time USSR ambassador to Washington Anatoly Dobrynin wrote that the leadership in Moscow thought Carter's pronouncement was "incredible" and one believes him. *In Confidence*, 448.

173. Carter, *Keeping Faith*, 473.

174. Ibid., 471–89; Vance, *Hard Choices*, 386–96; Brzezinski, *Power and Principle*, chap. 12.

175. Carter, *Keeping Faith*, 483.

176. Collins, *Soviet Invasion of Afghanistan*, 145.

177. On the Reagan Doctrine, see Bode, "Reagan Doctrine"; and Codevilla, "Reagan Doctrine"; George Shultz, "America and the Struggle for Freedom," *State Department Current Policy* 659 (Feb. 1985).

178. Arnold, *Afghanistan*, 18; see *New York Times*, May 3, 1983; Nov. 28, 1984;

Wall Street Journal, April 9, 1984; *Washington Post,* Jan. 3, 1985; *Economist,* Jan. 19, 1985; Cordesman and Wagner, *Lessons of Modern War,* 20; Ranelagh, *Agency,* 681; Amstutz, *Afghanistan,* 210; Bradsher, *Afghanistan and the Soviet Union,* 278.

179. Cordesman and Wagner, *Lessons of Modern War,* 83; Alexiev, *Inside the Soviet Army,* 62. "Soviet mine warfare against the mujahidin represent[ed] one more failed attempt to solve the difficult problems of counter-insurgency warfare with a simple, technological solution." McMichael, *Stumbling Bear,* 107.

180. U.S. Department of State, *Afghanistan,* 1.

181. Cordesman and Wagner, *Lessons of Modern War;* Jukes, "Soviet Armed Forces," 83; Grau and Gress, in Russian General Staff, *Soviet-Afghan War,* 310; Isby, *War in a Distant Country,* 65; Maley, "Geneva Accords," 16; Girardet, *Afghanistan,* 234.

182. Shroder and Assifi, "Afghan Mineral Resources," 128, quotation on 101.

183. Galeotti, *Afghanistan,* 226.

184. Arnold, *Fateful Pebble,* 112.

185. Soviet Central Asia is today the republics of Kazakhstan, Kyrgyzstan, Tajikistan, Turkmenistan, and Uzbekistan; Bennigsen, "Impact of the Afghan War," 295.

186. Bennigsen, "Mullahs, Mujahidin, and Soviet Muslims," 28–45; and the review article by Karpat, "Moscow and the 'Muslim Question,'" 71–80. See also Fuller, "Emergence of Central Asia."

187. Cordesman and Wagner, *Lessons of Modern War,* 95.

188. Daley, "Afghanistan," 496–513. An enlightening treatment of nonmilitary aspects of Soviet counterinsurgency in Afghanistan is Robbins, "Soviet Counterinsurgency."

189. U.S. Department of State, *Afghanistan,* 2.

190. Ibid., 5, 1. This "departure [from Afghanistan] would be the first-ever retreat by Soviet forces from a territory or country they dominated." Shultz, *Turmoil and Triumph,* 1086; see his description of the withdrawal, 1086–94.

191. The resistance parties opposed the accords, for at least two reasons: first, the illegitimate and illegal Kabul regime could not enter into any agreement with any state; second, they feared that the accords might foreshadow a lessening of world interest in Afghanistan's struggle, leaving the insurgents without further assistance.

192. "Socialism in One City" is a burlesque of Stalin's famously un-Marxist, un-Leninist mantra of "Socialism in One Country," in contrast to Trotsky's much more orthodox "permanent revolution," that is, carrying Bolshevism into central Europe. The State Department's *Afghanistan: Soviet Occupation and Withdrawal* contained these prognostications of the fall of Kabul: "Most observers believe that the Najibullah regime will not long survive the Soviet departure." "Most

experts agree that it [the Kabul Army] can survive no more than a matter of months after a complete Soviet withdrawal" (1, 7).

193. Rubin, "Fragmentation of Afghanistan," 163.

194. U.S. Department of State, *Afghanistan*, 161; Rubin, "Fragmentation of Afghanistan," 161.

195. Rashid, "Bloody Stalemate," 42; Rubin, "Fragmentation of Afghanistan," 186.

196. Yousaf and Adkin, *Bear Trap*, 227, 231, 228, 232, quotations on 228 and 232.

197. Urban, *War in Afghanistan*, 208, 210. As early as 1983, a women's militia unit played a role in the defense of Urgun, in Badakhshan Province.

198. U.S. Department of State, *Afghanistan*, 4.

199. Quinn-Judge, "Splitting the Faithful," 21; Rashid, "Highway Lifeline," 22.

200. Rashid, "Highway Lifeline," 22.

201. Jukes, "Soviet Armed Forces," 83.

202. Perhaps 50,000 were wounded, of whom more than 11,000 became invalids. Galeotti, *Afghanistan*, 68, 30, 97. Khrushchev said 1 million Soviet troops perished in the Finnish War. Nikita Khrushchev, *Khrushchev Remembers* (Boston, MA: Little, Brown, 1970), 155.

203. Maley, "Geneva Accords," 13.

5. Lessons Learned–or Not

1. Bianco, *Origins of the Chinese Revolution*, 203.

2. See Anthony James Joes, *Resisting Rebellion: The History and Politics of Counterinsurgency* (Lexington: Univ. Press of Kentucky, 2004), chap. 14, "The Myth of Maoist People's War."

3. See, inter alia, Johnson, *Autopsy on People's War*.

4. The French Communists received 5,154,000 votes in November 1946, 4,934,000 in June 1951, and 5,517,000 in January 1956. See Williams, *Crisis and Compromise*, 502.

5. O'Neill, *Insurgency and Terrorism*, 111; Record, *Beating Goliath*, xii, and see all of chap. 2. See also Jeffrey Record, "External Assistance: Enabler of Insurgent Success," *Parameters* 36 (Autumn 2006).

6. Castro tried to excuse the totalitarian dictatorship he set up in lieu of the oft-promised free elections as necessary to ward off U.S. hostility, but it was the minority nature of Castro's support that was the true cause of the dictatorship.

7. Russian General Staff, *Soviet Afghan War*, 72, 311.

8. McMichael, *Stumbling Bear*, 131, 129.

9. In recent decades, diaspora ethnic communities and organized crime have filled the role, to a degree, of assistance to insurgents from friendly states.

10. Consider the following table:

		Counterinsurgent Victory	
		Yes	**No**
	Yes	Malaya	Cuba (Batista)
		Boer War	
Counterinsurgent		Greece	
Numerical		Algeria	
Preponderance		Vendée	
	No	South Viet Nam	Spain
			Afghanistan
			French Viet Nam
			Japan-China

11. "The French used torture in Algeria; therefore they won because of torture" would (or at least should) earn a failing grade in any college course in logic. See Anthony James Joes, *Urban Guerrilla Warfare* (Lexington: Univ. Press of Kentucky, 2007).

12. C.E. Callwell, *Small Wars: Their Principles and Practice* (1906; Wakefield, England: EP, 1976), 126.

13. Colin Gray, *Irregular Enemies and the Essence of Strategy: Can the American Way of War Adapt?* (Carlisle, PA: Strategic Studies Institute, 2006); Nigel Aylwin-Foster, "Changing the Army for Counterinsurgency Operations," *Military Review* (Nov.–Dec. 2005); Andrew Krepinevich, *The Army and Vietnam* (Baltimore, MD: Johns Hopkins Univ. Press, 1986).

14. For language and other problems in the American effort to advise South Vietnamese Army units, see Cao Van Vien et al., *The U.S. Advisor* (Washington, DC: U.S. Army Center of Military History, 1980); Jeffrey J. Clarke, *Advice and Support: The Final Years* (Washington, DC: U.S. Army Center of Military History, 1988); Martin Dockery, *Lost in Translation: Vietnam: A Combat Advisor's Story* (Novato, CA: Presidio Press, 2004); Gerald C. Hickey, *The American Military Advisor and His Foreign Counterpart: The Case of Vietnam* (Santa Monica, CA: RAND, 1965); John G. Miller, *The Co-Vans: U.S. Marine Advisors in Vietnam* (Annapolis, MD: U.S. Naval Institute Press, 2000); Robert D. Ramsey, *Advising Indigenous Forces: American Advisors in Korea, Vietnam, and El Salvador* (Fort Leavenworth, KS: Combat Studies Institute Press, 2006); Kilcullen, *The Accidental Guerrilla*.

15. Jeffrey Record, *Japan's Decision for War in 1941: Some Enduring Lessons* (Carlisle, PA: Strategic Studies Institute, 2009), 53. And see Richard K. Betts, *Enemies of Intelligence: Knowledge and Power in American National Security* (New York: Columbia Univ. Press, 2007), 131.

16. See Mack, "Why Big Nations Lose Small Wars," 177. On this question of the difficulties of great powers in small wars, see Arreguin-Toft, *How the Weak Win Wars*; Gil Merom, *How Democracies Lose Small Wars: State, Society, and the Failure of France in Algeria, Israel in Lebanon, and the United States in Vietnam* (New York: Cambridge Univ. Press, 2003); and Record, *Beating Goliath*.

17. Recall that during the Vietnam conflict the media profoundly misinformed the U.S. electorate about, among other things, the nature of the opposition to President Diem, the 1968 New Hampshire Democratic presidential primary, and the Tet Offensive.

18. See Kilcullen, *Accidental Guerrilla*; and Joes, *Urban Guerrilla Warfare*.

19. If no host government properly so-called exists, the United States could encourage regional organizations or states, or as a last resort the United Nations, to restore civil order. If a U.S. administration judges such a course impossible or unsuitable and commits American forces to a combat role, it would be imperative to obtain support on the ground from states within the region or from the NATO allies, or both.

Bibliography

Aaron, Harold R. "The Seizure of Political Power in Cuba, 1956–1959." Ph.D. diss., Georgetown Univ., 1964.

Aguilar, Luis E. *Cuba 1933: Prologue to Revolution.* Ithaca, NY: Cornell Univ. Press, 1972.

Alexiev, Alexander. *Inside the Soviet Army in Afghanistan.* Santa Monica, CA: RAND, 1988.

Alexiev, Alexander, and S. Enders Wimbush, eds. *Ethnic Minorities in the Red Army: Asset or Liability?* Boulder, CO: Westview, 1988.

Allen, W.E.D., and Paul Muratoff. *Caucasian Battlefields.* Cambridge: Cambridge Univ. Press, 1953.

Ambrose, Stephen E. *Eisenhower.* Vol. 2, *The President.* New York: Simon and Schuster, 1984.

Ameringer, Charles D. *The Cuban Democratic Experience: The Autentico Years, 1944–1952.* Gainesville: Univ. Press of Florida, 2000.

Amin, A. Rosul. "The Sovietization of Afghanistan." In Klass, *Afghanistan.*

Amnesty International. *Afghanistan: Torture of Prisoners.* London: Amnesty International, 1986.

Amstutz, J. Bruce. *Afghanistan: The First Five Years of Soviet Occupation.* Washington, DC: National Defense Univ. Press, 1986.

Andreski, Stanislav. *Military Organization and Society.* Berkeley: Univ. of California Press, 1968.

Andrew, Christopher. *Defend the Realm: The Authorized History of MI5.* New York: Knopf, 2009.

Arendt, Hannah. *On Revolution.* New York: Viking, 1965.

Argote-Freyre, F. *Fulgencio Batista.* New Brunswick, NJ: Rutgers Univ. Press, 2006.

Arnold, Anthony. *Afghanistan's Two-Party Communism*. Stanford, CA: Hoover Institution, Stanford Univ., 1983.

———. *Afghanistan: The Soviet Invasion in Perspective*. Stanford, CA: Hoover Institution, Stanford Univ., 1985.

———. *The Fateful Pebble: Afghanistan's Role in the Fall of the Soviet Empire*. Novato, CA: Presidio, 1993.

Arnold, Anthony, and Rosanne Klass. "Afghanistan's Divided Communist Party." In Klass, *Afghanistan*.

Arreguin-Toft, Ivan. *How the Weak Win Wars: A Theory of Asymmetric Conflict*. New York: Cambridge Univ. Press, 2005.

Baddeley, John F. *The Russian Conquest of the Caucasus*. New York: Russell and Russell, 1969. Originally published in 1908.

Bao Dai. *Le Dragon d'Annam*. Paris: Plon, 1980.

Barnett, A. Doak. *China on the Eve of Communist Takeover*. New York: Praeger, 1963.

———, ed. *Chinese Communist Politics in Action*. Seattle: Univ. of Washington Press, 1969.

Barnhart, Michael A. "Japanese Intelligence before the Second World War: 'Best Case' Analysis." In *Knowing One's Enemies: Intelligence Assessment before the Two World Wars*, ed. Ernest R. May. Princeton, NJ: Princeton Univ. Press, 1984.

———. *Japan Prepares for Total War: The Search for Economic Security, 1919–1941*. Ithaca, NY: Cornell Univ. Press, 1987.

Barrett, David D. *The Dixie Mission: The United States Army Observer Group in Yenan, 1944*. Berkeley: Univ. of California Press, 1970.

Barrett, David P. "The Wang Jingwei Regime, 1940–1945: Continuities and Disjunctures with Nationalist China." In Barrett and Shyu, *Chinese Collaboration with Japan*.

Barrett, David P., and Larry Shyu, eds. *Chinese Collaboration with Japan, 1932–1945: The Limits of Accommodation*. Stanford, CA: Stanford Univ. Press, 2001.

Bartholomew-Feis, Dixee. *The OSS and Ho Chi Minh: Unexpected Allies in the War against Japan*. Lawrence: Univ. Press of Kansas, 2006.

Batista, Fulgencio. *Cuba Betrayed*. New York: Vantage, 1962.

Bator, Victor. *Vietnam: A Diplomatic Tragedy: The Origins of U.S. Involvement*. London: Faber and Faber, 1965.

Bauman, Robert F. "Russian-Soviet Unconventional Wars in the Caucasus, Central Asia, and Afghanistan." Leavenworth Paper no. 20, Combat Studies Institute, Fort Leavenworth, Kansas, 1993.

Beal, John Robinson. *Marshall in China*. Garden City, NY: Doubleday, 1970.

Beals, Carleton. *The Crime of Cuba*. Philadelphia: Lippincott, 1933.

Beckett, Ian F.W., ed. *The Roots of Counterinsurgency*. London: Blandford, 1988.

Bedeski, Robert. *State-Building in Modern China: The Kuomintang in the Prewar*

Period. China Research Monograph 18. Berkeley, CA: Center for Chinese Studies, 1981.

Benjamin, Jules R. *The United States and Cuba: Hegemony and Dependent Development, 1880–1934.* Pittsburgh, PA: Univ. of Pittsburgh Press, 1977.

———. *The United States and the Origins of the Cuban Revolution: An Empire of Liberty in an Age of National Liberation.* Princeton, NJ: Princeton Univ. Press, 1990.

Bennigsen, Alexandre. "The Impact of the Afghan War on Soviet Central Asia." In Klass, *Afghanistan.*

———. "Mullahs, Mujahidin, and Soviet Muslims." *Problems of Communism* 33 (Nov.–Dec. 1984).

———. *The Soviet Union and Muslim Guerrilla Wars, 1920–1981: The Lessons of Afghanistan.* Santa Monica, CA: RAND, 1981.

Bergère, Marie-Claire. *Sun Yat-sen.* Stanford, CA: Stanford Univ. Press, 1998.

Bianco, Lucien. *Origins of the Chinese Revolution, 1915–1949.* Trans. Muriel Bell. Stanford, CA: Stanford Univ. Press, 1971.

Bigeard, Marcel-Maurice. *Ma guerre d'Indochine.* Paris: Hachette, 1994.

Billings-Yun, Melanie. *Decision against War: Eisenhower and Dien Bien Phu, 1954.* New York: Columbia Univ. Press, 1980.

Blainey, Geoffrey. *The Causes of War.* New York: Free Press, 1988.

Bland, Larry I., ed. *George C. Marshall's Mediation Mission to China, December 1945–January 1947.* Lexington, VA: George C. Marshall Foundation, 1998.

Blank, Stephen J. *Operational and Strategic Lessons of the War in Afghanistan, 1979–1990.* Carlisle, PA: Strategic Studies Institute, 1990.

———. "Russian Forces in Afghanistan: Unlearning the Lessons of Vietnam." In *Responding to Low-Intensity Conflict Challenges,* ed. Stephen J. Blank, Lawrence E. Grinter, Karl P. Magyar, Lewis B. Ware, and Bynum E. Weathers. Maxwell Air Force Base, AL: Air Univ. Press, 1990.

Blum, Robert M. *Drawing the Line: The Origins of the American Containment Policy in East Asia.* New York: Norton, 1982.

Bodansky, Yossef. "Soviet Military Operations in Afghanistan." In Klass, *Afghanistan.*

Bodard, Lucien. *The Quicksand War: Prelude to Vietnam.* Boston: Little, Brown, 1967.

Bode, William R. "The Reagan Doctrine in Outline." In *Central America and the Reagan Doctrine,* ed. Walter F. Hahn. Boston: Univ. Press of America, 1987.

Bodin, Michel. *La France et ses soldats: Indochine, 1945–1954.* Paris: Harmattan, 1996.

Bodinier, Gilbert, ed. *La guerre d'Indochine, 1945–1954.* Vol. 1, *Le retour de la France en Indochine 1945–1946.* Vincennes, France: Service Historique de l'Armée de Terre 1987.

———, ed. *La Guerre d'Indochine, 1945–1954*. Vol. 2, *Indochine, 1947: Règlement politique ou solution militaire?* Vincennes, France: Service Historique de l'Armée de Terre, 1989.

Bonachea, Ramon, and Marta San Martín. *The Cuban Insurrection, 1952–1959*. New Brunswick, NJ: Transaction, 1975.

Bonsal, Philip W. *Cuba, Castro, and the United States*. Pittsburgh, PA: Univ. of Pittsburgh Press, 1971.

Boorman, Howard L., and Richard C. Howard. *Biographical Dictionary of Republican China*. 4 vols. New York: Columbia Univ. Press, 1967–71.

Borovik, Artyom. *The Hidden War*. New York: Atlantic Monthly Press, 1990.

Boyer de Latour, Pierre. *La martyre de l'armée française: De l'Indochine à l'Algérie*. Paris: Les Presses du Mail, 1962.

Boyle, John Hunter. *China and Japan at War, 1937–1945: The Politics of Collaboration*. Stanford, CA: Stanford Univ. Press, 1972.

Bradsher, Henry S. *Afghanistan and the Soviet Union*. Durham, NC: Duke Univ. Press, 1985.

Brandt, Conrad. *Stalin's Failure in China: 1924–1927*. 2nd ed. Cambridge, MA. Harvard Univ. Press, 1958.

Brandt, Conrad, Benjamin Schwartz, and John K. Fairbank. *A Documentary History of Chinese Communism*. Cambridge, MA: Harvard Univ. Press, 1952.

Brennan, Ray. *Castro, Cuba, and Justice*. Garden City, NY: Doubleday, 1959.

Brigot, André, and Olivier Roy. *The War in Afghanistan*. New York: Harvester-Wheatsheaf, 1988.

Brook, Timothy. *Collaboration: Japanese Agents and Local Elites in Wartime China*. London: Harvard Univ. Press, 2005.

Brzezinski, Zbigniew. *Power and Principle: Memoirs of the National Security Adviser*. New York: Farrar, Straus and Giroux, 1983.

Bui Diem. *In the Jaws of History*. Boston: Houghton Mifflin, 1987.

Bui Tin. *Following Ho Chi Minh: Memoirs of a North Vietnamese Colonel*. Honolulu: Univ. of Hawaii Press, 1995.

Bunker, Gerald. *The Peace Conspiracy: Wang Ching-wei and the China War, 1937–1941*. Cambridge, MA: Harvard Univ. Press, 1972.

Bureau of Intelligence and Research. "Afghanistan: Four Years of Occupation." U.S. Department of State, Washington, DC, 1983.

Butow, Robert J.C. *Tojo and the Coming of the War*. Princeton, NJ: Princeton Univ. Press, 1961.

Buttinger, Joseph. *A Dragon Defiant: A Short History of Vietnam*. New York: Praeger, 1972.

———. *Vietnam: A Dragon Embattled*. Vol. 1, *From Colonialism to the Viet Minh*. Vol. 2, *Vietnam at War*. New York: Praeger, 1967.

Cable, James. *The Geneva Conference of 1954 on Indochina.* New York: St. Martin's, 1986.

Cady, John F. *The Roots of French Imperialism in Eastern Asia.* Ithaca, NY: Cornell Univ. Press, 1954.

Cameron, Allan W., ed. *Viet-Nam Crisis: A Documentary History.* Ithaca, NY: Cornell Univ. Press, 1971.

Carlson, Evans Fordyce. *The Chinese Army.* New York: Institute of Pacific Relations, 1940.

Carrère d'Encausse, Hélène. *Islam and the Russian Empire: Reform and Revolution in Central Asia.* Berkeley: Univ. of California Press, 1988.

Carter, Jimmy: *Keeping Faith: Memoirs of a President.* New York: Bantam, 1982.

Carver, Michael. *War since 1945.* New York: Putnam, 1981.

Chaliand, Girard. "The Bargain War in Afghanistan." In *Guerrilla Strategies,* ed. Gerard Chaliand. Berkeley: Univ. of California Press, 1982.

Chang, Iris. *The Rape of Nanking: The Forgotten Holocaust.* New York: Basic Books, 1997.

Chappelle, Dickey. "How Castro Won." In *Modern Guerrilla Warfare,* ed. Franklin Mark Osanka. New York: Free Press, 1962.

Chapuis, Oscar. *The Last Emperors of Vietnam: From Tu Duc to Bao Dai.* Westport, CT: Greenwood, 2000.

Chassin, Lionel Max. *The Communist Conquest of China: A History of the Civil War, 1945–1949.* Cambridge, MA: Harvard Univ. Press, 1965. Originally published in 1952.

Chen, King C. *Vietnam and China, 1938–1954.* Princeton, NJ: Princeton Univ. Press, 1969.

Chen Jian. "China and the First Indochina War, 1950–1954." *China Quarterly* 133 (March 1993).

Chester, Edmund A. *A Sergeant Named Batista.* New York: Holt, 1954.

Ch'i, Hsi-sheng. "The Military Dimension, 1942–1945." In Hsiung and Levine, *China's Bitter Victory.*

———. *Nationalist China at War: Military Defeats and Political Collapse, 1937–45.* Ann Arbor: Univ. of Michigan Press, 1982.

———. *Warlord Politics in China, 1916–1928.* Stanford, CA: Stanford Univ. Press, 1976.

Chiang, Tsien-tseh. *The Nien Rebellion.* Seattle: Univ. of Washington Press, 1954.

Chiang Kai-shek. *China Fights On: War Messages of Chiang Kai-shek.* Vol. 1, *October 1938–January 1940.* Trans. Frank Wilson Price. Chungking: China Publishing Co., 1940.

———. *China's Destiny.* New York: Roy, 1947.

———. *Soviet Russia in China.* New York: Farrar, Straus and Cudahy, 1957.

Ch'ien Tuang-shen. *The Government and Politics of China, 1912–1949*. Stanford CA: Stanford Univ. Press, 1970.

Chorley, Katherine. *Armies and the Art of Revolution*. Boston: Beacon, 1973.

Chou Shun-hsin. *The Chinese Inflation, 1937–1949*. New York: Columbia Univ. Press, 1963.

Chung, Iris. *The Rape of Nanking: The Forgotten Holocaust*. New York: Basic Books, 1997.

Churchill, Winston. *The Second World War*. Vol. 4, *The Hinge of Fate*. Boston: Houghton-Mifflin, 1950.

Chu Teh. *China's Revolutionary Wars*. Peking: Foreign Languages Press, 1951.

———. *On the Battlefronts of the Liberated Areas*. Peking: Foreign Languages Press, 1952. Originally published in 1945.

Clayton, Anthony. *Wars of French Decolonization*. New York: Longmans, 1994.

Cloake, John. *Templer: Tiger of Malaya*. London: Harrap, 1985.

Clubb, O. Edmund. *Twentieth Century China*. 2nd ed. New York: Oxford Univ. Press, 1972.

Codevilla, Angelo. "The Regan Doctrine: It Awaits Implementation." In *Central America and the Reagan Doctrine*, ed. Walter F. Hahn. Boston: Univ. Press of America, 1987.

Coll, Steve. *Ghost Wars: The Secret History of the CIA, Afghanistan, and bin Laden, from the Soviet Invasion to September 10, 2001*. New York: Penguin, 2004.

Collins, Joseph J. *The Soviet Invasion of Afghanistan: A Study in the Use of Force in Soviet Foreign Policy*. Lexington, MA: Lexington Books, 1986.

Coox, Alvin D. *Nomonhan: Russia against Japan, 1939*. Stanford, CA: Stanford Univ. Press, 1985.

———. "The Pacific War." In Duus, *Cambridge History of Japan*.

Cordesman, Anthony H., and Abraham R. Wagner. *The Lessons of Modern War*. Vol. 3, *The Afghan and Falklands Conflicts*. Boulder, CO: Westview, 1990.

Cordovez, Diego, and Selig Harrison, eds. *Out of Afghanistan: The Inside Story of the Soviet Withdrawal*. New York: Oxford Univ. Press, 1995.

Crile, George. *Charlie Wilson's War: The Extraordinary Story of the Largest Covert Operation in History*. New York: Atlantic Monthly Press, 2003.

Crowley, James B. Introduction to *The China Quagmire: Japan's Expansion on the Asian Continent, 1933–1941*, ed. James William Morley. New York: Columbia Univ. Press, 1983.

———. *Japan's Quest for Autonomy: National Security and Foreign Policy, 1930–1938*. Princeton, NJ: Princeton Univ. Press, 1966.

Daley, T. "Afghanistan and Gorbachev's Global Foreign Policy." *Asian Survey* 29 (May 1989).

Dalloz, Jacques. *La guerre d'Indochine, 1945–1954*. Paris: Editions de Seuil, 1987.

Dansette, Adrien. *Leclerc*. Paris: Flammarion, 1952.

Davidson, Phillip B. *Vietnam at War: The History, 1946–1975*. Novato, CA: Presidio, 1988.

Dear, I.C.B., ed. *The Oxford Companion to World War II*. New York: Oxford Univ. Press, 1995.

De Gaulle, Charles. *The War Memoirs*. Vol. 3, *Salvation*. Trans. Richard Howard. New York: Simon and Schuster, 1960.

De Lee, Nigel. "The Far Eastern Experience." In Beckett, *Roots of Counterinsurgency*.

Democratic Republic of Viet Nam. *Ten Years of Fighting and Building of the Vietnamese People's Army*. Hanoi: Foreign Languages, 1955.

———. *Thirty Years of Struggle of the Party*. Hanoi: Foreign Languages, 1960.

De Palma, Anthony. *The Man Who Invented Fidel: Castro, Cuba, and Herbert Matthews of the New York Times*. New York: Public Affairs, 2007.

Deutscher, Isaac. *Trotsky: The Prophet Armed, 1879–1921*. New York: Vintage, 1965.

Devillers, Philippe. *Histoire du Viêt-Nam de 1940 à 1952*. 3rd ed. Paris: Editions du Seuil, 1952.

Dewart, Leslie. *Christianity and Revolution: The Lesson of Cuba*. New York: Herder and Herder, 1963.

Dinfreville, Jacques. *L'opération Indochine*. Editions Internationales, 1953.

Divine, Robert A. *Eisenhower and the Cold War*. New York: Oxford Univ. Press, 1981.

Dobrynin, Anatoly. *In Confidence: Moscow's Ambassador to America's Six Cold War Presidents (1962–1986)*. New York: Random House, 1995.

Dommen, Arthur. *The Indochinese Experience of the French and the Americans: Nationalism and Communism in Cambodia, Laos, and Vietnam*. Bloomington: Indiana Univ. Press, 2001.

Dorn, Frank. *The Sino-Japanese War, 1937–1941: From Marco Polo Bridge to Pearl Harbor*. New York: Macmillan, 1974.

Draper, Theodore. *Castroism: Theory and Practice*. New York: Praeger, 1965.

———. *Castro's Revolution: Myths and Realities*. New York: Praeger, 1962.

Duiker, William. *The Communist Road to Power in Vietnam*. Boulder, CO: Westview, 1981.

Duncanson, Dennis J. *Government and Revolution in Vietnam*. New York: Oxford Univ. Press, 1968.

Dunn, Peter M. *The First Vietnam War*. New York: St. Martin's, 1985.

Dupree, Louis. *Afghanistan*. Princeton, NJ: Princeton Univ. Press, 1973.

———. "Post-Withdrawal Afghanistan: Light at the End of the Tunnel." In Saikal and Maley, *Soviet Withdrawal*.

Durand, Henry Marion. *The First Afghan War and Its Causes*. London: Longman's, Green, 1879.

Duus, Peter, ed. *The Cambridge History of Japan*. Vol. 6, *The Twentieth Century*. New York: Cambridge Univ. Press, 1988.

Duus, Peter, Ramon H. Myers, and Mark R. Peattie, eds. *The Japanese Wartime Empire, 1931–1945*. Princeton, NJ: Princeton Univ. Press, 1996.

Eastman, Lloyd E. *The Abortive Revolution: China under Nationalist Rule, 1927–1937*. Cambridge, MA: Harvard Univ. Press, 1990.

———. "Nationalist China during the Sino-Japanese War, 1937–1945." In *Cambridge History of China*, vol. 13, *Republican China, 1912–1949*, ed. John K. Fairbank and Albert Feuerwerker. New York: Cambridge Univ. Press, 1986.

———. *Seeds of Destruction: Nationalist China in War and Revolution, 1937–1949*. Stanford, CA: Stanford Univ. Press, 1984.

Eastman, Lloyd E., Jerome Chen, Suzanne Pepper, and Lyman P. Van Slyke. *The Nationalist Era in China, 1927–1949*. Cambridge: Cambridge Univ. Press, 1991.

Edwards, David Busby. "Origins of the Anti-Soviet Jihad." In Farr and Merriam, *Afghan Resistance*.

Eisenhower, Dwight D. *The White House Years: Mandate for Change, 1953–1956*. Garden City, NY: Doubleday, 1963.

Elliott, David W.P. *The Vietnamese War: Revolution and Social Change in the Mekong Delta, 1930–1975*. Armonk, NY: M. E. Sharpe, 2003.

Elsbree, Willard H. *Japan's Role in Southeast Asian Nationalist Movements, 1940 to 1945*. Cambridge, MA: Harvard Univ. Press, 1953.

Ely, Paul. *Lessons of the War in Indochina*. Vol. 2. Santa Monica, CA: Rand, 1967.

———. *L'Indochine dans la Tourmente*. Paris: Plon, 1964.

Emerson, Rupert. *From Empire to Nation*. Boston, MA: Beacon, 1963.

Ermacora, Felix. "Report on the Situation of Human Rights in Afghanistan," reports to the United Nations Commission on Human Rights in Afghanistan, UN Documents No. E/CN.4/1985/21 (Feb. 19, 1985); No. A/40/843 (Nov. 5, 1985); No. E/CN.41986/24 (Feb. 17, 1986), United Nations, New York.

Fairbairn, Geoffrey. *Revolutionary Guerrilla Warfare: The Countryside Version*. Harmondsworth, England: Penguin, 1974.

Fairbank, John K. *The Great Chinese Revolution, 1800–1985*. New York: Harper and Row, 1986.

———. "Introduction: Maritime and Continental in China's History." In *The Cambridge History of China*, vol. 12, *Republican China 1912–1949, Part 1*, ed. John K. Fairbank. New York: Cambridge Univ. Press, 1983.

———. "The Reunification of China." In *The Cambridge History of China*, vol. 14, *The People's Republic, Part 1, The Emergence of Revolutionary China, 1949–1965*, ed. Denis Twitchett and John K. Fairbank. New York: Cambridge Univ. Press, 1987.

Fall, Bernard. *Hell in a Very Small Place*. Philadelphia, PA: Lippincott, 1967.

———. *Street without Joy*. Harrisburg, PA: Stackpole, 1964.

———. *The Two Vietnams: A Political and Military Analysis*. 2nd ed., rev. New York: Praeger, 1967.

Farber, Samuel. *Origins of the Cuban Revolution Reconsidered*. Chapel Hill: Univ. of North Carolina Press, 2006.

———. *Revolution and Reaction in Cuba, 1933–1960: A Political Sociology from Machado to Castro*. Middletown, CT: Wesleyan Univ. Press, 1976.

Farr, Grant M., and John G. Merriam, eds. *Afghan Resistance: The Politics of Survival*. Boulder, CO: Westview, 1987.

Feifer, Gregory. *The Great Gamble: The Soviet War in Afghanistan*. New York: Harper, 2009.

Feis, Herbert. *The China Tangle: The American Effort in China from Pearl Harbor to the Marshall Mission*. Princeton, NJ: Princeton Univ. Press, 1953.

Fenn, Charles. *Ho Chi Minh: A Biographical Introduction*. New York: Scribner's, 1973.

Fishel, Wesley, ed. *Vietnam: Anatomy of a Conflict*. Itasca, IL: Peacock, 1968.

Fletcher, Arnold. *Afghanistan: Highway of Conquest*. Ithaca, NY: Cornell Univ. Press, 1965.

Fogel, Joshua A. *The Nanjing Massacre*. Berkeley: Univ. of California Press, 2000.

Forbes, Archibald. *The Afghan Wars, 1839–1842 and 1878–1880*. New York: Scribner's, 1892.

Foreign Relations of the United States (FRUS). See U.S. Department of State.

Fuller, Graham E. "The Emergence of Central Asia." *Foreign Affairs* 69, no. 2 (Spring 1990).

Galeotti, Mark. *Afghanistan: The Soviet Union's Last War*. London: Frank Cass, 1995.

Galula, David. *Counterinsurgency Warfare: Theory and Practice*. New York: Praeger, 1964.

Gellman, Irwin F. *Roosevelt and Batista: Good Neighbor Diplomacy in Cuba, 1933–1945*. Albuquerque: Univ. of New Mexico Press, 1973.

Giap. See Vo Nguyen Giap.

Gillin, Donald G., and Charles Etter. "Staying On: Japanese Soldiers and Civilians in China, 1945–1949." *Journal of Asian Studies* 42 (May 1983).

Girardet, Edward. *Afghanistan: The Soviet War*. New York: St. Martin's, 1985.

Glantz, David M. Introduction to Grau, *Bear Went over the Mountain*.

Goldenberg, Boris. *The Cuban Revolution and Latin America*. New York: Praeger, 1965.

Gras, Yves. *Histoire de la guerre d'Indochine*. Paris: Denoel, 1992.

Grau, Lester W., ed. *The Bear Went over the Mountain: Soviet Combat Tactics in Afghanistan*. Portland, OR: Frank Cass, 1998.

Gray, Colin. *Modern Strategy*. New York: Oxford Univ. Press, 1999.

Gregorian, Vartan. *The Emergence of Modern Afghanistan: Politics of Reform and Modernization, 1880–1946*. Stanford, CA: Stanford Univ. Press, 1969.

Grew, Joseph C. *Turbulent Era: A Diplomatic Record of Forty Years, 1904–1945*. Ed. Walter Johnson. Boston: Houghton-Mifflin, 1952.

Griffith, Samuel B. *The Chinese People's Liberation Army*. New York: McGraw Hill, 1967.

Guevara, Ernesto. *Episodes of the Cuban Revolutionary War*. New York: Pathfinder, 1996.

Halperin, Ernest. *Fidel Castro's Road to Power*. Boston: MIT Press, 1970.

Hammer, Ellen J. *The Struggle for Indochina, 1940–1955*. Stanford, CA: Stanford Univ. Press, 1955.

Hammond, Thomas T. *Red Flag over Afghanistan: The Communist Coup, the Soviet Invasion, and the Consequences*. Boulder, CO: Westview, 1984.

Hanrahan, Gene Z. *Japanese Operations against Guerilla Forces*. Chevy Chase, MD: Operations Research Office, Johns Hopkins Univ., 1954.

Harding, Harry. "The Chinese State in Crisis." In *The Cambridge History of China*, vol. 15, *The People's Republic, Part 2, Revolutions within the Chinese Revolution, 1966–1982*, ed. Roderick McFarquhar and John K. Fairbank. New York: Cambridge Univ. Press, 1992.

Hargrove, Claude. "Fulgencio Batista: Politics of the Electoral Process in Cuba, 1933–1944." Ph.D. diss., Howard Univ., 1979.

Harries, Meirion, and Susie Harries. *Soldiers of the Sun: The Rise and Fall of the Japanese Army*. New York: Random House, 1991.

Harrison, Selig. "Soviet Occupation, Afghan Resistance and the American Response." In Cordovez and Harrison, *Out of Afghanistan*.

Hata, Ikuhiko. "Continental Expansion, 1905–1941." Trans. Alvin D. Coox. In *Cambridge History of Japan*, vol. 6. Cambridge: Cambridge Univ. Press, 1988.

Heathcote, T.A. *The Afghan Wars, 1839–1919*. London: Osprey, 1980.

Héduy, Philippe. *La guerre d'Indochine, 1945–1953*. Paris: Société de Production Littéraire, 1981.

Herring, George C., and Richard H. Immerman. "Eisenhower, Dulles, and Dien Bien Phu: 'The Day We Didn't Go to War' Revisited." *Journal of American History* 71 (1984).

Hess, Gary R. "Franklin Roosevelt and Indochina." *Journal of American History* 59 (1972).

Higgins, Marguerite. *Our Vietnam Nightmare*. New York: Harper and Row, 1965.

Hillam, Ray C. "Counterinsurgency: Lessons from the Early Chinese and Japanese Experience against the Communists." *Orbis* 12 (1968).

Hoang Van Chi. *From Colonialism to Communism: A Case History of North Vietnam*. New York: Praeger, 1964.

Ho Chi Minh. "The Path Which Led Me to Leninism." In *On Revolution,* by Ho Chi Minh, ed. Bernard Fall. New York: Praeger, 1967.

Hofheintz, Roy, Jr. "The Ecology of Chinese Communist Success: Rural Influence Patterns, 1923–1945." In Barnett, *Chinese Communist Politics in Action.*

Holmes, Leslie. "Afghanistan and Sino-Soviet Relations." In Saikal and Maley, *Soviet Withdrawal.*

Holubnychy, Lydia. *Michael Borodin and the Chinese Revolution, 1923–1925.* Ann Arbor, MI: Univ. Microfilms International, 1979.

Honey, J.P. *Genesis of a Tragedy: The Historical Background to the Vietnam War.* London: Benn, 1968.

Hooton, E.R. *The Greatest Tumult: The Chinese Civil War, 1936–1949.* Washington, DC: Brassey's, 1991.

Hosmer, Stephen T. "How Successful Has the Soviet Union Been in Protracted Third-World Conflict?" In *Guerrilla Warfare and Counterinsurgency: U.S.-Soviet Policy in the Third World,* ed. Richard Shultz, Uri Ra'anan, William J. Olson, and Robert L. Pfaltzgraff. Lexington, MA: Lexington Books, 1989.

Hsieh Jan-chih. *The Kuomintang: Selected Historical Documents, 1894–1969.* New York: St. John's Univ. Press, 1970.

Hsiung, James C., and Steven I. Levine, eds. *China's Bitter Victory: The War with Japan, 1937–1945.* Armonk, NY: M. E. Sharpe, 1992.

Hsu Long-hsuen and Chang Ming-kai. *History of the Sino-Japanese War, 1937–1945.* Taipei: Chung Wu, 1971.

Hue Tam Ho Tai. *Millenarianism and Peasant Politics in Vietnam.* Cambridge, MA: Harvard Univ. Press, 1983.

Hughes, Geraint. "A 'Post-War' War: The British Occupation of French Indochina, September 1945–March 1946." *Small Wars and Insurgencies* 17 (2006).

Hung-Mao Tien. *Government and Politics in Kuomintang China, 1927–1937.* Stanford, CA: Stanford Univ. Press, 1972.

Huntington, Samuel P. *Political Order in Changing Societies.* New Haven, CT: Yale Univ. Press, 1968.

Hu Pu-yu. *A Brief History of the Chinese National Revolutionary Forces.* Taipei: Chung Wu, 1971.

Hyman, Anthony. *Afghanistan under Soviet Domination, 1964–1981.* New York: St. Martin's, 1984.

Iriye, Akira. *The Origins of the Second World War in Asia and the Pacific.* New York: Longman, 1987.

Isaacs, Harold. *The Tragedy of the Chinese Revolution.* Stanford, CA: Stanford Univ. Press, 1961. Originally published in 1938.

Isby, David C. "Soviet Strategy and Tactics in Low Intensity Conflict." In *Guerrilla Warfare and Counterinsurgency: U.S.-Soviet Policy in the Third World,* ed.

Richard H. Shultz, Uri Ra'anan, William J. Olson, and Robert L. Pfaltzgraff. Lexington, MA: Lexington Books, 1989.

———. *War in a Distant Country: Afghanistan, Invasion, and Resistance.* London: Arms and Armour, 1989.

Jalali, Ali Ahmad, and Lester W. Grau. *Afghan Guerrilla Warfare: In the Words of the Mujahideen Fighters.* London: Compendium, 2001.

———. *The Other Side of the Mountain: Mujahideen Tactics in the Soviet-Afghan War.* Quantico, VA: U.S. Marine Corps, 1999.

James, Daniel. *Che Guevara: A Biography.* London: Allen and Unwin, 1970.

James, D. Clayton. "American and Japanese Strategies in the Pacific War." In *Makers of Modern Strategy: From Machiavelli to the Nuclear Age,* ed. Peter Paret. Princeton, NJ: Princeton Univ. Press, 1986.

Jansen, Marius B. *Japan and China: From War to Peace, 1894–1972.* Chicago: Rand McNally, 1975.

Johnson, Chalmers. *Autopsy on People's War.* Berkeley: Univ. of California Press, 1973.

———. *Peasant Nationalism and Communist Power.* Stanford, CA: Stanford Univ. Press, 1961.

———. *Revolutionary Change.* Boston: Little, Brown, 1966.

Jordan, Donald A. *The Northern Expedition: China's National Revolution, 1926–1928.* Honolulu: Univ. of Hawaii Press, 1976.

Jukes, Geoffrey. "The Soviet Armed Forces and the Afghan War." In Saikal and Maley, *Soviet Withdrawal.*

Kakar, Hassan M. *Afghanistan: The Soviet Invasion and the Afghan Response, 1979–1982.* Berkeley: Univ. of California Press, 1995.

Kaplan, Robert D. "Afghanistan: Post Mortem." *Atlantic,* April 1989.

———. *Soldiers of God: With the Mujahidin in Afghanistan.* Boston: Houghton Mifflin, 1990.

Karp, Craig. *Afghanistan: Eight Years of Soviet Occupation.* Washington, DC: U.S. Department of State, 1987.

———. *Afghanistan: Seven Years of Soviet Occupation.* Washington, DC: U.S. Department of State, 1986.

———. *Afghanistan: Six Years of Soviet Occupation.* Washington, DC: U.S. Department of State, 1985.

Karpat, Kemal. "Moscow and the 'Muslim Question.'" *Problems of Communism* 32 (Nov.–Dec. 1983).

Keegan, John. *Dien Bien Phu.* New York: Ballantine, 1974.

Kelly, George. *Lost Soldiers: The French Army and Empire in Crisis, 1947–1962.* Cambridge, MA: MIT Press, 1965.

Kilcullen, David. *The Accidental Guerrilla: Fighting Small Wars in the Midst of a Big One.* New York: Oxford Univ. Press, 2009.

Kirby, Stanley Woodburn. *The War against Japan.* Vol. 5. London: H.M. Stationery Office, 1969.

Klass, Rosanne, ed. *Afghanistan: The Great Game Revisited.* New York: Freedom House, 1987.

Klein, Donald W., and Anne B. Clark. *Biographic Dictionary of Chinese Communism, 1921–1965.* Cambridge, MA: Harvard Univ. Press, 1971.

Kline, Harvey F. "Cuba: The Politics of Socialist Revolution." In *Latin American Politics and Development*, ed. Howard J. Wiarda and Harvey F. Kline. Boston: Houghton Mifflin, 1979.

Krakowski, Elie. "Afghanistan and Soviet Global Interests." In Klass, *Afghanistan.*

Kuperman, Alan J. "The Stinger Missile and U.S. Intervention in Afghanistan." *Political Science Quarterly* 114 (1999).

Laber, Jeri, and Barnett Rubin. *"A Nation Is Dying": Afghanistan under the Soviets, 1979–1987.* Evanston, IL: Northwestern Univ. Press, 1988.

Lacouture, Jean, and Philippe Devillers. *La fin d'une guerre: Indochine 1954.* Paris: Editions du Seuil, 1960.

La Feber, Walter. "Roosevelt, Churchill, and Indochina: 1942–1945." *American Historical Review* 80 (1975).

Lam Quang Thi. *The Twenty-Five Year Century: A South Vietnamese General Remembers the Indochina War to the Fall of Saigon.* Denton: Univ. of North Texas Press, 2001.

Lancaster, Donald. *The Emancipation of French Indochina.* London: Oxford Univ. Press, 1961.

Langlais, Pierre. *Dien Bien Phu.* Paris: Editions France-Empire, 1963.

Laniel, Joseph. *Le drame Indochinois.* Paris: Plon, 1957.

Laqueur, Walter. *Guerrilla: A Historical and Critical Study.* Boston: Little, Brown, 1976.

Lazo, Mario. *Dagger in the Heart: American Policy Failures in Cuba.* New York: Funk and Wagnalls, 1968.

Lebra, Joyce. *Japanese-Trained Armies in Southeast Asia.* New York: Columbia Univ. Press, 1977.

Lee, Chong-Sik. *Counterinsurgency in Manchuria: The Japanese Experience, 1931–1940.* Santa Monica, CA: RAND, 1967.

Lenin, Vladimir I. "Left-Wing Communism: An Infantile Disorder." In *The Lenin Anthology*, ed. Robert C. Tucker. New York: Norton, 1975.

Leung, Edwin. *Historical Dictionary of Revolutionary China, 1839–1976.* Westport, CT: Greenwood, 1992.

Levine, Steven I. *Anvil of Victory: The Communist Revolution in Manchuria, 1945–1948.* New York: Columbia Univ. Press, 1987.

Li, Lincoln. *The Japanese Army in North China, 1937–1945: Problems of Political and Economic Control.* Tokyo: Oxford Univ. Press, 1975.

Linebarger, Paul M. *The China of Chiang Kai-shek: A Political Study.* Boston: World Peace Foundation, 1941.

———. *Sun Yat-sen and the Chinese Republic.* New York: Century, 1925.

Litwak, Robert S. "The Soviet Union in Afghanistan." In *Foreign Military Intervention: The Dynamics of Protracted Conflict,* ed. Ariel E. Levite, Bruce W. Jentleson, and Larry Berman. New York: Columbia Univ. Press, 1992.

Liu, Frederick Fu. *A Military History of Modern China, 1924–1949.* Princeton, NJ: Princeton Univ. Press, 1956.

Lockhart, Greg. *Nation in Arms: The Origins of the People's Army of Vietnam.* Boston: Allen and Unwin, 1989.

Lohbeck, Kurt. *Holy War, Unholy Victory: Eyewitness to the CIA's Secret War in Afghanistan.* Washington, DC: Regnery Gateway, 1993.

Lowe, Peter, ed. *The Vietnam War.* New York: St. Martin's, 1998.

Luttwak, Edward N. *The Grand Strategy of the Soviet Union.* New York: St. Martin's, 1983.

MacAleavy, Henry. *The Modern History of China.* London: Weidenfeld and Nicolson, 1968.

MacDonald, Peter. *Giap: The Victor in Vietnam.* New York: Norton, 1983.

Mack, Andrew. "Why Big Nations Lose Small Wars: The Politics of Asymmetric Conflict." *World Politics* 27 (1975).

Macrory, Patrick. *Signal Catastrophe: The Story of a Disastrous Retreat from Kabul: 1842.* London: Hodder and Stoughton, 1966.

Magnus, Ralph H., and Eden Naby. *Afghanistan: Mullah, Marx, and Mujahid.* Boulder, CO: Westview, 2000.

Maki, John M. *Conflict and Tension in the Far East: Key Documents, 1894–1960.* Seattle: Univ. of Washington Press, 1961.

Maley, William. *The Afghanistan Wars.* 2nd ed. New York: Palgrave, 2009.

———. "The Geneva Accords of April, 1988." In Saikal and Maley, *Soviet Withdrawal.*

Malhuret, Claude. "Report from Afghanistan." *Foreign Affairs* 62 (Winter 1984).

Malia, Martin. *The Soviet Tragedy: A History of Socialism in Russia, 1917–1991.* New York: Free Press, 1994.

Mao Tse-tung. *Basic Tactics.* Trans. Stuart Schram. New York: Praeger, 1966.

———. "On Protracted War." In Mao, *Selected Works,* vol. 2. New York: International, 1957.

———. "Problems of Strategy in China's Revolutionary War." In Mao, *Selected Works,* vol. 1. New York: International, 1957.

———. "Problems of Strategy in Guerrilla War against Japan." In Mao, *Selected Works,* vol. 2. New York: International, 1957.

————. *Selected Military Writings*. Peking: Foreign Languages Press, 1963.

————. *Selected Works of Mao Tse-tung*. Peking: Foreign Languages Press, 1967.

Marchand, Jean. *L'Indochine en guerre*. Paris: Pouzet, 1955.

Marks, Thomas A. *Counterrevolution in China*. London: Frank Cass, 1998.

Marr, David G. *Vietnam, 1945: The Quest for Power*. Berkeley: Univ. of California Press, 1995.

Massu, Jacques. *Sept ans avec Leclerc*. Paris: Plon, 1974.

Matthews, Herbert. *The Cuban Story*. New York: Braziller, 1961.

Maxon, Yale C. *Control of Japanese Foreign Policy: A Study of Civil-Military Rivalry, 1930–1945*. Berkeley: Univ. of California Press, 1957.

McAlister, John T. *Vietnam: The Origins of Revolution*. Garden City, NY: Doubleday Anchor, 1971.

McCord, Edward A. *The Power of the Gun: The Emergence of Modern Chinese Warlordism*. Berkeley: Univ. of California Press, 1993.

McMichael, Scott R. *Stumbling Bear: Soviet Military Performance in Afghanistan*. Washington, DC: Brassey's, 1991.

Michael, Franz H. *The Taiping Rebellion: History and Documents*. 3 vols. Seattle: Univ. of Washington Press, 1966–71.

Modelski, George. "The Viet Minh Complex." In *Communism and Revolution: The Strategic Uses of Political Violence*, ed. Cyril Black and Thomas P. Thornton. Princeton, NJ: Princeton Univ. Press, 1964.

Morison, Samuel Eliot. *History of United States Naval Operations in World War II*, vol. 3, *The Rising Sun in the Pacific, 1931–April 1942*. Boston: Little, Brown, 1948.

Morley, James William, ed. *The China Quagmire: Japan's Expansion on the Asian Continent, 1933–1941*. New York: Columbia Univ. Press, 1983.

Morton, Louis. "Japan's Decision for War." In *Command Decisions*, ed. Kent Roberts Greenfield. Washington, DC: Office of the Chief of Military History, 1960.

Mountbatten, Louis. *Report of the Combined Chiefs of Staff by the Supreme Allied Commander: Southeast Asia, 1943–1945*. London: H.M. Stationery Office, 1951.

Mus, Paul. *Sociologie d'une guerre*. Paris: Seuil, 1952.

Myers, Ramon H., and Mark R. Peattie. *The Japanese Colonial Empire, 1895–1945*. Princeton, NJ: Princeton Univ. Press, 1984.

Navarre, Henri. *Agonie de l'Indochine*. Paris: Plon, 1956.

Neville, Peter. *Britain in Vietnam: Prelude to Disaster, 1945–1946*. New York: Routledge, 2007.

Ngo Van Chieu. *Journal d'un combattant Vietminh*. Paris: Editions du Seuil, 1955.

Nixon, Richard. *No More Vietnams*. New York: Arbor House, 1985.

————. *RN: The Memoirs of Richard Nixon*. New York: Grosset and Dunlap, 1978.

Noorzoy, M. Siddieq. "Long-Term Soviet Economic Interests and Policies in Afghanistan." In Klass, *Afghanistan*.

O'Ballance, Edgar. *The Indo-China War, 1945–1954: A Study in Guerrilla Warfare.* London: Faber and Faber, 1964.

Odom, William. *The Collapse of the Soviet Military.* New Haven, CT: Yale Univ. Press, 1998.

O'Neill, Bard. *Insurgency and Terrorism: From Revolution to Apocalypse.* 2nd ed. Washington, DC: Potomac Books, 2005.

O'Neill, Robert J. *General Giap.* New York: Praeger, 1969.

Overy, Richard. *Why the Allies Won.* New York: Norton, 1995.

Panikkar, K.M. *Asia and Western Dominance.* New York: John Day, 1950.

Peck, Graham. *Two Kinds of Time.* Boston: Houghton Mifflin, 1950.

Pellissier, Pierre. *Dien Bien Phu.* Paris: Perrin, 2004.

Pepper, Suzanne. *Civil War in China: The Political Struggle, 1945–1949.* Berkeley: Univ. of California Press, 1978.

———. "The KMT-CCP Conflict, 1945–1949." In *The Cambridge History of China,* vol. 13, *Republican China, 1912–1949, Part 2,* ed. John K. Fairbank and Albert Feuerwerker. New York: Cambridge Univ. Press, 1986.

Perez, Louis A., Jr. *Army Politics in Cuba, 1898–1958.* Pittsburgh, PA: Univ. of Pittsburgh Press, 1976.

———. "Cuba, 1930–1959." In *The Cambridge History of Latin America,* vol. 7, ed. Leslie Bethell. Cambridge: Cambridge Univ. Press, 1990.

Pike, Douglas. *A History of Vietnamese Communism, 1925–1976.* Stanford, CA: Hoover Institution Press, Stanford Univ., 1978.

———. *PAVN: People's Army of Vietnam.* Novato, CA: Presidio, 1986.

Pimlott, John. "Ho Chi Minh's Triumph." In *War in Peace,* ed. Ashley Brown and Sam Elder. London: Orbis, 1981.

Popkin, Samuel L. *The Rational Peasant.* Berkeley: Univ. of California Press, 1979.

Porter, Bruce D. *The USSR in Third World Conflicts.* New York: Cambridge Univ. Press, 1984.

Pouget, Jean. *Nous étions à Dien Bien Phu.* Paris: Presses de la Cité, 1964.

Poullada, Leon B. "The Road to Crisis: 1919–1980." In Klass, *Afghanistan.*

Powell, Ralph L. *The Rise of Chinese Military Power, 1895–1912.* Princeton, NJ: Princeton Univ. Press, 1955.

Pye, Lucian. *China.* 4th ed. New York: HarperCollins, 1991.

———. "China: Erratic State, Frustrated Society." *Daedelus* 120 (1990).

———. "The Roots of Insurgency." In *Internal War,* ed. Harry Eckstein. New York: Free Press, 1964.

———. *Warlord Politics: Conflict and Coalition in the Modernization of Republican China.* New York: Praeger, 1971.

Pyle, Kenneth B. *Japan Rising: The Resurgence of Japanese Power and Purpose.* New York: Public Affairs, 2007.

Qiang Zhai. *China and the Vietnam Wars, 1950–1975.* Chapel Hill: Univ. of North Carolina Press, 2000.

Quinn-Judge, Sophia. "Splitting the Faithful." *Far Eastern Economic Review,* July 13, 1989.

Radvanyi, Janos. *Delusions and Reality: Gambits, Hoaxes, and Diplomatic Oneupmanship in Vietnam.* South Bend, IN: Gateway, 1978.

Randle, Robert F. *Geneva 1954: The Settlement of the Indochinese War.* Princeton, NJ: Princeton Univ. Press, 1969.

Ranelagh, John. *The Agency: The Rise and Decline of the CIA.* New York: Simon and Schuster, 1986.

Rashid, Ahmed. "A Bloody Stalemate." *Far Eastern Economic Review,* June 9, 1989.

———. "A Highway Lifeline." *Far Eastern Economic Review,* Oct. 26, 1989.

Rea, Kenneth W., and John C. Brewer. *The Forgotten Ambassador: The Reports of John Leighton Stuart, 1946–1949.* Boulder, CO: Westview, 1981.

Record, Jeffrey. *Beating Goliath: Why Insurgencies Win.* Washington, DC: Potomac Books, 2007.

Reitz, Deneyz. *Commando.* New York: Praeger, 1970. Originally published in 1929; composed in 1903.

Rhoads, Edward J.M. *Manchu and Han: Ethnic Relations and Political Power in Late Qing and Early Republican China, 1861–1928.* Seattle: Univ. of Washington Press, 2000.

Richards, D.S. *The Savage Frontier: A History of the Anglo-Afghan Wars.* London: Macmillan, 1990.

Robbins, James S. "Soviet Counterinsurgency in Afghanistan." Ph.D. diss., Tufts Univ., 1991.

Rocolle, Pierre. *Pourquoi Dien Bien Phu?* Paris: Flammarion, 1968.

Romanus, Charles F., and Riley Sunderland. *Time Runs Out in CBI.* Washington, DC: Office of the Chief of Military History, Department of the Army, 1959.

Rosen, Stephen Peter. "War Power and the Willingness to Suffer." In *Peace, War, and Numbers,* ed. Bruce Russett. Beverly Hills, CA: Sage, 1972.

Roy, Jules. *The Battle for Dien Bien Phu.* New York: Harper and Row, 1965.

Roy, M.N. *Revolution and Counterrevolution in China.* Calcutta: Renaissance, 1946.

Roy, Olivier. *Islam and Resistance in Afghanistan.* 2nd ed. New York: Cambridge Univ. Press, 1990.

Rubin, Barnett R. "The Fragmentation of Afghanistan." *Foreign Affairs* 68 (Winter 1989–90).

———. "Human Rights in Afghanistan." In Klass, *Afghanistan.*

Ruiz, Ramon Eduardo. *Cuba: The Making of a Revolution.* Amherst: Univ. of Massachusetts Press, 1968.

Russell, D.E.H. *Rebellion, Revolution, and Armed Forces*. New York: Academic Press, 1974.

Russian General Staff. *The Soviet-Afghan War: How a Superpower Fought and Lost*. Trans. and ed. Lester W. Grau and Michael A. Gress. Lawrence: Univ. Press of Kansas, 2002.

Ryan, Henry Butterfield. *The Fall of Che Guevara: A Story of Soldiers, Spies, and Diplomats*. New York: Oxford Univ. Press, 1998.

Saikal, Amin, and William Maley. Introduction to *The Soviet Withdrawal from Afghanistan*, ed. Amin Saikal and William Maley. New York: Cambridge Univ. Press, 1989.

———. *The Soviet Withdrawal from Afghanistan*, ed. Amin Saikal and William Maley. New York: Cambridge Univ. Press, 1989.

Sainteny, Jean. *Histoire d'une paix manqué: Indochine, 1945–1947*. Paris: Amiot-Dumont, 1953.

———. *Ho Chi Minh and His Viet Nam: A Personal Memoir*. Chicago: Cowles, 1972.

Salan, Raoul. *Mémoires: Fin d'un empire*. Paris: Presses de la Cité, 1970.

Sale, Florentia Wynch. *The First Afghan War*. Ed. Patrick Macrory. Hamden, CT: Archon, 1969.

Schaller, Michael. *The U.S. Crusade in China, 1938–1945*. New York: Columbia Univ. Press, 1978.

Schram, Stuart. *Mao Tse-tung*. Harmondsworth, England: Penguin, 1966.

Schwartz, Benjamin J. *Chinese Communism and the Rise of Mao*. Cambridge, MA: Harvard Univ. Press, 1951.

Sheridan, James E. *China in Disintegration: The Republican Era in China, 1912–1949*. New York: Free Press, 1975.

———. *Chinese Warlord: The Career of Feng Yu-hsiang*. Palo Alto, CA: Stanford Univ. Press, 1966.

———. "The Warlord Era: Politics and Militarism under the Peking Government, 1916–1928." In *The Cambridge History of China*, vol. 12, ed. John K. Fairbank and Denis Twitchett. New York: Cambridge Univ. Press, 1983.

Shieh, Milton J.T. *The Kuomintang: Selected Historical Documents, 1894–1969*. Jamaica, NY: St. John's Univ. Press, 1970.

Short, Anthony. *The Origins of the Vietnam War*. London: Longman, 1989.

Short, Philip. *Mao: A Life*. New York: Henry Holt, 2000.

Shroder, John F., and Abdul Tawab Assifi. "Afghan Mineral Resources and Soviet Exploitation." In Klass, *Afghanistan*.

Shultz, George P. *Turmoil and Triumph: My Years as Secretary of State*. New York: Scribner's, 1993.

Sih, Paul K.T. *Nationalist China during the Sino-Japanese War, 1937–1945*. Hicksville, NY: Exposition, 1977.

———, ed. *Strenuous Decade: China's Nation-Building Efforts, 1927–1937*. New York: St. John's Univ. Press, 1970.

Silverstein, Josef, ed. *Southeast Asia in World War II*. New Haven, CT: Yale Univ. Press, 1966.

Simpson, Howard R. *Dien Bien Phu: The Epic Battle America Forgot*. Washington, DC: Brassey's, 1996.

Skocpol, Theda. *States and Social Revolutions: A Comparative Analysis of France, Russia, and China*. New York: Cambridge Univ. Press, 1979.

Sliwinski, Marek. "Afghanistan: The Decimation of a People." *Orbis* 33 (1989).

Smith, Earl E.T. *The Fourth Floor*. New York: Random House, 1962.

Smith, R.B. *An International History of the Vietnam War*. Vol. 1, *Revolution and Containment, 1955–1961*. New York: St. Martin's, 1983.

Snow, Edgar. *Red Star over China*. New York: Random House, 1938.

Spector, Ronald B. *Advice and Support: The Early Years, 1941–1960*. Washington, DC: U.S. Army Center of Military History, 1983.

Spence, Jonathan D. *The Memory Palace of Mateo Ricci*. New York: Penguin, 1985.

———. *The Search for Modern China*. New York: Norton, 1990.

Stuart, John Leighton. *Fifty Years in China*. New York: Random House, 1954.

Suchlicki, Jaime. *Cuba: From Columbus to Castro*. Washington, DC: Brassey's, 1990.

Sullivan, Marianna P. *France's Vietnam Policy: A Study in French-American Relations*. Westport, CT: Greenwood, 1978.

Sun Shuyun. *The Long March: The True History of Communist China's Founding Myth*. New York: Doubleday, 2007.

Sun Tzu. *The Art of War*. Trans. Samuel B. Griffith. New York: Oxford Univ. Press, 1963.

Sun You-li. *China and the Origins of the Pacific War, 1931–1941*. New York: St. Martin's, 1993.

Sutton, Donald S. "German Advice and Residual Warlordism in the Nanking Decade: Influences on Nationalist Military Training and Strategy, 1928–1938." *China Quarterly* 91 (Sept. 1982).

———. *Provincial Militarism and the Chinese Republic: The Yunan Army, 1905–1925*. Ann Arbor: Univ. of Michigan Press, 1980.

Szulc, Tad. *Fidel: A Critical Portrait*. New York: Morrow, 1986.

Taber, Robert. *The War of the Flea: A Study of Guerrilla Warfare Theory and Practice*. New York: L. Stuart, 1965.

Tahir, Amin. "Afghan Resistance: Past, Present, and Future." *Asian Survey* 24 (April 1984).

Tang Tsou. *America's Failure in China, 1941–1950*. Chicago: Univ. of Chicago Press, 1963.

Tanham, George K. *Communist Revolutionary Warfare: From the Viet Minh to the Viet Cong.* New York: Praeger, 1967.

Taruc, Luis. *Born of the People.* Westport, CT: Greenwood, 1973. Originally published in 1953.

Tarzi, Shah M. "The Politics of the Afghan Resistance Movement: Cleavages, Disunity, and Fragmentation." *Asian Survey* 31 (1991).

Taylor, George. *Japanese Sponsored Regime in North China.* New York: Institute of Pacific Relations, 1939.

Taylor, Jay. *The Generalissimo: Chiang Kai-shek and the Struggle for Modern China.* Cambridge, MA: Harvard Univ. Press, 2009.

Teng Ssu-yu. *The Nien Army and Their Guerrilla Warfare, 1851–1868.* Paris: Mouton, 1961.

Thayer, Thomas C. *War without Fronts: The American Experience in Vietnam.* Boulder. CO: Westview, 1986.

Thomas, Hugh. *The Cuban Revolution.* New York: Harper and Row, 1977.

Thompson, Robert. *No Exit from Vietnam.* London: Chatto and Windus, 1969.

Thornton, Thomas P. "Foundations of Communist Revolutionary Doctrine." In *Communism and Revolution: The Strategic Uses of Political Violence,* ed. Cyril E. Black and Thomas P. Thornton. Princeton, NJ: Princeton Univ. Press, 1964.

Tong, Hollington K. *Chiang Kai-shek.* Taipei: China Publishing Co., 1953.

Tonnesson, Stein. *The Vietnamese Revolution of 1945: Roosevelt, Ho Chi Minh, and De Gaulle in a World at War.* London: Sage, 1991.

Trottier, Paul, and Craig Karp. *Afghanistan: Five Years of Occupation.* Special Report No. 120. Washington, DC: U.S. Department of State, 1984.

Truong Chinh. "The August Revolution." In *Primer for Revolt: The Communist Take-over in Vietnam,* by Truong Chinh. New York: Praeger, 1963.

Truong Nhu Tang. *A Vietcong Memoir.* New York: Harcourt, 1987.

Tuchman, Barbara. *Stilwell and the American Experience in China, 1911–1945.* New York: Macmillan, 1970.

Turner, Robert F. *Vietnamese Communism: Its Origin and Development.* Stanford, CA: Hoover Institution Press, Stanford Univ., 1975.

Ucko, David. *The New Counterinsurgency Era: Transforming the U.S. Military for Modern Wars.* Washington, DC: Georgetown Univ. Press, 2009.

Urban, Mark. *War in Afghanistan.* New York: St. Martin's, 1988.

U.S. Department of Defense. *The Pentagon Papers: The Defense Department History of United States Decisionmaking in Vietnam.* Senator Gravel edition, vol. 1. Boston: Beacon, 1971.

U.S. Department of State. *Afghanistan: Soviet Occupation and Withdrawal.* Washington, DC: U.S. Department of State, 1988.

———. *Foreign Relations of the United States, 1947.* Vol. 7. Washington, DC: U.S. Government Printing Office, 1972.

——. *Foreign Relations of the United States, 1949*. Vol. 8. Washington, DC: U.S. Government Printing Office, 1978.

——. *Foreign Relations of the United States, 1950*. Vol. 6. Washington, DC: U.S. Government Printing Office, 1976.

——. *Foreign Relations of the United States, 1952–1954*. Vol. 13. Washington, DC: U.S. Government Printing Office, 1982.

——. *Foreign Relations of the United States, 1955–1957*. Vol. 6, *American Republics Multilateral Relations: Mexico; the Caribbean*. Washington, DC: U.S. Government Printing Office, 1987.

——. *Foreign Relations of the United States, 1958–1960*. Vol. 6, *Cuba*. Washington, DC: U.S. Government Printing Office, 1991.

——. *Political Alignments of Vietnamese Nationalists*. OIR Report No. 3708, Oct. 1, 1949. Washington, DC: U.S. Department of State.

——. *United States Relations with China: With Special Reference to the Period 1944–1949*. Washington, DC, 1949. (See Van Slyke, *China White Paper*.)

Valenta, Jiri. "From Prague to Kabul: The Soviet Style of Invasion." *International Security* 5 (1980).

Vance, Cyrus. *Hard Choices*. New York: Simon and Schuster, 1982.

Van Hollen, Eliza. *Afghanistan: Three Years of Occupation*. Washington, DC: U.S. Department of State, 1982.

Van Slyke, Lyman. "China Incident." In Dear, *Oxford Companion*.

——. *China White Paper*. 2 vols. Stanford, CA: Stanford Univ. Press, 1967.

——, ed. *The Chinese Communist Movement: A Report of the United States War Department, July 1945*. Stanford, CA: Stanford Univ. Press, 1968.

——. "The Chinese Communist Movement during the Sino-Japanese War, 1937–1945." In *The Cambridge History of China*, vol. 13, part 2, ed. John K. Fairbank and Albert Feuerwerker. New York: Cambridge Univ. Press, 1986.

——. *Enemies and Friends: The United Front in Chinese Communist History*. Stanford, CA: Stanford Univ. Press, 1967.

Vertzberger, Yaakov. "Afghanistan in China's Policy." *Problems of Communism* 31 (May–June 1982).

Vo Nguyen Giap. *Dien Bien Phu*. Hanoi: Foreign Languages, 1954.

——. *Inside the Viet Minh*. Quantico, VA: Marine Corps Association, 1962.

Wakeman, Frederic, Jr., and Richard Louis Edmonds, eds. *Reappraising Republican China*. New York: Oxford Univ. Press, 1999.

Waller, John H. *Beyond the Khyber Pass: The Road to British Disaster in the First Afghan War*. Austin: Univ. of Texas Press, 1993.

Warner, Denis. *Certain Victory: How Hanoi Won the War*. Kansas City, KS: Sheed, Andrews, and McMeel, 1978.

——. *The Last Confucian*. New York: Macmillan, 1963.

Wedemeyer, Albert C. *Wedemeyer Reports!* New York: Holt, 1958.

Wei, William. *Counterrevolution in China: The Nationalists in Jiangxi during the Soviet Period.* Ann Arbor: Univ. of Michigan Press, 1985.

Werner, Jayne Susan. *Peasant Politics and Religious Sectarianism: Peasant and Priest in the Cao Dai in Vietnam.* New Haven, CT: Yale Southeast Asian Studies, 1981.

Westad, Odd Arne. *Decisive Encounters: The Chinese Civil War, 1946–1950.* Stanford, CA: Stanford Univ. Press, 2003.

Wheal, Elizabeth-Ann, Stephen Pope, and James Taylor. *A Dictionary of the Second World War.* New York: Peter Bedrick, 1990.

White, Theodore H., ed. *The Stilwell Papers.* Cambridge, MA: Da Capo, 1991.

White, Theodore H., and Annalee Jacoby. *Thunder out of China.* New York: Sloane, 1946.

Whiting, Allen S. *Soviet Policies in China, 1917–1924.* New York: Columbia Univ. Press, 1954.

Whitney, Robert. *State and Revolution in Cuba: Mass Mobilization and Political Change, 1920–1940.* Chapel Hill: Univ. of North Carolina Press, 2001.

Whitson, William W. *The Chinese High Command: A History of Communist Military Politics, 1927–1971.* New York: Praeger, 1973.

———. *Lessons from China.* N.p., n.d.

Whyte, Martin King. "Urban Life in the People's Republic." In *The Cambridge History of China,* vol. 15, ed. Roderick McFarquhar and John K. Fairbank. New York: Cambridge Univ. Press, 1992.

Wiarda, Howard J. "Cuba." In *Political Forces in Latin America,* ed. Ben G. Burnett and Kenneth F. Johnson. Belmont, CA: Wadsworth, 1970.

Wiest, Andrew. *Vietnam's Forgotten Army: Heroism and Betrayal in the ARVN.* New York: New York Univ. Press, 2008.

Wilbur, C. Martin. "The Nationalist Revolution: From Canton to Nanking, 1923–1928." In *The Cambridge History of China,* vol. 12, ed. John K. Fairbank and Denis Twitchett. New York: Cambridge Univ. Press, 1983.

———. *The Nationalist Revolution in China, 1923–1928.* Cambridge: Cambridge Univ. Press, 1983.

Williams, Philip. *Crisis and Compromise: Politics in the Fourth Republic.* London: Longmans, 1964.

Wilson, Dick. *The Long March, 1935: The Epic of Chinese Communism's Survival.* New York: Viking, 1971.

———. *When Tigers Fight: The Story of the Sino-Japanese War, 1937–1945.* New York: Viking, 1982.

Windrow, Martin. *The Last Valley: Dien Bien Phu and the French Defeat in Vietnam.* Cambridge, MA: Da Capo, 2004.

Woodside, Alexander. *Community and Revolution in Modern Vietnam.* Boston: Houghton Mifflin, 1976.

Worthing, Peter. *Occupation and Revolution: China and the Vietnamese August Revolution of 1945.* Berkeley: Univ. of California Press, 2001.

Wright, Mary C. "From Revolution to Restoration: The Evolution of Kuomintang Ideology." *Far Eastern Quarterly* 15 (1955).

———. *The Last Stand of Chinese Conservatism: The Tung-Chih Restoration, 1862–1874.* Stanford, CA: Stanford Univ. Press, 1967.

Wu Tien-wei. *The Sian Incident: A Pivotal Point in Modern Chinese History.* Ann Arbor: Univ. of Michigan Press, 1976.

Young, Arthur N. *China and the Helping Hand, 1937–1945.* Cambridge, MA: Harvard Univ. Press, 1963.

———. *China's Wartime Finance and Inflation, 1937–1945.* Cambridge, MA: Harvard Univ. Press, 1965.

Young, Ernest P. *The Presidency of Yuan Shih-k'ai: Liberalism and Dictatorship in Early Republican China.* Ann Arbor: Univ. of Michigan Press, 1977.

Young, Louise. *Japan's Total Empire: Manchuria and the Culture of Wartime Imperialism.* Berkeley: Univ. of California Press, 1998.

Yousaf, Mohammad, and Mark Adkin. *Afghanistan: The Bear Trap: The Defeat of a Superpower.* Havertown, PA: Casemate, 2001.

Zarrow, Peter. *China in War and Revolution, 1895–1949.* New York: Routledge, 2005.

Zhang Guo-tao. *Rise of the Chinese Communist Party.* 2 vols. Lawrence: Univ. Press of Kansas, 1971–72.

Index